Laurel J. Brinton and Alexander Bergs (Eds.)
The History of English
Volume 1

The History of English

—

Volume 1: Historical Outlines from Sound to Text

Edited by
Laurel J. Brinton and Alexander Bergs

DE GRUYTER
MOUTON

ISBN 978-3-11-052238-9
e-ISBN (PDF) 978-3-11-052528-1
e-ISBN (EPUB) 978-3-11-052303-4

Library of Congress Cataloging-in-Publication Data
A CIP catalog record for this book has been applied for at the Library of Congress.

Bibliographic information published by the Deutsche Nationalbibliothek
The Deutsche Nationalbibliothek lists this publication in the Deutsche Nationalbibliografie;
detailed bibliographic data are available on the Internet at: http://dnb.dnb.de.

© 2017 Walter de Gruyter GmbH, Berlin/Boston
Cover image: russwitherington1/iStock/Thinkstock
Typesetting: jürgen ullrich typosatz, Nördlingen
Printing: CPI Books GmbH; Leck
♾ Printed on acid-free paper
Printed in Germany

www.degruyter.com

Table of Contents

Abbreviations —— VII

Laurel J. Brinton and Alexander Bergs
Chapter 1: Introduction —— 1

Anne Curzan
Chapter 2: Periodization in the History of the English Language —— 8

Janet Grijzenhout
Chapter 3: Phonology —— 36

Donka Minkova
Chapter 4: Prosody —— 57

Dieter Kastovsky
Chapter 5: Morphology —— 77

Graeme Trousdale
Chapter 6: Syntax —— 102

Elizabeth Closs Traugott
Chapter 7: Semantics and Lexicon —— 123

Gabriele Knappe
Chapter 8: Idioms and Fixed Expressions —— 140

Andreas H. Jucker
Chapter 9: Pragmatics and Discourse —— 165

Carole Hough
Chapter 10: Onomastics —— 185

Hanna Rutkowska
Chapter 11: Orthography —— 200

Claudia Claridge
Chapter 12: Styles, Registers, Genres, Text Types —— 218

Claudia Lange
Chapter 13: Standards in the History of English —— 238

Index —— 253

Abbreviations

ACC	accusative case
ACT	active
ADJ	adjective
ADV	adverb
AN	Anglo-Norman
Angl.	Anglian
AUX	auxiliary
C	consonant
COMPR	comparative
DAT	dative case
DEM	demonstrative
DU	dual
EModE	Early Modern English
EWSax.	Early West Saxon
FEM	feminine
Fr.	French
GEN	genitive case
Ger.	German
Gk.	Greek
Go.	Gothic
Grmc.	Germanic
IE	Indo-European
IMP	imperative
IND	indicative
INF	infinitive
INFL	inflected
INSTR	instrumental case
Kent.	Kentish
LAEME	*A Linguistic Atlas of Early Middle English*
LALME	*A Linguistic Atlas of Late Mediaeval English*
Lt.	Latin
LModE	Late Modern English
LWSax.	Late West Saxon
MASC	masculine
ME	Middle English
MED	*Middle English Dictionary*
ModE	Modern English
NEG	negative

VIII — Abbreviations

NEUT	neuter
N	noun
NOM	nominative case
NP	noun phrase
O	object
OBJ	objective case
OE	Old English
OED	*Oxford English Dictionary*
OFr.	Old French
OHG	Old High German
ON	Old Norse
P	person
PASS	passive
PAST	past tense
PDE	Present-day English
PGrmc.	Proto-Germanic
PIE	Proto-Indo-European
PL	plural
PREP	preposition
PRON	pronoun
PRTC	participle
PRES	present tense
PRET	preterit
S	subject
SG	singular
SUBJ	subjunctive mood
SUP	superlative
SOV	subject-object-verb word order
SVO	subject-verb-object word order
T	tense
V	verb
v2	verb second
V	vowel
VO	verb-object word order
VP	verb phrase
WGrmc.	West Germanic
WSax.	West Saxon
>	changes to, becomes
<	derives from

Ø	no ending
*	reconstructed form, ungrammatical form
< >	spelling

Laurel J. Brinton and Alexander Bergs
Chapter 1:
Introduction

1 English Language Studies —— 1
2 Description of the Series —— 2
3 Description of this Volume —— 4
4 References —— 7

1 English Language Studies

The study of the English language has a lengthy history. The second half of the 18th century saw a phenomenal increase in the number of published grammars of the vernacular language, while the field of comparative linguistics arising in the 19th century was concerned in large part with the Germanic languages, including English. Moreover, in the field of theoretical linguistics English has played a truly central role. While there are no reliable statistics, it seems safe to say that the majority of studies in contemporary linguistics deal at least in part with English, and are also written in English.

During the 20th century, monumental works concerned with the English language, both synchronic and diachronic, were produced, following historical/comparative and more contemporary linguistic approaches. In keeping with developments on the field of general linguistics, today it is possible to find descriptions and analyses of the history and development of English from virtually any linguistic perspective: external, internal, generative, functional, sociolinguistic, pragmatic, comparative, phonological, morphological, syntactic, lexical, semantic. There are numerous "Histories of English" to cater to just about every (theoretical) taste, as well as detailed descriptions of historical periods, language levels, or theoretical frameworks of English and specialized studies of individual topics in the development of the language.

Work on the history of English has culminated most recently in the a series of edited handbooks and histories of English: the six-volume *Cambridge History of the English Language*, edited by Richard M. Hogg (1992–2001), *The Handbook of the History of English*, edited by Ans van Kemenade and Bettelou Los (2006), *The*

Laurel J. Brinton: Vancouver (Canada)
Alexander Bergs: Osnabrück (Germany)

Oxford History of English, edited by Lynda Mugglestone (2012 [2006]), *The Oxford Handbook of the History of English*, edited by Elizabeth Closs Traugott and Terttu Nevalainen (2012), the two-volume *English Historical Linguistics: An International Handbook*, edited by Alexander Bergs and Laurel J. Brinton (2012), and most recently *The Cambridge Handbook of English Historical Linguistics*, edited by Päiva Pahta and Merja Kytö (2015).

While study of the history of any language begins with texts, increasingly scholars are turning to dictionaries and corpora of English that are available online or electronically. The third edition of the *Oxford English Dictionary* (OED) online, while still undergoing revision, is now fully integrated with the *Historical Thesaurus*. The *Middle English Dictionary* (MED), completed in 2001, is freely available online along with the *Corpus of Middle English Prose and Verse*. The pioneer historical corpus of English, *The Helsinki Corpus of English Texts*, was first released to scholars in 1991. The *Dictionary of Old English Web Corpus*, containing all Old English texts, is searchable online. ARCHER, *A Representative Corpus of English Registers 1650–1900*, accessible at a number of universities, provides a balanced selection of historical texts in electronic form. COHA, a 400-million-word, balanced *Corpus of Historical American English 1810–2009*, was launched online in 2010. Smaller corpora, such as the *Corpus of English Dialogues 1560–1760*, the *Lampeter Corpus of Early Modern English Tracts*, the *Corpus of Early English Correspondence*, the *Corpus of Early English Medical Writing*, the *Corpus of Late Modern English 3.0*, and the newly expanded *Old Bailey Corpus*, have made more specialized corpora – covering more periods and more text types – available to scholars. Archives of historical newspapers online, including the *Zurich English Newspaper Corpus* and the *Rostock Newspaper Corpus*, provide another source of electronic data. Finally, syntactically annotated corpora for historical stages of English are being produced, including *The York-Helsinki Parsed Corpus of Old English Poetry*, *The York-Toronto-Helsinki Parsed Corpus of Old English Prose*, *The Penn-Helsinki Parsed Corpus of Middle English*, and *The Penn-Helsinki Parsed Corpus of Early Modern English*. (For information on all of the corpora listed here, see http://www.helsinki.fi/varieng/CoRD/corpora/)

2 Description of the Series

The two-volume *English Historical Linguistics: An International Handbook* (Bergs and Brinton 2012) serves as the textual basis for the current five-volume reader series *The History of English*. The aim of this series is to make selected papers from this important handbook accessible and affordable for a wider audience, and in particular for younger scholars and students, and to allow their use in the classroom. Each chapter is written by a recognized specialist in the topic and includes extensive bibliography suitable for a range of levels and interests.

While conventional histories of English (e.g., Brinton and Arnovick 2016) are almost universally organized chronologically, the six-volume *Cambridge History of English* (Hogg 1992–2001) is organized by linguistic level, as is the shortened version (Hogg and Denison 2006) and to a lesser extent *The Handbook of the History of English* (van Kemanade and Los 2006). Volumes 1 to 4 of this series likewise follow this pattern:

Volume 1: The History of English: Historical Outlines from Sound to Text provides a comprehensive overview of the history of English and explores key questions and debates. The volume begins with a re-evaluation of the concept of periodization in the history of English. This is followed by overviews of changes in the traditional areas of phonology, morphology, syntax, and semantics as well as chapters covering areas less often treated in histories of English, including prosody, idioms and fixed expressions, pragmatics and discourse, onomastics, orthography, style/register/text types, and standardization.

Volume 2: The History of English: Old English provides an in-depth account of Old English. Individual chapters review the state of the art in phonological, morphological, syntactic, and semantic studies of Old English. Key areas of debate, including dialectology, language contact, standardization, and literary language, are also explored. The volume sets the scene with a chapter on pre-Old English and ends with a chapter discussing textual resources available for the study of earlier English.

Volume 3: The History of English: Middle English provides a wide-ranging account of Middle English. Not only are the traditional areas of linguistic study explored in state-of-the-art chapters on Middle English phonology morphology, syntax, and semantics, but the volume also covers less traditional areas of study, including Middle English creolization, sociolinguistics, literary language (including the language of Chaucer), pragmatics and discourse, dialectology, standardization, language contact, and multilingualism.

Volume 4: The History of English: Early Modern English provides a comprehensive account of Early Modern English. In seventeen chapters, this volume not only presents detailed outlines of the traditional language levels, such as phonology, morphology, syntax, semantics and pragmatics, but it also explores key questions and debates, such as *do*-periphrasis, the Great Vowel Shift, pronouns and relativization, literary language (including the language of Shakespeare), and sociolinguistics, including language contact and standardization.

The last volume in the series turns its attention to the spread of English worldwide. **Volume 5: The History of English: Varieties of English** is one of the first detailed expositions of the history of different varieties of English. It explores language variation and varieties of English from an historical perspective, covering theoretical topics such as diffusion and supra-regionalization as well as concrete descriptions of the internal and external historical developments of more than a dozen varieties of English including American English, African American Vernacular English, Received Pronunciation, Estuary English, and English in Canada, Africa, India, Wales, among many others.

Taking into account the important developments in the study of English effected by the availability of electronic corpora, this series of readers on *The History of English* offers a comprehensive, interdisciplinary, and theory-neutral synopsis of the field. It is meant to facilitate both research and teaching by offering up-to-date overviews of all the relevant aspects of the historical linguistics of English and by referring scholars, teachers, and students to more in-depth coverage. To that end, many chapters have been updated from the 2012 edition to include more recent publications.

3 Description of this volume

This volume begins with a chapter by **Anne Curzan** on the problematic question of "Periodization" in the history of English – a topic assumed but typically not explicitly discussed in histories of English. Reviewing schemas of periodization from the late 19th century to the present, the chapter queries the bases for the period divisions, whether they are differentiated by internal linguistic criteria (by the retention of archaic features or the development of innovative ones, or both), by extralinguistic (political/historical/cultural) criteria, or by some combination of these criteria. The chapter concludes that the historical periods are "important and useful scholarly fictions".

Janet Grijzenhout begins her chapter on "Phonology" by describing the major processes of change within the phonological system, including the addition and loss of phonemes, the emergence of allophonic rules, and the rise of phonotactic constraints. On this basis, the chapter then traces changes from the Proto-Indo-European to Germanic to Old English consonant systems and, more briefly, the vowel system. The chapter on "Prosody" by **Donka Minkova** traces word and phrasal stress through the history of English: Old English alliterative versification provides the basis for reconstructing the meter and prosody of the period; lexical borrowing from French and Latin then has a profound effect on the prosody of Middle English, while Present-day English prosody represents a hybrid system consisting of words following the Germanic Stress rules and those following the Latin Stress Rule.

Dieter Kastovsky sees a major typological restructuring at work in the development of English "Morphology", in large part due to the loss of unstressed final syllables, from root-based to stem-based to word-based (i.e., invariant base and phonologically-conditioned inflection). Irregularities in Present-day inflections represent preservations of the earlier stem-based system, while irregular word formations are often based on non-native languages with similar stem-based systems. Beginning with Present-day inflectional and derivational and word formation systems, the chapter then traces these systems from Proto-Indo-European to Germanic to Old English and beyond. Dividing "Syntax" is "the syntactic history of English" (i.e., examination of a particular development in English, based on a set of evidence) and "English historical syntax" (i.e., comparison of change in English with change in other varieties in order to understand general principles of language change), **Graeme Trousdale** looks at a number of syntactic changes globally in the history of English. Using the first approach, the chapter looks at word order changes, the modal auxiliaries, and the impersonal construction; using the second approach it considers syntactic borrowing (e.g. from Celtic), reanalysis (grammaticalization), and analogy.

In "Semantics and lexicon", **Elizabeth Closs Traugott** focuses on semantic change in the history of English from a cognitive perspective, including the concepts of metaphor, conceptual metonymy, and invited inferencing (i.e. the Invited Inferencing Theory of Semantic Change) as well an collocational relations between words ("semantic prosody") and collostructional analysis. Certain types of semantic changes may predominate in certain period. Grammatical and lexical semantic changes differ in a number of respects but are often similarly motivated. The chapter concludes by discussing change in the lexicon. In the study of "Idioms and Fixed Expressions" two different questions arise, according to **Gabriele Knappe**, how do principles of language change affect fixed expressions and collocations and, vice versa, how do fixed expressions influence language change in a broader perspective? In addressing the first question, the chapter examines issues such as the metalinguistic sources of phraseological units, the identification of such units in older texts, the origins of such units, and their changes over time. In addressing the second question, the chapter points out, for example, how string frequency might have triggered the Great Vowel Shift or how various collocations may have contribute to the shift from *thou* to *you*.

In her chapter on "Onomastics", **Carole Hough** argues that place names and personal names may offer evidence of semantic content in earlier periods that is not afforded by other historical sources as well as exemplify phonological and morphological processes of change, it remains unclear onomastic forms reflect ordinary vocabulary or are quite specialized forms of language. The chapter first reviews place name and personal name evidence from Old English and then looks at their transmission over time, arguing that this evidence may "both supplement and extend those [insights] offered by other areas of language". The intricacies of English "Orthography" are explored by **Hanna Rutkowska**. Before providing an inventory of all of the graphemes of English and their historical development, the chapter places English orthography within the taxonomy of writing systems and introduces the concept of the 'grapheme'. Orthography as a source of phonological evidence is discussed, as is the social importance place on orthography.

Two chapters concern more global elements of language. **Andreas H. Jucker**, in "Pragmatics and Discourse", distinguishes between pragmatics as the process of language use and discourse as its product. In its broadest sense, pragmatics can explain all social aspects of interaction, as they exist in earlier periods or change over time. Research in historical pragmatics in English has thus focused on interactive elements such as discourse markers, interjections, terms of address, and speech acts. Historical discourse studies encompass both historical dialogue as well as varieties of discourse (e.g. legal, scientific, or news discourse). Research on "Styles, registers, genres, text types" is treated by **Claudia Claridge**. After a definition of terms, the chapter begins with a brief history of the registers of legal English and scientific language. Stylistic changes in the history of English are seen as in large part resulting from standardization and from alternations between more 'oral' and more 'literate' styles, as exemplified by the change from the more courtly style of the fifteenth and sixteenth century to the 'plain style' of the seventeenth century. Historical discourse analysis focuses either on the study of genres or discourse domains (e.g. letters) at a particular (historical) point in time or on changes in those genres and domains over time. One might also be interested in how linguistic change is constrained or restricted by text type.

In the final chapter of the text, "Standards in the History of English", **Claudia Lange** suggests that there are two ways of conceptualizing standardization: as a process (e.g. involving minimization of variation and elaboration of function) or as an ideology (e.g. involving promotion of the standard and demotion of other varieties). The chapter surveys the existence and development of standards from Old English to Late Modern English. It concludes that the ideology of standardization is losing ground in Present-day English.

The length of the chapters obviously precludes a complete treatment of each topic; rather, the chapters raise central questions and issues relevant to each domain and exemplify these with relevant historical cases from the history of English.

4 References

Bergs, Alexander and Laurel J. Brinton. 2012. *English Historical Linguistics: An International Handbook.* 2 vols. (HSK 34.1-34.2.) Berlin/New York: De Gruyter Mouton.
Brinton, Laurel J. and Leslie K. Arnovick. 2016. *The English Language: A Linguistic History.* 3rd edn. Toronto: Oxford University Press.
Hogg, Richard (ed.). 1992–2001. *The Cambridge History of the English Language.* 6 vols. Cambridge: Cambridge University Press.
Hogg, Richard and David Denison (eds.). 2006. *A History of the English Language.* Cambridge: Cambridge University Press.
Kemenade, Ans van and Bettelou Los (eds.). 2006. *The Handbook of the History of English.* Chichester: Wiley-Blackwell.
Kytö, Merja and Päiva Pahta (eds.). 2015. *The Cambridge Handbook of English Historical Linguistics.* Cambridge: Cambridge University Press.
Nevalainen, Terrtu and Elizabeth Closs Traugott (eds.). 2012. *The Oxford Handbook of the History of English.* Oxford: Oxford University Press.
Mugglestone, Lynda (ed.). 2012. *The Oxford History of English.* Updated edn. Oxford: Oxford University Press. [First published 2006]

Anne Curzan
Chapter 2:
Periodization in the History of the English Language

1 Introduction —— 9
2 The rationale for periodization —— 10
3 Critiques of periodization in the history of English —— 11
4 Origins of canonical periods in the history of English —— 13
5 Debates over criteria for periodization —— 21
6 Debates over boundary dates for historical periods —— 24
7 Reference work perspectives on periodization —— 29
8 Final reflections: the need for one solution? —— 32
9 References —— 33

Abstract: The question of periodization in language, and in the history of the English language specifically, has brought into conversation some of the most eminent historical linguists and historians of English over the past two centuries, dating back to Jacob Grimm, and has raised some of the most fundamental questions one can ask about the history of English, including: What is "English"? This chapter surveys both critical scholarship on periodization in the history of English and published histories of English to summarize the development and current status of the now canonical three-/four-part historical model and to address the theoretical and pragmatic questions that periodization has raised for historians of English. Issues at the crux of scholarly debates include: how the concept of periodization can be reconciled with the realities of language variation and change; the proper criteria for identifying historical periods and/or period boundaries; the best boundary dates to use for both canonical and non-canonical historical models; and the definition of the stated object of inquiry, "English". In its conclusion, the chapter offers some reflections about the state of the discussion, the extent to which "solutions" are needed, and possible future directions.

Anne Curzan: Ann Arbor (USA)

DOI 10.1515/9783110525281-002

1 Introduction

The history of the English language, in theory, could be broken up into as many historical periods as the imagination allows. Defined historical periods could span a year, a decade, a generation, a century, or multiple centuries. Or, again in theory, the history of English could be told as one continuous narrative, with no defined historical periods at all. It could, instead, be told as the continuous history of English sounds, grammar, vocabulary, and so on. In practice, however, most histories of English rely on historical periods as a heuristic, a means for parsing, interpreting, and narrating language change. Since the 19th century, the history of English has traditionally been broken into three or four major historical periods (depending on whether early and later Modern English are viewed as one period or two), each spanning several centuries: Old English (OE), Middle English (ME), Early Modern English (EModE), and Modern English (ModE). How did the almost infinite possibilities for periodization in the history of English become so dramatically limited through the canonization of one particular schema? And to what extent has that schema been challenged?

The question of periodization in language, and in the history of the English language specifically, has brought into conversation some of the most eminent historical linguists and historians of English over the past two centuries, dating back to Jacob Grimm in the early 19th century. Later that century, Henry Sweet and James A. H. Murray established some of the canonical foundations; in a flurry of articles in the past two decades, central figures in history of English scholarship such as Norman Blake, Jacek Fisiak, Manfred Görlach, and Roger Lass have all weighed in on the question. This scholarly conversation has raised some of the most fundamental questions about the history of English, including: What is "English"? And what qualifies as "linguistic" evidence? This chapter surveys both critical scholarship on periodization in the history of English and published histories of English (a) to summarize the development and current status of the now canonical three-/four-part historical model, and (b) to address the theoretical and pragmatic questions that periodization has raised for historians of English. Issues at the crux of scholarly debates include: how the concept of periodization can be reconciled with the realities of language variation and change; the proper criteria for identifying historical periods and/or period boundaries; the best dates to use for both canonical and non-canonical historical models; and the definition of the stated object of inquiry, "English". In its conclusion, this chapter offers some reflections about the state of the discussion, the extent to which "solutions" are needed, and possible future directions.

2 The rationale for periodization

In practice, scholars across many fields have reached general consensus about the usefulness of periodization as an interpretive device. Periodization has become standard in all forms of history, including literary and linguistic history, although the dates for period breaks vary across disciplines. As detailed below, the periodization of the history of the English language sometimes dovetails and sometimes deviates from the periodization of English literary history.

To clarify the terminology, Nicolaisen (1997: 160) usefully distinguishes periodization from stratification: stratification involves "the mostly pragmatic aspect of the chopping up of continuous change", often by a set length of time (for example, unlike most histories of English, Strang [1970] structures the historical narrative by two hundred-year blocks: 1970–1770, 1770–1570, etc.); periodization, by contrast, involves "certain interpretative and evaluative ingredients" in the definition of historical periods. Of key importance is the recognition that periodization is inherently an artificial, interpretive device imposed upon history, be that the history of a people, a culture, a nation, literature, art, or language. It allows scholars and their audiences to create meaningful schemas for organizing historical information, and once certain periodizations become canonical, they become part of the history itself: part of telling a responsible history is explaining how that history has been told by preceding scholars.

In linguistics, historical periodization is often justified through the analogy with the practice of drawing isoglosses in dialectology (Fife 1992; Lass 1994; Wright 1999). As Wright (1999: 25) puts it: "Periodizations are the chronological counterpart of the nearly necessary fictions used in dialectology". Dialect variation occurs more continuously than the isoglosses on any dialect map suggest, yet isoglosses capture something important about the coming together of dividing lines for multiple distinctive variables along a particular regional boundary. Isoglosses obviously require a level of idealization, both about the coherence of a dialect within a given region and about the distinctiveness of that dialect from a neighboring one along a given boundary. Dialectologists do not rely solely, if at all, on purely geographical factors to draw dialect boundaries, although geographical features such as bodies of water and mountain ranges are known to sometimes correspond to dialect boundaries given their effects on population movements and contact between speech communities.

Periodization relies on similar idealizations about the coherence of a particular chronological period, as well as about the ability to categorize linguistic features/change into binary categories that correspond to a chronological boundary. In other words, period breaks, like isoglosses, can suggest the presence of a given linguistic feature in one historical period and its absence in the subsequent one, whereas language change also typically demonstrates a gradient effect, with new and old features overlapping and fuzzy boundaries. Also similar to practices in dialectology, while language historians rarely take external political or social events as adequate for marking chronological boundaries, looking also if not primarily at "purely linguistic" factors, some significant historical events are known to have had dramatic effects on languages and may, as a result, coincide with the historical breaks or boundaries imposed on the language's history.

The imposition of artificial, interpretive schemas onto a continuous entity, be that a language in all its variation at one moment in time or a language as it changes over its history, and the idealization required to do so inherently involve limitations, which have been critiqued in detail for more than a century by historians of the English language.

3 Critiques of periodization in the history of English

A handful of scholars have directly challenged the concept of periodization as a premise in the history of the English language (Hockett 1957; Jones 1972; Wright 1999), but most critiques of periodization have focused more specifically on how historical periods are presented in histories of English and the potential misleading implications of named historical periods. Fisiak (1994: 47), based on a survey of over one hundred relevant texts such as histories of English and historical grammars, presents one of the most detailed examinations of, and critiques of, scholars' justifications of periodization. He finds that stages in the history of English are usually justified by "such vague notions as 'convenience' (... by far the most widely used justification among historians of English ...), 'clarity of presentation', 'pedagogical' or other unspecified 'advantages'". Of particular concern are claims such as that in Millward and Hayes's (2012 [1989]: 18) canonical textbook *A Biography of the English Language* that the dating of breaks at events such as the Norman Conquest or printing is "neither accidental or arbitrary": for Fisiak, such wording suggests too strong a correlation between external events and language change and may go so far as to imply cataclysmic change in the language around a specific date.

Many scholars over the past half century have raised similar concerns about the ways in which the creation of historical periods with discrete chronological boundaries can create the false impression that the language was stable for several centuries during that period and then underwent fairly dramatic change over a short period of time right around the boundary date. Scholars of language variation and change know this picture of language change to be false: language change occurs (a) continually, with older forms competing with newer forms at any given moment in time; and (b) gradually, often below the level of consciousness for the speakers involved. At any moment in time, parts of a language's grammar (including phonology and morphosyntax) demonstrate greater stability and parts are in flux; and speakers are forever creatively manipulating a language's lexical resources to create new words. While factors such as language contact or social upheaval can accelerate language change for a given speech community, the rate and spread of change is still probably better described as gradual than cataclysmic. Hockett (1957: 63) usefully explains how periodization can belie this linguistic reality: "It does not occur to the layman, however, to doubt that in general a period of stability and a period of transition can be distinguished; it does not occur to him that *every* stage in the history of a language is perhaps at one and the same time one of stability and also one of transition".

Closely related to this misperception about how language change works is what Wright (1999: 26) calls the "structuralist fallacy": "the assumption that if there happens to exist now a single name for a linguistic state in the past, there must have existed then a complete single language system which that name is used to refer to". As all scholars acknowledge, the description of any language variety, be that a historical stage in a language or a dialect of a language, is an idealization: in order to create a coherent description, linguists must assume a level of homogeneity and stability. As modern sociolinguistics has convincingly demonstrated, within any speech community, there will be variation. It is as false to suggest a coherent variety called Early Modern English as to describe Southern American English as one coherent regional dialect of American English. Yet language scholars do both because it is equally true that an idealized prototype of that variety of English (which may or may not correspond to the actual language of any one speaker or speech community) is definably distinct from other varieties of English. Change at different levels of language also occurs at different rates and at different times. For example, in the Early Modern English period, the rise of periphrastic *do* and the Great Vowel Shift did not perfectly coincide chronologically, happened at different rates in different dialects, and spread according to different sociolinguistic patterns; yet generic descriptions of "Early Modern English" will include both as characteristics of "the language" during that period. History of English scholars must also always take into account the limitations of the available evidence: the surviving written record does not necessarily accurately reflect changes in the spoken language and typically captures more conservative forms. In addition, histories of English, to enhance coherence, tend to tell the history of only selected dialects, specifically those that functioned as standards and/or are the ancestors of Standard English, creating a sense of a teleological progression – and as a result a deceiving sense that the history of English is the history of how we arrived at Standard English rather than the history of all the many varieties of English, past and present (cf. Milroy 1992, 1999).

The canonical names for stages in the history of English can also create false impressions about the nature of language and of language change, specifically in terms of the teleology they can imply. The term "middle" in Middle English suggests the movement of the language from a beginning, through a middle, to an end, through this transitional period. As Hockett asserts above, all periods can and should be seen as transitions, and Modern English is just one more stage in the language's history, not in any way an endpoint. If one imagines a horizontal timeline, the middle of any language's history is also always shifting to the right as the language continues (Lass 2000); if "Middle English" retains that name for several more centuries, it will be much closer to Old English than to the English of that future moment – i.e., it will no longer clearly be in the middle of the language's history, no matter whether one starts that in the 5th century or the 8th. The other canonical names for periods in the history of English are equally problematic. A period can only be "old" from the perspective of a future moment; as Nicolaisen (1997: 165) points out: "[...] each phase of a language is 'modern' to its speakers in its contemporary setting", which highlights both the problem with "old" and "modern". At some point, scholars will need to draw a boundary to end Modern English (cf. Curzan 2000), which means that either the new period will become the "modern" period and what we now know as Modern English will need a new name, or the new period will be forced into a label such as "Postmodern English". To draw such a boundary, however, scholars will need to use criteria different from those Henry Sweet employed over 130 years ago when he first proposed "Modern English" as the third major historical period of English.

4 Origins of canonical periods in the history of English

Henry Sweet, the renowned phonetician and philologist working in the late 19th century, is generally acknowledged as the creator of the now canonical historical framework of Old, Middle, and Modern English, and most recent scholarship on the topic uses his work as a starting point. However, James A. H. Murray, Sweet's colleague in London's philological circles, seems to be equally important in the development of the canonical periodization, as detailed below, offering not only dates for period breaks but also an alternative perspective on the appropriate criteria for setting those boundaries. There were, of course, also other models proposed during the period that did not become canonical. For example, Oliphant (1886) offers a ten-period model in *The New English* and structures his chapters around authors (e.g., "Caxton's English", "Dryden's English").

Before Sweet and Murray, 19th-century scholars generally relied on a two-period model with five subperiods, schematized by Fisiak (1994: 48) as follows:

Anglo-Saxon	Anglo-Saxon	7th century –1150
	Half-(Semi-)Saxon	1150–1250
English	Old English	1250–1350
	Middle English	1350–1500
	Modern English	1500–

This model can be traced back to Jacob Grimm's division of Germanic languages into Old, Middle, and New/Modern phases from 1819 (Matthews 2000) and to his 1830 two-period model for English: Anglo-Saxon (up to the end of 12th century) and "English", with Old English spanning the 13th and 14th centuries and English from the 14th century onwards (Fisiak 1994). The term "Anglo-Saxon" can be dated back to the 16th century, and 19th-century scholars developed the term "Semi-Saxon" to describe texts that weren't Anglo-Saxon but were not "English" either (Lass 2000). Murray (1910) traces *Anglo-Saxon* back to *Angul-Seaxan* 'English Saxon' (in contrast to the Saxons of the continent), first adopted by 16th- and 17th-century scholars studying the works of Alfred and Ælfric. Many modern scholars, including Henry Sweet, have expressed concerns about the term *Anglo-Saxon*, from the false suggestion that the language of that period was spoken only by the Angles and the Saxons or that it was a mixture of those two Germanic dialects, to the inappropriate break in language continuity it may imply between the earliest forms of the Germanic dialect(s) spoken in the British Isles and what later is called "English". Lass (2000: 14) dates the first appearance of the term "Middle English" to 1839, in Thomas Wright's *Literature and Language under the Anglo-Saxons*; Matthews (2000: 3) notes that the term "Middle English" remained rare until the 1870s and was not uniformly used after that for several decades.

Henry Sweet (1874), in *A History of English Sounds*, supports the rejection by fellow scholars of *Anglo-Saxon* and argues against any loose application of "Old English": it should be reserved for the inflectional stage of the language. This premise leads him to the following proposal for periodization, which laid the groundwork for the model still employed today:

> I propose, therefore, to start with the three main divisions of *Old, Middle,* and *Modern,* based mainly on the inflectional characteristics of each stage. Old English is the period of *full* inflections (*nama, gifan, caru*), Middle English of *levelled* inflections (*naame, given, caare*), and Modern English of *lost* inflections (*naam, giv, caar*). We have besides two periods of

transition, one in which *nama* and *name* exist side by side, and another in which final *e* is beginning to drop (Sweet 1874: 56),

Nowhere in this first edition does Sweet provide specific dates for these three historical periods, although he refers to "the Transition English [between Old and Middle] of the twelfth century" (Sweet 1874: 39). Later in the book he distinguishes five periods of Modern English with specific dates – e.g., the *Earliest* (1450–1500), the *Early* (1550–1650) – all described purely by phonological characteristics, specifically the development of vowels.

Fourteen years later, in the second edition of *A History of English Sounds*, Sweet (1888) retains the loss of inflections as the determinative criterion for periodization and adds dates for the three major periods, as well as "early", "late", and "transitional" subperiods:

> It is impossible to draw any absolutely definite line between ME and OE on the one side and MnE on the other, but, roughly speaking, fully developed ME may be said to extend from 1150 to 1450, the period between 1200 and 1400 being especially well marked and well represented by written documents. The period from 1050 to 1150 may be distinguished as *Old Transition* (OTr), that from 1450 to 1500 as *Middle Transition* (MlTr). The difficulty of drawing a line is increased by the varying speed of change of the different dialects. [...] Taking the SthE [Southern English] dialects as the standard we may call everything before 1300 *early Middle English* (eME), everything after 1300 *late Middle English* (lME) (Sweet 1874: 154).

Equally interesting, but rarely noted, is Sweet's reworked description of the line between late Middle and early Modern English, in which he broadens the criteria to include not only phonology and inflections but also historical events. He writes:

> It is still more difficult to draw a definite line between late Middle and early Modern E. than between OE and eME. The most marked criterion is, no doubt, the loss of final *e* in *nāme*, *nāmes* etc. The loss of final *e* – of which we see the beginnings in Ch[aucer], and which was completely carried out by the middle of the 15th cent. – broke down the metrical system brought to perfection by Chaucer, and made a new departure necessary. The break between old and new was made more abrupt by the social confusion caused by the Wars of the Roses (1450–71), which, at the same time, helped to level differences of dialect – at least, in the upper classes. When printing was introduced – in 1476 – the language had almost completely settled down into its Modern, as distinguished from its Middle, stage. The diffusion of printed books made the want of a common literary language more and more felt, and, at the same time, greatly facilitated the realization of the ideal – an ideal which was, however, not fully realized till the appearance of Tindal's translation of the New Testament in 1525 – a work which is wholly modern both in vocabulary and diction (Sweet 1874: 199).

Sweet is quoted by subsequent scholars as advocating solely inflectional criteria for periodization, but here he clearly introduces historical events as factors in periodization, working in conjunction with language-internal factors. It is impossible to know what prompted this revision in the second edition, but it is hard not to hear echoes of James A. H. Murray's framing of the historical periods, published ten years before.

In between the two editions of Sweet's *A History of English Sounds*, James A. H. Murray, shortly to become chief editor of the *Oxford English Dictionary*, wrote the entry "English Language" for the ninth edition of *Encyclopedia Britannica*, published in 1879. Murray's piece appears to be ground-breaking both for presenting a more detailed periodization of the language, with dates, and for offering an alternative to the purely internal criteria that underlie Sweet's original model. But Sweet does not mention it in the second edition of *A History of English Sounds*, and Murray's work is not picked up in any of the subsequent critical linguistic scholarship on periodization in the history of English. (An excerpt from Murray's entry does appear in Matthews's [2000] collection of primary texts focused on the construction of "Middle English". I am indebted to Richard W. Bailey for first bringing Murray's entry to my attention.) Yet it is hard to imagine Sweet did not know the work. Sweet reviewed Murray's book *The Dialects of the Southern Counties of Scotland* in 1874, and Sweet and Murray were in fairly extensive contact in the late 1870s as negotiations with Oxford University Press over a contract for the *New English Dictionary* came to a head (see E. K. M. Murray 1977).

Murray begins the entry with many of the now standard caveats about periodization: the drawing of distinct lines for successive stages is inherently artificial; the progression of a history of English is disrupted by shifts in focus on different dialects as central; language change is gradual and therefore hinders precise dating; changes happen in some dialects earlier than others. Murray then summarizes Sweet's three-part distinction based on inflectional loss, notes that each period can be divided into an early and late period, and presents the following model with approximate dates, noting that the dates varied considerably for different dialects (recall that Sweet does not provide exact dates in the first edition):

Old English or Anglo-Saxon	–1100
Transition Old English, or "Semi-Saxon"	1100–1200
Early Middle English, or "Early English"	1200–1300
Late Middle English	1300–1400
Early Modern English, "Tudor English"	1485–1611
Modern English	1611–onward

Murray goes on to explain that some carry Transition Old English down to 1250, Early Middle English to 1350, and Late Middle English 1350 to 1485. He then adds: "But the division given above, which was, I believe, first proposed by Mr Sweet, represents better the development of the language" (Murray 1879: 392).

Perhaps more importantly, Murray's detailed notes on the rationale for the boundary dates include a mixture of internal and external criteria, a striking departure from Sweet's use of purely internal criteria in the first edition of *A History of English Sounds*. For example, Murray writes of the first boundary date: "The Old English period is usually considered as terminating 1100, – that is, with the death of the generation who saw the Norman Conquest" (Murray 1879: 393). The precise boundary for the end of Middle English at 1485 is explained as follows: "[...] and the year 1485, which witnessed the establishment of the Tudor dynasty, may be conveniently put as that which closed the Middle English transition, and introduced Modern English" (Murray 1879: 398). The transition to Early Modern English, however, is also described using internal criteria: Early Modern English captures the decay and disappearance of final *e* and most syllabic inflections, such that "[i]n the productions of Caxton's press, we see the passage from Middle to Modern English completed" (Murray 1879: 398). As opposed to, or in addition to, Sweet's description of Middle English as the period of leveled inflections, Murray describes it as "the Dialectal period of the language" (Murray 1879: 394). This description of the boundary date for Modern English effectively captures the mix of criteria that characterize Murray's model:

> The date of 1611, which coincides with the end of Shakespeare's literary work, and marks the appearance of the Authorized Version of the Bible [...], may be taken as marking the close of Tudor English. The language was thenceforth Modern in structure, style and expression, although the spelling did not settle down to present usage till about the Restoration (Murray 1879: 399).

In the eleventh edition, Murray shifts the date to "the Revolution of 1688" and adds: "The latter date also marks the disappearance from literature of a large number of words, chiefly of such as were derived from Latin during the 16th and 17th centuries. Of these nearly all that survived 1688 are still in use" (Murray 1910: 596). At times, Murray's wording can suggest an oddly precise use of boundary dates:

> This shifting of the literary vocabulary and gradual fixing of the literary spelling, which went on between 1611, when the language became modern in structure, and 1689, when it became modern also in form, suggests for this period the name of Seventeenth-Century Transition (Murray 1879: 596).

Murray also provides a visual representation of the language's periodization (see Figure 2.1), which juxtaposes the chronological names (with Sweet's terminology about full/leveled/lost inflexions) with literary developments in three major dialects of English. A second image appears in the eleventh edition of *Encyclopaedia Britannica* in 1910, which captures the influence of other languages on different historical periods and includes notes on both literary and historical developments during various periods (see Figure 2.2).

CHRONOLOGICAL NOMENCLATURE			LITERARY DEVELOPMENT OF THE LEADING DIALECTS.		
Divisions.	Subdivisions.	Dates.	Northern English.	Midland English.	Southern English.
OLD ENGLISH (Full Inflexions.)	OLD ENGLISH or ANGLO-SAXON.	500 — Old Anglian. 600 700 — Old Northumbrian. 800 900 1000 1100	Cædmon, 660. Cynewulf? Bæda, 734. Durham Glosses, 950–975.	? Old Mercian. Rushworth Gloss, ? 975–1000.	Old Saxon and Kentish. (Laws of Ethelbert, 600.) (Laws of Ine, 700.) Epinal Glossary? Literary West-Saxon or Anglo-Saxon. Alfred, 885. Rhymes in Saxon Chron., 937–979. Ælfric, 1000. Wulfstan, 1016. Worcester Chronicle, 1043–79.
MIDDLE ENGLISH (Levelled Inflexions.)	OLD ENGLISH TRANSITION (SEMI-SAXON.)	1200	Early Northern	Early	Early Southern English. Chronicle, 1123–31. Chronicle, 1154. Ormulum, 1200. Cotton Homilies, 1150. Hatton Gospels, 1170. Layamon, 1203.
	EARLY MIDDLE ENGLISH, (EARLY ENGLISH.)	1300	Cursor Mundi.	Genesis and Exodus, 1230–50. Harrowing of Hell, 1280. Robt. of Brunne, 1303.	Ancren Riwle, 1220? Procl. of Henry III., 1258. Robt. Gloucester. 1300.
	LATE MIDDLE ENGLISH.	1400	English. Early Scotch. Hampole, 1350. Barbour, 1375.	English. Mandeville, 1356. Wycliffe, Chaucer.	Ayenbite, 1340. Trevisa, 1387.
	MIDDLE ENGLISH TRANSITION.	1485	Wyntoun, 1420.	Lydgate, 1425. Caxton, 1477–90.	
MODERN ENGLISH (Lost Inflexions.)	EARLY MODERN ENGLISH. TUDOR ENGLISH.	1500 1611	Middle Scotch. Dunbar, 1500. Lyndesay. James VI., 1590.	Standard English. Tyndal, 1525. Shakespeare, 1590–1613.	(Edgar in *Lear*.)
	MODERN ENGLISH.	1700 1800	Modern Scotch. Allan Ramsay, 1717. Burns, 1790. Scott.	Milton, 1626–71. Dryden, 1663–1700. Addison, 1717. Johnson, 1750. Coleridge, 1805. Macaulay. Tennyson.	Exmoor Scolding, 1746. Barnes, 1844.

Figure 2.1: A visual representation of the English language's periodization, from James A. H. Murray's original entry in the *Encyclopaedia Britannica* (Murray 1879: 402).

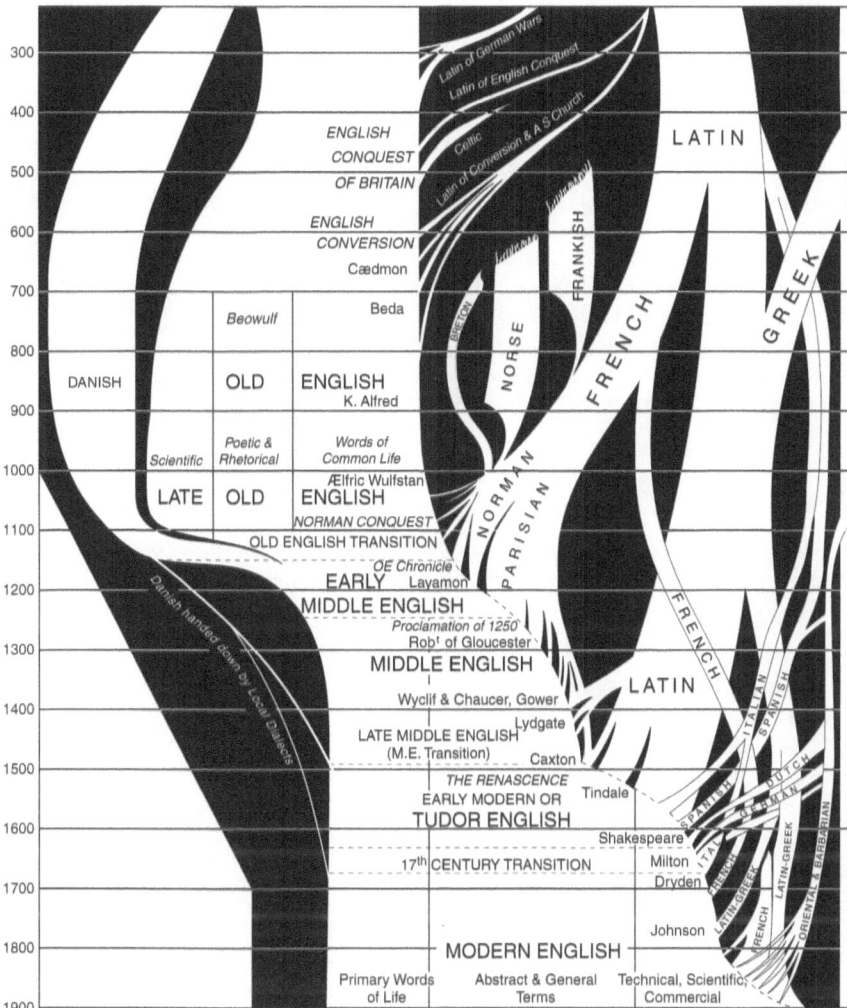

Figure 2.2: An additional visual representation of the English language's periodization, showing the influence of other languages, in James A. H. Murray's revised entry in the *Encyclopaedia Britannica* (Murray 1910: 597).

Henry Sweet's final representation of the historical periods in the history of English, published in *A New Grammar of English* (1892), looks strikingly close to Murray's in terms of dates:

> For the sake of convenience we distinguish three main stages in the history of the language, namely Old English (OE), Middle English (ME), and Modern English (MnE). OE may be

defined as the period of *full* endings (*mōna, sunne, sunu, stānas*), ME as the period of *levelled* endings (*mōne, sunne, sune, stōnes*), MnE as the period of *lost* endings (*moon, sun, son, stones* = stounz). We further distinguish periods of transition between these main stages, each of which latter is further divided into an early and a late period. The dates of these periods are, roughly, as follows:

Early Old English (E. of Alfred)	700–900
Late Old English (E. of Aelfric)	900–1100
Transition Old English (E. of Layamon)	1100–1200
Early Middle English (E. of the Ancren Riwle)	1200–1300
Late Middle English (E. of Chaucer)	1300–1400
Transition Middle English (Caxton E.)	1400–1500
Early Modern English (Tudor E.; E. of Shakespere)	1500–1650
Late Modern English	1650–

(Sweet 1892: 211)

By 1910, however, when the eleventh edition of *Encyclopaedia Britannica* was published, Murray had shifted the dates for the transition between Old and Middle English back, closer to Sweet's (1888) version (he also adds the 17th-century transition):

Old English or Anglo-Saxon	–1100
Transition Old English, or 'Semi-Saxon'	1100–1150
Early Middle English	1150–1250
(Normal) Middle English	1250–1400
Late and Transition Middle English	1400–1485
Early Modern or Tudor English	1485–1611
Seventeenth century transition	1611–1688
Modern or current English	1689–

As captured by these detailed excerpts, the now canonical historical periods have been, since their inception, scholarly fictions. They are important and useful scholarly fictions, which is why they have continued to be the focus of academic discussion and debate. The dates have been and continue to be negotiable and negotiated, shifting fifty years one way or the other, and fundamental to that negotiation are the criteria for determining a period break.

Murray's foundational work in this scholarly conversation, however, remains unmentioned in Kemp Malone's 1930 article "When did Middle English begin?", which has been cited subsequently as the first piece of critical scholarship to address the question of periodization. Malone focuses on revising Sweet's model, primarily in terms of the dating of Middle English but also in terms of criteria. Malone accepts Sweet's central focus on the leveling of inflections for periodization, although he argues that while Sweet frames his model as based on morphosyntactic criteria (i.e., the leveling of inflections), he is actually describing a phonetic change: the leveling and ensuing loss of vowels in final unstressed syllables. The question then becomes when that leveling began. By examining four Southern manuscripts from the 10th century (the Vercelli Book, the Exeter Book, the Junius Codex, and the *Beowulf* Codex), Malone establishes the existence of many clear cases of leveling of the vowel (and some deletion of the final nasal) in the 10th century. He concludes: "The transition period from Old to Middle English is not the twelfth century, as the grammarians used to think, nor even the eleventh, as most of them think today, but rather the tenth" (117). Lass (2000), more than 60 years later, provides evidence that Sweet's criteria are an idealization as there is already leveling in Old English. He writes:

> The main point is that there is a lot of messiness in weak vowel spellings, and the typically 'Middle' <-e> accounts for more than half the unhistorical spellings [in OE]. [...] Sweet's criteria are a little out of line with what the texts show: his 'transition' period here may be a little late (on his own criteria): if Middle English is the period of levelled inflections, then *Peterborough Chronicle* is not really 'transitional' at all, but as much Middle English as Sweet's choice of texts for 'Early Middle English' (Lass 2000: 23–24).

Malone sets the terms of the debate on Sweet's ground, with Sweet's early work alone as the foil rather than in conjunction with Murray's broader vision of the factors involved in periodization. Malone hypothesizes that Sweet's model met with such success due to the "neatness and simplicity of this scheme" (110), and his revision of the model adjusts dates and the description of the criteria but not the overall simplicity of the scheme. Critical scholarship in the second half of the twentieth century, however, has created more complex models, adding more internal criteria as well as in many cases external criteria.

5 Debates over criteria for periodization

The greatest bone of contention about the criteria for periodization has been the use of "external" versus "internal" criteria – a debate that could be reframed at a more general level as what counts as "linguistic" criteria. At one extreme are the scholars who define "linguistic criteria" as purely intralinguistic criteria: phonological, morphological, syntactic, and lexical developments in the language (although lexical criteria typically receive scant attention – see Lutz (2002) for an exception). For example, Fisiak (1994) explicitly equates "linguistic" and "structural"; Lass (2000: 20), in justifying his test for the concept of "middle" in Germanic languages, describes a language-internal point of view as "surely what we ought to be primarily interested in", in which case "only the typological characters count". At the other extreme are scholars adopting a more sociolinguistic perspective that acknowledges the role that social factors play in language change, in addition to internal factors. For example, Görlach (1989: 98) challenges the narrower typological definition of "purely linguistic" in his explanation of proper periodization. He begins with this assertion: "It will therefore be useful to look for purely linguistic criteria for a linguistic definition of English language history, and only then determine whether a boundary based on linguistic criteria squares with what other disciplines have to suggest". He then describes three levels of linguistic criteria:

> (1) structural (important developments in phonology, morphology, syntax, and orthography and lexis which, taken together, result in a markedly different language before and after the watershed), (2) societal (language planning, standardization, ranges of functions and domains), (3) attitudinal (evaluation by speakers of earlier forms of their language, or of their vernacular as compared with French or Latin) (Görlach 1989: 99).

In other words, the "purely linguistic" includes the highly sociolinguistic.

Periodization based exclusively or primarily on intralinguistic considerations is often framed as the more traditional, if not canonical, approach. The many advocates of this approach trace it back to Sweet, although they often expand the scope of relevant criteria far beyond Sweet's (and subsequently Malone's) focus on the loss of inflectional endings, stressing the persuasiveness of cumulative internal evidence. The descriptions of historical periods should capture, they argue, a set of internal features that distinguish the period from those on either side; or as Nicolaisen (1997: 167) describes the goal: "[...] the establishment of essentially *linguistic* periods, isolated and connected on the basis of cumulative linguistic data". Not all these scholars dismiss extralinguistic factors, but they emphasize the internal. In fact, Nicolaisen goes on to note:

> Such a procedure in no way compels us [...] to take into account only intra-systemic developments within English itself but would also reckon with extra-systemic influences from outside as a result of contact [...]. Initially all data involved in the process of 'periodization' should, however, be intra-linguistic while extra-linguistic evidence should be accorded secondary status without having its importance diminished (Nicolaisen 1997: 167–168).

Lass (2000) has proposed one of the most detailed schemes for categorizing intralinguistic developments in Germanic languages in order to test the concept of "middle", which he concludes is an identifiable entity. His "archaism matrix" charts the loss versus retention of ten features, including phonological features (e.g., root-initial accent, at least three distinct vowel qualities in weak inflectional syllables) and morphosyntactic features (e.g., adjective inflection, person/number marking on the verb, distinct dative in at least some nouns, grammatical gender). Kitson (1997), however, in an extended argument for a later boundary between Old and Middle English, returns to a single phonological feature: the retention of the front/back unstressed vowel distinction, which he posits as a cornerstone for the maintenance of inflections (or to put it differently, the critical obstacle to the full leveling of inflections). This approach is most obviously reminiscent of Malone's work.

As these descriptions capture, many models based on intralinguistic features focus primarily on the retention versus loss of archaic features, a weakness in the eyes of some scholars, who advocate equal attention to the development of new features. Nicolaisen (1997: 167) summarizes: "proper periodization should take into account both the old and the new, both continuity and change, both inertia and innovation". Along these lines, Fife (1992: 7) argues for a prototype-based model: "Given some nucleus of cohesive grammatical behavior which serves as the prototype for a historical period, further examples of the language can be judged as either central or peripheral examples of this schematic grammar". The description of the nucleus of each period is not necessarily dependent on preceding or subsequent ones – in other words, the description may be independent of concepts such as retention and loss.

One of the complications of relying primarily or solely on internal criteria is that different levels of structure can suggest different chronological divisions. Whereas the leveling of unstressed vowels and the leveling of inflectional endings are intertwined, later developments such as the Great Vowel Shift, the simplification of many initial consonant clusters, the rise of periphrastic *do*, and the demise of third-singular present tense -*(e)th* do not work together to suggest clear chronological boundaries. And scholars can and have made persuasive arguments for privileging different categories of evidence, from the phonological to the syntactic. For example, although Malone and Kitson focus on phonological evidence, Fife (1992) argues that phonology is too subject to dialect variation to be reliable as a signal of structure change and privileges instead morphology, followed by syntax, lexicon, and phonology.

Internal criteria sometimes also fail to account comprehensively or consistently for period distinctions. For example, while inflectional criteria can arguably help distinguish Old, Middle, and Modern English, they fail to distinguish Early Modern from Modern English – a boundary that has, at this point, become canonical yet difficult to account for purely on internal grounds. In addition, if the loss of inflections is the sole criterion for periodization in the history of English, then Modern English has the potential to stretch on for many more centuries – until, if this were to happen, English completes the cycle that some historical linguists posit and undergoes dramatic cliticization to become more synthetic.

As noted above, most recent arguments for the inclusion of external factors advocate using them in conjunction with internal factors, sometimes noting their convenience as boundary markers but usually emphasizing that periods should demonstrate structural coherence based on internal criteria. Fisiak (1994) counters that the internal and external are intertwined, and Görlach's definition of "linguistic" criteria encompasses both the internal and external. By sharp contrast, Wright (1999: 33) is one of the few scholars to argue for using solely external criteria – although these must be more than "mere chronological accidents" – because internal changes are too slow to make meaningful periods. He concludes with this strong assertion: "If [...] historical linguists wish to base successive periodizations on internal considerations alone, there seems to be no reason to have any periodizations at all. Maybe that would be for the best. It is easy to be mesmerized by the differences and fail to see the great continuities" (Wright 1999: 37).

If one of the central concerns about responsible periodization is highlighting the artificial nature of the boundary, there is something to be said for external criteria. If presented correctly, external events are clearly not a linguistic line in the sand, dividing a period of the language with specific internal features from a period without those specific internal features. Historical events as period boundaries suggest that these external forces had significant implications for the development of the language (i.e., they are not randomly selected or simply imported from other disciplines) but do not have to imply cataclysmic change.

Depending on the criteria scholars employ, the boundary dates for the major periods in the history of English shift, although not all that dramatically except in the rare case when a scholar attempts to fully reconceptualize the enterprise.

6 Debates over boundary dates for historical periods

To tell the history of English, one has to start somewhere, which raises the thorny question of whether English, or any other language (creoles perhaps being the exception), really has a beginning. Strang (1970) avoids the issue in her history of English by moving backwards through time, but most histories of English settle on CE 449 (the date provided in historical chronicles for the first invasions by the Angles, Saxons, and Jutes), the rounded-up date CE 450, or the vaguer "5th century". The traditional rationale is that once these Germanic tribes were isolated on the British Isles, their dialect(s) of English began to change in ways different from Germanic dialects on the continent – although, of course, for several centuries the dialects were probably mutually comprehensible. To say that English "starts" in CE 449, however, is as problematic, Nicolaisen (1997) points out, as saying that American English began in 1607 with the settlement of Jamestown.

The boundary dates for the period called "Middle English" have been the most hotly contested. As a dividing line between Old and Middle English, the year 1066, the year of the Norman Conquest, stands as a given in literary history (Georgianna 2003) and has been used by some in linguistics as a boundary since Alexander Ellis and Henry Sweet (Penzl 1994). For historians of English who entertain external factors as potential boundary dates, the Norman Conquest is an obvious candidate. To make it a boundary is not to say that this historical event had immediate or cataclysmic effects on the language (although the wording in some histories of English does seem to suggest this); it is to say that it was a historical event with great import for the history of the language and its speakers. While many of the structural changes between Old and Middle English were not caused by the Norman Conquest, some were probably accelerated by it. The lexicon was clearly dramatically affected over time by the rule of the Norman French, and English prosody, phonology, etc. also show its influence. Sociolinguistically, the Norman Conquest radically altered the status of English in the British Isles, the written and literary tradition, and much more.

The impact of Old Norse and the Scandinavian raids from the 9th century on tends to get minimized by this focus on the Norman Conquest. Nicolaisen (1997: 169) notes:

> It has always surprised me that the extensive Scandinavian influence on English from the tenth to the twelfth centuries has never been regarded as 'period-making,' as something straddling Later Old English and Early Middle English, whereas it has usually been taken for granted that the equivalent Norman French influence stands on the threshold of Middle English [...]

Some of the recent scholarship on the "Middle English creole question" has tried to highlight Scandinavian influence on Old English, and while none of this scholarship proposes specifically moving the dates for Middle English, they do attempt to disrupt the sense that the history of English is a straightforward, linear progression of "one language" from one stage to the next; instead, they argue, contact with other languages can have such a strong impact that the resulting form of the language cannot be categorized as simply as a genetic descendant (in the historical linguistic sense) of the earlier variety (cf. Poussa 1982; Görlach 1986; Dalton-Puffer 1995; Danchev 1997).

Historians of English focused primarily on internal factors have proposed different boundaries for Middle English, rarely 1066, depending on the factors under investigation. As mentioned above, Malone proposes a date as early as the

10th century. Nicolaisen (1997: 170–171) comes up with the limits of 1000 and 1400 based on his intralinguistic criteria: leveled vowels in unstressed final syllables, concomitant loss of inflectional differentiation, influx of large number of French (Fr.) loanwords and several loan-sounds, a vowel system not yet affected by Great Vowel Shift. Kitson (1997), through a detailed analysis of linguistic evidence in texts from the area between Wiltshire and Herefordshire, argues for 1200 as the earliest boundary date for Middle English, echoing Sweet (1888) and Murray (1910). Up until that point, scribes show evidence of maintaining a front/back unstressed vowel distinction; as long as this distinction is maintained, Kitson argues, the shift to a language with fully leveled inflections was not irrevocable (see, however, Lass's note in Section 4 about the second continuation of the *Peterborough Chronicle*, dated 1132–1154).

As to when Middle English ends, external evidence can be used to point to 1476, when the printing press was introduced into England – an event that allowed the mass production of texts, with a significant impact on language standardization, the form of the book, conceptions of authorship, literacy rates, popular education, and more. Henry VII's ascension to the English throne in 1485, marking the beginning of the Tudor dynasty, provides another possible boundary date. Some histories round up to 1500 and others use "the (late) 15th century". Görlach (1989: 103), using his fairly expansive definition of linguistic criteria, argues for an earlier date: "It seems to me that the phonological evidence in combination with the expanded functions of English (with all the consequences in orthography and spelling) and the growing standardization of the English language *in England* from 1430 onwards leave no better choice for a boundary than at 1430–1450".

One of the fundamental challenges for all the proposed dates above that rely to any extent on internal criteria is how much linguists can know about the spoken language from the remaining written evidence. For linguists, the history of "English" implies a focus on the spoken language, as the spoken is taken to be the most basic form of any language. Yet the evidence is entirely written – and often literary. And literary figures tend to be invoked often in linguistic descriptions of the early history of English. In a move not picked up by subsequent scholars, perhaps because the schema is not simple and does not allow one coherent narrative, Hockett (1957: 65) tries to separate the history of spoken from written English, giving weight to both; and he offers a significantly different chart to capture the development and periodization of the language. The diagram, adapted from Ernst Pulgram's adaptation of Kurt Sethe's work, shows diverging timelines for the written and spoken language (see Figure 2.3). Hockett's explanation of the period breaks, which draws on criteria quite different from most previous or subsequent scholarship, merits quoting at length:

> This line begins just before 700 A.D., because that date, so far as we know, is the earliest at which anyone wrote English. Down to the time of Alfred, the "writing" line slants approximately as does the "speech" line, since no very firm orthographic habits had become fixed, so that habits of writing tended to be modified to fit changing habits of speech. Yet the two lines are somewhat separated: even at this very early period, English writing did not reflect speech with complete accuracy. With Alfred, the "writing" line begins to slope downwards more gently, becoming further and further removed from the "speech" line. This is because Alfred's highly prestigious writings set an orthographic and stylistic habit, which tended to persist in the face of changing habits of speech. The Norman Conquest leads rather quickly to an end of this older orthographic practice; the new "writing" line which begins approximately at this time represents the rather drastically altered orthographic habits developed under the influence of the French-trained scribes. I have begun this line somewhat closer to the "speech" line at the time, on the assumption – of which I am not certain – that the rather radical change in writing habits led, at least at first, to a somewhat closer matching of contemporary speech. From this time until Caxton and printing, the "writing" line follows more or less inadequately the changing pattern of speech, never getting very close to it, yet constantly being modified in the direction of it. But with Caxton, and the introduction of printing, there soon comes about the real deep-freeze on English spelling-habits which has persisted to our own day (Hockett 1957: 65–66).

Hockett also offers a way to think about the place of central literary figures as part of his very strong critique of debates over the boundaries of historical periods:

> We should never be caught arguing, with each other or with ourselves, whether Layamon is "really" Old English or "really" Middle English – and certainly we should never call his writing "transition" Old English, for the word "transition" is extremely dangerous. We should not even make any such compromise statement as that "Layamon shows certain surviving traces of Old English, but begins to foreshadow what later is to emerge as Middle English". This statement is all right except for the use, in this particular context, of the terms "Old English" and "Middle English". Replace "Old English" by "the English of Alfred" or "the English of Ælfric", and replace "Middle English" by "Chaucerian English", the statement is valid enough. Alfredian English and Chaucerian English are non-contiguous and non-overlapping time slices in the history of the language (Hockett 1957: 66).

This proposal acknowledges the ways in which literature like Chaucer's and Layamon's provides prototypes for different historical forms of English – and the terminology Hockett suggests highlights linguists' dependence on the written, as well as the literary, as the source of information about the early development of English.

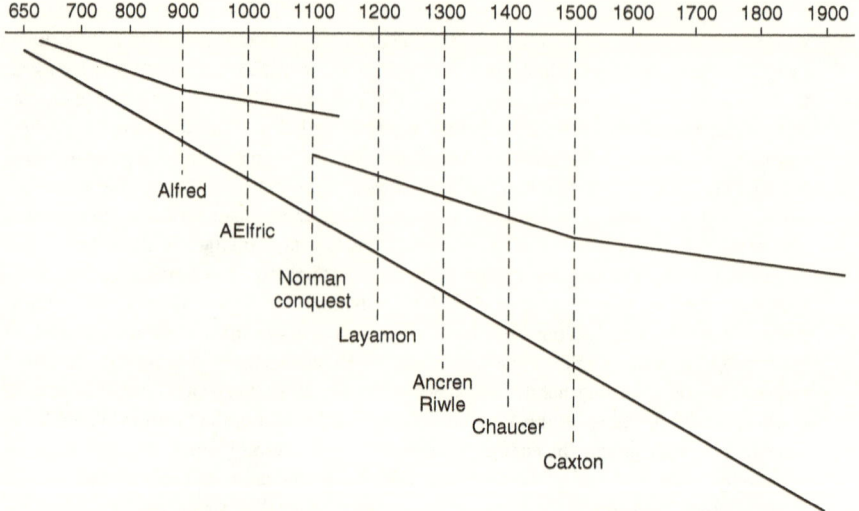

Figure 2.3: A visual representation of the diverging development of spoken English (bottom sloping line) and written English (top line, sloping at a gentler angle due to the implementation of written standards), with a break from older orthographic practices at the time of the Norman Conquest (Hockett 1957: 65)

Blake (1994) asks for perhaps an even more radical rethinking of how historical linguists tell the history of English: he argues that histories of English should explicitly be arranged around the history of the standard(s). He criticizes histories of English that assume the standard as "English" without acknowledgment, and he urges all historians of the language to clarify what they mean by English, which can be viewed as much as an abstract concept as an identifiable collection of linguistic data. The power of the standard to set an example for writers, Blake argues, makes it central to the history of the language, and attention to the standard usefully allows a junction of external and internal factors "in so far as the spread of a standard arises from external factors, but the standard itself is a matter of linguistic features" (Blake 1994: 39). This perspective redraws some of the period boundaries. As Blake explains, "[...] then English can have started only when the first standard was used outside its geographical area even if standardised languages were in use before then" (1994: 39), and King Alfred's rule in the 9th century provides the first real standard for English as well as the sense that English is a national language. The start date for Middle English is pushed forward: "So a historical division of the language ought to extend 'Old English' until this ideal [the West Saxon standard] ceases to be a force, something which we can probably date to the late twelfth or early thirteenth century" (Blake 1994: 41). The Middle English period, characterized by the lack of a national standard, ends around 1400 with the rise of attempts to create a new national standard. Blake then raises the critical question of how one breaks Modern English, once a standard language has been established. He argues for 1660, the date of Restoration (vs. Görlach's 1700, which marks the "end of remaining syntactic redundancies and of the use of Latin for expository prose"): "What characterises the earliest part of Early Modern English is the establishment of a standard spelling system in printed material" (Blake 1994: 42). Before then, for example, in Shakespeare's First Folio of 1623, standardized spelling may be an ideal but not a fact (Blake 1994: 42). Blake creates three subsequent periods based on developments with the standard, including intellectual attitudes: 1660–1798, characterized by attempts to codify the language and to establish the principles for having and promoting a standard language; 1798–World War I, notable for the attempt to impose these norms through the educational system; and World War I–present, a period during which the standard has been under attack and is no longer accepted unquestioningly (cf. Crystal 2004, 2012).

These later periods have received much less attention in the published scholarship, perhaps in part because many scholars have assumed a three-part division, with Modern English extending from the end of Middle English onwards. The break between the Early and Late periods has, it seems, been treated less as a linguistic question – i.e., as a boundary to be determined on purely linguistic grounds, however one defines linguistic. The date is often put near the end of the 18th century, the time of the Industrial Revolution, if not precisely at 1776 with the Declaration of Independence and subsequent attempts to establish a distinctly American English. This assumption of a three-part division, however, may no longer be appropriate if we examine recent reference works on the history of English. And, of course, reference works can have as great an impact on general understandings of the history of English as any piece of critical scholarship.

7 Reference work perspectives on periodization

Perhaps the most authoritative resource published on the History of English over the past two decades is the six-volume *Cambridge History of the English Language* (CHEL), the first four volumes of which provide comprehensive treatments of the four major historical periods, with the last two volumes organized around geography. The first four volumes use cultural, political, and economic factors to delineate four major periods: to 1066, 1066–1476, 1476–1776, 1776–Present. The project editor Richard Hogg explains these divisions in the preface and notes that linguistic changes, of course, often run across volumes but are typically treated in only one. This editorial decision, however, does not go unchallenged: the Middle

English volume editor Norman Blake (1992: 1) states that the political and historical events delimiting his volume, while perhaps significant in the long term, "are hardly appropriate as guides to the dating of periods in it".

History of English textbooks from the past few decades can be either criticized or celebrated for the hodge-podge of criteria from which they typically draw to explain the stages in the history of English. The criteria can include: phonological changes, morphosyntactic changes, lexical developments, major historical events, literary developments and/or specific literary figures, cultural shifts, and sociolinguistic factors. Many standard history of English textbooks – as well as introductory linguistics textbooks that address the history of English – rely on a four-part periodization of English similar to CHEL (cf. Fennell 2001; Curzan and Adams 2012; Millward and Hayes 2012; van Gelderen 2014), and some employ period names that no longer suggest a subdivided Modern period: Old English, Middle English, Early Modern English, Present Day English (Fennell 2001; Millward and Hayes 2012). A few standard textbooks maintain the three-period model (cf. Baugh and Cable 2013; Finegan 2015), but the table of contents of Baugh and Cable's text does not suggest a straightforward three-part model: not only do the Norman Conquest and the re-establishment of English after 1200 receive separate chapters from "Middle English", the history of English after 1500 is broken into the Renaissance (1500–1650), the Appeal to Authority (1650–1800), and the Nineteenth and Twentieth Centuries.

The division of the language since the Renaissance is more variable than the now highly standardized use of Old English and Middle English. Mugglestone's (2012) collection of essays on the history of English, for example, has chapters based on chronological periods, including both Renaissance English and Tudor English as well as 19th-century English, and chapters delimited by language-related traditions, such as "English at the Onset of the Normative Tradition". These five hundred years, much closer to the present moment with a language that is structurally and lexically more familiar, seem to encourage more experimentation with its divisions as well as more specificity, often based on extralinguistic criteria.

Mugglestone's volume also echoes Sweet's and Murray's emphasis on transitions. Mugglestone explains in the Introduction: "it is the working-out of change in progress – of transitions in usage – which preoccupies other chapters. The history of English is, in this sense, not a series of static states but, at each and every point in time, patterns of variation reveal the cross-currents of change, whether in the gradual marginalization or loss of older forms, alongside the rise of newer and incoming ones" (Mugglestone 2012: 4).

Other recent histories of English suggest this fuzziness of transitions by studiously avoiding dates whenever possible – and in the process offer a creative solution to a vexing problem. Crystal (2004) and Lerer (2007), both written for a wider audience, mix chapters that employ traditional names such Old and Middle English (but without dates) and those that do not (e.g., Crystal's "A trilingual nation"), and Crystal includes chapters explicitly on transitions. Crystal does, however, tackle the question of boundary dates for Middle English directly:

> When was Middle English? The question is as difficult to answer as "When were the Middle Ages?" Some people define it with reference to historical events, usually selecting the Norman invasion of 1066 as its starting-point and the beginning of the Tudor dynasty, the accession of Henry VII in 1485, as its close. Some use a mixture of literary, linguistic, and cultural criteria, starting with the earliest texts that show significant differences from Old English towards the end of the twelfth century, and finishing with Caxton's introduction of printing towards the end of the fifteenth (1476). Some take 1100 as the starting-point; some leave it as late as 1200. But no one feels really comfortable with an identification in terms of boundary-points. As the name "Middle" suggests, we are dealing with a period of transition between two eras that each has stronger definition: Old English and Modern English. Before this period we encounter a language which is chiefly Old Germanic in its character – in its sounds, spellings, grammar, and vocabulary. After this period we have a language which displays a very different kind of structure [...], with major changes having taken place in each of these areas, many deriving from the influence of French. From a modern perspective, we can sum up the effects of the Middle English period in a single word: it made the English language "familiar" (Crystal 2004: 105).

Through this detailed explanation of the problem, Crystal skillfully succeeds in not providing boundary dates himself – in other words, he acknowledges the problem but does not pretend to settle it or even suggest that the problem requires a solution. Lerer (2007: 54) focuses on prototypically Middle English without trying to specify when the period began; he opens the Middle English chapter with: "By the middle of the thirteenth century, the English language of both script and street was palpably different from the English at the time of the Conquest".

Of particular note, almost all these recent texts treat the question of the periodization of English directly, often with notable nuance even if the treatment is, of necessity, brief. For example, in her 2014 textbook, van Gelderen outlines the various possibilities for the end boundary date at the beginning of the Middle English chapter, mentioning both external and internal criteria:

> Several different points in time can be considered as the end of Middle English: 1400, when the Great Vowel Shift starts; 1476, when printing is introduced; or 1485, when Henry VII comes to the throne. Here, we will consider the year 1500, when the most radical morphological and syntactic changes are complete, as the end of Middle English (van Gelderen 2014: 115).

Others carefully explain the use of historical events for boundary dates, as Burnley (1992) does in the following two excerpts about the use of 1066 as a boundary date:

> The beginnings of Middle English might plausibly be associated with the invasion of 1066, after which England found itself host to a second language, Norman French, alongside the English used by the majority. But to equate the beginning of Middle English with Norman Conquest would be only partly true, and to understand why this is the case it is necessary to outline some of the major differences between the stages of the language which modern scholars have called Old and Middle English (Burnley 2000: 65).
>
> It is evident from this brief discussion [...] that the emergence of the language changes associated with the beginning of Middle English were only loosely connected with the Norman Conquest. In many cases, the dialect writing that the Conquest initiated simply revealed changes which had been in progress for more than two centuries, or diversity which had already been part of pre-Conquest Old English (Burnley 2000: 68).

Although these modern textbooks do not agree on the dates or the criteria for periodization, most of them do seem to agree on a now arguably established tradition of foregrounding the question of periodization even as they rely on it to tell their linguistic and cultural narratives.

8 Final reflections: the need for one solution?

When historians of English talk explicitly about the process of periodization, they often include the importance of recognizing that periodization and the boundaries that it creates are "arbitrary". But "arbitrary" is the wrong word. The boundaries are artificial but not arbitrary. As this chapter has detailed, scholars have paid meticulous attention to the criteria for creating boundaries, even if they have not always come to consensus. Histories of English have not traditionally imposed "arbitrary" boundaries: even if the criteria have not been discussed explicitly in the text, histories of English have generally relied on identifiable internal and external criteria, as well as an established historiographic tradition, for their periodization.

One could argue that we do not all have to agree on the one "correct" periodization for the history of English. The benefit of doing so is the consistency of the historiographic tradition. But over a century's worth of historians of English have yet to achieve full consensus on periodization, and the historiographic tradition has not suffered greatly. The greatest debates involve little more than a century on either side of canonical dates for the boundaries of Middle English. There is much less consistency about the periodization of English after the 15th century, but as these centuries fade into the past, periodization of them will probably stabilize.

Over the past few decades, scholars have offered almost as many solutions as they have critiques when it comes to periodization, and each solution has merits. Fisiak (1994) emphasizes the need to distinguish between "Middle English period" and "Middle English language", rather than collapse them into "Middle English". As mentioned in Section 6, Hockett (1957) highlights the benefits of naming periods by authors (e.g., "the language of Chaucer") as this implies non-contiguous periods. Some textbook writers have provided models for describing prototypical features of canonical stages such as Old and Middle English without providing boundary dates. Wright (1999) advocates avoiding language names altogether, using temporal and locative phrases instead – for example, "in England in the 12th century" rather than "in Middle English" – which would "thereby eliminate the hypostatization implicit in the use of language labels" (Wright 1999: 39). But all these various solutions should not be taken to say that all textbooks need to be rewritten.

The critical lesson is that historians of English, particularly those writing reference works, need to be explicit about how they are establishing periods in the history of the language – the internal and/or external criteria they are employing and the implications. Historians of English should take responsibility for explicating all the fundamental terms on which periodization relies, from "English" to each subperiod thereof – "Old English", "Middle English", "Early Modern English", "Present Day English", and whatever other terms they employ – as well as the criteria they have selected for creating boundaries. Based on the criteria that linguists establish as central, there is no reason that the periodization of the history of the English language would correspond exactly to English literary history, but it is equally possible that literary history could be a factor in telling the history of English.

In the end, many of the fundamental questions about periodization in the history of English boil down to what counts as "linguistic" history. Historical sociolinguistics encourages us to take the broadest view, which allows the weighting of the external and internal as both important to the speakers who have lived the history of the English language and recognizes the centrality of language variation as part of language change. The English language changes through its use by real speakers in real time, and ideally any periodization of English will capture the history of the structure and of the speakers of the English language in all its many varieties, both spoken and written.

9 References

Baugh, Albert and Thomas Cable. 2013. *A History of the English Language*. 6th edn. New York: Pearson.
Blake, Norman. 1992. Introduction. In: Blake (ed.), 1–22.
Blake, Norman (ed.). 1992. *The Cambridge History of the English Language*. Vol. II, *1066–1476*. Cambridge: Cambridge University Press

Blake, Norman F. 1994. Premisses and periods in a history of English. In: Fernández, Márquez, and Calvo (eds.), 37–46.

Burnley, David. 2000. *The History of the English Language: A Sourcebook*. 2nd edn. London/New York: Longman.

Crystal, David. 2004. *The Stories of English*. New York: Overlook.

Crystal, David. 2012. Into the twenty-first century. In: Lynda Mugglestone (ed.), *The Oxford History of English*, 488–513. Updated edn. Oxford: Oxford University Press.

Curzan, Anne. 2000. The end of Modern English? *American Speech* 75(3): 299–301.

Curzan, Anne and Michael Adams. 2012. *How English Works: A Linguistic Introduction*. 3rd edn. Boston: Pearson Longman.

Dalton-Puffer, Christiane. 1995. Middle English is a creole and its opposite: On the value of plausible speculation. In: Jacek Fisiak (ed.), *Linguistic Change under Contact Conditions*, 35–50. Berlin/New York: Mouton de Gruyter.

Danchev, Andrei. 1997. The Middle English creolization hypothesis revisited. In: Fisiak (ed.), 79–108.

Fennell, Barbara A. 2001. *A History of English: A Sociolinguistic Approach*. Oxford/Malden, MA: Blackwell.

Fernández, Francisco, Miguel Fuster Márquez, and Juan José Calvo (eds.). 1994. *English Historical Linguistics 1992: Papers from the 7th International Conference on English Historical Linguistics, Valencia, 22–26 September 1992*. Amsterdam/Philadelphia: John Benjamins.

Fife, James. 1992. On defining linguistics periods: Gradients and nuclei. *Word* 43(1): 1–14.

Finegan, Edward. 2015. *Language: Its Structure and Use*. 7th edn. Stamford, CT: Cengage.

Fisiak, Jacek. 1994. Linguistic reality of Middle English. In: Fernández, Márquez, and Calvo (eds.), 47–61.

Fisiak, Jacek (ed). 1997. *Studies in Middle English Linguistics*. Berlin/New York: Mouton de Gruyter.

van Gelderen, Elly. 2014. *History of the English Language*. Revised edn. Amsterdam/Philadelphia: John Benjamins.

Georgianna, Linda. 2003. Periodization and politics: The case of the missing twelfth century in English literary history. *Modern Language Quarterly* 64(2): 153–168.

Görlach, Manfred. 1986. Middle English – A creole? In: Dieter Kastovsky and Aleksander Szwedek (eds.), *Linguistics Across Historical and Geographical Boundaries*, Vol. 1, 329–344. Berlin/New York: Mouton de Gruyter.

Görlach, Manfred. 1989. Fifteenth-century English – Middle English or Early Modern English? In: J. Lachlan Mackenize and Richard Todd (eds.), *In Other Words: Transcultural Studies in Philology, Translation, and Lexicology presented to Hans Heinrich Meier on the Occasion of his Sixty-fifth Birthday*, 97–106. Dordrecht, Holland/Providence, RI: Foris.

Hockett, Charles F. 1957. The terminology of historical linguistics. *Studies in Linguistics* 12(3–4): 57–73.

Jones, Charles. 1972. *Introduction to Middle English*. New York: Holt, Rinehart and Winston.

Kitson, Peter R. 1997. When did Middle English begin? Later than you think! In: Fisiak (ed.), 221–269.

Lass, Roger. 1994. Phonology and morphology. In: Blake (ed.), 56–186.

Lass, Roger. 2000. Language periodization and the concept of 'middle'. In: Irma Taavitsainen, Terttu Nevalainen, Päivi Pahta, and Matti Rissanen (eds.), *Placing Middle English in Context*, 7–41. Berlin/New York: Mouton de Gruyter.

Lerer, Seth. 2007. *Inventing English: A Portable History of the Language*. New York: Columbia University Press.
Lutz, Angelika. 2002. When did English begin? In: Teresa Fanego, Belén Méndez-Naya, and Elena Seoane (eds.), *Sounds, Words, Texts and Change: Selected Papers from 11 ICEHL, Santiago de Compostela, 7–11 September 2000*, 145–170. Amsterdam/Philadelphia: John Benjamins.
Malone, Kemp. 1930. When did Middle English begin? In: James Taft Hatfield, Werner Leopold, and A. J. Friedrich Zieglschmid (eds.), *Curme Volume of Linguistic Studies*, 110–117. Baltimore: Waverly.
Matthews, David. 2000. *The Invention of Middle English: An Anthology of Primary Sources*. University Park, PA: The Pennsylvania State University Press.
Millward, C. M and Mary Hayes. 2012. *A Biography of the English Language*. 3rd edn. Boston: Wadsworth.
Milroy, James. 1992. *Linguistic Variation and Change: On the Historical Sociolinguistics of English*. Oxford/Cambridge, MA: Blackwell.
Milroy, James. 1999. The consequences of standardisation in descriptive linguistics. In: Tony Bex and Richard J. Watts (eds.), *Standard English: The Widening Debate*, 16–39. New York: Routledge.
Mugglestone, Lynda (ed.). 2012. *The Oxford History of English*. Updated edn. Oxford: Oxford University Press.
Murray, James A. H. 1879. English language. In: *Encyclopaedia Britannica*, Vol. VIII. 9th edn. Edinburgh: Adam and Charles Black.
Murray, James A. H. 1910. English language. In: *Encyclopedia Britannica*, Vol. IX. 11th edn. Cambridge: Cambridge University Press.
Murray, K. M. Elizabeth. 1977. *Caught in the Web of Words: James Murray and the Oxford English Dictionary*. New Haven: Yale University Press.
Nicolaisen, Wilhelm F. H. 1997. Periodization in the history of English. *General Linguistics* 35 (1–4): 157–176.
Oliphant, T. L. Kington. 1886. *The New English*. London/New York: Macmillan.
Penzl, Herbert. 1994. Periodization in language history: Early Modern English and the other periods. In: Dieter Kastovsky (ed.), *Studies in Early Modern English*, 261–268. Berlin/New York: Mouton de Gruyter.
Poussa, Patricia. 1982. The evolution of early Standard English: The creolization hypothesis. *Studia Anglica Posnaniensia* XIV: 69–85.
Strang, Barbara M. H. 1970. *A History of English*. London: Methuen.
Sweet, Henry. 1874. *A History of English Sounds from the Earliest Period*. Oxford: Oxford University Press.
Sweet, Henry. 1888. *A History of English Sounds from the Earliest Period with Full Word-Lists*. Oxford: Oxford University Press.
Sweet, Henry. 1892. *A New Grammar of English, Logical and Historical*. Vol. 1: *Introduction, Phonology, and Accidence*. Oxford: Clarendon Press.
Wright, Roger. 1999. Periodization and how to avoid it. In: Robert J. Blake, Diana L. Ranson, and Roger Wright (eds.), *Essays in Hispanic Linguistics Dedicated to Paul M. Lloyd*, 25–41. Newark, DE: Juan de la Cuesta.

Janet Grijzenhout
Chapter 3:
Phonology

1 Introduction to some basic terms and developments in phonological theory —— 37
2 Stability and instability in consonant inventories —— 40
3 The future of looking back in time on sound changes —— 51
4 Summary —— 54
5 References —— 55

Abstract: Changes in the sound system of a language may involve many different aspects. First, phonemes may be added to an inventory, they may become obsolete, or they may change their shape. Second, allophonic rules may emerge (e.g. "voice intersonorant fricatives"), disappear, or change. Third, phonotactic restrictions may be added (e.g. no syllable-initial /kn/ sequences, so that such clusters are reduced to one sound), or change their effect (e.g. the ban on /kn/ sequences may be resolved by epenthesis). Fourth, prosodic structure may change (resulting in, for instance, stress shift) and, fifth, morphophonological alternations (e.g. ablaut and umlaut) may start to play a different role or they may vanish (e.g. when morphology is regularized). This chapter will first briefly introduce the field of phonology as envisaged by structuralists and generative linguists. Section 2 discusses some changes in the consonant inventory, the allophonic variations, and the phonotactic restrictions in the history of the English language and shows that many of these changes are interrelated in the sense that a change in one component triggers an effect in another component. Section 3 expresses some ideas on the future of looking back on changes in the sound system, and Section 4 summarizes the chapter.

Janet Grijzenhout: Konstanz (Germany)

1 Introduction to some basic terms and developments in phonological theory

The ability of speakers to distinguish separate segments in a string of speech sounds is an important part of the knowledge that language users have about their native language. Speakers of English realize that the words *pin, thin, bin,* and *fin* differ only in the first sound and they may use this knowledge in rhyme, alliteration and in games with nonsense words (e.g. "Annie the pannie the thanny", "Simon the bimon the fimon"). The sounds represented by *p, th, b,* and *f* have a function in English, i.e. these speech sounds – together with approximately 35 others – are the minimal units that can distinguish meaning in English. The smallest elements that can cause a change in meaning are called "distinctive sounds" or "phonemes". Jones (1967: vi) mentions that the French word "phonème" appears to have been invented by the Frenchman L. Havet, who used it in 1876 to mean "speech sound". At the beginning of the 20th century the term "phoneme" acquired a more abstract meaning and referred to the minimal unit in speech that can function to distinguish meaning.

A theory of the phoneme began to be developed at the turn of the 20th century – especially in the works of Baudouin de Courtenay (1895) and de Saussure (1916) – and became one of the important research interests of structural linguistics in the first half of the 20th century. In a statement submitted to the First International Congress of Linguistics meeting in The Hague in 1928, Roman Jakobson, Sergej Karcevskij, Nikolaj Sergeevič Trubetzkoy, and other members of the Prague School emphasized that a scientific description of a language must include a characterization of its phonological system, i.e. the repertory, pertinent to that language, of the distinctive contrasts among its speech sounds (see Jakobson 1971 [1962]). Thus, an important goal of structural phonology in Europe – as well as in North America – was to establish the phoneme inventories of languages. The method used to establish the phoneme inventory of a language is to systematically compare words with different meanings that differ in one sound only. Such word pairs are called "minimal pairs".

Furthermore, the international congress held that the field of language change should not be confined to studying isolated changes; rather, changes should be considered in terms of the linguistic system which undergoes them. As Waugh (1976: 21) puts it, according to the Prague School, "we must understand the structure before the change begins, the structure after it takes place, the sense of the change undergone in respect to the undergoing system, the level at which the change takes place (e.g. distinctive feature or phoneme) and the effects of the change on the system".

One of the main concerns of Roman Jakobson became to develop a theory of phonology that would predict exactly those distinctive sounds that can be found in the world's languages, and he hypothesized that there is a limited number of phonological (or "distinctive") features – approximately 15 – that characterize the sounds of human languages (see, e.g., Jakobson 1939; Jakobson et al. 1951; Jakobson and Halle 1956). In the system that Jakobson and his colleagues developed, each phoneme is represented by a set of features such as [grave]/[acute] and [flat]/[nonflat] which are unrelated (i.e. not grouped into smaller sets) and binary. For Jakobson, speech sounds are characterized by features and for him it followed that sound changes should involve features or phonemes too: a sound change is a change in the distribution of a phonological feature or phoneme within a system. With Sapir (1921) before him, Jakobson posited that if in a system /p, t, k/, one segment has changed (e.g. /p/ to /b/), the outcome is asymmetric (/b, t, k/). The simplest way to restore the symmetry is an analogous change of the other members in the system (e.g. /t, k/ → /d, g/). Should the resulting pattern already exist, then the system of oppositions can only survive if the older series (in our example /b, d, g/) itself undergoes a change (e.g. spirantization). In this hypothetical example, the stops specified as being voiceless gradually changed into voiced stops – i.e. the feature that expresses voicing in stops changed – and the older voiced stops became fricatives – i.e. for voiced stops the feature that specified complete obstruction in the vocal tract changed into a feature that specifies incomplete obstruction ([+continuant]). In this case, the phonological sound change alters the relationship between two elements from /p/ versus /b/ to /b/ versus /v/. Jakobson also allowed for sound changes that lead to the elimination of a phonological contrast or to the formation of a contrast and we will encounter English examples of modification, elimination, and creation of phonological contrasts in the remainder of this chapter.

Speech sounds may be articulated differently depending on the position in the word. For example, the initial sound in the word *pin* (and the non-word *pannie*) is pronounced with a puff of air (called "aspiration"), which is lacking in the word *spin*. If we were to replace the sound *p* in *pin* and *pannie* by the corresponding *p*-sound in *spin* or *spaniel*, or by the unaspirated *p*-sound used in Dutch *pin*, the words would sound odd to native speakers of English, but *pin* would still mean 'a short thin piece of metal used for fastening things together'. Aspiration thus does not change the meaning of the words in question, but it is part of the grammar that speakers of Present-day English employ. The phonological rule that applies in this case would be "in word-initial position, add the feature [spread glottis] (for aspiration) to segments specified as [stiff vocal folds] underlyingly". Speech sounds that do not cause a change in meaning, but are realizations of one sound in different contexts (e.g. aspirated [p^h] in absolute word-initial position versus unaspirated [p] preceded by /s/) are called "allophones" (a term that was invented about 1934 by Benjamin Lee Whorf). To explain sound alternations in particular contexts, it is useful to distinguish the underlying representation from the actual realization (or "surface representation"): the former is put between slashes ("/ /") and the latter is put between square brackets ("[ ]"). For example, the underlying form of the English regular past tense marker spelled -ed is /d/ (as in *fail*[d], *love*[d]). Underlying /d/ is realized with an epenthetic vowel after a stem that ends in an alveolar stop (*need* [ɪd], *want*[ɪd]) and it is realized without voicing – i.e. as [t] – after a stem-final voiceless obstruent (as in *kiss*[t], *walk*[t]). In generative frameworks, the surface form (or "output") is derived from the underlying form (or "input") by phonological rules and in Optimality Theory (OT), i.e. the surface form that violates the least highly ranked constraints compared to alternative surface forms is selected as the "optimal" one for phonetic realization. In generative phonology, changes in allophonic variation may thus involve a change in rule applications, whereas in OT, allophonic changes involve a reranking of universal constraints in the language specific grammar.

Apart from the knowledge about which sounds are part of the sound system of a language and the knowledge about the realization of sounds in particular contexts, speakers also have clear intuitions about how sounds are organized to form words, i.e. how some sounds may combine with other sounds in the language. Speakers of English know that /p/ may combine with /s/ – as in *spin* – whereas the *th*-sound may not (**sthin*). Changes in the phonotactics of the English language have occurred throughout its history and we will consider a few of them in this chapter.

Some phonological phenomena have scope over larger domains than one segment, e.g. a syllable, or take effect at a morphosyntactic boundary. An example of the first kind of phenomenon is word stress (see Minkova, Chapter 4, which discusses the development of word and phrasal stress from Old to Present-day English). As an example of a phonological phenomenon that applies across a morphosyntactic boundary, English consonant-intrusion can be mentioned here. To avoid two vowels becoming adjacent, some varieties of English have the option of inserting a sonorant consonant. Which particular sound is inserted depends on the preceding vowel: the glide /j/ is inserted after a front high vowel (e.g. *I see [j] it*), /w/ is inserted after a back high vowel (e.g. *too [w] old*) and an *r*-sound is inserted when a non-high vowel-final word is followed by a suffix or a word that is vowel-initial (e.g. *I saw [r] it*), for instance in the Eastern Massachusetts dialect (McCarthy 1993: 170–171). Thus, the epenthetic consonant is a sonorant and the preceding vowel determines whether it is realized as /j/, /w/, or rhotic /r/.

The present chapter is mainly concerned with segmental phonology, i.e. the study of the function, behavior, and organization of speech sounds in one language and across languages. The three factors mentioned immediately above are part of the knowledge that speakers have about the sound system of their native language (see, e.g., Goldsmith 1995: 1–13; Lass 1984). The problem for historical linguistics is of course that there are no speakers of earlier stages of the language alive. Fortunately, in many cases they left traces of their speech in written records (manuscripts, grammars, etc.) and where written records are absent, it is often possible to reconstruct phonological systems by comparing different languages and language varieties that derived from the language period we are interested in. The present chapter examines some changes in the phoneme inventory, the allophonic variations, and the phonotactic restrictions in the history of the English language. It is not our ambition to investigate all phonological properties; we will concentrate on only a few properties that concern speech sounds and that have changed over time in the history of the English language as spoken in England. The most well-known phonological changes in the history of English are changes in the vowel system such as the Great Vowel Shift. Since these are thoroughly treated in all standard textbooks, we will here concentrate on changes in the consonant inventory, allophonic variation of consonants, and phonotactic restrictions on consonant clusters. The chapter on prosody (see Minkova, Chapter 4) complements this one and considers phenomena that cannot be restricted to single speech sounds (e.g. word and phrasal stress assignment).

2 Stability and instability in consonant inventories

At the turn of the 20th century, the major goal of historical linguistics was to reconstruct phonological systems and rules of language stages of which we have no direct evidence. According to an extreme version of the Neogrammarian doctrine, historical study was the only genuinely scientific approach to the facts of language. By examining sound changes, the Neogrammarians tried to find out why modern languages have developed the way they have and how they relate to other languages. The Neogrammarians maintained that language change is systematic and takes place without exceptions. For example, it was already observed by e.g. Friedrich von Schlegel in 1801 that Latin (Lt.) words that start with a labial plosive (e.g. *ped, pisces*) correspond to words that start with a labial fricative in Germanic languages (English *foot, fish*; German *Fuss, Fish*) and that words beginning in <t> (/t/) or <c> (/k/) in Latin would have <þ> (/θ/) or <h> (/x/ or /h/) in early stages of Germanic languages. The Neogrammarians deduced from these observations that the voiceless stops /p, t, k/ in the common ancestor of these languages (i.e. Indo-European) remained unchanged in Latin, but became voiceless fricatives in Germanic. By applying their method of systematically comparing sounds in certain positions of similar words in different languages, the Neogrammarians constructed family trees of related languages. Even though it is still common to refer to language family trees and say that, for instance, English, German, Dutch, and Frisian belong to the "branch" of West-Germanic languages and are "sister" languages, few people today would support the idea that the origin of the languages that we now know can be traced back to one common ancestor (see, e.g., Aitchison 2013: 24–35, Wunderlich 2008). Nevertheless, the important contribution of Neogrammarians to linguistic research is the insight that some sound changes do not take place arbitrarily, but that classes of sounds in a particular linguistic context may undergo a certain change.

To illustrate how consonant inventories may change over time, consider as an example the inventory of obstruents that the Neogrammarians assumed for Indo-European (PIE) (1a) and its descendant Proto-Germanic (PGrmc.) (1b):

(1) a. Indo-European obstruents
/p, t, kʲ, k, kʷ/
/b, d, gʲ, g, gʷ/
/bʰ, dʰ, gʰʲ, gʰ, gʰʷ/
/s, h/
and geminate stops after short vowels

b. Proto-Germanic obstruents
/f, θ, xʲ, x, xʷ/
/p, t, kʲ, k, kʷ/
/b, d, gʲ, g, gʷ/
/s, h/
geminate stops after short vowels

What remained "stable" in the transition from the Indo-European obstruent inventory to the Proto-Germanic one is the number of phonemes: both systems distinguish 17 obstruents. What changed was the set of phonemes. Proto-Germanic has fewer laryngeal contrasts, but more contrasts in manner of articulation for the different places of articulation as a result of a set of consonant shifts – commonly referred to collectively as "Grimm's Law" – whereby the Indo-European voiceless stops spirantized and became voiceless fricatives, the unaspirated stops underwent a strengthening process and became voiceless aspirated stops and, finally, the so-called "breathy voiced" stops were deaspirated and became voiced unaspirated stops (e.g. Harbert 2007: 41–88; for a phonological account of parts of this consonant shift see, e.g., Iverson and Salmons 1995). This type of sound change is an example of what Jakobson would consider a modification of a phonological contrast: it altered the relationship from voiceless stop to voiced stop and from voiced stop to breathy voiced stop into the opposition voiceless fricative versus voiceless stop and voiceless stop versus voiced stop.

We can only speculate as to why the system changed the way it did. The internal change from voiceless stops to voiceless fricatives in one branch of a language family may perhaps be attributed to the fact that voiceless /p, t, k/ are perceptually close to voiced /b, d, g/ whereas the fricatives /f, θ, x/ and the stops /b, d, g/ are more distinct. One hypothesis may thus be that in order to make the two classes more perceptually distinct, one class was "enhanced" by spirantization. However, Proto-Celtic kept the /p, t, k/ versus /b, d, g/ contrast and conflated (or "merged") /b, d, g/ and /b^h, d^h, g^h/, so that two perceptually close classes emerged as in (2a, b):

(2) a. Indo-European obstruents
  /p, t, k^j, k, k^w/
  /b, d, g^j, g, g^w/
  /b^h, d^h, g^{hj}, g^h, g^{hw}/
  /s, h/
  and geminate stops

b. Proto-Celtic obstruents
  /(p), t, (k^j), k, k^w/
  /b, d, (g^j), g, (g^w)/

  /s, h/
  and geminate stops

In this case, what remained "stable" (i.e. the "pertinent" properties) are the different manners of articulation. The unstable or "transient" property is the reduction in the number of phonemes: Proto-Celtic exhibits fewer laryngeal contrasts and – due to depalatalization and delabialization – fewer places of articulation. This type of sound change is an example of what Jakobson would consider elimination of a phonological contrast. The change altered the three-way opposition from voiceless stop to voiced stop to breathy voiced stop into a two-way contrast between voiceless stop and voiced stop.

The question why Proto-Germanic opted to enhance the contrast by spirantization of one class, whereas Proto-Celtic kept the /p, t, k/ versus /b, d, g/ contrast and conflated /b, d, g/ and /b^h, d^h, g^h/ is notoriously difficult to answer. In the framework of Optimality Theory as introduced in the early 1990s in different works by McCarthy, Prince, and Smolensky (McCarthy and Prince 1993a, 1993b, 1995; Prince and Smolensky 1993), the suggestion is made that the desire to satisfy "perceptual distance" to accommodate the needs of the hearer was valued more in Proto-Germanic than the constraint "avoid marked elements" (i.e. fricatives are universally more marked than stops and thus disfavored in phoneme inventories). In contrast, the constraints "faithfulness to manner" and "minimize phoneme inventory" (i.e. the so-called "principle of economy") gradually gained more weight and thus became more important than "perceptual distance" in Proto-Celtic. Of course this only says what happened in different language communities and not why it happened. As an autonomous reviewer pointed out, we cannot answer the question why "perceptual distance" was more valued in one language family and less in another and why the "principle of economy" came to play a more important role in some language communities, because we do not know the reasons for variation preferences in speech communities.

2.1 Stability and instability in consonant inventories related to phonotactics

Proto-Germanic is the ancestor of Old English. In (3) we compare the inventory of obstruents assumed by the Neogrammarians for Proto-Germanic and the inventory of Old English.

(3) a. Proto-Germanic obstruents
/p, t, kʲ, k, kʷ/
/b, d, gʲ, g, gʷ/
/f, θ, xʲ, x, xʷ/
/s, h/
and geminate stops
after short vowels

b. Old English obstruents
/p, t, kʲ, k/
/b, d, gʲ, g/
/f, θ, xʲ, x/
/s, ʃ, h/
and geminate consonants (except /h/, /ʃ/ and /r/) after short vowels

The effect of OE consonant gemination in intervocalic position was to create a closed syllable. Geminate consonants were lost before the 13th century.

Note first of all that labiovelar stops and fricatives are not assumed for Old English. The spelling of OE *cwēn* 'queen, wife of a king' and *cwæþ* 'said, spoke, called, named, proclaimed' suggests that /kʷ/ was a legitimate sound or sound sequence. Rather than being analyzed as one phoneme, the spelling <cw> suggests that we are dealing with a consonant cluster of a velar stop followed by a labiovelar approximant /w/ (due to the influence of Anglo-Norman scribes, the spelling <cw> changed into <qu> in the Middle English period). Some scholars do assume palatalized velar stops and fricatives in the Old English consonant inventory, but these were most probably fronted realizations of the velar obstruents before front vowels.

We will now focus on the fact that before the change from Proto-Germanic to Old English, there are some asymmetries in the consonant system. The ones we will have a closer look at are:
(i) only velar obstruents have a labialized counterpart (e.g. /k/ contrasts with /kʷ/, but /t/ does not contrast with /tʷ/) and

(ii) only alveolar stops and fricatives are followed by /w/ (cf. OE *twa* 'two', *twelf* 'twelve', *twentig* 'twenty', *betwix* 'between', and *sweord* 'sword'; /w/ disappeared in some initial /tw/ and /sw/ clusters preceding a round back vowel in late Middle English and Early Modern English, so that <w> is a "silent" letter in the words *two* and *sword* today).

If it is true that the labiovelar segments were reanalyzed as consonant clusters of a velar stop followed by a labiovelar approximant at an early stage of Old English, the phoneme inventory changed in that labiovelar obstruents gradually became obsolete and the phonotactics changed as a consequence: the language now allowed alveolar and velar obstruents followed by a labiovelar approximant in the onset of a syllable. Clusters with labial obstruents followed by /w/ did not emerge, presumably due to a ban on identical places of articulation in two adjacent onset consonants, i.e. a so-called "OCP-effect" (Obligatory Contour Principle), which prohibits /pw/, /fw/, /tl/, /dl/, etc. as possible word-initial clusters.

The change described above from a complex phoneme to a consonant cluster is one example of how the loss of a phoneme was compensated for by relaxing the phonotactics. The reverse state of affairs is also attested: at least in one case, a phonotactic restriction ("disallow sequences of /s/ immediately followed by /k/") resulted in the emergence of a new phoneme. Some sequences of alveolar /s/ followed by the velar stop /k/ were at some point no longer pronounced as /sk/ by the Anglo-Saxons, but rather as the alveopalatal sound /ʃ/ (as in the words *ship, sheep, shoe* and *fish*). It is often argued that in Old English, the change from /sk/ to /ʃ/ was the result of palatalization (see below). However, palatalization occurred in the context of front vowels, whereas /sk/ clusters seem to have become alveopalatal fricatives in more environments, for instance, word-initially independent of the quality of the following vowel, word-medially (except where the cluster is not tautosyllabic before back vowels, e.g., *aiskojan → *ascian* 'to ask' where <sc> represents /sk/) and word-finally. A similar assimilation process must have applied in the German language as well, since words of the same origin – so-called "cognates" – are also pronounced with an alveopalatal fricative in this language (as in the German [Ger.] words *Schiff* 'ship', *Schaff* 'sheep', *Schuh* 'shoe', and *Fisch* 'fish'). Other West-Germanic languages such as Frisian and Dutch still have initial consonant clusters in these words (e.g. Frisian [skip] and Dutch [sxɪp] for 'ship').

In different Germanic systems, /sk/-clusters are more or less stable. For instance, in the history of Icelandic, /sk/ remained fairly stable, whereas /sk/ was less stable in the history of English and very unstable in the history of German, where such clusters are now extremely rare. Even though these three languages derived from a common origin, they put different restrictions on consonant clusters in their respective histories. We conjecture here that Icelandic retained /sk/ clusters because they were highly frequent and could be syllabified as coda-onset clusters in most environments (e.g. *fis.kur* 'fish-NOM', *fis.kinn* 'the fish-ACC'); they are retained in environments where other languages would ban them because of analogy (e.g. in *fisk* 'fish-ACC') – here the cluster is not modified in analogy to the form *fiskur* 'fish-NOM'). In English, /sk/ clusters were modified at a particular stage in the history of the language and they were reintroduced when a large number of loanwords from Old Norse, Latin, etc. entered the language which had /sk/-clusters. Finally, in German, /sk/ clusters underwent a change that also affected most loans (presumably because German never borrowed as many words which involved /sk/-clusters as English did, so that the driving force to reintroduce them – i.e. the renewed relative frequency of /sk/-sequences – did not apply here; only a very few loanwords, all of Greek (Gk.) origin, retained the /sk/ cluster, e.g. Ger. *Skelett* 'skeleton').

Theoretically, there are many ways to resolve the ban on /sk/ clusters, e.g. metathesis (/sk/ → /ks/), prosthesis (/sk/ → /ɛsk/), epenthesis (/sk/ → /sək/), simplification (/sk/ → /s/ or /sk/ → /k/), gemination (/sk/ → /ss/ or /kk/), change of the place or manner of articulation of one of the consonants in the cluster (/sk/ → /sx/), or merger, so that the place of articulation of one segment survives and the manner of articulation of the other segment survives (/sk/ → /t/ or /sk/ → /ʃ/). The open question is why a language opts for which solution. The first possibility, metathesis, is not favored in word-initial positions, because the result does not make a better word-onset than the original cluster. Prosthesis is often found in a context of a preceding consonant, so that the preceding consonant can fill the onset position and the prosthesized vowel can form the nucleus of a new syllable of which /s/ can be the coda consonant. Prosthesis is attested in texts from the 2nd century onwards in word-initial /s/ plus voiceless stop clusters after consonants in Romance languages. This process gradually spread to all contexts in which word-initial /s/ is followed by a stop (e.g. Fr. *esprit* 'spirit' and Spanish *estado* 'state'). English has borrowed a considerable number of words with initial /ɛs/ plus stop clusters from Romance (e.g. *escape*). Epenthesis is an option that second language users often employ to remedy syllable structures that do not occur in the native language. Simplification of /s/ plus consonant clusters is an option that is often found in early child speech. Kiparsky (2003: 329) points out that assimilation of consonant clusters resulting in gemination seems to happen in languages that already have geminates, whereas languages without pre-existing geminates prefer to simplify clusters. A change of manner of articulation of the second consonant (/sk/ → /sx/) has taken place in Dutch. The merger of the segments /s/ and /k/ into one that shares properties with both consonants such as /t/ – which like /s/ is alveolar and which like /k/ is a stop – is unlikely, because the single consonant /t/ does not reflect the perceptually distinct stridency of the original /sk/ cluster. In Old English, the strident nature of the first element in the cluster is preserved and the alveolar fricative is retracted in the context of the following back consonant which is left unrealized (/sk/ → /ʃ/). This process introduces a new segment: the system did not accommodate alveopalatals before the change took place and the effect of the change is thus an extension of the consonant inventory. Note that we do not need to assume the introduction of a novel distinctive feature for this change if we assume that velar sounds are specified for the feature [back]; alveopalatal fricatives may be then specified for [strident] as well as [back], so that the contrast between /s/ [strident], /ʃ/ [strident, back] and /x/ [back] can be expressed by features that were already distinctive in the phonology of speakers of English.

One of the most interesting aspects of linguistic change is the fact that some units resist change. In Romance languages, prosthesis affected not only /sk/, but also /sp/ and /st/. In English, only /sk/ underwent a change. The fact that /sk/ is modified whereas /sp/ and /st/ do not results in an asymmetry in the system: now only labial and alveolar stops follow /s/; velar stops no longer do. However, the change from word-initial /sk/ → [ʃ] did not apply across the board and was not permanent. Consider in this respect that under the influence of Scandinavian invaders and Latin scholars, loanwords were introduced into the language which started with /sk/ clusters and these clusters were not modified, but borrowed as such into the English language (e.g. *skill* and *sky*, which are loans from Old Norse).

The temporary ban on /sk/ clusters resulted in a change in the linguistic system. The change /sk/ → [ʃ] itself was short lived, but it had a long-lasting effect. In Jakobson's terminology, this sound change is the "formation of a contrast": the effect of the change on the system is the creation of a new contrast within the class of fricatives (such that alveolar /s/, for instance, now contrasts with alveopalatal /ʃ/).

2.2 Stability and instability in consonant inventories related to allophonic variation

In many varieties of Old English, most notably West Saxon and Northumbrian, the Germanic voiceless velar stop /k/ gradually developed into the voiceless palatal affricate [tʃ] in the following three contexts:
- if initial followed by a front vowel or /j/ (e.g. OE *cild* [kild] → [kʲild] → [tʃild] 'child'; OE short vowels lengthened sometime around the 10th century if they were preceded by /ld/ clusters. Long vowels later underwent the Great Vowel Shift (e.g. OE /kīld/ → EModE /tʃaɪld/).

- if medial preceded and followed by a front vowel (e.g. OE *cwice* 'quitch') and
- if final preceded by front vowel (e.g. OE *ic* [ɪk] → [ɪtʃ] 'I').

The voiced velar stop /g/ underwent a similar process: if followed by a front vowel it was realized as /j/ (e.g. **georn* → *[j]ern* 'eager'). The voiced stop /g/ was palatalized if preceded by a front vowel (OE *bricg* [brɪg] → [brɪgʲ] → [brɪdʒ] 'bridge'), or between a nasal and /j/ (e.g. **sangjan* → *sen*[dʒ]*an* 'to singe'), or when geminated before /j/ (e.g. **laggian* → *lecgan* 'to lay', where <cg> represents /dʒ/). At the time when palatalization of /k/ and /g/ to [kʲ] and [gʲ]/[j] took place, the consonant inventory was stable and no phonological contrast was introduced. Rather, the segments /k/ and /g/ had allophonic variants which they did not have before.

In later stages in the history of English, we find velar stops before front vowels both in words of Germanic origin and in borrowed words. With respect to words of Germanic origin consider that for instance PGrmc. **kunningaz* had a velar stop before a back vowel. At the time that palatalization applied in Old English, the velar stop was still followed by a back vowel. Later, the vowel in question was affected by a process commonly referred to as "i-mutation", by which stressed long and short back vowels were fronted in the context of a following high front segment ([i], [j], [y]): PGrmc. **kunningaz* > OE *kynning* (mostly written as <cyning>) 'king'. After i-mutation, the process of palatalization did not apply and for this reason, many words of Germanic origin have a velar stop followed by a front vowel. Also note that palatalization of velar stops did not take place in Scandinavian borrowings (e.g. Present-day English *kid, kettle, dike, give, get, egg*). Thus, [tʃ] and [dʒ] are not allophonic variants of the phonemes /k/ and /g/ in Modern English. Instead, after the rule of palatalization ceased to play a role in the phonology of Old English and after borrowings from Scandinavian and other languages and after the change from [kʲ, gʲ] to [tʃ, dʒ], the consonant inventory is expanded, i.e. a new system emerged in which the phonemes /k/ and /g/ contrast with the phonemes /tʃ/ and /dʒ/, respectively.

There is a lot of debate over the realization of velar fricatives. Most textbooks maintain that OE /x/ was realized as [h] word-initially before vowels and before the sonorants /n, l, r, w/, it was pronounced as [x] medially and finally except after front vowels, and it was realized as palatal [ç] after front vowels. The variant [ç] gradually vocalized in all southern English dialects, resulting in compensatory lengthening of a preceding short vowel, which was later affected by the Great Vowel Shift (e.g. [ɪç] → [iː] → [ai] in words like *knight*, and *night*). In late Middle English, the variant [x] was labialized and changed into [f] when following round vowels (mostly /u/) in some dialects (cf. ModE *enough* where <gh> = /f/) and gradually disappeared entirely in other phonological contexts. With respect to the direction of phonological change, it is interesting to reflect on the following developments: in some variants of English, /xt/ changed into /ft/ after a short back vowel (cf. ModE *draught*), whereas in the early history of Dutch, monomorphemic /ft/ was disfavored and realized as /xt/ (compare Ger. *Luft* 'air' and *Kraft* 'power' to Dutch *lucht* and *kracht* and English *soft* and *after* to Dutch *zacht* 'soft' and *achter* 'after, behind' where <ch> represenets [x]). It is thus impossible to say that postvocalic /xt/ is generally less favored than postvocalic /ft/. Rather, both /xt/ and /ft/ are "unstable" clusters and the one may turn into the other, depending on the local conditions within a language at a certain time: English developed in such a way that velar fricatives became disfavored (i.e. they became obsolete by replacement by other segments or by omission), whereas at a certain time, Dutch extended the distribution of velar fricatives (e.g. the Germanic voiced velar plosive is realized as /x/ in most dialects of Modern Dutch).

Another consonantal innovation in Old English concerns allophonic variation among the fricatives: the singleton (or "short") voiceless fricatives /f, θ, s/ became voiced word-medially in the context of other voiced phonemes, as in (4):

(4) SG PL
wulf *wulfas* (<f> = /v/) 'wolf'
smiþ (<þ> = /θ/) *smiþas* (<þ> = /ð/) 'smith'
hūs *hūsa* (<s> = /z/) 'house'

After this allophonic rule had taken effect, no singleton voiceless fricatives were realized in word-medial position after a vowel. Old English intervocalic geminate consonants were degeminated later and this change gave rise to the phonemic opposition between short voiced and voiceless fricatives in word-medial positions. Thus, the addition of the phonological rule of degemination to the grammar generated segments (in this case singleton fricatives) that might have been the input of the phonological rule of intervocalic voicing. The fact that the degeminated fricatives did not undergo voicing indicates that the former allophonic rule ceased to have an effect. The result of these developments was that in word-medial positions, the opposition geminate versus singleton fricative was replaced by the opposition voiceless versus voiced fricative.

The word-final contrast between voiced and voiceless fricatives developed through schwa-reduction of full vowels in unstressed position and eventual loss of final schwa between 1100 and 1300, i.e. the fricatives that were voiced by an allophonic rule before, were no longer followed by a vowel, but occurred in word-final position. The initial voiced fricatives /v/ and /z/ originated primarily from Norman-French borrowings in Middle English (e.g. *valour* 'valor', *veel* 'veal', and *zele* 'zeal').

The result of the allophonic variation in Old English between voiceless and voiced fricatives combined with the loss of geminate consonants and the loss of word-final schwa and the introduction of /v/ and /z/ in initial position with borrowings from French resulted in a system where voiceless and voiced fricatives are distinctive.

2.3 Changes in phonotactics without effects on the consonant inventory

In describing phonotactic restrictions, it is generally agreed in phonological theory that the concept of "sonority" plays a crucial role. Sievers (1881) and Jespersen (1904) introduced the Sonority Sequencing Principle to explain the fact that, within a syllable, the less sonorous segments are found at the periphery and the most sonorous sounds are found in the syllable peak. The idea that sonority is not an absolute property, but rather a relative one, gave rise to the notion of "strength hierarchies" (e.g. Lass 1970) and a "sonority scale". In the sonority scale presented in (5), the degree of sonority of segments increases from left to right:

(5) *Sonority scale for some segments*

⎯⎯⎯⎯⎯⎯⎯⎯⎯⎯⎯⎯⎯⎯⎯⎯⎯⎯⎯⎯⎯⎯⎯⎯⎯⎯⎯⎯⎯⎯⎯▶

p, t, k, b, d, g   f, s, ʃ, x   m, n   l, r   j, w   i, u e, o a
stops   fricatives   nasals liquids glides vowels of different height

In Old English, possible syllable-initial consonant clusters only needed to show a slight increase of sonority. In stressed syllables, initial clusters of voiceless /k/ and /x/ or voiced /g/ followed by a nasal (/kn/, /gn/, /xn/) or clusters of the glide /w/ followed by a sound which was of the same degree of sonority (a rolled /r/) were as common as clusters with a steeper increase of sonority such as stop-liquid clusters. Lutz (1992) suggests that initial clusters with unfavorable phonotactics may result in different changes such as

(i) the loss of the initial consonant of the cluster (e.g. ME *wlispen* → 14th/15th centuries *lisp* and ME *fnēsen* → 14th/15th centuries *neeze* 'sneeze'),
(ii) the replacement of the initial consonant by a consonant that forms a more favorable consonant sequence (e.g. OE *wlott* → 14th century *blot*), and
(iii) loss of words that start with such unfavorable clusters (e.g. OE *wlank* 'proud', *wrabble* 'squirm', and *gnede* 'misery' became obsolete in the 15th and 16th centuries).

The syllable-initial clusters /xn/, /xl/, and /xr/ were lost within a short time span between the OE and the ME periods. The initial clusters /kn/, /gn/, and /wr/ were spelled and probably still pronounced as such when the writing system became more and more standardized after the introduction of Caxton's printing press in the late 15th century. The reduction of /wr/ to /r/ probably took place relatively early (possibly starting in late Middle English). Shakespeare's puns on *knight–night*, *knot–not* and *wring–ring* indicate that the initial sound in such clusters was either no longer pronounced during his time, or that there was variation between the pronunciation with and without the initial consonant. In the course of the 16th century, the phonotactics of the language gradually changed in such a way that sonority distances in syllable-initial clusters became larger: except for word-initial clusters with /s/ (*spy*, *stop*, *sky*, *sneeze*), the only permissible onset clusters after Shakespeare's time are those in which a stop or fricative is followed by a liquid or a glide (as in the words *dry*, *fly*, *cue*, *queen*). In 17th-century educated English, the reduction of /kn/ and /gn/ to /n/ was completed and other dialectal varieties followed. In Present-day English, words that are borrowed from other languages that start with such impermissible clusters are modified by English speakers in such a way that both sounds of the cluster are realized. However, the ban on having syllable-initial /kn/ or /gn/ clusters still exists. In order to realize both members of the clusters, the strategy that speakers use today is to insert a vowel between the two consonants. Thus, the Hebrew word *Knesset* and the German name *Knopf*, for instance, are both pronounced with initial /kən/ in Present-day English (see Green 1997: 25–28). Thus, the Present-day repair strategy for unfavorable phonotactics is vowel epenthesis.

2.4 Stability and instability in the vowel inventory and the effect on phonotactics

Middle English diphthongs /iʊ/ (occurring in words like *chew*, *due*, and *hue*) and /eʊ/ (occurring in words like *beauty*, *dew*, and *few*) eventually collapsed under /juː/. In the diphthong /iʊ/, the first part was reanalyzed as the glide /j/ and assigned to the onset, while /ʊ/ turned into /uː/ to compensate for the loss of vowel quantity in the late 16th century. In the diphthong /eʊ/, the first member was gradually raised to /i/ after the 16th century. In the 18th century, the element /i/ was reanalyzed as a glide and the element /ʊ/ was tensed and lengthened, so that the original contrast between /iʊ/ and /eʊ/ was lost by the end of the 19th century in most dialects of English. The question is whether the original diphthongs palatalized the preceding consonant (as in d^jue and d^jew), or whether the original diphthongs are now realized as sequences of the palatal glide /j/

followed by the high back vowel /uː/. Consider in this respect that consonants with and without a following /j/ are not allophones of a phoneme, because – as the (6) illustrates – there are also instances of consonants followed by a high back vowel without the intervening palatal glide /j/:

(6) *Syllable-initial sonorant + /j/ clusters in Present-day British English*
    a. music   [mjuːzɪk]   versus   moose   [muːs]
    b. nude   [njuːd]   versus   noon   [nuːn]
    c. lurid   [ljuːrɪd]   versus   lunatic   [luːnətɪk]

Interestingly, even though the palatal glide [j] may follow [l] in word-initial position in Present-day British English, we never find that a cluster of a non-strident obstruent plus [l] is followed by [j]. Hence, there is no [j] between [l] and a following vowel in words like *plumage, blue, clue, glue*, but, according to Harris (1994: 61), some speakers have one in *slew*. This fact has important consequences for the analysis of English syllable structure. In particular, we might conclude from this observation that /j/ should not be analyzed as a secondary place of articulation. If it were, the explanation for the fact that a palatal glide may be present in single consonants, but not in some consonant clusters would be cumbersome. Instead, the phoneme /j/ is a consonantal segment which may occupy one position in the onset. Apart from /s/-initial clusters, the English onset may be filled by at most two positions and three-consonantal clusters such as */plj/, */blj/, */klj/ or */glj/ would violate this restriction. Note that American English introduced a further restriction on initial clusters with /j/: it bans clusters in which a coronal consonant is followed by a palatal glide /j/ (as in the words *tune, dune, suit, new*). Since a palatal place of articulation is a sub-class of coronals, this ban may be interpreted as an OCP-effect (see Section 2.1).

3 The future of looking back in time on sound changes

For Roman Jakobson and many phonologists after him, "phonology is the study of the properties of the sound systems which speakers must learn or internalize in order to use language for the purpose of communication" (Hyman 1975: 1). The word "systems" implies the notion of "stability" and suggests that the properties of sound systems are stable. However, as we saw in this chapter, little in phonology seems to be stable. For communication to be successful, speakers and hearers must share linguistic knowledge (e.g. knowledge of how sounds are used by the speaker). When we compare different stages of a language, we find that the properties of sounds that speakers use are not stable at all but nevertheless, communication between speakers and hearers functions well. How is this possible? Part of the answer lies in the fact that phonological properties of human languages are flexible and constrained only by what our vocal tract allows us to produce and by what our ears allow us to perceive. For instance, to differentiate voiceless stops from voiced ones, the following properties may vary: the length of the preceding vowel, the formants of a preceding and following vowel, the duration of the stop's closure phase (i.e. closure duration), the presence/absence of vocal fold vibration during the closure phase (so-called "closure voicing"), the voicing lag or "VOT", i.e. the time between the release of the closure phase and the onset of vocal fold vibration (with a large scale to choose from), burst intensity, burst duration, and more. In English, the major cues to distinguish laryngeal classes of stops are the length of the preceding vowel and the VOT values of the stops in question: voiced stops are preceded by a relatively long vowel duration and have a relatively short voicing lag whereas voiceless stops are preceded by a comparatively shorter vowel and have a longer voicing lag when initial in a word. Pohl and Grijzenhout (2010 and references therein) suggest that in German, a difference in voicing lag is the major cue to maintaining the contrast, whereas in Dutch closure voicing and the duration of the closure phase seem to matter most to identify a voiceless or voiced stop and in Swiss German closure duration alone contrasts two classes of stops. Thus, in the modern Germanic languages, each language favors a different cue or set of cues (and the speakers may have different mental representations for the contrast in question). Children must "learn" to pay attention to the relevant cues in their language and then "internalize" that information – i.e. to build mental representations – to use it to convey meaning. Later generations may shift the attention to another cue or cues and this shift may be very small and hardly noticeable at first. When this shift is used by more speakers of a community, it may cause temporal or permanent change. For example, Dutch seems to shift from closure voicing and closure duration to differences in VOT as the major cue to maintain the distinction; the contrast between /p/ and /b/ remains, but its instantiation is different and it may lead to different mental representations for future generations. Thus, one source of change in the sound system is its inherent variability and flexibility which allows speakers to highlight relevant phonological properties and vary the irrelevant properties of sounds. Hearers too are able to ignore irrelevant phonetic detail (i.e. they abstract away from much information in the acoustic signal) and they pick up on just a few properties of the speech signal that make a distinction between two sounds. The system may change to enhance, create, or omit a contrast (e.g. a system with positive VOT distinctions of 10ms versus 80ms may become a system with negative VOT and positive VOT, or there may be room to add another VOT contrast or the contrast may vanish over time). Part of the answer why change occurs is thus: because the system is flexible, change is preprogrammed.

The next question is when does change occur? The Neogrammarians advocated the view that change is "spontaneous" and others also find an answer in sociological factors (e.g. peer group pressure, the need to be different from your neighbor, the need to borrow words from your neighbor). Human beings live in groups. In order for the group to be successful, it has either to blend in with other groups (so that a language contact situation may result in language change), or to compete with other groups (so that variations emerge within one dialect or language which may eventually lead to language split) or – when the group becomes too big – to form subgroups with their own identity (and, hence, their own language variety). This is a continuing or "dynamic" process. Languages will always change and there is enough flexibility in the speech signal to allow them to do just that.

The question that many people raise is why some languages seem to resist change or change relatively slowly, whereas others seem to change more rapidly. To illustrate the point, we would here like to compare the histories of Icelandic and English. Icelandic is spoken in a relatively isolated part of the world where it did not come in contact with many other languages (one possible source of language change). Moreover, as Kristján Árnason (p.c.) once pointed out to me, there has been a long tradition of a conscious effort to maintain the language and not to allow innovations or to "imitate" the Danes and the Germans. Dialectal variations that emerged in smaller communities in Iceland were stigmatized and gave way to the standard dialects spoken by the majority. Moreover, the population is small enough for language planning committees to be able to impose their recommendations and social pressure has a major effect on the relative stability of the language. In contrast, ever since the Anglo-Saxons landed on the British Isles, the English language has been exposed to foreign influences and this has had a major effect on the relative instability of some of its properties. There have been many attempts to preserve or "improve" the language, but such attempts apparently have been less successful than in Iceland. As late as at the turn of the 20th century, phoneticians like Daniel Jones attempted to develop a theory of sound systems that would help second language learners to acquire the accurate pronunciation of words in a foreign language (Jones 1917). Moreover, phonetics as the study of sound systems was considered to be useful in helping to improve the pronunciation of native speakers. George Bernard Shaw certainly contributed to this view in 1912 when he made Professor Higgins teach Eliza Doolittle the "proper" pronunciation of words in his popular play *Pygmalion*. Such attempts have proven to be futile: there is no proper pronunciation of English and the many speakers of the language will never employ exactly the same pronunciation of all sounds. English has always had many dialects: some are conservative and have archaic features, whereas others are more progressive and are open to innovations. Both types of dialects have considerable numbers of speakers for whom it is advantageous (from a sociolinguistic perspective) to use the dialectal variety. Also, since the 16th century, the language has expanded to new territories and the distance between the British Isles may have lead to independent developments between varieties of English spoken throughout the world. There are thus many reasons why English has changed so much over the centuries and why there is so much diversity. The future of looking back on English sound change lies in the fact that English is a global language with a rapidly growing number of speakers and for this reason alone, interest in its ever changing sound system will not vanish.

Even a voluminous handbook of English would still be incomplete in that not all changes which have occurred in the English language could be illustrated and discussed. Improved techniques, the availability of more extensive corpora, etc. will in the near future certainly result in extending our knowledge of which aspects triggered which kind of change in the history of the English language. Linguists like Aditi Lahiri and Frans Plank (p.c.), however, hold that it is actually more surprising that some aspects of a language are stable and do not change (or change relatively slowly or only within a relatively small area), i.e. the future of looking back on linguistic change also lies in the interest in which properties of language are unstable and highly variable compared to properties that are stable or invariable in the sense that they resist change or change slowly. This is a relatively underexplored field.

4 Summary

Phonology is the study of the properties of sounds which speakers use to convey meaning. As pointed out in Section 1, a primary goal of structural and generative phonology is to investigate the function of speech sounds, i.e. to establish and compare phoneme inventories of languages. In this chapter, we have seen examples of phonemes that changed their shape (e.g. voiceless stops becoming fricatives according to Grimm's Law), phonemes that were added to the English inventory (e.g. alveopalatal fricatives), and phonemes that became obsolete (e.g. /k^w/, /x/).

We have also looked into the behavior of speech sounds: some allophonic rules (e.g. voicing of fricatives in the context of other voiced segments) emerged at some stage and disappeared again later. Section 2.2 discussed two examples of allophonic variants that developed into phonemes (alveopalatal affricates and voiced fricatives, respectively).

Another goal of phonology is to account for the distribution of speech sounds. For English, we have seen that changes in phonotactics may be temporal (e.g. the ban on /sk/) and that the effect of a phonotactic restriction may give rise to a new phoneme (e.g. /ʃ/). Some phonotactic restrictions may be added relatively late in the history of a language (e.g. the ban against /kn/ clusters) and may change their effect (from deletion of a segment in the cluster to insertion of a vowel to break up the cluster). Sometimes, a change in the phoneme inventory may result in the addition of new phonotactics (e.g. changes from the diphthongs /iʊ/ and /eʊ/ to the monophthong /u:/ preceded by /j/ which can form a complex onset with any single consonant).

In many cases, a merger of two consonants into one may result in a new phoneme for which the distinctive features are already part of the system (/sk/ → /ʃ/), allophonic rules and borrowings may also create new phonemes (e.g. voiced fricatives) and a change from a complex phoneme into a simplex one may result in new phonotactics.

5 References

Aitchison, Jean. 2013 [1981]. *Language Change: Progress or Decay?* 4th edn. Cambridge: Cambridge University Press.
Baudouin de Courtenay, Jan Niecisław. 1895. *Versuch einer Theorie phonetischer Alternationen.* Strasbourg: Trübner.
Goldsmith, John A. 1995. Phonological theory. In: John A. Goldsmith (ed.), *The Handbook of Phonological Theory*, 1–23. Cambridge, MA/Oxford: Blackwell.
Green, Anthony Dubach. 1997. *The Prosodic Structure of Irish, Scots Gaelic, and Manx.* Ph.D. dissertation, Cornell University.
Harbert, Wayne. 2007. *The Germanic Languages.* Cambridge: Cambridge University Press.
Harris, John. 1994. *English Sound Structure.* Cambridge, MA: Blackwell.
Hyman, Larry M. 1975. *Phonology: Theory and Analysis.* New York: Holt, Rinehart and Winston.
Iverson, Gregory K. and Joseph C. Salmons. 1995. Aspiration and laryngeal representation in Germanic. *Phonology* 12: 369–396.
Jakobson, Roman. 1939. Observations sur la classement phonologique des consonnes. *Proceedings of the 3rd International Congress of Phonetic Sciences*: 34–41.
Jakobson, Roman. 1971 [1962]. Retrospect. In: *Selected Writings I: Phonological Studies*, 631–658. The Hague: Mouton.
Jakobson, Roman, Gunnar Fant, and Morris Halle. 1951. *Preliminaries to Speech Analysis.* Cambridge, MA: MIT Press.
Jakobson, Roman and Morris Halle. 1956. *Fundamentals of Language.* The Hague: Mouton.
Jespersen, Otto. 1904. *Lehrbuch der Phonetik.* Leipzig: Teubner.

Jones, Daniel. 1917. *An English Pronouncing Dictionary*. London: Dent.
Jones, Daniel. 1967. *The Phoneme; its Nature and Use*. 3rd edn. Cambridge: W. Heffer & Sons Ltd.
Kiparsky, Paul. 2003. The phonological basis of sound change. In: Brian D. Joseph and Richard D. Janda (eds.), *The Handbook of Historical Linguistics*, 313–343. Malden, MA: Blackwell.
Lass, Roger. 1970. Boundaries as obstruents: Old English voicing assimilation and universal strength hierarchies. *Journal of Linguistics* 7: 15–30.
Lass, Roger. 1984. *Phonology: An Introduction to Basic Concepts*. Cambridge: Cambridge University Press.
Lutz, Angelika. 1992. Lexical and morphological consequences of phonotactic change in the history of English. In: Matti Rissanen, Ossi Ihalainen, Tertta Nevalainen, and Irma Taavitsainen (eds.), *History of Englishes*, 156–166. Berlin/New York: Mouton de Gruyter.
McCarthy, John J. 1993. A case of surface constraint violation. *Canadian Journal of Linguistics* 38: 169–195.
McCarthy, John J. and Alan S. Prince. 1993a. Generalized Alignment. In: Geert Booij and Jaap van Marle (eds.), *Yearbook of Morphology 1993*, 79–153. Dordrecht: Kluwer.
McCarthy, John J. and Alan S. Prince. 1993b. *Prosodic Morphology I: Constraint Interaction and satisfaction*. Ms., University of Massachusetts, Amherst and Rutgers University.
McCarthy, John J. and Alan S. Prince. 1995. Faithfulness and reduplicative identity. In: Jill N. Beckman, Suzanne Urbanczyk, and Laura W. Dickey (eds.), *University of Massachusetts Occasional Papers* 18: 249–384.
Pohl, Muna and Janet Grijzenhout. 2010. Phrase-medial bilabial stops in three West Germanic languages. *Linguistische Berichte* 222: 141–167.
Prince, Alan and Paul Smolensky. 1993. *Optimality Theory: Constraint Interaction in Generative Grammar*. Ms., Technical Report no. 2, Rutgers University Center for Cognitive Science, Cambridge, MA, MIT Press.
Sapir, Edward. 1921. *Language: An Introduction to the Study of Speech*. New York: Harcourt, Brace; downloaded from http://www.bartleby.com/186/.
de Saussure, Ferdinand. 1916. *Course de linguistique générale*. Paris: Payot.
Sievers, Eduard. 1881. *Grundzüge der Phonetik. Zur Einführung in das Studium der Lautlehre der Indogermanischen Sprachen*. Leipzig: Von Breitkopf & Härtel.
Waugh, Linda R. 1976. *Roman Jakobson's Science of Language*. Lisse: The Peter de Ridder Press.
Wunderlich, Dieter. 2008. Spekulationen zum Anfang von Sprache. *Zeitschrift für Sprachwissenschaft* 27: 229–265.

Donka Minkova
Chapter 4:
Prosody

1 Definition of terms —— 57
2 Syllable structure and syllable weight —— 58
3 Historical sources of information for prosodic reconstruction —— 59
4 Old English meter and prosody —— 60
5 Middle English meter and prosody —— 67
6 Post-Middle English prosodic innovations —— 72
7 References —— 75

Abstract: The chapter traces the development of word and phrasal stress from Old to Present-day English. Section 1 and Section 2 define the terms needed to describe the prosodic patterns of speech and address the notions of syllable structure and syllable weight. Section 3 surveys the methodological bases for prosodic reconstruction, focusing specifically on the interplay between meter and language in the recovery of rhythmic patterns in speech. Old English meter and prosody are covered in Section 4, where the basic principles of Old English alliterative versification provide the foundation for reconstructing word and phrasal stress. Middle English meter and prosody are covered in Section 5, again with specific references to metrical form, word stress, and phrasal stress. The section includes a discussion of the effect of lexical borrowing from French and Latin on the prosody of English. Section 6 is devoted to the major prosodic changes in English during and after the Renaissance.

1 Definition of terms

The term "prosody", as used in this chapter, refers to the properties and the organization of syllables into words, phrases, and sentences in speech. Outside of linguistics, the term prosody can also be used with reference to the study of verse and its properties; for the conventionalized rhythmic structures of verse we reserve the term "meter". The prosodic properties of speech are "suprasegmen-

---

Donka Minkova: Los Angeles (USA)

tal": their domain is larger than individual speech sounds, which are organized into higher-level units that are independently pronounceable, namely "syllables". The ability to divide an utterance into syllables is part of the intuitive knowledge that speakers have of their language. Very importantly, syllables are the carriers of "stress", the contrastive intensity that marks some syllables as more or less prominent. Phonetically, stress is associated with the use of a greater amount of respiratory energy on a syllable, increased tension of the vocal folds, and loudness. In terms of metrical structure, the prominent position is called an "ictus" (S); ictic positions are usually, but not always, filled by stressed syllables, while "non-ictic" (W) positions attract unstressed syllables.

Stress is binary in the sense that syllables are either stressed or unstressed. Further, a stress may range from a full primary/main stress, here marked with ´ (acute), to various levels of non-primary stress, here marked with ` (grave). Although informally we speak of "stressed" and "unstressed" vowels, and we place the stress marks over the vowels for typographic convenience, it is important to bear in mind that stress is a property of the entire syllable.

2 Syllable structure and syllable weight

The syllable is the smallest pronounceable prosodic unit, but it is also structurally complex in that it is further decomposable. At the core of the syllable is its "nucleus" or "peak", the segment of highest sonority in the string. Every syllable has to have one and only one nucleus, usually a vowel or a diphthong, but sometimes also a syllabic sonorant /r̩, l̩, m̩, n̩/. Consonants or consonant clusters to the left of the nucleus constitute the syllable "onset", and the consonants following the nucleus make up the "coda". The onset and the coda are not obligatory elements of the syllable. Universally, a filled onset is preferred to a filled coda. A coda consonant can contribute to the "weight" of a syllable, whereas an onset is commonly considered weight-neutral.

The division of a string of sounds into syllables follows the "Maximal Onset Principle". According to that principle, a single consonant between two vowels fills the onset of the syllable to the right (syllable divisions are marked with a period): *rea.son, e.ne.my, de.hu.mi.di.fy*. A two-consonant cluster is either divided or not, depending on whether the resulting onset is also a possible word-initial cluster: *com.post, prag.ma.tic, fic.tion*, but *hi.sto.ry, pa.tri.ot*. Three consonants between vowels are split again depending on the nature of the resulting cluster: *emp.ty, friend.ly, coun.try, um.bre.lla, a.strin.gent, o.sprey*. The Maximal Onset Principle does not apply across prosodically independent words, so *boil eggs* is not **boi.leggs*.

Syllable weight is a prosodic property tightly associated with stress: universally, heavy syllables attract stress and syllables that carry stress are likely to become heavy. In English a "heavy syllable" is any syllable whose peak is a long vowel or a diphthong: *see.saw, pay.ee,* or any syllable that ends in a consonant: *com.pul.sion, prac.tice*. A "light syllable" has a short vowel in the peak and no coda: *A.me.ri.ca, re.pli.ca*. In practice, in Present-day English all syllables except those ending in /ɪ, ɛ, æ, ʊ, ʌ, ə/ are heavy. Monosyllabic major class words (*clue, club, day, fry, three, wet*) cannot have a light syllable; it follows that /*clɛ, *frɪ, *sʊ/ would not be possible English words, while /clɛs, frɪn, sʊg/ are possible words which are accidental gaps in our vocabulary (see Minkova 2013: 39–45).

3 Historical sources of information for prosodic reconstruction

Reconstructing the prosodic properties of the earlier stages of English is a complex task. The types of segmental changes that occur in stressed and unstressed syllables are very dissimilar. Vowel lengthening, vowel shifting, and gemination typically occur in stressed syllables, while vowel reduction and loss and consonant lenition are expected in unstressed syllables. If we find textual evidence of such processes, we can make prosodic inferences: the progressive reduction and loss of the prefix *ge-* (OE *geriden* > ME *iriden* > PDE *ridden* 'ridden') is good evidence that *ge-* was unstressed in Old English and Middle English. Similarly, Middle English spellings *luved, luvd* for earlier *luvede* 'loved' indicate reliably that the form was initially stressed. Our most direct source of information about the prosodic structure of earlier English, however, comes from the way in which the forms of speech are matched to the structural positions in verse.

The greatest challenge for the use of verse as the primary evidence for prosodic reconstruction is circularity: since there are no records of instructions on what is permitted in early versification, we rely on templates extrapolated from the surviving poetic corpus. Our understanding of how the metrical templates worked is thus founded on a web of typological inferences about language and meter with no possibility of direct verification. The way we avoid *ignotum per ignotius*, explaining 'the unknown by means of the more unknown' is by applying testable quantitative and typological criteria to the formulation of the rules of meter and the reconstruction of prosodic patterns. The statistical data on some features, e.g., in 26,088 verses of OE poetry, only 36, or 0.001%, lack alliteration (Hutcheson 1995: 169), justify reliance on alliteration as the binding principle in the alliterative long line, here marked in boldface. Moreover, testably unstressed syllables, such as inflectional syllables, never alliterate, which makes the co-occurrence of stress and alliteration a solid source of prosodic reconstruction. No matter what theory of Old English meter one adopts, there can be no doubt that in *Beowulf* (henceforth *Beo*) 102: *wæs se grímma gæst / Gréndel haten* 'was the grim ghost / Grendel called', the words *grímma* and *Gréndel* are initially stressed. Typologically too, all Germanic languages, including Present-day English, stress native unprefixed words on the first syllable; we can safely project that back to Old English and posit root-initial stress on *cýning* 'king', *démaþ* 'they judge', *hǽðen* 'heathen', *sóþe* 'truly'. The alignment of the main stress with the left edge of a simplex word in early English is known as the "Germanic Stress Rule" (GSR).

Statistical and typological grounding of prosody-meter correspondences is our best recourse in spite of some inherent uncertainties. The historical poetic corpus presents cases where deviations from an established norm may be interpreted as deliberate creative choices. A poet may force an unstressed syllable into an ictic position to fit the expectations of the template: thus Chaucer rhymes *felawe : awe, biddyng : thing*. This convention of versification is of no use to us in trying to reconstruct the prosodic contour of Germanic *felawe* or *biddyng* in speech – the words were always initially stressed. On the other hand, Chaucerian rhymes such as *honour : flour, servise : wyse* have, all too freely, been taken as evidence for non-initial stress on the Romance borrowings *honour* and *servise*. Such evidence has to be evaluated carefully and compared to the evidence of the placement of such words in line-medial position. Similarly, placing *réady, únder, máketh* at the left edge of an iambic (W S) line is a metrical inversion which breaks the monotony of repeated identical structures, but it tells us nothing new or special about the prosody of these native words. However, placing loans such as *citees, justice, poynaunt* line-initially is open to both WS and SW metrical scansion and can be considered good evidence that such words maintain their Romance stress contour. We will return to these metrical issues in Section 5.1. For now we just note that decisions on the prosodic history of loanwords will have to be based on fine-grained and comprehensive coverage of the placement of individual items in the verse.

4 Old English meter and prosody

Germanic and Old English versification is notoriously difficult to model. Although new theories of Old English meter continue to appear, most recently in Getty (2002), Bredehoft (2005), and Teresawa (2011), no new approach rivals the descriptive adequacy and scholarly acceptance of the observations and patterns in Sievers (1893); see Stockwell and Minkova (1997), Minkova (2008a).

4.1 Basic principles of Old English alliterative verse

Sievers's hypothesis about the metrical structure of Old English verse rests on the following configurations:
- a line consists of two verses, the "on-verse" ("a-verse") and the "off-verse", ("b-verse"), linked by alliteration;
- each verse contains two feet and at least four positions;
- each foot contains an ictus (S), also known as a "lift", and at least one non-ictic position (W), also known as a "dip".

This allows us to represent the structure of the line as in Figure 4.1, where the numbers at the bottom stand for positions:

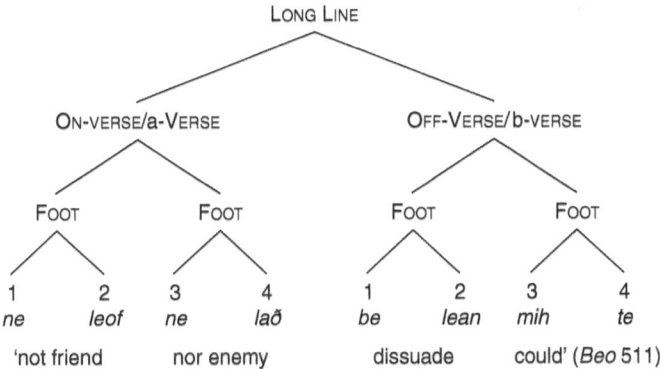

Figure 4.1: The structure of the Old English verse line

The binary representation in Figure 4.1 is an abstraction based on the minimal line structure in terms of syllable count. The prominence relations are unspecified; within the feet, lifts and dips can appear in either order. Each position is ideally filled by a single syllable, and an S position must be filled by at least one syllable. Unlike the familiar notion of classical metrical feet, positions and feet in Old English verse may be of uneven size, due mainly to the expandability of the non-final weak positions in each verse, thus in *þégnas syndon geþwǽre* 'thanes are united' (*Beo* 1230a) the template S W S W has the first W position filled by four unstressed syllables: *-nas syn.don ge-*. The one-to-one correspondence between a syllable and a position may be disregarded for S-positions under special metrical conditions; this is known as "resolution". Resolution is a metrical equivalence: one and only one heavy syllable can fill a lift, but a light syllable and any other syllable may jointly fill a lift to avoid an unacceptable metrical violation, such as an expanded dip at the right edge of the verse. Thus in the S W S W verse *réceda under róderum* 'of halls under heavens' (*Beo* 310a), the syllables *ró.de-* are metrically subsumed under the second S position to avoid the unacceptable matching of the last W to *-de.rum*.

The conventions of alliteration which help us separate relevant from irrelevant metrical information are:
- in the on-verse both S positions may alliterate.
- in the off-verse only the first S position is allowed to alliterate.

Nearly all verses are complete syntactic units. The smallest linguistic units that occupy a verse are compounds, e.g. *þeodcyninga* 'of tribe-kings' (*Beo* 2a), *wilgesiþas* 'willing companions' (*Beo* 23a), *landgemyrcu* 'shore-boundaries' (*Beo* 209b). Most often, however, a verse is coextensive with a clause or a syntactic phrase: *Hi hine þa ætberon / to brimes faroðe* 'they him then carried / to the sea's current' (*Beo* 28).

An intriguing convention, not fully understood, describes the hierarchy of syntactic elements within the verse with respect to alliteration. In a verse where the S-positions are filled by a noun and a verb, the noun will consistently be strong, whether it is an NP-VP string as in *Him ða Scyld gewat* 'Then Scyld departed' (*Beo* 26a), or a VP-NP: *Gebad wintra worn* 'Lived to see winters many' (*Beo* 264a). This alliterative regularity is known as Sievers's "Rule of Precedence" (Sievers 1893: Sections 22–29); it states that if an inflected verb precedes a noun it does not have to alliterate, that it must not alliterate if the noun does not alliterate too, and that a non-alliterating noun can never be followed by an alliterating finite verb. The rule does not exclude double alliteration: *þenden wordum weold* 'when with words ruled' (*Beo* 30a), *geafon on garsecg* 'gave in ocean' (*Beo* 49a), so projecting the Rule of Precedence on to the prosody of Old English speech is not always straightforward. The significance of alliteration in the reconstruction of phrasal and utterance prosodic contours will be discussed further in Section 4.3.

4.2 Old English word stress

As noted in Section 3, Old English word stress falls on the first stressed syllable of word roots. The acoustic prominence of stress is thus, unsurprisingly, an important and consistent morphological boundary signal. All root-initial syllables are stressed. The weight of the root-initial syllable is irrelevant; both heavy and light syllables can be stressed: *drí.fan* 'drive', *fúl.tum* 'help', *mén.gan* 'mix', *só.na* 'soon' (heavy), and *cý.ning* 'king', *gá.fol* 'tax' *mé.du* 'mead', *scá.mu*, 'shame' (light). A very important difference between Old English and Present-day English is the stability of stress on the first root syllable in a derivational set: while suffix-induced stress-shifts in Present-day English can leave root-initial syllables completely stressless: *chronic–chronólogy, ídiot–idiótic, sólid–solídity*, Old English word roots are always marked by the presence of stress:

géogoð	*géogoðhad*	*wóruld*	*wóruldlic*
'youth'	'youth-hood'	'world'	'worldly'
hláford	*hláfordscipe*	*wúldor*	*wúldorfull*
'lord'	'lordship'	'glory'	'glorious'

The addition of suffixes in Old English never affects the primary prominence. The suffixes themselves can bear some degree of non-primary stress because they can be ictic, but they are automatically excluded from the positions of obligatory alliteration, the first ictic positions in each verse.

Inflectional suffixes are always unstressed, while derivational suffixes exhibit complex behavior in the verse and it is likely that their prosodic realization in speech was gradient, ranging from non-primary stress to absence of stress. The variability is attested both synchronically and diachronically. The position of the suffix with regard to the word boundary is of relevance, and so is vowel quality and quantity. When inflected, heavy suffixes with non-high vowels (*-lēas-* '-less', *-dōm-* '-dom', *-fæst-* '-fast', *-hād-* '-hood') are regularly scanned as lifts, e.g. *wísdòme heold* 'with wisdom ruled' (*Beo* 1959b), *of cíldhàde* 'from childhood' (*Elene* 914a), but uninflected *-dōm* '-dom', *-fæst* '-fast' are not ictic: *word ond wisdom* 'word and wisdom' (*Andreas* 569a), *wísfæst wórdum* 'wise with words' (*Beo* 626a). The placement of the word linearly in the verse is also significant: the suffixes *-sum* '-some', *-scipe* '-ship', *-ian* '-en' (v) occupy ictic positions only in the coda of the verse; for full coverage see Fulk (1992: 197–216).

Further indeterminacies arise from the difficulty of assigning suffixal status to morphological units which are also attested as independent words: *dōm, fæst, full, hād, lēas* are separate lexical entries, and their semantic autonomy may be related to the preservation of stress. Additionally, as demonstrated in Minkova and Stockwell (2005), the full prosodic history of native suffixes has to refer to rhythmic factors linked to the types and frequency of derived words in the lexicon. Thus the equally productive OE suffixes *-hād* and *-dōm* would be expected to emerge either both with a full vowel, or both with a reduced vowel in Early Modern English. However, in Middle English close to 70% of the *-dom* derivatives followed a monosyllabic root (*earldom, freedom, kingdom, wisdom*), where stress-clash avoidance resulted in de-stressing of the suffix to [-dəm/-dm̩], while during the same period 73% of *-hood* derivatives had a disyllabic stem (*bishophood, maidenhood, womanhood*), allowing the preservation of secondary stress on the affix and raising of the long vowel to [uː] prior to 17th-century shortening to [-hʊd]. In summary, all factors identified above – syllable weight, vowel quality or quantity, semantic independence, and rhythmically induced changes – must be considered in the account of Old English suffixal stress.

Derivational affixes often have their diachronic roots in independent words. Within the larger family of affixes, suffixes are cross-linguistically more likely to lose their independent word status than prefixes, and therefore one would expect more word-like behavior from prefixes. Identifying the exact range of prefixes in Old English is a widely recognized problem, precisely because outside of the invariably bound forms: *æf-, and-, be-, ed-, fær-, for-, ge-, mis-*, etc., there is no clear-cut divide between prefixes such as *ofer-, on-, wiþ-, ymb-* and words. Moreover, the metrical treatment of both bound and free prefixal forms may differ for nouns and adjectives, where main stress aligns with the left edge of the whole word, leaving the root with secondary stress, and verbs and adverbs, where the main stress is kept on the root: compare *swylce óncỳþðe* 'such grief' (*Beo* 830a) to *he onféng hraþe* 'he seized quickly' (*Beo* 748b).

As argued in Minkova (2008b), both syllable weight and the grammatical nature of the base are determiners of stress in OE prefixation. Light prefixes behave like clitics; they do not form independent prosodic words and are consistently unstressed, while prefixes capable of forming independent prosodic words get stressed in accord with the word class of the derivative (see Figure 4.2).

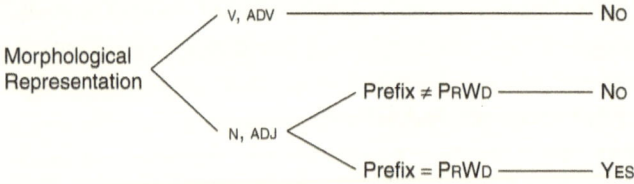

Figure 4.2: Prefixal stress in Old English (adapted from Minkova 2008b: 36)

The principle of root-initial stress persists in compounding, where roots get their first syllables stressed as if they were independent words. Within the larger domain of compounds the stress to the left is primary, marking off the left boundary of the entire word, while compound-internal stresses are secondary. In the verse, the obligatory alliteration is consistently placed on the first stressed syllable onset, e.g. *ofer* **h**rónràde 'over whale-road' (*Beo* 10a), **w**óroldàre forgeaf 'worldly honor gave' (*Beo* 17b). The second stressed syllable may alliterate only if the first stress alliterates too: *wið* **þ**éodþrèaum 'against people's calamity' (*Beo* 178a), **h**éardhìc-

gende 'hard-minded' (*Beo* 394a). Such self-alliterating compounds are restricted to the on-verse by definition, since alliteration is prohibited from the second ictus in the off-verse. This restriction does not extend to affixal elements, thus *láðlìce* 'hatefully' is found at the right edge of the off-verse. The inference is clear: in **þéod**þrèa 'people-calamity', **héard**hìcgend 'hard-minded', both roots retain their semantic independence and strong prosodic prominence. Such forms present an analytical problem: they are interpretable both as compounds and as freely formed syntactic phrases. Another difficulty comes from the fact that many of the self-alliterating compounds in the Old English corpus are *hapax legomena*, single-instance forms: *béarn-gebỳrdo* 'child-bearing', *éall-ìren* 'all of iron', *fén-frèoðo* 'marsh refuge', *grýre-gèatwe* 'terrifying armor', *grýre-gìest* 'terrible visitor', *héard-hìcgend* 'hard-minded, *héoro-hòcyht* 'savagely hooked', *hílde-hlæ̀mm* 'battle crash', *swát-swàðu* 'bloody track', *sýn-snæ̀d* 'huge cut', *þéodþrèa* 'people-calamity' are some examples of such unique forms in *Beowulf*. The status of these constructions is an area deserving further inquiry; cf. Giegerich (2009) who shows that end-stress on noun-noun compounds in Present-day English: *steel bridge, apple pie, Madison Avenue*, may reflect the syntactic provenance of incompletely lexicalized forms, and that nominals of the form attribute-head can be both lexical and syntactic.

4.3 Old English phrasal stress

In connected speech words are grouped together in larger prosodic constituents: clitic and phrasal groups. Clitic groups are made up of a fully stressed head-word and a clitic, an unstressed function word such as an article, a preposition, a conjunction, or a pronoun: *the bóok, at schóol*, etc., are clitic groups. Such groups behave in the same way in Old English: se *ríca* 'the ruler', on **béarme** 'on bosom'.

The stressed words in a sentence are syntactically organized into noun-, verb-, adverb- and adjective phrases, coordinate phrases, and clauses. In Present-day English such syntactic units are right-prominent; i.e., the highest prominence is on the rightmost stressed syllable, while other stresses are secondary: *càreful respónse, drìve cárefully, vèry cáreful, qùick and cáreful, Bèn cáres*.

Recovering the corresponding prosodic features of Old English from the existing textual records is challenging, and therefore the issue of phrasal prosody is under-researched and controversial. We know with certainty that the poets treated finite verbs differently from nouns; see Section 4.1 for Sievers's Rule of Precedence. Clause-final intransitive verbs (*oþþæt sǽl alàmp* 'until time came' (*Beo* 622b)) are metrically weaker, but this convention may not match speech prosody. Clause-initial finite verbs may be skipped by the alliteration, e.g. *Còm þa to récede* 'came then to building' (*Beo* 720a), *Forgèaf þa Béowulfe* 'gave then to Beowulf' (*Beo* 1020a), although the verbs also occupy ictic positions. Like the second elements of compounds, finite verbs may alliterate only if the other stressed word in the verse alliterates: **w**èox under **w**ólcnum 'waxed under the clouds' (*Beo* 8a), ... **w**órdum **w**èold '... with words ruled' (*Beo* 30a). Throughout the modern Continental West Germanic languages and in older Germanic, complements are stronger than their verbs, irrespective of the linear order. This typological comparison and the consistency with which complement-verb prosodic relations are observed in the verse – the complement always alliterates – is a good argument for projecting this prosodic contour to Old English.

Prominence in noun and adjective phrases and coordinate phrases is not directly recoverable from the verse. In this area the rules of alliteration may be more of a handicap than help. The frequent assumption that obligatory alliteration on the first word in such phrases (*lange hwile* 'a long while' (*Beo* 16a), ... **h**ond ond rond '... hand and shield' (*Beo* 656a)) translates directly into left prominence in the prosody is unfounded. The linear alliterative arrangement is a purely metrical convention, as can be seen from the freedom with which the poet switches components to fit the scheme in the line: **G**eata dryhten 'lord of the Geats' (*Beo* 2561b) vs. **d**ryhten Geata (*Beo* 2901a); **m**adma fela 'of treasures many' (*Beo* 36a) vs. **f**ela missera 'many of half-years' (*Beo* 153b), **m**anig oðerne 'many other (men)' (*Beo* 1860b) vs. **æ**þeling manig 'hero many' (*Beo* 1112b). Some other facts also prompt skepticism about the link between alliteration and linguistic prominence: the default contour (no special focus) for noun phrases and coordinate phrases in the modern Germanic languages is right-prominent; for German see Selkirk (1984: 225–230). Right-hand prominence is attested also in copulative combinations of the type *Anglo-Sáxon, Native Canádian*; they also typically align with syntactically coordinated phrases. The density of double alliteration in on-verses co-extensive with noun + prepositional phrase (*bat under beorge* 'boat under cliff' [*Beo* 211a]) and in conjoined phrases (*word ond wísdom* 'word and wisdom' [*Andreas* 569a]), exceeds by far the overall 47% ratio of double alliteration in the on-verse, as reported in Hutcheson (1995: 112). This asymmetrical distribution precludes a linguistic bias towards left-prominence, but does not rule our equal or right-hand prominence. The absence of double alliteration in the off-verse can only be metrically determined; see Russom (1987: 114), Hutcheson (1995: 271). The most economical account that does not require a historical shift, therefore, is that the right-prominent prosodic contour of phrasal stress has been in the language since Old English times (Minkova and Stockwell 1997).

5 Middle English meter and prosody

The Norman Conquest of 1066 coincides roughly with the abandonment of the structural principles of Classical Old English alliterative versification. The last surviving pieces of alliterative poetry that conform to the norms outlined in Section 4.1 are two short poems: *Durham*, c.1100, and *The Grave*, c.1150. Early Middle English compositions such as *The Proverbs of Alfred*, *The Worcester Fragments of the Soul's Address to the Body*, *The Bestiary*, and Lagamon's *Brut*, are "hybrid" compositions, mixing rhyme, alliteration and syllable-counting in often erratic patterns. Being grounded in the prosodic pattern of stress on the first root syllable, alliteration as a cohesive device survived, and a significant portion of the literary activity in the 14th century was channeled into the reinvention and composition of alliterative verse, culminating in masterpieces like *Sir Gawain and the Green Knight*, *Piers Plowman*, and *The Alliterative Morte Arthure*. At the same time new modes of versification based on rhyme, stress alternation, and syllable counting were gaining popularity. The relative rigidity of the new forms provides a solid basis for reconstructing the prosodic properties of Middle English.

5.1 Middle English metrical innovations: isosyllabicity, rhyme, iambic feet

Verses of equal numbers of syllables – "isosyllabic verses" – are not uncommon in Old English poetry, but the recurrence was not structurally regulated; a verse could have from a minimum of four to fourteen syllables. Isosyllabism is an imported metrical feature in Middle English. Schemes based on the iteration of isosyllabic lines – the octosyllabic line, the septenarius, and, with Chaucer, the decasyllabic iambic pentameter – are at the core of Middle English verse composition. All of these forms allow an unstressed syllable after the last ictus; such "extrametrical" syllables are outside the metrical template and their presence or absence does not affect the isosyllabicity of the line. The lines were often linked in couplets or larger groups by end-rhymes. Rhyming did appear occasionally as an ornamentation in Old English verse, but the influence of Anglo-Norman made it the verse-line marker of choice.

The third component of the new type of versification is the "iamb", a binary sequence of a weak and a strong position (W S). Iambic feet could occur in Old English verse as a subset of a larger right-strong metrical type: the first three feet in *ne léof ne láð / beléan mihte* 'not friend nor enemy / dissuade could' (*Beo* 511; see Figure 4.1), happen to be iambs. In Middle English isosyllabic verse, however, the iamb became the dominant metrical foot. The earliest post-Conquest long non-alliterative compositions, *The Owl and the Nightingale* and *The Ormulum*, both late 12th century, are strictly iambic. Chaucer's poetic works are also iambic. (All Middle English verse examples in this chapter are from Chaucer; abbreviations are from *The Riverside Chaucer* [Benson ed. 1987: 779].)

The reconstruction of stress based on the new type of versification is most reliable line-medially. The interplay between prosody and meter at the two edges of the line is complicated by specific properties of the first and the last foot. The left edge of the line is rhythmically malleable, so that the expected W S / W S metrical cadence of the first two feet may be filled by:

- a prosodic /s w w s/. An inverted foot S W followed by a regular W S foot is known as a "triple": *Thón.ked be Gód ...* (*WBT* 5), *Ún.der his belt ...* (*GP* 105). Triples may appear elsewhere in the line, but the probability of a triple decreases sharply from left to right.
- a prosodic /s w s w/, resulting in trochaic inversion in both feet: *Spóones and stóoles and ...* (*WBT* 288). Occasionally whole lines can be trochaic: *Bléssinge hálles, chámbres, kíchenes, bóures* (*WBT* 869).
- by /Ø s w s/, where the W of the first foot is unfilled and the line is headless: **Twénty bóokes**, *clad in blak or reed* (*GP* 294), **Swére and lýen**, *as a womman kan* (*WBT* 228).

The strong position in the rightmost foot of the line, where the rhyme is located, is metrically demanding in that it enforces prominence on the syllable filling that position. This is a verse convention, possibly observed in recitation, but it does not carry over into the prosody of speech. In Middle English rhyming practice, some suffixes appear to acquire metrically-induced secondary stress: *bóldelỳ, drónkenèsse*. The metrical strictness of the last strong position is such that it can even invert the prosodic contour of a native derived word by suppressing the primary stress and using the suffix as the single carrier of prominence, as in: *... and make a thyng : ... at his writỳng* (*GP* 325–326), *... in hir drónkenèsse : ... that I took witnèsse* (*WBT* 381–382). The convention is linguistically motivated only to the extent that derivational suffixes, but *not* grammatical suffixes, are subject to such metrical promotion.

The fashion for iambic versification in Middle English was a cultural import from the Continent, but it could not have been adopted with such ease if the prosodic conditions had not been favorable. The gradual loss of final <-e> and inflections in Middle English resulted in a growing number of words realized as monosyllables, allowing flexibility in the prosody-to-meter matching. Increased use of prepositions compensating for inflectional loss created new W S clitic groups: *at níght, to rést, with chéer*. Prefixed verbs and adverbs supplied another set of natural iambic structures: *befóre, forgíve, perfórm, asléep*. Phrasal stress continued to be right-strong; phrases made up of stressed monosyllables easily match an iambic foot: *five bóoks, tall mén, full glád, God knóws*. The poets also draw from an inventory of handy "fillers", semantically dispensable monosyllabic words, e.g. *and, now, for, some*, and the grammatically redundant "pleonastic" *this, that*. Thus, although individual underived words retained root-initial stress, in connected speech metrical W S cadences were frequent and easy to construct; this permits an effortless "fit" between language and meter.

Except for the metrical conventions at the line edges, iambic verse provides a reliable framework for reconstructing the stress of Middle English words on the basis of meter-to-prosody correspondences.

5.2 Native and non-native word stress in Middle English

The continuing stability of the GSR, aligning primary stress with the left edge of all words and with the left edge of the root for prefixed verbs and adverbs, is easily demonstrated in verse, as in *dróppyng, hóuses, smóke, chídyng, wýves, máken* in Chaucer's *Wife of Bath's Tale* (*WBT*), 278–279:

> Thow seyst that dróppyng hóuses, and eek smóke,
> And chídyng wýves máken men to flee

Words derived by suffixation also show the expected main stress on the leftmost root syllable, as *kíngship, wísdom, wítness, hóly, blíssful*: *The hóoly blísful ...* (*GP* 17). Again predictably, the first syllable of compounds is regularly aligned with a metrical S: *... for ány **léchecràft*** (*KnT* 2745), *with wílde **thónder-dỳnt** ...* (*WBT* 276), *to bé me **wárde-còrs** ...* (*WBT* 359). Compounds usually start in even (S) positions, but since both roots carry a degree of prominence, if the first part is monosyllabic, it can be placed in W, while the second root is in S, e.g. *Óf **clooth-mákyng** she hadde swich an haunt* (*GP* 447, headless), *He wás **shortshóldred**, brood, a thikke knarre* (*GP* 549).

Phrasal stress is not testable in iambic verse if there is a buffer weak syllable between the stressed syllables: *of sóndry fólk* (*GP* 25), *and máde fórward* (*GP* 33), *týme and spáce* (*GP* 35). Monosyllabic adjectives in noun phrases do provide some corroboration for continuing right-prominent phrasal stress: *ne pólax, **né short knýf*** (*KnT* 2544), *Gret swéryng is* (*PardT* 631), but the stress-alternating nature of the verse and the availability of optional *-e* and metrical slot-fillers obscure the picture. As argued in Minkova and Stockwell (1997), there is no good reason to posit any dramatic changes in the prosody of phrasal stress from Old English to Present-day English. Even if we assume a more level phrasal stress in Old English than in Present-day English, the right-hand prominence of Old French and Anglo-Norman would have contributed to the present contour.

The introduction of a large non-native component into the vocabulary of Middle English is a central theme in any account of the history of English word stress. The non-native vocabulary of Old English never exceeded about 3%, while the portion of the Romance vocabulary at the end of the Middle English period is estimated at about 25%. Once again, attestations in verse provide our best test for the realization of loanwords in the spoken language. Thus we can safely posit initial stress on *seson* in: *Bifil that in that **séson** on a day* (*GP* 19), *And eek the lusty **séson** of that May* (*KnT* 2484). The word was first attested in English 1340–1370 (OED, Proffitt [ed.] 2000–), roughly during Chaucer's lifetime (1343–1400), yet out of the 15 times Chaucer uses the word in *The Canterbury Tales* and in *Troilus and Criseyde*, there is one single attestation of the word in rhyme (*... thy declinacion : ... tyme and his seson* (*FrT* 1033–1034)) where one could possibly posit right prominence. Such evidence suggests that a metrical promotion to *sesòn* is not different from the treatment of native *writỳng, witnèsse* discussed in Section 5.1, i.e., there is no reason to differentiate between native and borrowed words at the line end. The 13th-century loanword *country* is used 45 times in *CT* and in *Tr*, 21 of which are in rhyme position and are realized as end stressed. Of the 24 line-internal attestations, however, there is not a single example of end stress on the word; they are all of the type illustrated by *SumT* 1710: *A msrsshy **cóntree** called holdernesse*. Such findings lead to a serious methodological amendment to the way of collecting verse data for prosodic reconstruction. As argued in Minkova (2000, 2006), the blanket assumption that the verse-final foot provides reliable information on stress is flawed. When we take rhyme position out of the picture, the rate of assimilation of the foreign prosodic contours to the native stem-initial prominence is significantly faster than has been previously acknowledged.

The new Romance words coming into the language after the Conquest could be direct loans from the Classical languages, or they could be coming via Anglo-Norman or Old French. Latin (and Greek-via-Latin) disyllabic words would be stressed initially by default: *áxle, érgo, hýmnal, hérpes, mórtar, stúpor, ónyx* were all borrowed in Middle English. According to the Latin Stress Rule, in words of more than two syllables stress falls on the penultimate syllable if it is heavy, otherwise, on the antepenultimate syllable. The Latin Stress Rule in polysyllabic words is thus weight-sensitive, but since many early Latin borrowings lost their inflectional markers (*-a, -(t)is, -us, -um*, etc.), the picture was often obscured, thus *júncture* < *junctūra, húman* < *humānus*.

Anglo-Norman and Old French words were stressed depending on the weight of the final syllable: if heavy, the final syllable attracts stress: *author, chaplain, jargon, merchant*. Light final syllables are unstressed: *able, chambre, piece*. Since final syllables containing schwa are unstressable, in initially polysyllabic words like *bataille, folye, justice, servise, visage* the stress was on the penultimate, as in Latin.

The extent to which weight-sensitivity at the right edge of the new words affected the prosody of Middle English has often been overestimated, mostly because of misinterpretation of the verse evidence; see Section 5.1. Both disyllabic and trisyllabic pre-Renaissance borrowings show a strong tendency of leftward stress-shifting, in conformity with the GSR, as in *juncture, human, chaplain, merchant, battle, folly, novice, service*. The leftward stress-shift disregards syllable weight; indeed in many cases the stress shifts leftwards from a heavy to a light syllable, as in *chaplain, battle, folly, justice, novice*. Table 4.1 shows the stress profiles of borrowed disyllabic simplex nouns and adjectives in alliterative and syllable-counting verse; the search ignores attestations in the final foot of iambic verse:

Table 4.1: Romance loans in Middle English verse (from Minkova 2006: 114)

Text	Tokens	Initial Stress	Non-initial Stress
Sir Gawain and the Green Knight	283	276/97.5%	7/2.5%
The Siege of Jerusalem	87	84/96.5%	3/3.4%
Troilus and Criseyde	266	223/84%	43/16%
Henryson's poetry	151	137/90.7%	14/9.3%

It is evident that the initial wave of borrowing did not upset the stem demarcation on the left. Verbs in which the prefixation is transparent behave like the native prefixed verbs discussed in Section 4.2.: **Perfóurme** *it out* ... (*Tr* III 417), *ye nát* **discóvere** *me* (*MerT* 1942). Prefixed nouns and adjectives vary. Chaucer uses both initial and final stress on *proverb*, a word first recorded in his works (OED): *Wel may that be a* **próverbe** ... (*WBT* 284), *And therfore this* **provérbe** *is* ... (*RvT* 4319). Etymologically non-transparent prefixed nouns and adjectives tend to follow the native rule: *Ben humble* **súbgit** ... (*Tr* II 828), ... *in joye and* **pérfit** *heele* (*KnT* 1271). The history of stress on prefixed loanwords in Middle English is an area which has not been fully researched yet – it is an inquiry that promises to throw light on the continuity and/or reintroduction of functional stress-shifts in English of the type *ábstract* (N, ADJ)–*abstráct* (V); *récord* (N)–*recórd* (V).

In iambic verse, polysyllabic words may be hard to fit to a metrical frame of alternating prominences. In Section 5.1 we noted how native suffixes appear to acquire metrically induced secondary stress: *bóldelỳ, drónkenèsse, dóutelèes, mártyrdòm*. The combination of dominant word-initial stress and the rhythmic preference for stress alternation in borrowed words produces a comparable effect in the new Romance vocabulary: the linguistic /w w s/ in the source language is realized in English as /s w s/: *àmoróuse, chàritée, làxatíf, òpposít, òrisóun, plèntevóus, règióun,* only in this case it is probably the left edge of the word that carried secondary stress at first, judging from the strong preference for placement of such words in rhyme position: *wróoth was shé : chàritée* (*GP* 451–452), *whít : òpposít* (*KnT* 1893–1894), *hóus : plèntevóus* (*GP* 343–344), *adóun : règióun* (*KnT* 2081–2082). The switch from word-initial secondary to primary stress on such trisyllabic words probably started during Middle English, but the precise dating is not recoverable from iambic verse, where both primary and secondary stresses may fill S-positions. The preservation of some degree of stress on the final syllable in Romance loans comfortably beyond Middle English is well documented in Early Modern English, see Dobson (1957: 830–860).

The placement of secondary stress on the initial syllable of four-syllable words with an unstressable final syllable: *dìgestíble : Bíble* (*GP* 437–438) *sàcrifice : wíse* (*KnT* 2369–2370), *dýe : of bìgamýe* (*WBT* 85–86) is also attributable to the principle of rhythmic stress alternation enhanced by the native left-edge prominence pattern. If the final syllable is stressable, the additional stress appears on the second syllable to the left: *relìgióun : tóun* (*GP* 477–478), *comàndemént : ysént* (*KnT* 2869–2870). The Middle English stress alternation and the eventual demotion and loss of the original primary stress in the foreign vocabulary was attributed to the school pronunciation of Latin in Middle English by Danielsson (1948: 26–29, 39–54) who used the term *countertonic accentuation* to describe the shift of e.g. post-Classical Latin *melancholía* (1375) to *mélanchòly*, in line with the native model of *máidenhòd, drónkenèsse*.

6 Post-Middle English prosodic innovations

The rise of literacy in Early Modern English was accompanied by a parallel rapid expansion of the lexicon. Barber (1997: 219–220) estimates that as many as 95 new words were recorded in English during each decade between 1500 and 1700; his counts are based on sampling entries in the OED. This exceeds by far the rate of borrowing in Middle English, which he estimates at 17 new words per decade, using the same methodology. Two-thirds of the new forms in Early Modern English were based on already recorded roots and affixes and about one third were straight borrowings. The large majority of these words were coined or adopted by English speakers who were proficient in Latin and Greek and who would therefore automatically apply the Latin Stress Rule to the novel "English" forms: *ablátion, cathédral, demócracy, meánder, términus*. The density of these forms and the shared literate understanding of their prosody gave rise to a new, parallel model of stress in English, which is weight sensitive, and which can apply to new words such as *Óregon* (1765, possibly Connecticut pidgin Algonquian, OED *kaínga* 'village' (Maori, 1820), *palachínka* 'pancake' (Slavic, 1884).

The tenacity of the GSR continued during the Early Modern English period in spite of the unprecedented influx of foreign loans, however. Consolidation of the primary stress on the initial syllable of the stem went beyond the disyllabic shifts recorded in Section 5.2 and affected trisyllabic nouns and adjectives: *ámorous, chárity, láxative, ópposite, órison, plénteous, région* have changed their Chaucerian pronunciation in accord with the GSR, similarly *ínfantry, mércury, órient, cálendar, génial*. Stress shift to the initial syllable often proceeds in spite of the etymological heaviness of the penultimate syllable, as in the early loans *ámorous, fórtunate, ínfantry, ínterval, órient* and many post-Middle English forms such as *vértebra* (1615), *tálisman* (1638), *sýnergy* (1660), *Cávendish* (1839), *bádminton* (1845), *állergy* (1911), *bóondòggle* (1935).

The emerging picture is complexly layered: the prosody of native words follows the Old English left-alignment of word or stem with the main stress. The non-native vocabulary displays hybrid patterns, and no single model covers all realizations without exceptions, so we can only define strong tendencies. New words can fall in with the native left-strong Germanic model, or they can follow a weight-sensitive model whereby stress in non-derived words is assigned by word class and by syllable weight. Verbs with heavy final syllables are generally end-stressed, e.g. *paráde, dený, maintáin, oblíge, protéct*. Nouns may be stressed depending on the weight of the penultimate syllable in accord with the Latin Stress Rule: *agénda, cánopy, horízon, ínfidel, Torónto*. Although the considerable overlap between the patterns noted in Section 5.2. for disyllabic nouns and adjectives continues, end-stressed nouns like *abýss, baróque, cabál, canál, duréss, elíte, maláise, ravíne* do occur. The extent to which such words retain their prosodic "foreignness" may vary in British and American English. Table 4.2 shows some examples with first attestation dates from the OED; some of these are simply "majority" pronunciations in variation with the alternative pronunciation.

Table 4.2: Stress differences between American and British English

American English	Date	British English
ínquiry	(1440)	*inquíry*
pólice (also políce)	(1450)	*políce*
frústrate	(1447)	*frustráte*
premíer	(1500)	*prémier*
móustache	(1585)	*moustáche*
debrís	(1708)	*débris*
café	(1802)	*cáfe*
garáge	(1902)	*gárage*

The hybridity of the Present-day English stress system is also evident in the variability of stress patterns within the last century. Bauer (1994: 96–103) records items which have undergone a recent shift to penultimate stress, e.g. *ábdomen, ácumen, ánchovy, étiquette, molýbdenum, précedence, quándary, sécretive, sónorous, vágary*. He notes a further complicating factor: stress placement in derived words can ignore the nature of the suffix and preserve the prosody of a pre-existing and frequently used base, thus *cápital, prefér* are the bases which trigger the change of old *capítalist* to current *cápitalist*, and of old *préferable* to *preférable*.

As noted in Section 4.2, suffixation in Old English was never associated with main-stress reduction; the highest level of prominence for derivational suffixes was secondary stress. The adoption of a large number of foreign affixed words along with their prosodic contours changed this situation. Present-day English suffixes can attract main stress themselves or they can trigger the placement of main stress on one or two syllables to the left of the suffix. Among the suffixes attracting primary stress and reducing the original stress of the base to secondary stress are: *-ette* (1849), as in *màjorétte, -een* (1551) as in *vèlvetéen, -ese* (1898), as in *jòurnalése, -eer* (1704) as in *mòuntainéer*. Final main stress appears also on word endings that may not be etymologically productive suffixes: *-ade* as in *lèmonáde, -ique* as in *boutíque, -oo* as in *kàngaróo*.

Main stress usually falls on the syllable immediately preceding the suffixes *-ic, -id, -ion, -ity/-ety: numéric, carótid, rebéllion, tranquílity*. Among the borrowed suffixes that place the main stress on the antepenultimate syllable of the derived word are *-acy, -ast, -ose, -tude: demócracy, icónoclast, cómatose, simílitude*. The antepenultimate is stressed also in combining forms such as *-ólogy, -ósophy, -ógraphy, -ólatry, -ócracy* etc. These new patterns of stress-assignment extend to native roots under foreign suffixation as in *Icelándic* (1674), *weatherólogy* (1823), *speedómeter* (1904), *Chàplinésque* (1921). The placement of stress in derived words has been the subject of much linguistic research. A good descriptive coverage is found in Fudge (1984); the analytical problems are addressed in Giegerich (1999).

Another innovation in the post-Renaissance period is the growing productivity of functional stress-shifting in homographic pairs, the *áddict* (N)–*addíct* (V), *présent* (N)–*presént* (V), *pólice* (N)–*police* (V) model, where the shift of stress from one part of speech to another is no longer a matter of prefixation, as in the native shifts in *úpset* (N), *óverhang* (N). The new stress-shifts do not require compositionality; on the other hand, they are directional (right-to-left) and subject to syllabic and segmental restrictions on the base, not applicable to the native pairs (Minkova 2009).

In conclusion, the prosody of Present-day English presents a mixture of word-stress patterns, some inherited from Old English, some introduced in Early

Modern English. What we share with Old English is an uninterrupted line of left-edge marking of compounds, unstressable function words and head-prominence in clitic groups, and right-hand phrasal prominence. Many relevant details in the prosodic history of English remain under-researched: we lack good documentation of the prosodic behavior of borrowings in Middle English and we still need to evaluate the relevance of competing factors such as phonological composition, frequency, morphological marking and transparency, social prestige, spelling. The relationship between innovations in verse form and prosodic innovations is also of considerable linguistic and cultural interest. Other areas that invite further inquiry are the prosodic patterns in the regional and ethnic varieties of English, and the contact-induced changes in the English spoken in countries where it is an official second language.

7 References

Barber, Charles. 1997. *Early Modern English*. Edinburgh: Edinburgh University Press.
Bauer, Laurie. 1994. *Watching English Change*. London: Longman.
Benson, Larry D. (ed.). 1987. *The Riverside Chaucer*. 3rd edn. Boston: Houghton Mifflin.
Bredehoft, Thomas. 2005. *Early English Metre*. Toronto: University of Toronto Press.
Danielsson, Bror. 1948. *Studies on the Accentuation of Polysyllabic Latin, Greek, and Romance Loan-Words in English: With Special Reference to those Ending in* -able, -ate, -ator, -ible, -ic, -ical, and -ize. Stockholm: Almqvist and Wiksell.
Dobson, Eric J. 1957. *English Pronunciation 1500–1700*. Vol. II. Oxford: Clarendon Press.
Fudge, Eric. 1984. *English Word-Stress*. London: George Allen & Unwin.
Fulk, Robert D. 1992. *A History of Old English Meter*. Philadelphia: University of Pennsylvania Press.
Getty, Michael. 2002. *The Metre of Beowulf. A Constraint-Based Approach*. Berlin/New York: Mouton de Gruyter.
Giegerich, Heinz. 1999. *Lexical Strata in English. Morphological Causes, Phonological Effects*. Cambridge: Cambridge University Press.
Giegerich, Heinz. 2009. Compounding and lexicalism. In: Rochelle Lieber and Pavol Štekauer (eds.), *The Oxford Handbook of Compounding*, 178–200. Oxford: Oxford University Press.
Hutcheson, Bellenden Rand. 1995. *Old English Poetic Metre*. Cambridge: D. S. Brewer.
Minkova, Donka. 2000. Middle English prosodic innovations and their testability in verse. In: Irma Taavitsainen, Terttu Nevalainen, Päivi Pahta, and Matti Rissanen (eds.), *Placing Middle English in Context*, 431–461. Berlin/New York: Mouton de Gruyter.
Minkova, Donka. 2006. Old and Middle English prosody. In: Ans van Kemenade and Bettelou Los (eds.), *The Handbook of the History of English*, 95–125. Oxford: Blackwell.
Minkova, Donka. 2008a. Review of Thomas Bredehoft, *Early English Metre*. *Speculum* 83(3): 673–675.
Minkova, Donka. 2008b. Prefixation and stress in Old English. *Word Structure* 1(1): 21–52.
Minkova, Donka. 2009. Continuity or re-invention in functional stress-shifting. Paper presented at ICEHL 15, Munich.

Minkova, Donka. 2013. *A Historical Phonology of English*. Edinburgh: Edinburgh University Press.
Minkova, Donka and Robert Stockwell. 1997. Against the *emergence* of the nuclear stress rule in Middle English. In: Jacek Fisiak (ed.), *Studies in Middle English*, 301–335. Berlin/New York: Mouton de Gruyter.
Minkova, Donka and Robert Stockwell. 2005. Clash avoidance in morphologically derived words in Middle English. (Why [-hʊd] but [-dəm])? In: Nikolaus Ritt and Herbert Schendl (eds.), *Rethinking Middle English. Linguistic and Literary Approaches*, 263–280. Bern: Peter Lang.
Proffitt, Michael (ed.). 2000–. *The Oxford English Dictionary*. 3rd edn. online. Oxford University Press. www.oed.com
Russom, Geoffrey. 1987. *Old English Meter and Linguistic Theory*. Cambridge: Cambridge University Press.
Selkirk, Elisabeth O. 1984. *Phonology and Syntax: The Relation Between Sound and Structure*. Cambridge, MA: MIT Press.
Sievers, Eduard. 1893. *Altgermanische Metrik*. Halle: Niemeyer.
Stockwell, Robert and Donka Minkova. 1997. Prosody. In: Robert Bjork and John Niles (eds.), *A* Beowulf *Handbook*, 55–85. Lincoln: University of Nebraska Press.
Teresawa, Jun. 2011. *Old English Metre: An Introduction*. (Toronto Anglo-Saxon Series, Vol. 7.) Toronto: University of Toronto Press.

Dieter Kastovsky
Chapter 5:
Morphology

1   Introduction —— 77
2   Morphological typology —— 79
3   Modern English —— 81
4   History —— 89
5   References —— 99

Abstract: Modern English morphology is the result of a long-range typological restructuring, triggered by phonological changes in connection with the emergence of the Germanic language family, leading to an erosion of unstressed final syllables. As a result, the originally root-based morphology became stem-based and finally word-based. Also morphology was originally characterized by pervasive phonologically conditioned morphophonemic alternations, which gradually became morphologically conditioned, because of phonological changes. This was replaced by a simplified system with base invariancy and phonologically conditioned alternations of inflectional endings as a default case characterizing the regular inflection of nouns, verbs and adjectives. The irregular patterns continue properties of the original system and can be interpreted as stem-based with morphologically conditioned alternations of the base form. This is also true of many non-native word-formation patterns, which have been borrowed from stem-based languages such as French, Latin or Greek and have re-introduced base alternation into English derivational morphology.

1 Introduction

Modern English morphology is the result of several millennia of linguistic change, which has transformed its ancestor, Indo-European morphology, into a completely different morphological type. These changes often left relics behind, which like tombstones commemorate earlier stages, as e.g. irregular verbs of the type *write : wrote : written*, which go back to Indo-European ablaut alternations, or irregular

---

Dieter Kastovsky †: Vienna (Austria)

noun plurals like *mouse* : *mice*, *goose* : *geese*, *oxen*, which reflect old Indo-Germanic and Germanic inflectional classes. Similarly, the stress alternation between verbal *òverflów* and nominal *óverflòw*, etc. can be traced back to a combination of the Germanic innovation of initial stress and syntactically governed stress distribution in Proto-Germanic (cf. Minkova 2008a, 2008b), eventually acting as a landing site for Romance loans like *recórd* v and *récord* N. This new Germanic stress system is also held responsible for the loss of unstressed syllables, many of which were carriers of morphological information, the result being a language with little inflection left. On the other hand, there are also typological innovations like the vowel and/or consonant alternations in *sane* : *sanity, serene* : *serenity, Japán* : *Jàpanése, hístory* : *históric* : *hìstorícity, eléctric* : *elèctrícity, close* : *closure*, resulting from the integration of non-native (Romance, Latin and Neo-Latin) word-formation patterns into English with a concomitant variable stress system, which reverses the original typological drift towards a non-alternating relation between bases and derivatives and is reminiscent of Indo-European, where variable stress/accent produced variable vowel quality/quantity (ablaut). It is such long-range developments and their typological consequences that will be dealt with in the following.

The existing literature, e.g. Brunner (1960–62), Wełna (1996), the respective chapters in Hogg (1992), Blake (1992), or Hogg and Denison (2006), pay only cursory attention to these typological changes. Moreover, they reflect the Neogrammarian tradition of looking backwards to the Indo-European and Germanic morphological structures, interpreting later patterns in terms of older structures as having undergone losses rather than as acquiring structural innovations. As a consequence, morphological restructuring is often not topicalized enough or assumed to have occurred much later than it actually did.

A good example is Brunner's (1962: 3–10) treatment of Old English nominal inflection. He makes a point of describing this in terms of Indo-European inflectional classes involving stem-formatives like IE -*o*- (= Grmc. -*a*-), IE -*ō*- (= Grmc. -*ā*-), etc., arguing that reference to the Indo-European categories rather than the Germanic ones is preferable in order to emphasize the fact that the Germanic declinations correspond exactly to the declinations of other Indo-European languages. The synchronic relevance of classifying Old English nouns in terms of Indo-European *o*- or *ā*-stems, etc. is simply taken for granted and never questioned, which obscures a profound typological change between Indo-European and Old English, viz. the shift from root-based to stem-based and even word-based morphology and the demise of the stem-formatives as a functional category. Even though this approach allows for restructurings, it would tend to place them at a later period than when they actually occurred. What is needed, therefore, is a Janus-like approach: this should take into account both where a synchronic linguistic stage comes from (= retrospective), but also in which direction it is moving (= prospective).

2 Morphological typology

2.1 Traditional typology

Morphological typology as introduced by the Schlegels (Schlegel, Friedrich 1808; Schlegel, August W. 1818) and Humboldt (1827–29) covered only inflectional morphology and was based on two overlapping scales with one parameter each. The first parameter resulted in the distinction between analytic languages, where grammatical functions are expressed word-externally by prepositions, auxiliaries, etc., and synthetic languages, where grammatical functions are expressed word-internally by inflection, incorporation, etc. The second parameter was based on how grammatical functions are represented formally and resulted in the distinction between isolating, agglutinating, inflectional, and incorporating languages. In isolating languages, grammatical functions are expressed word-externally; i.e. this type coincides with the analytic one, and languages belonging to this type have no inflectional morphology. The other three are sub-types of the synthetic type. In agglutinating languages, there is a one-to-one correspondence between a grammatical category and its exponent, as, e.g., in Turkish, in Finnish or in English, where number and case are expressed consecutively, if the plural is irregular, cf. (1):

(1) ox   en   s   **gee**se   s   boy   s   Ø
          PL   GEN   PL   GEN   PL   GEN

In inflectional languages, one morphological exponent represents more than one grammatical category, functioning as a portmanteau morph, cf. Lt. *am-ō* 'I love' (*-ō* = 1P [person] SG [number] PRES [tense] IND [mood] ACT [voice]), or OE *cyning-as* (*-as* = PL [number] + NOM/ACC [case]). In incorporating languages, grammatical functions such as subject, object, adverbial complement are integrated into the predicate itself together with their nominal carriers; this might be postulated for recent English formations such as *machine-translate*, *thought-read*, *flight-test*, etc. (cf. Section 3.2.2.)

2.2 Extended typology

These parameters only partially characterize the overall *gestalt* of the morphology of a language and therefore have to be supplemented by further aspects, which will lead to a more differentiated picture. The following additional parameters have proved useful (cf. Kastovsky 1997, 2006a, 2006b):
- morphological status of the input to the morphological processes (word, stem, root)
- number and status of inflectional classes
- formal representation of inflectional and derivational markers
- status and function of morphophonemic/allomorphic alternations
- position of affixes/position of the head
- existence and status of morphological levels (e.g. native vs. foreign)

The first parameter requires a comment. I will adopt the distinction between "lexeme" (= dictionary entry), "word-form" (inflectional form of a lexeme), and "word" (actual representation of a lexeme via word-form in an utterance as independent syntactic element or free form) from Matthews (1974: 20–26) and Lyons (1977: 18–25). "Word-formation" ("derivational morphology") is therefore actually "lexeme-formation", but I will retain the former term for convenience's sake. What is crucial is the status of the lexeme representation which acts as input to inflectional and derivational processes, the "base form". This is defined as that lexeme representation from which all word-forms and the result of word-formational processes can be derived. Thus, word-formation and inflectional morphology are interdependent: the input to word-formation processes, and the demarcation between inflection and derivation, depends on the typological status of inflection.

For this, the following distinction is suggested:
a. word-based morphology: The base form can function as a word (free form) in an utterance without the addition of additional morphological (inflectional or derivational) material, e.g. ModE *cat(-s)*, *cheat(-ed)*, *beat(-ing)*, *sleep(-er)*.
b. stem-based morphology: The base form does not occur as an independent word, but requires additional inflectional and/or derivational morphological material in order to function as a word. It is a bound form (= stem), cf. OE *luf-* (*-ian*, *-ast*, *-od-e*, etc.), *luf-estr-*(*-e*) 'female lover', Grmc. **dag-*(*-az*) 'day, NOM SG', ModE *scient-*(*-ist*) vs. *science*, *dramat-*(*-ic*) vs. *drama*, *astr-o-naut*, *telepathy*; thus *luf-*, *luf-estr-*, **dag-*, *dramat-*, *astr-*, *-naut*, *tele-*, *-pathy* are stems.
c. root-based morphology: Here the input to morphological processes is even more abstract and requires additional morphological material to become a stem, to which the genuinely inflectional endings can be added in order to

produce a word. Such roots can either be affiliated to a particular word-class, or they can be word-class neutral. In this case the word-class affiliation is added by a word-formative process, cf. IE roots like *wVr- 'bend, turn' (cf. Lt. *uer-t-ere* 'turn', OE *weor-þ-an* 'become', *wyr-m* 'worm', etc.), with V standing for the ablaut vowel, whose shape is determined by the morphological process in question. Whether Indo-European roots were word-class specific or neutral is not quite clear, but not relevant for our purposes.

Terminology varies considerably in this respect, cf., e.g., Bauer (1983: 20–21; 1992: 252–253), Giegerich (1999), or Huddleston and Pullum (2002: 1624–1625). The terminology used here is geared to the history of Indo-European morphology, with its shift from a root-based to a stem-based and a (partly) word-based system. I will therefore use the term "stem" for what some linguists call "root" also with reference to English, i.e. for a lexical element which is bound and which can only occur as a word with additional morphological material, as, e.g., *scient-*, *dramat-*, *tele-*, *-pathy*. The term "root" will be restricted to the Indo-European period and is not relevant for the Indo-European daughter languages.

The ultimate starting point of English was a root-based morphology (Indo-European), which became stem-based in the transition to Germanic. In the transition from Germanic to Old English, inflection became partly word-based, and this eventually became the dominant typological trait of Modern English.

3 Modern English

3.1 Inflectional morphology

3.1.1 Inflectional morphology vs. word-formation

In Modern English, there is a fairly neat division between inflectional morphology and word-formation, except for adverb formation in *-ly*, which is ambivalent. Since *-ly* produces a change of word-class (ADJ > ADV), it is usually treated as derivational. But on account of the complementary distribution of adverbs and adjectives as in (2)

(2) *He smokes heavily* : *He is a heavy smoker.*

it could also be treated as inflectional, parallel to nominal case inflection, cf. Hockett (1958: 211). This is probably why Marchand (1969) did not include adverb formation in his handbook.

3.1.2 Regular vs. irregular inflectional morphology

Inflectional morphology of verbs and nouns is based on a default system consisting of two inflectional classes: regular and irregular. Regular inflection is fully predictable. It is word-based, base-invariant, and the morphophonemic alternations of the inflectional endings are phonologically conditioned: 3P SG, plural and genitive have the allomorphs: /z/ (underlying form and default), e.g. *kids* /kɪdz/; /ɪz/ (vowel insertion after base-final coronal sibilants), e.g. *kisses* /kɪsɪz/; and /s/ (devoicing after base-final voiceless consonants), e.g. *bets* /bets/. Preterit and past participle have the allomorphs: /d/ (underlying and default), e.g. *loved* /lʌvd/; /ɪd/ (vowel insertion after base-final alveolar stops), e.g. *hated* /heɪtɪd/; and devoicing after base-final voiceless consonants, e.g. *kissed* /kɪst/.

Irregular verbs and nouns can be grouped into various sub-classes (classification in the grammars varies considerably); they have either variable bases or phonologically unpredictable inflectional allomorphs, or both, and are relics of historically earlier stages, cf. (3a, b):

(3) a. *keep* /kiːp/ : *kep-t* /kep-t/ (variable base, regular inflectional allomorph),
   deal /diːl/ : *deal-t* /del-t/ (variable base and unpredictable inflectional allomorph /t/),
   shut : *shut-Ø* (invariable base, unpredictable inflectional allomorph Ø),
   write : *wrote* : *writt-en, sing* : *sang* : *sung, bleed* : *bled* : *bled*
   (unpredictable inflectional allomorphs, viz. replacives, *-en*);
 b. *leaf* /liːf/ : *leav-es* /liːv-z/ (variable base, regular inflectional allomorph),
   ox : *ox-en* (invariable base, unpredictable inflectional allomorph),
   mouse : *mice, child* : *child-ren, fung-us* : *fung-i* (unpredictable inflectional allomorphs)

The status of /kep/, /del/, /liːv/ /tʃɪld/ is arguable. On the one hand, these are allomorphs of the lexeme representations /kiːp/, /diːl/, /liːf/, /tʃaɪld/, which are words. But since they only occur together with inflectional morphemes, these allomorphs might be regarded as stems, i.e. these lexemes have both a word-based and a stem-based morphological representation. This is similar to the derivational pattern *science* : *scient-ist, drama* : *dramat-ic,* where the lexical base is represented as a word, but also has an allomorph which occurs in derivatives and which has to be regarded as a stem. *Write* : *wrote* : *written,* or *mouse* : *mice* are word-based with a replacive morph representing the inflectional morpheme, which in the case of *writt-en* might be interpreted as discontinuous, consisting of the replacive /aɪ →ɪ/ and the suffix *-en*. In this case, the morphophonemic alternation is morphologically relevant and expresses a morphological contrast, whereas in the cases of *keep : kept, leaf : leaves*, etc. the morphophonemic alternation is non-functional. Synchronic classifications do not always reflect historical developments. Thus, Modern English *sing : sang, write : wrote* and *bleed : bled* all have replacives as tense and participle markers, but with *sing* and *write* the replacive reflects an Indo-European ablaut alternation, whereas with *bleed : bled* the alternation has the same origin as that occurring in *keep : kept, deal : dealt*, viz. shortening of long vowels before certain consonant clusters in late Old English. But with *bleed : bled* the alternation has become morphologically distinctive because of the lack of any other overt exponent of tense/participle, whereas the alternation in *keep : kept* might be treated as morphologically non-distinctive. On the other hand, *bleed : bled* and *shut : shut* share the same history with regard to the loss of the original past tense/past participle ending, cf. OE *blēd-d-e, ge-blēd-(ed), scyt-t-e, ge-scyt-t-(ed)*: the ending was lost (= replaced by zero, cf. Kastovsky 1980), when gemination was lost in Middle English; but with *bleed : bled*, a formal contrast had arisen thanks to vowel shortening in the preterit/past participle, which was morphologized, whereas with *shut* no formal contrast remained, which results in a zero allomorph for preterit and past participle.

3.1.3 Inflectional morphology of nouns

For nouns, the following morphological categories are relevant: number, case, class. Gender does not figure as an inflectional category but is determined by the nature of the referent (= natural gender), in contradistinction to Old English, where it was a relevant grammatical category in the organization of inflectional paradigms. For its loss, cf. Kastovsky (1999).

The category of number is primary; the category of case (genitive) is secondary and dissociated from number, i.e. has a separate exponent, in contradistinction to Old English, where the two categories were fused, cf. *cyning-as* NOM/ACC PL, *cyning-um* DAT PL. In view of structures such as *the Queen of England's castles*, where the genitive attaches to the whole NP rather than to its head *Queen*, the genitive might be regarded as a clitic, and not as an inflection.

The category of class relates to the formal expression of plural, which involves a default system: regular plurals with base invariance and phonologically determined plural allomorphs, and irregular plurals, which deviate from this, cf. (3b).

3.1.4 Inflectional morphology of verbs

For verbs, the following inflectional categories are relevant: tense, number, person, mood, finiteness, class.

On the basis of the degree to which these categories are exploited, the verb system can be subclassified into three subcategories, each with distinct properties: 1) modal verbs, 2) lexical verbs, 3) the copula *be*.

Modal verbs are the continuation of the Germanic preterit presents, which have undergone a shift towards a separate category in Middle and Early Modern English. They only exploit the tense dimension, i.e. they have no infinitive or participle forms, no person/number marking and no mood contrast. The verbs in question are *can, may, shall, will, must, ought to* and, to a certain extent, *dare, need*. Semantically speaking, the tense contrast is problematic, since the morphological opposition *can : could, may : might*, etc. most of the time does not really signal 'past' vs. 'non-past', but rather a different degree of modality. In view of their specific morphological and semantic properties, the modal verbs are treated as a separate category.

Lexical verbs are characterized by the contrast between an unmarked base form (which also functions as infinitive and non-preterit), the 3P SG, and the marked preterit, present participle, and past participle.

The copula *be* has the richest morphology with a person/number contrast in the preterit, and person distinctions marking first, second and third person in the non-past.

With the lexical verbs, person and number are expressed jointly, but they only have a person/number marker in the 3P SG non-preterit, which might better be regarded as an agreement morpheme rather than a person/number morpheme proper.

The morphological dimension of mood involves the categories indicative, subjunctive, and imperative, where the morphological marking is reduced to the absence of the agreement morpheme, whereas in Old English there were full-fledged separate paradigms.

Inflectional class is an inherent property of the verb, determines how it forms the preterit and the second participle, and is based on a default system. Regular verbs are the default case: they are base-invariant and select the phonologically conditioned allomorphs /d/, /t/ and /ɪd/. The irregular verbs (c.200) involve a modification of the base form (allomorphy), or select a non-phonologically conditioned representation of the past tense and past participle morphemes or both.

3.2 Word-formation

Modern English word-formation includes the following processes: compounding, affixation (prefixation, suffixation and zero-derivation/conversion), clipping, blending, acronyms, sound symbolism; for a comprehensive, somewhat dated but still relevant survey cf. Marchand (1969).

It can be argued (Kastovsky 2009b) that most of these word-formation processes are prototypical patterns arranged on a scale of progressively less independent constituents, cf. (4):

(4) word compounding > stem compounding > clipping and clipping compounds > affixation (word-/stem-based) > blending (splinters)) > acronyms

3.2.1 Compounding

English compounds are conventionally defined as combinations of full words resulting in a new lexical unit, e.g. *bird cage, flatfish, earthquake, house-keeping, law-breaker, sunrise, writing table, dance hall; color-blind, icy-cold, heart-breaking, easy-going, man-made*, etc. These illustrate nominal and adjectival compounds, most of which have been in the language since pre-Old English. The status of verbal compounds is problematic. Marchand (1969: 96) accepts as compounds only verbs with a locative particle like *overdo, underestimate*, and *outdo*, but with some reservations because of semantic problems with the first constituents, which make them look like semi-prefixes. These continue Old English formations with inseparable particles originally having a purely locative meaning, which was later extended metaphorically to 'excess', 'deficiency'. For the type *stagemanage, playact, spoonfeed, newcreate*, Marchand (1969: 104) assumes backderivation from nouns such as *stage-manager, playacting, spoonfed, newcreated*, since the Germanic languages never had a genuinely productive verbal compound pattern. But in the last decades, the situation has changed, and a verbal compound pattern based on incorporation is apparently taking over, which no longer needs a nominal base as a source, cf. *quick-march, new-form, slow-step, slow-kill, dark-adapt, quick-frost, sure-kill, hard-learn, quick-check; quantum-teleport, knee-jerk, machine-translate, thought-read, flight-test, depth-bomb, finger-tap, hull-walk, flash-vaporize, flash-freeze*, randomly culled from science fiction novels published in the last 15 years. Even v + v compounds are catching on, cf. *think-hiss, whisper-hiss, touch-share, wobble-hop, glide-walk, skim-glide, bend-swivel* (in the form *bent-swivelled*), *strip-search, hop-step, strip-mine* from the same kind of source (cf. Wald and Besserman 2002).

The compound principle as such is old and goes back to Indo-European, probably even to its oldest layer before the development of certain inflectional and syntactic categories like full relative clauses (cf. Kastovsky 2009a). Therefore, at this stage compounds do not seem to have consisted of full-fledged words, but of roots and stems (with stem-formatives). At a later stage syntactic groups consisting of full-fledged words with case marking of the first member expressing its semantic-syntactic relation to the second member seem to have coalesced to compound patterns, carrying along their original first-member inflectional endings. These eventually lost their syntactic function and became mere morphological linking elements like the original stem-formatives, cf. ModE *driver's seat, bull's eye* or Ger. *Universitätsbibliothek, Kindergarten, Frauenkirche*.

3.2.2 Stem-compounds

Formations such as *astr-o-naut, Mars-naut, astr-o-physics, agr-o-chemical, agr-i-culture; hyper-active, hyper-emia, omn-i-présent, omn-i-scient, hepat-itis, wakeup-itis, astr-o-logy, ex-o-bio-logy, megal-o-mania, star-mania* belong to the non-native level of English word-formation. Their constituents have been dubbed "combining forms" in the *Oxford English Dictionary* for want of a better term at the time of its inception, but there has never been a satisfactory definition of this heterogeneous category (cf., e.g., Prćić 2005, 2007, Kastovsky 2009b). This term is misleading, covering a number of different phenomena, and should therefore be discarded. Instead, we should recognize the existence of stem-compounds in English, i.e. compounds whose constituents are lexeme representations without word-status, a pattern inherited from languages like Latin or Greek. Formations such as *astr-o-naut, agr-i-culture, omn-i-scient*, etc. thus contain stems, and the middle element is – historically speaking – a stem-formative, but today functions as a linking element as is the case with *-s-* in word-compounds. Elements like *-logy* also go back to such stems, but have developed into suffixes, just as OE *dōm* in *kingdom, stardom* or OE *hād* in *childhood, statehood*, where *dōm, hād* had originally been independent words which developed into suffixes. Similarly, elements like *ante-, anti-, auto-, mono-*, etc., originally independent lexemes in the source languages, have developed into prefixes. And the elements *Ameri-* or *Euro-* in *Euro-City* can be regarded as clipped stems (< *Ameri(ca), Euro(pa)*), which can also be used in compounding.

3.2.3 Affixation

Let me now turn to affixation. There are three basic sources for affixes:
a. bleaching and grammaticalization of lexemes as compound constituents, as in *-dom, -hood*, or *for-, be-* and many other prefixes going back to locative particles;
b. borrowing from other languages, as was the case with the majority of ModE prefixes (e.g. *ante-, auto-, co-, counter-, de-, dis-, ex-, hyper-, in-, mono-, non-, post-, pre-, re-, sub-*, and many others) and also suffixes (e.g. *-able, -age, -al, -ance, -ation, -ery, -ess, -ify, -ism, -ist, -ity, -ize, -ment, -ory*, and many others);
c. secretion, as in *-teria <cafe-tería (> caketeria, washeteria), -gate < Watergate (> Irangate, zippergate), -burger < hamburger (> beef-burger > burger)*, etc.

The latter two sources, borrowing and secretion, are closely related, because the borrowing of a non-native affix also involves secretion, since the borrowed affixal element has to be recognized as a separate morphological unit before it can become productive.

The demarcation between compounding and affixation is fluid because of the diachronic shift from lexeme to affix, resulting in a bridge category "semi-affix", e.g. *-monger, -like, -wise* (Marchand 1969: 356–358), or *out-, over-, under-* in their metaphorical meaning. On the other hand, affixes might also turn into lexemes, cf. *burger, mini, extra*.

3.2.4 Zero-derivation

There is one word-formation process whose status is controversial, but which I interpret as a sub-type of suffixation, i.e. derivation by means of a zero morpheme, as in *salt* N > *salt* V, *clean* ADJ > *clean* V, *cheat* V > *cheat* N, *walk* V > *walk*. Several approaches have been suggested to account for this process; the following two seem to be the most prominent ones. The older is "conversion", which assumes that this process is different from normal suffixation and simply consists of converting a lexeme belonging to one word class, e.g. *salt* N, to a lexeme belonging to another word class, *salt* V. Connected with this is the view that this is a recent phenomenon in English, which only became really productive after the loss of inflectional endings (cf., e.g., Biese 1941). The second approach assumes that this is a regular derivational process following the binary determinant/determinatum schema of word-formation, except that the derivational element is not overtly present, but is there in content; this is formally expressed by assuming a zero morpheme as the derivational element, which allows one to account for the semantic addition involved in this process. It is parallel to suffixal derivation, cf. *carbon* N > *carbon-ize* V 'provide with carbon' = *salt* N > *salt-Ø* V 'provide with salt', *black* ADJ > *black-en* V 'make black' = *clean* ADJ > *clean-Ø* V 'make clean', *teach* V > *teach-er* N 'someone who teaches' = *cheat* V > *cheat-Ø* N 'someone who cheats', *walk* V > *walk-ing* N 'action of walking' = *walk* V > *walk-Ø* N 'act of walking' (Marchand 1969: 359–364). This interpretation presupposes a neat distinction between inflection and derivation, where inflectional endings have no derivational force, and therefore allows us to treat as zero-derivations also instances where the derived word is accompanied by inflectional affixes, as in OE $ār_N$ 'honor' > $ār_N$-$Ø_V$-ian_{INF} 'to honor', $dēop_{ADJ}$ 'deep' > $dēop_{ADJ}$-$Ø_V$-ian_{INF} 'to deepen', $feoht_V$-an_{INF} 'to fight' > $feoht_V$-$Ø_N$-$e_{NOM.SG}$ 'fight'. The latter approach, apart from taking into consideration the semantics of the derivational process, also has the advantage of reflecting the historical development, because in all the instances where today we would have to assume zero-derivation, there originally was some derivational marker in the guise of a stem-formative, which was lost due to phonetic attrition and was "replaced by zero" (cf. Kastovsky 1980, 1996).

3.2.5 Blending

The end of the scale is made up by blending, which is a heterogeneous category and consists of formations where both parts consist of curtailed lexemes, e.g. (5a, b, c).

(5) a. *Chunnel* = *Ch-(annel)* + *(t)-unnel*
        motel = *mo-(tor[ist])* + *(ho)-tel*
    b. *Oxbridge* = *Ox-(ford)* + *(Cam)-bridge*
        transceiver = *trans-(mitter)* + *(re)-ceiver*
    c. *smog* = *sm-(oke)* + *(f)-og*
        brunch = *br-(eakfast)* + *(l)-unch*
        slithy = *sli-(m)* + *(li)the* + *y*
        chortle (*chuckle* + *snort*)

Examples (5a, b) echo the structure of regular determinative compounds, except that both constituents are clipped. *Oxbridge, transceiver* are clipped dvandva compounds, which denote a combination (union) of the respective referents, i.e. *Oxbridge* 'the universities of Oxford and Cambridge' is comparable to *Austro-Hungary* 'an entity which consists of both Austria and Hungary', similarly *concavo-convex*. This compound type is an innovation in English, borrowed from Latin and Greek. The formations in (5a, b) are usually treated on the same footing as (5c), but this does not seem to be correct. While the examples in (5a, b) echo regular compound structures, those in (5c) do not. They denote a referent which is a mixture or crossbreed of the referents of the constituent lexemes. They have no direct counterpart in compounding and seem to be a relatively recent development alongside the tremendous rise of acronyms like *aids, laser, NATO, FBI, CIA*, which form the endpoint of the scale in (4).

3.2.6 Typological properties

Let me conclude this section with a few general remarks on the typological properties of Modern English word-formation. The input to Modern English word-formation can be words (at the native level), stems (at the non-native level), both of which can be curtailed (clipped) in clipping-compounds and blends. This implies that there are different morphological levels with different properties. The native level is characterized by base invariancy (no alternations), affix-invariancy (except for phonologically determined alternations) and stress always located on the first constituent (= German stress rule) except for verbal prefixes as in *ùntíe*. The non-native level allows for both stem and affix variation as well as variable stress position coupled with vowel alternation, cf. *intolerable* : *impossible* : *illegible*, *Japán* : *Jàpanése*, etc.

As in all Germanic languages, the standard constituent sequence in word-formations is determinant/determinatum (modifier/head). There is one controversial area, however, viz. prefix formations of the type *defrost, disarm, unbutton*. Some linguists (e.g. Lieber 1983: 253) assume that the prefixes here act as heads in order to account for the change of word-class involved, thus reversing the standard sequence of modifier/head. This analysis coincides, interestingly, with the rejection of zero derivation as a productive derivational process; rather the relationship between the involved lexical items is described as a static lexical correspondence. But as has been argued above, zero-derivation might be regarded as a sub-type of suffixal derivation, and in the case of the prefixal verbs *defrost, disarm, unbutton*, the second part might also be regarded as zero-derived, functioning as a head, which would make the prefix a modifier, as befits.

4 History

4.1 Indo-European

Some features of Modern English morphology go back to Indo-European, e.g. ablaut like *sing* : *sang* : *sung*, but also the division into strong and weak verbs and the various inflectional classes of nouns. Therefore, a look at Indo-European might be useful. Its central morphological category was the root, a monosyllabic consonantal skeleton with a vowel slot (conventionally assumed to have been /e/ with its ablaut alternants) and certain restrictions on the co-occurrence of consonants in onset and coda position (cf. Clackson 2007: 69–71). The actual nominal, adjectival, or verbal paradigms were derived by adding stem-forming elements and/or other derivational elements again followed by stem-formatives, to which the inflectional endings proper were added, as in (6):

(6) root + stem-formative (+ derivational affix + secondary stem-formative elements) + inflection proper

From such roots primary nouns and primary verbs were formed. There was no directional connection between verb and derived noun, or noun and derived verb; both were indirectly related via a common root, from which they were derived by independent morphological processes. This relationship characterizes the ancestors of the strong verbs and the related nouns and adjectives. From these primary derivatives further, secondary derivatives could be formed (see Figure 5.1).

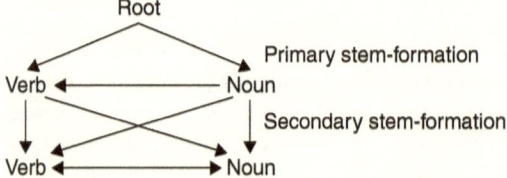

Figure 5.1: Derivational relationship between IE roots, noun stems, and verb stems

The Indo-European verb system was characterized by a mixture of aspectual and temporal categories such as present, imperfect, perfect, aorist, etc., and mode of action categories such as iterative, intensive, durative, inchoative, etc. In Modern English or German, these categories are separated as either belonging to inflection (tense, aspect) or derivation (mode of action/aktionsart). In Indo-European, however, no such separation was possible, and these aspect/mode of action categories were derived directly from the root, resulting in stems (see Figure 5.2).

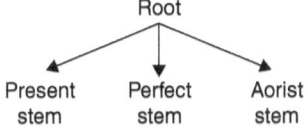

Figure 5.2: Verbal stems in Indo-European

Aspect formation and the person/number inflection of these primary verbs were characterized by morphologically-governed stress alternations, which produced non-functional differences of vowel quality and quantity, called ablaut. This is the source of the Germanic system of strong verbs, consisting of six classes (and one additional class of reduplicative verbs fitting into the same pattern), which are based on the syllable-structure of the root, viz. ablaut vowel + syllable coda in (7):

(7) Class 1:   -ViT-   Class 2:   -VuT-   Class 3:   -VL/NT-
    Class 4:   -VL/N-   Class 5:   -VT-   Class 6:   -VH-
    (V = ablaut vowel, T = obstruent, L = liquid, N = nasal, H = laryngeal)

The secondary derived verbs, i.e. those derived from primary nouns, verbs, or adjectives, but not directly from roots, only occurred in the non-perfective (= present) aspect. They are the ancestors of the Germanic weak verbs containing stem-formatives like *-j-* and *-ōj-* characterizing class 1 and 2 weak verbs.

4.2 Germanic to Old English: verbal system

One major Germanic innovation was a shift from an aspectual to a tense system. This coincided with the shift to initial accent, and both may have been due to language contact, maybe with Finno-Ugric. Initial stress deprived ablaut of its phonological conditioning, and the shift from aspect to tense required a systematic marking of the new preterit tense. For this, two types of exponents emerged. One is connected to the secondary (weak) verbs, which only had present aspect/tense forms. They developed an affixal "dental preterit", together with an affix for the past participle. The source of the latter was the Indo-European participial *-to-* suffix; the source of the former is not clear (cf. Tops 1974). The most popular theory is grammaticalization of a periphrastic construction with *do* (IE *d^he-*), but there are a number of phonological problems with this. The second type was the functionalization of the originally non-functional ablaut alternations to express the new category, i.e. the making use of junk (Lass 1990). But this was somewhat unsystematic, because original perfect forms were mixed with aorist forms, resulting in a pattern with over- and under-differentiation. Thus, in class III (*helpan* : *healp* : *hulpon* : *geholpen*) the preterit is over-differentiated, because the different ablaut forms are non-functional, since the personal endings would be sufficient to signal the necessary distinctions. But in class I (*wrītan* : *wrāt* : *writon* : *gewriten*), there is under-differentiation, because some preterit forms and the past participle have the same vowel. This situation proved unstable and was levelled out in Middle English, along with a loss of many strong verbs or their shift to the regular (= originally weak) class. Moreover, the transparent syllable structure on which this system had been based had lost its transparency in Old English due to numerous sound changes. It is therefore arguably possible to treat the Old English strong verbs already as irregular, i.e. to assume that the switch from a system based on the distinction between weak verbs characterized by stem-formatives and strong verbs characterized by ablaut without a stem-formative to a system based on the dichotomy of regular and irregular verbs had already occurred in Old or even in pre-Old English (cf. Kastovsky 1997).

The weak verbs were originally derived from nouns, adjectives or verbs by various stem-formatives, which are still recognizable in Gothic (Go.), cf. (8):

(8) Class 1:   -j-/-i-   (Go. *sat-j-an*, OE *sett-an*)
    Class 2:   -ōj-/-ō-   (Go. *salb-ô-n*, OE *sealf-ian*)
    Class 3:   -ē(j)-   (Go. *hab-an*, OE *habb-an*)
    Class 4:   -nō-   (Go. *full-n-an*, ?OE *beorht-n-ian*)

Classes 1 and 2 survive in Old English. Remnants of class 3, e.g. *libban, lifde* 'live', *habban, hæfde* 'have', *hyċgan, hogode* 'think' are best treated as irregular. Class 4 seems to have survived with -*n*- having been re-interpreted as a derivational suffix, e.g. *beorht-n-ian* < OE *beorht* ADJ, the antecedent of the -*en*-suffix in *blacken, redden, fasten*, etc. At this stage, the stem formative had a dual function: it acted as a derivational morpheme like -*ize*, -*ify*, -*en*, but it also had an inflectional function characterizing a particular inflectional class.

Gradually, the weak verbs lost their status as a derived category (cf. Kastovsky 1996). Many of them were reinterpreted as basic, partly because their derivational base was lost, partly due to semantic reinterpretation. The ablaut nouns related to strong verbs usually denoted agents, actions, results or instruments related to the underlying verbal action. These lexical-semantic categories are typically deverbal. Now these deverbal nouns often served as the basis for secondary verbal derivatives, e.g. *faran* 'to go, travel' > *fōr* 'going, journey' > *fēran* 'go, come, depart' (= 'make a journey'). In this way, many pairs of the type action noun > verb 'perform action', agent noun > verb 'act as agent' came into existence. For these, however, the direction of derivation was just the opposite of the one relating the basic nouns to their strong verbs and in many instances came to be reinterpreted in the same way as in back-derivations such as *peddler* > *peddle* 'act like a peddler' → *peddle* > *peddler* 'someone who peddles' because of *write* > *writer* 'someone who writes'. Such reinterpretations eventually established a general pattern of nominal derivation from weak verbs, so that these lost their exclusively derived character, cf. the following examples of clearly deverbal nouns in (9):

(9) *hwistlian* 'to whistle' > *hwistle* 'whistle'
  cnyllan 'to strike, knock, ring a bell' > *cnyll* 'clang, stroke of a bell'
  huntian 'to hunt' > *hunta* 'hunter'

While in Germanic and pre-Old English the stem formatives were clearly recognizable throughout the respective paradigms, this was no longer true of Old English, where they have fused with the person/number endings, cf. *trymm-an* 'to strengthen' < *trum* 'strong', *lufian* 'to experience love' < *lufu* 'love', *dēman* 'to pass judgement' < *dōm* 'judgment', *nerian* 'to save'; see Table 5.1.

Table 5.1: Typical paradigms of Old English class 1 and class 2 weak verbs

	Stem	+	Person/Number/Inf.		Stem	+	Person/Number/Inf.
Class 1	trymm	+	an_{INF}	Class 2	luf	+	ian_{INF}
	trymm	+	$e_{1P\ SG}$		luf	+	$ie_{1P\ SG}$
	trym	+	$est_{2P\ SG}$		luf	+	$ast_{2P\ SG}$
	trym	+	$eð_{3P\ SG}$		luf	+	$að_{3P\ SG}$
	trymm	+	$að_{PL}$		luf	+	$iað_{PL}$
	dēm	+	an_{INF}				
	dēm	+	$e_{1P\ SG}$				
	dēm	+	$st_{2P\ SG}$				
	dēm	+	$þ_{3P\ SG}$				
	dēm	+	$að_{PL}$				
	ner	+	ian_{INF}				
	ner	+	$ie_{1P\ SG}$				
	ner	+	$est_{2P\ SG}$				
	ner	+	$(e)þ_{3P\ SG}$				
	ner	+	$iað_{PL}$				

The stems of class 1 may exhibit morphologically conditioned allomorphy caused by West Germanic Consonant Lengthening (e.g. *trymm-an* : *trym-est* : *trym-ed-e*); so did the person/number morphemes in both classes. The choice of the latter was determined by the class membership of the verb, which was an inherent feature of the stem, no longer linked to an overt class-defining stem-formative, i.e. external class characterization had become holistic, i.e. paradigm-dependent.

In the past tense and the past participle, the two classes still seemed to be kept apart by the reflexes of the original stem formatives /e/ and /o/, as in (10):

(10) a. Class 1: trym+e+d$_{PAST}$+e$_{1P\ SG}$ trym+e+d+est$_{2P\ SG}$ trym+e+d+on$_{PL}$ ge$_{PP}$+trym+e+d$_{PP}$
     b. Class 2: luf+o+d$_{PAST}$+e$_{1P\ SG}$ luf+o+d$_{PAST}$+est$_{2P\ SG}$ luf+o+d+on$_{PL}$ ge$_{PP}$+luf+o+d$_{PP}$

This analysis we find implicitly or explicitly in the traditional handbooks, and it is the primary basis for the distinction of the two classes. But it is questionable synchronically, especially in view of the increased number of class shifts, beginning with the overlap of the *nerian-* and the *lufian-*type, but eventually going far beyond it. The morphological structure postulated for the present without a stem-formative must have also been extended to the preterit already in the course of the early Old English period. This was certainly a gradual process, and there was a transition period of morphological indeterminacy. But by the end of the 9th century, if not even earlier (the earliest class shifts might make this date more precise), the change had been complete, and the phonological relics of the stem-formatives had been reinterpreted as part of the underlying representation of the preterit/past participle morpheme, i.e. (11):

(11) trym+e+d$_{PAST}$+e > trym+ed$_{PAST}$+e
     luf+o+d$_{PAST}$+e > luf+od$_{PAST}$+e

This was facilitated by the pre-Old English syncopation of /i/ in class 1 when preceded by a heavy stem or dental stops (i.e. Siever's Law/High Vowel Deletion), cf. *dēm-d-e, set-t-e*, as against *ner+e+d+e*. With *fæstan,* vowel deletion resulted in an ungrammatical cluster /fæst+t+e/, which was simplified to /st/ with concomitant loss of the representation of the preterit and past participle morpheme, i.e. *fæst+Ø+e*. This is the first zero allomorph of the preterit/past participle, i.e. the antecedent of the type *cut : cut : cut*. More instances arose through the loss of geminates in Middle English, when forms like OE *set+t+t+e* developed into *set +Ø(+e)*.

This development had a very important morphological side effect. The stem formatives had had a dual function, derivational and inflectional. With their loss, inflection became lexically determined (implicational), and the derivational function was no longer expressed overtly: overt derivation became zero-derivation. At the same time, the fuzzy delimitation between inflection and derivation became clear-cut. Incidentally, zero-derivation was the only process for creating denominal verbs, since the *-n-*suffix only derived deadjectival verbs. It was only in Middle and Early Modern English that new suffixes were introduced through borrowing, viz. *-ate, -ify,* and *-ize.*

Towards the end of the Old English period, the only class whose morphological behavior was fully predictable was class 2. Verbs of class 1 exhibited morphophonemic/morphological alternations, partly old, partly created by the Late Old English vowel lengthening and shortening processes, which are the germ of a subset of the Modern English irregular verbs (type *keep* : *kept*). The underlying form of the past tense and past participle morpheme originally had not contained a vowel but was preceded by the stem-formative, but the re-interpretation postulated in (11) above created a new underlying form with a vowel, /ed/ and /od/. While /od/ was stable, /ed/ allowed deletion of the vowel in certain, originally predictable environments. This deletion process was gradually extended and became phonologically unpredictable. At the same time, /ed/ and /od/ merged in /əd/, which elevated vowel-deletion to a class distinctive feature. We now have two classes: one that deletes the vowel, and one that does not. In the course of Middle English, vowel deletion was gradually generalized, at first controlled by stylistic and rhythmic factors, until it became the rule except after base-final alveolar stops. At this stage, the vowel deletion process must have been re-interpreted as a vowel-insertion process (rule inversion).

There is one further important development, viz. the loss of the infinitive ending, which is already attested in the North at a relatively early stage, and gradually spreads to the South. This introduced word-based morphology also to the verb morphology, whereas it had evolved in noun morphology already in pre-Old English.

4.3 Germanic to Old English: nominal system

Let me now turn to nominal inflection. A typical reconstructed Indo-European paradigm, e.g. the masculine *o*-stems, would have the structure shown in Table 5.2.

Table 5.2: Reconstructed IE masculine o-stem (= Grmc. a-stem) paradigm of 'day'

		root	stem-formative	inflection
SG	NOM	*$dʰóg^{hw}$	o	s
	ACC	*$dʰóg^{hw}$	o	m
	GEN	*$dʰog^{hw}$	é/ó	so
	DAT	*$dʰog^{hw}$	∅/ó:	í/i
PL	NOM	*$dʰóg^{hw}$ *$dʰog^{hw}$	o:	s(es)
			ó:	s(es)
	ACC	*$dʰóg^{hw}$	o	ns
	GEN	*$dʰog^{hw}$	ó:/(?é:)	m
	DAT	*$dʰóg^{hw}$	o	mis

Again, the stem-formatives had both derivational and inflectional function and exhibited allomorphic ablaut alternations. At this stage, the stem-formatives had a consistent, predictable exponent.

In Germanic, this variable system was replaced by non-variable initial stress, which destroyed the phonological conditioning of ablaut and led to a gradual weakening and loss of inflectional syllables. This resulted in the reconstructed Germanic paradigm shown in Table 5.3 based on Voyles (1982).

Table 5.3: Reconstructed Grmc. a-stem (= IE o-stem) paradigm of 'day'

SG	NOM	*dág + az	PL	NOM	*dág + o:s / dág + o:z
	ACC	*dág + a		ACC	*dág + ã
	GEN	*dág + es		GEN	*dág + õ:
	DAT	*dág + e:		DAT	*dág + amz

Here it is no longer plausible to segment a stem-formative separate from the inflectional endings using conventional methods of morphological analysis, i.e. the original morphological structure had been destroyed. In forms such as SG ACC *dag-a, SG DAT *dag-e:, PL ACC *dag-ã, PL GEN *dag-õ, the original case/number endings had been lost, and in the interest of paradigm symmetry it can be assumed that the stem-formative was re-interpreted as a new case/number ending, thereby losing its original function. In the other forms, there is also no consistent representation of the old stem-formative. This resulted in a new set of inflectional endings with a concomitant shift from a ternary root + stem-formative + inflection to a binary stem + inflection structure.

Further restructuring took place in the transition to Old English, as seen in the paradigm given in Table 5.4.

Table 5.4: OE a-stem

SG	NOM	dæg	PL	NOM	dag + as
	ACC	dæg		ACC	dag + as
	GEN	dæg + es		GEN	dag + a
	DAT	dæg + e		DAT	dag + um

With these masculine nouns and the corresponding neuters, e.g. *scip*, the accusative singular had lost its exponent, resulting in a base form which could function as a word without any additional morphological material. This part of nominal inflection thus had become word-based. Since these paradigms contained the majority of nouns, they attracted more and more nouns from other paradigms, e.g. from the original *-ja-* and *-i-*stems, where a form like *end-e* came to be reinterpreted as *ende*, with *-e* losing its inflectional function as nominative singular and becoming part of the unmarked base form, parallel to *cyning*. At this stage, however, morphology was still inflectional: the two inflectional categories of number and case were fused in one exponent.

4.4 Post Old English

At the end of the Old English period a number of new developments happened. These have primarily to do with the merger of unstressed vowels in schwa, i.e. *luf-u* > *luf-e* /lufə/ (original "-ō-stem"), *gum-a* > *gum-e* /gumə/ (original "-n-stem"), etc., which had still been stem-based with *-u* and *-a* functioning as nominative singulars. This development makes these forms look like the continuation of the original strong *-ja-* and *-i-*masculines, whose (originally inflectional) ending *-e* > /ə/ had already been re-interpreted as part of the base. These originally stem-based forms underwent the same reinterpretation and were integrated into the emerging generalized word-based noun morphology. Another development concerned the other inflectional forms, especially the singular genitive and dative as well as the plural nominative and accusative of these stem-based nouns. With the reduction of the final vowels to /ə/ these forms were now identical with the unmarked singular nominative, i.e. they had become endingless. It is therefore not surprising that the salient singular *-s*-genitive was gradually transferred to these nouns and also to other inflectional classes. At the same time, these nouns also adopted *-s*-forms in the plural nominative/accusative. This suggests that the ending *-es* had come to be reinterpreted as a general marker of the category plural only, without any additional case function. The same apparently happened to the ending *-en* characterizing the weak masculines of the type *gum-a(n)*. This brings about a crucial typological realignment: the categories of number and case became dissociated, because otherwise the analogical transfer of a case ending in the singular and of a plural ending independent of a case function (plural nominative/accusative) cannot be explained. This means that already at the end of the Old English period noun inflection had become completely word-based. The gradual marginalization of the dative (both singular and plural) must have started at this period as well. It had become a basically preposition-controlled ending, whose presence or absence was more and more governed by metrical-stylistic requirements (cf. Lass 1992: 110). This indicates that its actual grammatical function had been lost at this stage (or had at least been considerably weakened), cf. comparable 19th century Ger. *dem Hund-e* > *dem Hund*.

The Middle English period is characterized by the gradual generalization of the -s-plural, since eventually most of the -n-plurals (exceptions such as *ox-en, childr-en, brethr-en* are the last remnants today) adopted this plural form. Similarly, the -s-genitive singular came to be generalized. The genitive plural poses a problem, because there had never been an -s-genitive in the plural, but the irregular plural nouns – as well as the group genitive – adopted this form. For a possible explanation, cf. Kastovsky (2008).

The only other remarkable restructuring between Middle English and Modern English (probably in the transition from Middle English to Early Modern English) concerns the relationship between the regular allomorphs of the plural and genitive morphemes. Originally, i.e. until Middle English, their underlying representation contained a vowel, probably /e/ or /ə/, which was raised to /ɪ/ in certain varieties. During the Middle English period, this vowel could be deleted for rhythmic reasons, so that its presence or absence became optional, except before a coronal sibilant. Eventually, this vowel deletion became the rule, just as with verbs. This generalization of the vowel deletion led to rule-inversion: the vowelless allomorph came to be interpreted as underlying, and vowel-insertion replaced vowel-deletion, controlled by phonotactic requirements.

In Old English, adjectives agreed with the nominal head with regard to number, gender and case. Moreover, there were two types of inflection, so-called "weak" inflection after demonstratives, and "strong" inflection without a determiner, which was a Germanic innovation. But adjectival inflection became unstable towards the end of the Old English period and was lost in Middle English, clearly as a result of the general breakdown of NP inflection.

4.5 Word-formation

Let me conclude with a few remarks on word-formation. One striking feature is the almost total loss of ablaut nouns and adjectives related to strong verbs with corresponding ablaut alternations of the type *write : writ, sing : song*. These had formed part of the Old English core vocabulary, as they still do in German. In English, however, they were gradually replaced by base-invariant derivatives, since native word-formation – like regular inflection – adopted base invariancy as its basic principle. The massive borrowing of Romance and Latin vocabulary in Middle and Early Modern English, however, reintroduced base alternations at a new non-native level.

Another remarkable phenomenon is the demise of most Old English verbal prefixes, many of which had become semantically opaque already in Old English (cf. Hiltunen 1983). They were gradually replaced by non-native patterns, which dominate much more in prefixation than in suffixation.

Finally, the rise of a new compound type, viz. *washing machine, swimming pool* in should be mentioned. This has to be seen in connection with the rise of the new *-ing*-participle/gerund, which replaced the old *-ende*-participle. But, as many other Middle English developments in this area, this still needs more detailed investigation (cf. Kastovsky 2007).

5 References

Bauer, Laurie. 1983. *English Word-Formation*. Cambridge: Cambridge University Press.
Bauer, Laurie. 1992. *Introducing Linguistic Morphology*. Edinburgh: Edinburgh University Press.
Biese, Y. M. 1941. *Origin and Development of Conversions in English*. Helsinki: Finnish Academy of Sciences.
Blake, Norman (ed.). 1992. *The Cambridge History of the English Language*. Vol. II. *1066–1476*. Cambridge: Cambridge University Press.
Brunner, Karl. 1960–62. *Die englische Sprache. Ihre geschichtliche Entwicklung*. 2 Bd. 2. Aufl. Tübingen: Niemeyer.
Clackson, James. 2007. *Indo-European Linguistics. An Introduction*. Cambridge: Cambridge University Press.
Giegerich, Heinz J. 1999. *Lexical Strata in English: Morphological Causes, Phonological Effects*. Cambridge: Cambridge University Press.
Hiltunen, Risto. 1983. *The Decline of the Prefixes and the Beginnings of the English Phrasal Verb. The Evidence from Some Old and Early Middle English Texts*. Turku: Turun Yliopisto.
Hockett, Charles. 1958. *A Course in Modern Linguistics*. New York: MacMillan.
Hogg, Richard M. (ed.). 1992. *The Cambridge History of the English Language*. Vol. I. *The Beginnings to 1066*. Cambridge: Cambridge University Press.
Hogg, Richard and David Denison (eds.). 2006. *A History of the English Language*. Cambridge: Cambridge University Press.
Huddleston, Rodney and Geoffrey K. Pullum. 2002. *The Cambridge Grammar of the English Language*. Cambridge: Cambridge University Press.
Kastovsky, Dieter. 1980. Zero in morphology. A means of making up for phonological losses? In: Jacek Fisiak (ed.), *Historical Morphology*, 213–250. The Hague: Mouton.
Kastovsky, Dieter. 1996. Verbal derivation in English: A historical survey. Or: Much ado about nothing. In: Derek Britton (ed.), *English Historical Linguistics 1994*, 93–117. Amsterdam/Philadelphia: John Benjamins.
Kastovsky, Dieter. 1997. Morphological classification in English historical linguistics: The interplay of diachrony, synchrony and morphological theory. In: Terttu Nevalainen and Leena Kahlas-Tarkka (eds.), *To Explain the Present. Studies in the Changing English Language in Honour of Matti Rissanen*, 63–75. Helsinki: Société Néophilologique de Helsinki.
Kastovsky, Dieter. 1999. Inflectional classes, morphological restructuring, and the dissolution of Old English grammatical gender. In: Barbara Unterbeck and Matti Rissanen (eds.), *Gender in Grammar and Cognition*. Vol. 2. *Manifestations of Gender*, 709–727. Berlin/New York: Mouton de Gruyter.

Kastovsky, Dieter. 2006a. Historical morphology from a typological point of view: Examples from English. In: Terttu Nevalainen (ed.), *Types of Variation: Diachronic, Dialectal and Typological Interfaces*, 53–80. Amsterdam/Philadelphia: John Benjamins.

Kastovsky, Dieter. 2006b. Typological changes in derivational morphology. In: Ans van Kemenade and Bettelou Los (eds.), *The Handbook of the History of English*, 151–176. Oxford: Blackwell.

Kastovsky, Dieter. 2007. Middle English word-formation: A list of desiderata. In: Gabriella Mazzon (ed.), *Studies in Middle English. Forms and Meanings*, 41–56. Frankfurt: Peter Lang.

Kastovsky, Dieter. 2008. The genesis of the Modern English genitive plural: Structural and phonostylistic factors. In: József Andor, Béla Hollósy, Tibor Laczkó, and Péter Pelyvás (eds.), *When Grammar Minds Language and Literature. Festschrift for Prof. Béla Korponay on the Occasion of his 80th Birthday*, 263–273. Debrecen: Institute of English and American Studies, University of Debrecen.

Kastovsky, Dieter. 2009a. Diachronic aspects. In: Rochelle Lieber and Pavol Štekauer (eds.), *The Oxford Handbook of Compounding*, 323–340. Oxford: Oxford University Press.

Kastovsky, Dieter. 2009b. English word-formation, combining forms and neo-classical compounds: A reassessment. In: *Current Issues in Unity and Diversity of Languages. Selected Papers from the CILT 18, Held at Korea University in Seoul on July 21–26, 2008*, 724–734. Seoul: Korea University.

Lass, Roger. 1990. How to do things with junk: Exaptation in language evolution. *Journal of Linguistics* 26: 79–102.

Lieber, Rochelle. 1983. Argument linking and compounds in English. *Linguistic Inquiry* 14: 251–286.

Lyons, John. 1977. *Semantics*. 2 vols. Cambridge: Cambridge University Press.

Marchand, Hans. 1969. *The Categories and Types of Present-Day English Word-Formation*. 2nd rev. edn. München: Beck.

Matthews, Peter H. 1974. *Morphology*. Cambridge: Cambridge University Press. [2nd edn. 1991].

Minkova, Donka. 2008a. Prefixation and stress in Old English. *Word Structure* 1: 21–52.

Minkova, Donka. 2008b. Continuity or re-invention in functional stress-shifting. Paper presented at the 15th International Conference on English Historical Linguistics, Munich, August 24–30, 2008.

Prćić, Tvrtko. 2005. Prefixes vs initial combining forms in English: A lexicographic perspective. *International Journal of Lexicography* 18: 313–334.

Prćić, Tvrtko. 2007. Headhood of suffixes and final combining forms in English word formation. *Acta Linguistica Hungarica* 54: 381–392.

Schlegel, August Wilhelm. 1818. *Observations sur le langage et la littérature provençales*. Paris.

Schlegel, Friedrich. 1808. *Über die Sprache und Weisheit der Indier: Ein Beitrag zur Begründung der Altertumskunde*. Heidelberg: Winter.

Tops, Guy A. J. 1974. *The Origin of the Germanic Dental Preterit. A Critical Research History since 1912*. Leiden: Brill.

von Humboldt, Wilhelm. 1827–29. *Über die Verschiedenheit des menschlichen Sprachbaues*. Bonn.

Voyles, Joseph B. 1992. *Early Germanic Grammar. Pre-, Proto- and Post-Germanic Languages*. San Diego: Academic Press.

Wald, Benji and Lawrence Besserman. 2002. The emergence of the verb-verb compound in twentieth century English and twentieth century linguistics. In: Donka Minkova and

Robert Stockwell (eds.), *Studies in the History of the English Language. A Millennial Perspective*, 417–447. Berlin/New York: Mouton de Gruyter.

Wełna, Jerzy. 1996. *English Historical Morphology*. Warszawa: Wydawnictwa Uniwersytetu Warszawskiego.

Graeme Trousdale
Chapter 6:
Syntax

1   Introduction: the syntactic history of English and English historical syntax —— 102
2   The syntactic history of English —— 106
3   English historical syntax —— 111
4   Summary —— 118
5   References —— 119

Abstract: Syntactic change in English can be considered in a number of ways, depending on whether the aim of the research is to find out more about the ways in which English has changed over time, or whether it is to find out more about general constraints on change in the syntactic component of human language by using evidence from diachronic varieties of English. Adapting a proposal from Honeybone (2008), on phonological change in English, this chapter is concerned with both the syntactic history of English and English historical syntax, and discusses evidence from a range of varieties of the language (both contemporary and historical). Changes discussed in the chapter include the development of word order patterns, the evolution of auxiliaries, and the category "subject" in English. Both formal and functional theories of language change are considered, along with some discussion of the roles played by borrowing, reanalysis, and analogy in shaping change in English syntax.

1 Introduction: the syntactic history of English and English historical syntax

This section presents an overview of the ways in which the syntax of English has changed, providing a rather global approach to syntactic change. The overview is divided into two parts, the syntactic history of English (Section 2) and English historical syntax (Section 3), following a similar distinction regarding the evolution of English phonology proposed by Honeybone (2008). To illustrate this

Graeme Trousdale: Edinburgh (UK)

distinction, consider the development of the tense auxiliary *do* in the history of the language. There are a number of questions one might ask about this particular change, including:
- based on the textual evidence available to us, what do we know of the regional and textual provenance of this change?
- to what extent do current varieties of English display similar or divergent patterns with respect to the use of *do*-support?
- how can we relate the development of *do*-support to other changes affecting auxiliary verbs in English, such as the modals and the aspect and voice auxiliaries?
- is this change typologically odd?
- what does this change tell us about properties of verbs and their dependents?
- how does this affect our understanding of constraints on syntactic change, or of more general issues such as reanalysis and analogy/extension?

The first three questions relate to the syntactic history of English, since answers to such questions will tell us something about a particular development in a particular set of varieties, based on a particular set of evidence. By contrast, the last three questions relate to English historical syntax, since answers to such questions will tell us something about general properties of human language undergoing change, comparing data from (varieties of) English with other varieties as evidence for universal tendencies.

It is important to keep the syntactic history of English distinct from English historical syntax, because different questions need to be asked in each case. The importance of the distinction does not lie in a difference between description and explanation: it is wrong to say that work in the syntactic history of English does not concern itself with explaining patterns of change, and equally wrong to say that matters of description are irrelevant to those working on English historical syntax. Both approaches require the appropriate use of appropriate data, and both require "theorizing", but not necessarily in the same way. In a discussion of contemporary dialect variation and theoretical syntax, Adger and Trousdale (2007: 261) note that dialect syntax in its sociolinguistic context provides a challenge for syntactic theory because it "raises important questions regarding what the theory is actually modelling": and the same holds true for English historical syntax. Furthermore, although the syntactic history of English and English historical syntax are distinct, they are related.

This can be exemplified by situations of language contact. An accurate account of the historical syntax of English will describe the many ways in which contact with other languages (from the Celtic substratum which has been said to have had a significant effect on the evolution of British English [see various papers in Filppula et al. 2008], to the new Asian varieties which have emerged in the later modern period); but contact linguistics more generally interfaces with linguistic theory, so these developments also have a role to play in English historical linguistics (not least in the way in which phonological, morphological, and syntactic changes are themselves related, and even accelerated, in contact situations). The various inputs to a child acquiring a particular variety may differ significantly depending on the degree of imperfect second language learning which may characterize the adult's output. Exogenous changes, brought about by borrowing from one variety into another, serve as part of the input system to subsequent generations acquiring the language (who may have no knowledge that a particular form is the consequence of borrowing), which may prompt a series of endogenous changes. However one wishes to describe this phenomenon in theoretical terms – parameter resetting, constraint reranking, constructional entrenchment, and so on – the relation between the syntactic history of English and English historical syntax is at the heart of much of the new research in this field of linguistic enquiry.

My reason for detailing this distinction at some length is because much research remains to be done, despite advances made in both fields. Some work which (in part or in whole) addresses grammatical change in English is more clearly aligned with the syntactic history of English (e.g. Mitchell 1985); similarly a lot of work on historical syntax uses English as a source of data, an understandable decision given the wealth of historical material available for analysis (e.g. Lightfoot 1999); the vast majority of research includes some aspects of both (e.g. the various syntax chapters in *The Cambridge History of the English Language* [Hogg (ed.) 1992–2001]). However, there is still much in the domain of the syntactic history of English which remains to be uncovered; similarly, work in English historical syntax is also rapidly evolving. Some, perhaps most, research into English historical syntax follows mainstream work on Chomskyan generative syntax, though there is increasing work within Optimality Theory, and construction grammars of various kinds, as discussed in Section 3 below. Furthermore, some research counts as an excellent representation of both kinds of historical work, in which we discover more about both the historical development of English syntax, and the interface of these developments with more general issues in syntactic (and linguistic) theory (e.g. Warner 1993 and Allen 1995).

The remainder of this introduction is concerned with some other issues of relevance to syntactic change in English. Some of these issues concern categorizations of various kinds. First, there are the rather problematic issues of what we mean by terms such as "the English language" or an "Old English dialect" when considering the changes that have occurred. Who counts as a native speaker of contemporary English, and at what arbitrary point in time do we separate Old

English from Middle English, for instance? Second, what evidence do we use to document the changes we observe, and how coherent are these (spoken or written) text types as instances of a single category? Comparing a Kentish charter from the 9th century with a contemporary text message written in Singlish may well indicate some of the ways in which English syntax has changed in the course of over a millennium, but we need to bear in mind not simply diachronic change, but also provenance, text type, intended communicative function, and the like.

Matters such as these are perhaps more directly relevant to the syntactic history of English than to English historical syntax, but recent work on the earlier syntax of English, using the various parsed corpora, has associated different dialect patterns with both endogenous constraints and instances of language contact. A good example concerns the effects of Viking invasions on the more northerly dialects of Old English and Middle English. In terms of the particular history of English, we can witness not only place name evidence of settlements and the like, but also the structural consequences of prolonged contact with Old Norse, in the more rapid loss of inflections witnessed in texts from northern parts of England, in comparison with texts with a more southerly provenance. The syntactic consequences of this contact are far reaching, including variation in the position of finite verbs (the v2 constraint), with northern varieties of Middle English as a COMPLEMENTIZER PHRASE-V2 type, and southern varieties as INFLECTION PHRASE-V2 (Kroch et al. 2000), and, following from that, the identification of the functional projection under CP in Old English as AgrSP (Subject Agreement Phrase) (Haeberli 2000). This snapshot is intended to illustrate how it is possible to connect, via a series of steps, particular features of the syntactic history of English to highly theory-specific accounts in English historical syntax. While it is helpful to separate the syntactic history of English from English historical syntax, it is also useful to see how the two relate to one another.

Very little mention is made in what follows of the methodologies adopted in accounts of syntactic change, from the primarily philological to the primarily theoretical; equally, I have decided for reasons of space not to discuss many of the ways in which the use of computerized corpora has revolutionized how work on grammatical change in English is conducted. However, both of these issues are addressed briefly in the conclusion. For further discussion of good practice in historical syntax research, see Fischer (2007: 11–52). In an overview chapter such as this, it is possible only to deal with a small subset of syntactic changes. There are three main changes I concentrate on (ov/vo word order, the loss of impersonals and the establishment of the category "modal"), linking these where possible to other changes in the system, and showing how various theoretical issues can be addressed by considering these particular changes.

2 The syntactic history of English

The syntactic history of English, based on the extant materials available to us, reveals some issues of continuity throughout the history of language, e.g. the availability of pre- and post-modification of nouns in both Old English and Present-day English, and some aspects of change, e.g. the use of the sequence [mə] with the first person singular pronoun to indicate futurity in some non-standard varieties of English, as in *I'm a get a drink*. Before I go on to discuss some particular features of linguistic change, it is important to consider some aspects of the way in which the story of English is told in many historical accounts. Typically, the story is that of the evolution of forms which constitute the standard variety – explanations are given to work out why it is that the most geographically generalized and conventionalized of forms have come to take the shape that they have. There are a number of reasons for this. For instance, much work in syntactic theory has used English as a data source, and particularly, has used the idiolect of the researcher as a way of judging grammaticality, which typically reflects the middle-class, educated variety of English that typifies the standard. This is of particular relevance to English historical syntax, but still features in accounts of the history of a particular language. By way of example, we can consider the history of word order in English.

2.1 Word order changes

Most research on word order in clauses has been concerned with three particular phenomena, the v2 constraint, verb raising, and ov word order, illustrated by (1), (2), and (3) respectively:

(1) *On his dagum   sende   Gregorius us   fulluht*
    In his day-DAT.PL send-3P.SG.PAST Gregory 1P.PL.DAT baptism
    'In his time, Gregory sent us Christianity' (ChronA2 18.565.1; Haeberli 2002: 88)

(2) *To hwæm   locige   ic buton to ðæm   eaðmodum*
    To who-DAT look-1P.SG.PRES I except to the-DAT humble-DAT.PL
    'To whom do I look except to the humble?' (CP 41.299.18; Fischer et al. 2000: 67)

(3) *He ne mæg his agne aberan*
    He NEG can his own support-INF
    'He cannot support his own' (CP 7.53.1; Moerenhout and van der Wurff 2005: 85)

The loss of v2, ov word order, and v-to-t raising has been central in much work in English historical syntax (for useful summaries within a principles and parameters model, see Fischer et al. 2000). The first two changes are typically used to explain why English word order has become more "fixed". Exceptions to the rule in contemporary standard English are noted (e.g. in clauses beginning with negative adverbs, as in *Never have I heard such rubbish*), but typically, the story ends there. However, word order in "English" continues to evolve. The syntactic history of English is a history of contact, and in some contact varieties we see a continuation of variation in terms of v2 and verb raising in (4) and (5):

(4) *if you want we can go earlier because # at four thirty starts the quiz* (German-English bilingual; Eppler 1999: 303)

(5) *What he has eaten?* (Indian vernacular English; Bhatt 2000: 74)

Do we include such patterns as part of the syntactic history of English? To a large extent the answer to that question depends on the degree of conventionalization in different communities. Example (4) might be a "one-off" case of interference between the competing grammars of a single bilingual (though as we will see in Section 3, the notion of competing grammars among monolinguals has been highly influential in theorizing earlier stages of word order variation and change), thus an innovation rather than a change (since the latter requires spread). But (5) is rather well established as a feature of a particular variety of English spoken by a substantial number of people. Because so much of the syntactic history of English is concerned with the tracing of what is now the standard for inner circle varieties of the language, many of the "big stories" in the syntactic history tend to come to the same conclusion, by relating what has happened to give us the contemporary standard forms.

2.2 The English modals

There are also a number of questions regarding the extent of continuity in the history of the language. A useful example here comes from another of the more widely discussed changes, the story of the English modals (again a topic of relevance to both the syntactic history of English, and English historical syntax: for a useful overview of both the relevant data and different theoretical accounts, see Denison 1993: 292–339). The story of the modals is one of divergence, in which a series of (formally) slightly anomalous verbs became (formally and functionally) even more anomalous over time. Although part of a set of preterit-presents in Old English, the ancestors of modern modals had more verb-like formal properties than the Present-day English modals do, such as the ability to take an object complement and to appear in non-finite form, with these properties gradually being lost over time. Allied to the formal development is a functional change, such that these verbs come to encode aspects of the speaker's viewpoint, whether that be the intention to lay down some sort of obligation on the hearer (in deontic modality) or the assessment of the veracity of the proposition encoded elsewhere in the clause (in epistemic modality), functions which had previously been coded by subjunctive inflectional endings on verbs.

The story of the modals does not involve an orderly transition from lexical verb to auxiliary (AUX). This is shown most clearly by the findings of Warner (1993), who emphasizes the apparent messiness of the development. For example, instead of developing more auxiliary-like properties in the transition from Old English to Middle English, the modals in some ways become more verb like (e.g. OE *sculan and cunnan develop new present tense forms sculeþ and cunneþ), and different dialects of Middle English show changes at different times and in different ways. What Warner's study suggests is that the category of auxiliary (and the subcategory of modals) becomes strengthened in the history of English (see also Hudson 1997), by showing bonds between the various forms that were to emerge as auxiliaries (e.g. negative contraction in nolde 'would not', næs 'was not', nabbe 'have not'). Warner argues that the key development is that the auxiliary category becomes more well-defined (a more basic level category), in part in terms of its interaction with other phenomena (e.g. the appearance of tag questions, negative clitics, and the position of unstressed adverbs). Towards the end of Middle English (roughly at the turn of the 15th century), the differentiation between auxiliaries and verbs becomes sharper.

A further issue regarding continuity concerns the existence of "double modal" constructions in some contemporary varieties of English, as illustrated by (6) and (7):

(6) *Could you might possibly use a teller machine?* (Southern US English; Mishoe and Montgomery 1994: 11)

(7) *Oh no, they're double-glazed. They wouldn't could [break]* (Tyneside English; McDonald 1981)

Such forms are well-attested in earlier varieties of English, as we see in (8):

(8) &   hwu   muge   we   þone   weig   cunnen
    and   how   may   we   the-MASC.SG.ACC   way   can-INF

'And how can we know the way?' (Jn [Warn 30]; Fischer and van der Wurff 2006: 147)

and there is some debate regarding the extent to which the contemporary forms should be seen as continuations from earlier stages of the language, or as independent developments. Of relevance here is the fact that the syntax and semantics of modal combinations in those varieties of British English which allow them (i.e. dialects of north-eastern England and central Scotland) are rather different from those in the southern United States dialects. So it may be that we have continuation in the case of the British dialects, but independent development in the American ones (see further Nagle 1994).

2.3 Subjects and the impersonal construction

My final example to illustrate the centrality of variation in the syntactic history of English concerns the category of "subject". While it is certainly the case that there are some instances of "subjectless" clauses in early English:

(9) norþan   sniwde
    from-north   snow-3P.SG.PAST
    'It snowed from the north' (*Seafarer* 31)

such unambiguous examples are restricted either to a particular lexical set (weather verbs) (9) or to a particular kind of information packaging (impersonal passives) (10):

(10) ðætte   forðy   to ungemetlice   ne   sie
     that   therefore   too greatly   not   be-3P.SG.PRES.SUBJ
     geliðod   ðæm   scyldgan
     let-off-PAST.PRTC   the-DAT   guilty-DAT
     'that therefore it must be let off too greatly to the guilty' (CP 20.149.24; Fischer et al. 2000: 39)

In cases of co-ordination such as (11):

(11) *and him*   *comon*   *englas*   *to,*
     and 3P.SG.MASC.DAT   come-PL.PAST   angels-PL.NOM/ACC   to
     and him   *ðenodon*
     and 3P.SG.MASC.DAT   served

'and angels came to him, and served him' (*ÆCHom* I, 11.174.17; Fischer et al. 2000: 39)

the absence of the subject in the second clause is predictable from the discourse context, and such VP coordination is equally common in Present-day English. More crucial are the well-known impersonal constructions such as in (12):

(12) him   ofhreow   þæs   mannes
     3SG.MASC.DAT rue-3P.SG.PAST the-GEN   man-GEN
     'He pitied the man' (*ÆCHom* I, 8.192.16; Denison 1993: 85)

in which neither argument is marked as nominative. Such constructions have been thoroughly discussed in the literature (most comprehensively by Allen 1995), and highlight the problematic notion of "subject" as a category for earlier English. One widely held view is that the loss of impersonal constructions is a consequence of case loss (see, e.g., Lightfoot 1991), where assignment of inherent/lexical (dative) case to experiencers prevents structural case assignment. The question remains, however, as to whether dative or genitive noun phrases in such constructions constitute subjects. Evidence from raising and co-ordination, as in (13) and (14) respectively:

(13) him   sceal sceamian   ætforan gode   ælmihtigum
     3P.SG.MASC.DAT shall shame-INF before   God-DAT almighty-DAT
     'he shall be ashamed before God almighty' (*ÆLS* [Ash Wednesday] 12.169 Visser 1970: 23)

(14) ac   gode   ne   licode   na   heora   geleafleast ...
     but god-DAT NEG please-3P.SG.PAST NEG 3P.PL.GEN faithlessness ...
     ac   asende   him   to fyr   of   heofnum
     but send-3P.SG.PAST   3P.PL.DAT   to fire-ACC from heavens-DAT
     'But their faithlessness did not please God ... but [he] sent them fire from heaven' (*ÆCHom* II, 20.644.71; Denison 1993: 89)

suggests that dative noun phrases had some subject properties; however, the category of subject was not as fully grammaticalized as it is in Present-day English, which may be associated with a more general grammaticalization of the transitive construction (Trousdale 2008). Anderson (1997: 216–224) proposes a different analysis, in which the change involves a gradual coalescence of morphosyntactic and syntactic subject. The distinction between the two can be illustrated by existential clauses such as *there are books on the shelf*, where *books* is the syntactic subject, *there* the morphosyntactic subject (controlling concord). In Anderson's analysis, earlier English optionally marked morphosyntactic subjecthood, though raising in (13) suggests that the dative NP is a syntactic subject. Turning to the situation in contemporary English, as Anderson (1997: 224) observes, instances such as *there's books on the shelf* suggest the wide systemic spread of the coalescence of morphosyntactic and syntactic subject. But even subjectlessness has not disappeared entirely. We find it in particular (albeit restricted) kinds of written or spoken discourse, such as diary entries of the kind *went home, ate dinner, fell asleep* (Haegeman 1997), or in casual dialogue (A: *How many people were at the party?* B: *Dunno, couldn't say*), where it is understood that the subject is first person singular.

There are many other aspects of the syntactic history of English which I do not have the space to deal with here (for an excellent summary, see Fischer and van der Wurff 2006; for authoritative treatment of individual periods, see the various syntax chapters of *The Cambridge History of the English Language* [Hogg (ed.) 1992–2001]). There are also many other topics which are still awaiting detailed treatment. Some of these are highly specific. For instance, what is the precise history of the ditransitive construction where both objects are pronouns (e.g. *he sent it her* vs. *he sent her it*)? What do we know about the spread of the progressive with stative verbs (e.g. *I'm loving your new look*), and how widespread is this in the new Englishes? Why does *þa* trigger V2 more consistently than *þonne* in OE? What is the spread of the indirect passive in the later history of English (and why was the spread so slow)? There are also general questions relating to on-going changes: for instance, what features characterise the syntax of emergent contact varieties involving English? Answers to these and other questions will clarify even further the various features of change in the syntactic history of English.

3 English historical syntax

In this section, I look at some of the ways in which data from the history of English has been used to explore more general issues in syntactic change. I will use some of the changes discussed in Section 2 to indicate how the syntactic history of English and English historical syntax overlap, and bring in some further data to highlight some of the other relevant issues. In discussing cross-linguistic patterns, Harris and Campbell (1995: 50) state that there are three mechanisms of syntactic change: borrowing, reanalysis, and extension. I deal with each in turn, though for reasons of space I say less about borrowing than about the other mechanisms of change, and I give generally accepted definitions of each mechanism. Borrowing, in its strictest sense, occurs when the "replication of the syntactic pattern is incorporated into the borrowing language through the influence of a host pattern found in a contact language" (Harris and Campbell 1995: 51); reanalysis involves "change in the structure of an expression or class of expressions that does not involve any immediate or intrinsic modification of its surface manifestation" (Langacker 1977: 58), while extension is the reverse, involving changes "in the surface manifestation of a pattern [...] which does not involve immediate or intrinsic modification of its underlying structure" (Harris and Campbell 1995: 51). Harris and Campbell see extension as part of analogy, but avoid using this second term because it has a range of meanings in the literature. The critical issue is whether the analogy involves some exemplar or not, as discussed below: exemplar-based analogy may be equated with extension, but "non-exemplar based analogy" is rather different, as Kiparsky (2012) has argued.

3.1 Borrowing

Research on borrowing in the earlier history of the language (i.e. on English spoken in Britain) has considered both borrowing from other languages and borrowing from different dialects of English. In terms of language contact, for earlier English, syntactic borrowing from the Celtic substratum (Filppula et al. 2008) and from Old Norse (McWhorter 2002) has been suggested, and the effects of long-term contact with Vikings in the north of England have been shown to be widespread (see further below). An interesting case regarding borrowing from Latin concerns the development of accusative with infinitive constructions in Middle English: Fischer (1989) suggests that Latin borrowing alone was not responsible for the change, though the existence of such constructions in Latin may have facilitated some aspects of its spread. The later history of language contact involving English has more to do with English beyond Britain, particularly in the development of African American English, and a range of pidgin and creole languages. Dialect contact has also been influential in the development of particular morphosyntactic features of both British English, and other Englishes, e.g. in the spread of *do*-support, and the variation between -*th*, -*s* and zero as inflections on third person singular indicative verbs (Nevalainen and Raumolin-Brunberg 2003).

3.2 Reanalysis

Reanalysis and extension/analogy have been at the centre of much of the work in English historical syntax. In research on many of the changes discussed here (e.g. OV/VO word order, loss of the impersonal construction, and the establishment of the category modal), two rather different claims have been made. One is that change is catastrophic, the other is that it is gradual. This raises the question of what we mean by syntactic change, and different kinds of grammarians are likely to give different answers to that question. I deal first with formal approaches to syntactic change, and how these approaches deal with the issue of reanalysis. Later in this section, I consider functional accounts of reanalysis in syntactic change.

For many formal grammarians, what changes is the system, the set of parameters (or features on lexical items) which determine well-formedness in a particular manifestation of human language. In this approach to change, the primary focus is on acquisition, on how a child acquiring a particular language comes to set parameters in a particular way, given a particular set of inputs. Acquisition is the locus of reanalysis, as the language learner sets the parameters of his or her grammar, based on the primary linguistic data. The notion of parameters has changed as Chomskyan theory has developed, with specific consequences for this particular theory of syntax and our understanding of syntactic change more generally, and parametric change has been suggested by some (e.g. Pintzuk et al. 2000) to be reduced to the creation and combination of feature bundles in lexical items. This diachronic notion of the locus of change correlates with other Minimalist work on synchronic dialectal variation (e.g. Adger 2007 on variation in Buckie Scots). Increased use of corpora in formalist accounts of change, combined with particular discussions of dialectal differences in the implementation of changes (e.g. Kroch and Taylor 1997 on verb movement in Middle English) has rather altered some of the perceptions of the importance of E(xternalized)-language data in accounting for I(nternalized)-language changes. Formalist attempts to associate statistical patterns in corpora/E-language to changes in a particular individual, mental system/I-language have re-evaluated some of the claims regarding the ways in which reanalysis is actualized.

Nonetheless, reanalysis is the primary mechanism of change in most formal accounts, a mechanism of change which is also discussed in the more functionalist grammaticalization literature. Indeed Roberts and Roussou (2003), adopting a Minimalist theory of language structure, argue that grammaticalization is an epiphenomenon, since it is simply a particular case of parametric change involving reanalysis – the production of functional material from lexical material (primary grammaticalization) or other functional material (secondary grammaticalization) – and structural simplification. This focus on functional heads – and the notion that functional heads are the "magnets" which trigger Move (Chomsky 1995) – is also used to explain patterns of word-order variation, a linguistic feature which Meillet (1958 [1912]) also considered to be associated with grammaticalization. However, while Roberts and Roussou identify similarities between patterns of word order variation and instances of grammaticalization, they also show how the two are distinct. For instance, in their Minimalist model, all of the word order changes mentioned in the previous section – the loss of v2, the loss of verb-raising/v-to-t, and the shift from ov to vo – involve "loss of movement to a higher functional position" (Roberts and Roussou 2003: 206). Loss of movement also characterizes the development of the modals (Roberts and Roussou 2003: 195), which unlike the others is an instance of grammaticalization. They therefore identify five significant differences between the two instances of loss of movement, one of which entails grammaticalization, the other of which does not, for example:

a. only the grammaticalization of the modals creates a "new realization for t (t^*_{Merge})" (Roberts and Roussou 2003: 207)
b. the word order changes involve a reanalysis to a lower functional head (e.g. c(omplementizer)-to-t), the modals to a higher one (i.e. v-to-t)
c. loss of v-to-t affects all lexical verbs, but the changes in the modals affect only a subset (but see Hudson 1997 for an alternative analysis which dispenses with v-to-t movement)
d. upward reanalysis only is associated with bleaching and phonetic attrition (though this seems rather a stipulation than anything explanatory)
e. upward reanalysis can be cyclical.

Associated with this account of parameter resetting is the notion of grammar competition (Kroch 1989) as an explanation of language change. In grammar competition, an individual speaker is said to display patterns of variation that cannot be the product of operations of a single grammar. In a principles and parameters model, it is impossible for an individual speaker to have one grammar that both allows verb raising and simultaneously disallows it: the "switch" for the v-to-t parameter cannot be set at both "on" and "off" in one individual grammar. In more recent Chomskyan theory, as noted above, the focus of grammar competition has shifted to features of lexical items (and in cases of variation, how the same lexical item surfaces with apparently contradictory feature markings). A further issue associated with grammar competition is the Constant Rate Effect (Kroch 1989), a phenomenon used to link frequency with rates of change: for any change involving grammar competition, while the change may occur more frequently in one syntactic context than in another, the rate of change across different contexts remains the same. Different rates of change indicate that there is likely to be more than one change involved. Grammar competition has been used as an explanation for word order changes such as the loss of ov. In an elegant study (which also illustrates the usefulness of computerized corpora in syntactic change), Pintzuk and Taylor (2006) provide quantitative evidence that, although vo order occurs with different kinds of objects (positive, quantified, and negative) all affected by different kinds of factors (such as length and thematic role), the rates of change are different, and so cannot be explained simply in terms of grammar competition; rather, there is both (a) grammar competition between head initial and head final VPS and (b) addition stylistic motivations for object-movement. Crucially, the corpus data provide no evidence of negative objects postposing with OV grammars, and little evidence of positive objects preposing with VO grammars. The rise of VO and the demise of OV, in this account, is due to not only the loss of the OV grammar, but also the loss of the movement rule in VO generated grammars. Given that the rate of loss of the preposing movement rule is different for different kinds of objects (i.e. positive or quantified), Pintzuk and Taylor account for the gradual nature of the actualization of the changes in the history of the language.

In such an approach to change, the actualization of change may be gradual, and this gradualness may be systemic (changes may occur in a particular syntactic context before spreading to another), spatial (affecting the idiolects of one geographical area before another), stylistic (originating in a particular speech context, or register), social (occurring in the language of a particular subgroup in the speech community before being transmitted to another subgroup), or any combination of these. However, the reanalysis itself is "abrupt and catastrophic" (Lightfoot 1999: 88), and what changes is grammar.

By contrast, in some functionalist analyses of grammatical change, what changes is use. Indeed, in usage-based models (Kemmer and Barlow 2000) the relationship between form and function is something of a feedback loop, where "usage feeds into the creation of grammar, just as much as grammar determines the shape of usage" (Bybee 2006: 730); the frequency of use affects the mental representation of language, such that "grammar is the cognitive organization of one's experience with language" (Bybee 2006: 711). In models of language structure such as these, reanalysis occurs, but it is not restricted to changes of features or resetting parameters; instead, what is involved in change is form-function reanalysis, alterations to "the form-meaning mapping in a grammatical construction" (Croft 2000: 118). This notion of reanalysis is central to Hollmann's work on the development of the *have* causative in English (e.g. *my boss had me work late*) arising from an "affecting event" construction (e.g. *he wolde haue his reign endure and last*), in which Hollmann argues that the form-function reanalysis is based on alternative construals: the pragmatics of an experiential event allow for a causative interpretation where the experiencer is understood to be more powerful than the other participant in the process (Hollmann 2003: 87): compare (15) and (16):

(15) *I often have my boss come in when I'm sleeping* (= 'It often happens that my boss comes in when I'm sleeping')

(16) *My boss often has me come in when he's sleeping* (= 'My boss forces me to come in when he's sleeping')

While both examples could be interpreted as either causative or as "affecting event" constructions, (15) seems more likely as an affecting event, and (16) as a causative, because of the different power relations inherent in an employer-employee relationship. Hollmann's account shows how a cluster of constructions involving *have* with a different (formal) complement had a similar function to the emerging *have* causative in late Middle English. Reanalysis here, then, is conceived as accommodation attempts: speakers and hearers negotiating the relationship between the forms and functions of constructions while trying to maintain their conventionalized uses (see further Croft 2000: 118). Change in this sense is most likely to be gradual, because it may involve incremental changes at all parts of a construction.

We can consider such an instance of gradual change in the development of the English determiner. In their discussion of the elements of the noun phrase, Fischer and van der Wurff (2006: 114) argue that there has been little change in the order of the various dependents, suggesting that there has been no new functional slot in the history of the language. This position runs counter to that of Denison (2006: 288), who suggests that, rather, parallel to the development of the category Modal in English, the "evidence for the existence of D[eterminer] is much shakier in earlier English", and somewhat problematic even in contemporary English. Categorization – both the general cognitive process and the language-specific outcomes – has been, and continues to be, an important issue in general linguistics, but it is of particular concern in historical work, where issues of synchronic gradience at time 1, and diachronic gradualness, either temporally (i.e. between time 1 and time 2), or structurally (e.g. between a change in some aspect of meaning and a change in some aspect of form), or sociolinguistically (e.g. in the spread between groups of speakers, or registers), are of considerable importance, as noted above. Specifically in the syntactic history of English, we certainly see a strengthening of the category "determiner" over time. We see this development most sharply, perhaps, in the development of articles, the most grammaticalized of determiners. In this development, English is like many other languages, in that the definite article *the* has arisen from a demonstrative, while the indefinite article *a(n)* has arisen from the numeral "one" (OE *an*). In less formal contemporary English, the use of *some* with a singular count noun (as in *Some guy called earlier*) we witness a further typical grammaticalization path, through which an indefinite article emerges from and becomes layered with an earlier quantifier (OE *sum*). The absence of such clearly grammaticalized articles in the Old English period does not, of course, mean that speakers of the language at that time could not express definiteness; the difference was simply in the means of expression: strong forms of adjectives typically indicated indefiniteness, as in (17):

(17) ðurh   boclic-*e*   lare
     through   book-like   teaching
     'by teaching with books' (*ÆCHom* Pref. 175.68)

while weak forms (often with a demonstrative, suggesting incipient grammaticalization even at the earliest stages of the language) typically indicated definiteness (18):

(18) *se*   *frumsceapen-**a***   *mann*
     DEM.NOM.SG.MASC   first-created-NOM.SG.MASC   man
     'the first man' (*ÆCHom* I 7.240.250)

In other words, what has remained stable is the capacity to mark particular "things" as (in)definite; what has changed is the means by which this is marked. Put another way, speakers of English have always had some way of grounding nominals, but over time they have chosen to do this using different linguistic strategies: the function is constant, the form changes. This observation from history is of relevance not just to our understanding of the categories of Present-day English, but more generally for our understanding of the nature of categories. Particularly, it brings into question whether categories may be determined by syntax alone (see Anderson 1997 and Aarts 2007 for different views on this), and it helps us to understand the relationship between gradience and gradualness in grammatical change (Traugott and Trousdale 2010). The crystallization of articles forms part of a more general development in the gradual evolution of the category "determiner" in Denison's account; many of these crystallizations may be considered as instances of grammaticalization, including the deictification of post-determiners such as *various* and *several* (Davidse and Breban 2006).

3.3 Analogy

Analogy has been an equally debated concept in syntactic change. Both reanalysis and analogy have been widely debated in the grammaticalization literature (see Hopper and Traugott 2003 for a useful summary); recently Fischer (2007) has called for a greater focus on the role of analogy in grammaticalization (arguing, for example, that in early Modern English *be going to* joins the token set of [AUX V] based on analogy with other future markers like *will*), while

Kiparsky (2012) has equated non-exemplar based analogy with grammaticalization. Fischer's model presents an interesting synthesis between iconic and indexical relations, between types and tokens (and relevant sets for each), and between the various paradigmatic and syntagmatic processes in grammaticalization; the model also raises the important issue of whether reanalysis results in a totally new structure, but see also Meillet (1958 [1912]) on analogy, grammaticalization and the creation of new forms. Kiparsky's distinction between exemplar based and non-exemplar based analogy make very interesting predictions for unidirectionality in syntactic change. Because exemplar-based analogy is local (language-specific), there are exceptions to it, but it is nonetheless an attempt by the language user to simplify the grammar by abandoning redundancies; by contrast, the only "model" for non-exemplar analogy has to be the most general of grammatical constraints, universal grammar itself. It is this non-exemplar based analogy that is more commonly known as grammaticalization in the sense of Meillet (1958 [1912]): the creation of new forms. For Kiparsky, then, analogy and grammaticalization both instantiate types of grammar optimization. From a functionalist perspective, a rather different way of unifying reanalysis and analogy comes from grammatical constructionalization, the entrenchment of schematic constructions through a series of discrete reanalyses, motivated by pattern matching – recall the definition of reanalysis provided by Croft (2000) above, as a "change to the form-meaning mapping of a grammatical construction" – this series of discrete reanalyses give the appearance of gradual change, and can be exemplified by a series of changes in English grammar, including the development of degree modifiers (Denison 2002; Traugott 2008a) and cleft constructions (Traugott 2008b; Patten 2010).

4 Summary

The one thing that is constant about the history of English syntax is variation. But questions still remain regarding the best way of capturing and modelling that variation optimally. Certainly work using computerized corpora has revolutionized what can be done in the quantitative (and qualitative) analysis of syntactic change. In relation to the history of English syntax, this has been most firmly established in work that intersects with the generative approach to diachronic syntax, as we have seen; but more recently, in cognitive linguistics, we see the use of corpora to explain patterns of collostructional variation and change in new Englishes (Mukherjee and Gries 2009) and in other languages (Hilpert 2008). This has the potential to be a very illuminating way of exploring many of the major issues in syntactic change from a cognitive, usage-based perspective.

In the overall history of the syntax of the language, we see constant processes of renewal, as similar functions come to be coded in different ways. Particularly, we see renewal as part of grammaticalization, such that terms expressed by means of inflection at one stage in the language come to be expressed periphrastically, by means of the syntax, at a subsequent stage. The importance of contact on particular developments in English syntax cannot be understated. First, it played a significant role in the development of the determiner and auxiliary system, and on the establishment of particular word orders, in the earlier history of English; but second, and equally importantly, as English continues to be used in different communities around the world, speakers of the new varieties which emerge from contact with other languages conventionalise new patterns, so a subsequent wave of variation begins. Such external factors combine with system-internal changes – loss of phonological contrasts, and increased morphological syncretism – and lead to a series of restructurings. Thus histories of the syntax of English must take into account both the particular social and linguistic context in which speakers have used, and continue to use, varieties of English, and the more general patterns of syntactic change which can be witnessed in any human language. Both kinds of change require theorization and explanation, and neither can be achieved by appeal solely to local customs of use, or solely to cross-linguistic tendencies.

Acknowledgments: I would like to thank Laurel Brinton and Elizabeth Traugott for their very helpful comments on an earlier version of this chapter.

5 References

Aarts, Bas. 2007. *Syntactic Gradience*. Oxford: Oxford University Press.
Adger, David. 2007. Combinatorial variability. *Journal of Linguistics* 42: 503–530.
Adger, David and Graeme Trousdale. 2007. Variation in English syntax: Theoretical implications. *English Language and Linguistics* 11: 261–278.
Allen, Cynthia L. 1995. *Case Marking and Reanalysis*. Oxford: Clarendon.
Anderson, John M. 1997. *A Notional Theory of Syntactic Categories*. Cambridge: Cambridge University Press.
Bhatt, Rakesh M. 2000. Optimal expressions in Indian English. *English Language and Linguistics* 4: 69–95.
Bybee, Joan. 2006. From usage to grammar: The mind's response to repetition. *Language* 82: 711–733.
Chomsky, Noam. 1995. *The Minimalist Program*. Cambridge, MA: MIT Press.
Croft, William. 2000. *Explaining Language Change*. London: Longman.
Davidse, Kristin and Tine Breban. 2006. *Deictification: The Development of Postdeterminer Uses of Adjectives*. Preprint no. 250. Department of Linguistics, KU Leuven.
Denison, David. 1993. *English Historical Syntax: Verbal Constructions*. London: Longman.

Denison, David. 2002. History of the *sort of* construction family. Paper presented at the International Conference on Construction Grammar 2, Helsinki, 7 September 2002. http://www.humanities.manchester.ac.uk/medialibrary/llc/files/david-denison/Helsinki_ICCG2.pdf; last accessed 3 January 2017.

Denison, David. 2006. Category change and gradience in the determiner system. In: van Kemenade and Los (eds.), 279–304.

Eppler, Eva. 1999. Word order in German English mixed discourse. *UCL Working Papers in Linguistics* 11: 285–308

Filppula, Markku, Juhani Klemola, and Heli Paulasto (eds.). 2008. *English and Celtic in Contact*. London: Routledge.

Fischer, Olga. 1989. The origin and spread of the accusative and infinitive construction in English. *Folia Linguistica Historica* 8: 143–217.

Fischer, Olga. 2007. *Morphosyntactic Change: Functional and Formal Perspectives*. Oxford: Oxford University Press.

Fischer, Olga, Ans van Kemenade, Willem Koopman, and Wim van der Wurff. 2000. *The Syntax of Early English*. Cambridge: Cambridge University Press.

Fischer, Olga and Wim van der Wurff. 2006. Syntax. In: Richard Hogg and David Denison (eds.), *A History of the English Language*, 109–198. Cambridge: Cambridge University Press.

Haeberli, Eric. 2000. Adjuncts and the syntax of subjects in Old and Middle English. In: Pintzuk, Tsoulas, and Warner (eds.), 109–131.

Haeberli, Eric. 2002. Inflectional morphology and the loss of verb second in English. In: David Lightfoot (ed.), *Syntactic Effects of Morphological Change*, 88–106. Oxford: Oxford University Press.

Haegeman, Liliane. 1997. Register variation, truncation, and subject omission in English and French. *English Language and Linguistics* 1: 233–270.

Harris, Alice C. and Lyle Campbell. 1995. *Historical Syntax in Cross-linguistic Perspective*. Cambridge: Cambridge University Press.

Hilpert, Martin. 2008. *Germanic Future Constructions: A Usage-based Approach to Language Change*. Amsterdam/Philadelphia: John Benjamins.

Hogg, Richard M. (ed.). 1992–2001. *The Cambridge History of the English Language*. Cambridge: Cambridge University Press

Hollmann, Willem. 2003. *Synchrony and Diachrony of English Periphrastic Causatives: A Cognitive Perspective*. Ph.D. dissertation, University of Manchester.

Honeybone, Patrick. 2008. Historical phonology: Phonological variation and language change. Keynote seminar, Nordic Language Variation Network. University of Bergen/Flåm.

Hopper, Paul J. and Elizabeth Closs Traugott. 2003. *Grammaticalization*. 2nd edn. Cambridge: Cambridge University Press.

Hudson, Richard. 1997. The rise of auxiliary *do*: Verb-non-raising or category strengthening? *Transactions of the Philological Society* 95: 41–72.

Kemenade, Ans van and Bettelou Los (eds.). 2006. *The Handbook of the History of English*. Oxford: Blackwell.

Kemmer, Suzanne and Michael Barlow. 2000. Introduction: A usage-based conception of grammar. In: Michael Barlow and Suzanne Kemmer, (eds.), *Usage-based Models of Language*, 7–28. Stanford: CSLI.

Kiparsky, Paul. 2012. Grammaticalization as optimization. In: Dianne Jonas, John Whitman, and Andrew Garrett (eds.), *Grammatical Change: Origins, Nature, Outcomes*, 15–51. Oxford: Oxford University Press.

Kroch, Anthony. 1989. Reflexes of grammar in patterns of language change. *Language Variation and Change* 1: 199–244.
Kroch, Anthony and Ann Taylor. 1997. Verb movement in Old and Middle English: Dialect variation and language contact. In: Ans van Kemenade and Nigel Vincent (eds.), *Parameters of Morphosyntactic Change*, 297–325. Cambridge: Cambridge University Press.
Kroch, Anthony, Ann Taylor, and Donald Ringe. 2000. The Middle English Verb-Second constraint: A case study in language contact and language change. In: Susan C. Herring, Pieter van Reenen, and Lene Schøsler (eds.), *Textual Parameters in Older Languages*, 353–391. Amsterdam/Philadelphia: John Benjamins.
Langacker, Ronald W. 1977. Syntactic reanalysis. In: Charles Li (ed.), *Mechanisms of Syntactic Change*, 57–139. Austin: University of Texas Press.
Lightfoot, David. 1991. *How to Set Parameters: Arguments from Language Change*. Cambridge, MA: MIT Press.
Lightfoot, David. 1999. *The Development of Language: Acquisition, Change, and Evolution*. Oxford: Blackwell.
McDonald, Christine. 1981. *Variation in the Use of Modal Verbs with Special Reference to Tyneside English*. Ph.D. dissertation, University of Newcastle upon Tyne.
McWhorter, John. 2002. What happened to English? *Diachronica* 19: 217–272.
Meillet, Antoine. 1958 [1912]. L'evolution des formes grammaticales. Reprinted in: *Linguistique Historique et Linguistique Générale*, 130–158. Paris: Champion.
Mishoe, Margaret and Michael Montgomery. 1994. The pragmatics of multiple modal variation in North and South Carolina. *American Speech* 69: 3–29.
Mitchell, Bruce. 1985. *Old English Syntax*. 2 vols. Oxford: Clarendon.
Moerenhout, Mike and Wim van der Wurff. 2005. Object-verb order in early sixteenth-century English prose: An exploratory study. *English Language and Linguistics* 9: 83–114.
Mukherjee, Joybrato and Stefan Th. Gries. 2009. Collostructional nativisation in New Englishes: Verb-construction associations in the International Corpus of English. *English World Wide* 30: 27–51.
Nagle, Stephen J. 1994. The English double modal conspiracy. *Diachronica* 11: 199–212.
Nevalainen, Terttu and Helena Raumolin-Brunberg. 2003. *Historical Sociolinguistics*. London: Longman.
Patten, Amanda L. 2010. Grammaticalization and the *it*-cleft construction. In: Traugott and Trousdale (eds.), 221–243.
Pintzuk, Susan and Ann Taylor. 2006. The loss of OV order in the history of English. In: van Kemenade and Los (eds.), 249–278.
Pintzuk, Susan, George Tsoulas, and Anthony Warner. 2000. Syntactic change: Theory and method. In: Pintzuk, Tsoulas, and Warner (eds.), 1–22.
Pintzuk, Susan, George Tsoulas, and Anthony Warner (eds.). 2000. *Diachronic Syntax: Models and Mechanisms*. Oxford: Oxford University Press.
Roberts, Ian and Anna Roussou. 2003. *Syntactic Change: A Minimalist Approach to Grammaticalization*. Cambridge: Cambridge University Press.
Traugott, Elizabeth Closs. 2008a. Grammaticalization, constructions and the incremental development of language: Suggestions from the development of degree modifiers in English. In: Regine Eckardt, Gerhard Jäger, and Tonjes Veenstra (eds.), *Variation, Selection, Development: Probing the Evolutionary Model of Language Change*, 219–252. Berlin/New York: Mouton de Gruyter.

Traugott, Elizabeth Closs. 2008b. "All that he endeavoured to prove was ...": On the emergence of grammatical constructions in dialogic contexts. In: Ruth Kempson and Robin Cooper (eds.), *Language in Flux: Dialogue Coordination, Language Variation, Change and Evolution*, 143–177. London: Kings College Publications.

Traugott, Elizabeth Closs and Graeme Trousdale. 2010. Gradience, gradualness and grammaticalization: How do they intersect? In: Traugott and Trousdale (eds.), 19–44.

Traugott, Elizabeth Closs and Graeme Trousdale (eds.). 2010. *Gradience, Gradualness and Grammaticalization*. Amsterdam/Philadelphia: John Benjamins.

Trousdale, Graeme. 2008. Words and constructions in grammaticalization: The end of the English impersonal construction. In: Susan M. Fitzmaurice and Donka Minkova (eds.), *Studies in the History of the English Language IV: Empirical and Analytical Advances in the Study of English Language Change*, 301–326. Berlin/New York: Mouton de Gruyter.

Visser, F. Th. 1970. *An Historical Syntax of the English Language. Part One: Syntactical Units with One Verb*. Leiden: E. J. Brill.

Warner, Anthony. 1993. *English Auxiliaries: Structure and History*. Cambridge: Cambridge University Press.

Elizabeth Closs Traugott
Chapter 7:
Semantics and Lexicon

1   Introduction —— 123
2   Cognitive semantics and metaphor —— 125
3   Invited inferencing and conceptual metonymy —— 127
4   Collocation and collostructional analysis —— 129
5   Productivity of semantic changes at specific periods —— 130
6   Differences between lexical and grammatical changes —— 132
7   Changes in the lexicon —— 133
8   Future prospects —— 136
9   References —— 136

Abstract: Selected topics in research on semantic change are discussed with focus on work based in Cognitive Linguistics and neo-Gricean pragmatics. Recent work on metaphor and metonymy, grammaticalization, subjectification, and collostructional analysis are highlighted and shown to provide theoretical underpinnings for some traditional taxonomies of semantic change. As the inventory of form-meaning pairs in a language, the historical lexicon reflects semantic change; it also reflects how vocabulary size has changed in English, and how borrowings have affected the typological ways in which meanings are packaged into words.

1 Introduction

While meaning or "semantics" has been a central concern of philosophy since early Greek times, semantic change has been a subject of investigation for little more than a hundred years. A landmark work is Bréal (1964 [1897]), in which a taxonomy of semantic changes was developed (and revised in structuralist terms by Ullmann 1964) that has in essence been repeated in most textbooks and handbooks on language change (e.g. Hock and Joseph 2009 [1996]; Campbell 2013 [2004]; Fortson 2003). Key concepts include change due to metaphor (e.g. *tissue* 'woven cloth' > 'aggregation of cells in animals or plants') and metonymy (e.g. *board* 'table' > 'people sitting around a table, governing body'), pejoration (*conceit*

Elizabeth Closs Traugott: Palo Alto (USA)

'(self)concept' > 'overestimation of one's qualities') and amelioration (e.g. ME *nice* 'foolish' > 'pleasant'), narrowing (e.g. OE *mete* '(solid) food' > 'food derived from animals') and broadening (e.g. ME *bridde* 'nestling' > *bird*), and taboo avoidance (e.g. 16th century *toilet* 'cloth' > 17th century 'cloth covering for dressing-table' > 18th century 'dressing-table' > 19th century 'lavatory' (a euphemistic use) > 20th century 'bathroom fixture'). Often several types of change affect one item, e.g. the changes to *toilet* involve first narrowing (restriction to a certain type of cloth), metonymy (object for object covering it, a subtype of whole for part), taboo avoidance, and then further narrowing. Such examples suggest that semantic change is haphazard and unpredictable.

Central to Bréal's theory of semantics and semantic change was the importance not only of reference to objects in the world but also of what we now call "sense" (meaning defined in terms of linguistic relations), and of polysemy (related meanings associated with the same form). With the advent of structuralism, differences in sense came to be thought of in terms of "lexical fields" consisting of tightly-knit sets of words with similar meaning, such as terms for intellectual cleverness, colors, or kinship (for examples and references, many of them German, see Ullmann 1964: 243–253). In much of this work it was assumed that there were relatively fixed components of meaning, and that they could be organized in different ways across languages and times. In the latter part of the 20th century, semantic change came to be rethought in terms of more flexible sets of semantic properties. For example, one can think of how the term *car* fits into a "semantic space" devoted to vehicles like *tank, plane*, with respect to such factors as their constituent parts (metal, tires), shape, purpose, and how they are driven. Such factors are called "qualia" in Pustejovsky's (1995) Generative Lexicon theory. The flexibility of categories is highlighted in work on prototypes and categories with fuzzy boundaries that change over time (see Geeraerts 1997; Grondelaers et al. 2007). Research on cognitive semantics, Gricean pragmatics, and grammaticalization showed that semantic change was more frequently replicated and "regular" than had often been assumed, and the advent of electronic corpora made fine-grained analysis of change in context possible.

Meaning change can be conceptualized along two dimensions. One is "semasiological": attention is paid to how meaning changes, while form remains reasonably constant (but subject to phonological change). The questions are, what meanings does a word have, how are they related, and how did they arise over time? Most of the changes listed in the taxonomies were thought of in terms of semasiology. The other dimension is "onomasiological": attention is paid to relations that hold between the lexical items in semantic space and which forms come to express a certain meaning. This is the principle behind Buck's (1949) dictionary of synonyms in Indo-European languages. It is also one of the principles behind the *Historical Thesaurus of the Oxford English Dictionary* (Kay et al. 2009). Current work on onomasiology concerns a wide-ranging set of concepts from expressions of emotion such as anger and pain (see Díaz Vera 2002), to intelligence and stupidity (Allan 2008), adjectives of difference like *distinct, several* (Breban 2008), and modality, especially as expressed by semi-modals like *have to, dare (to)* (Krug 2000).

The meaning of a word is only part of what we know about it. We also know its morphosyntactic structure, its phonology, what register it belongs to, perhaps what language it was borrowed from, etc. These complex sets of information are specified in the "lexicon", the inventory of form-meaning pairs in a language. This chapter ends with some discussion of the lexicon from a historical perspective (see Section 7).

In this chapter I focus on aspects of recent research on semantic change, mostly from a cognitive perspective. A broader range of topics can be found in Traugott (2017), an annotated bibliography of semantic change.

2 Cognitive semantics and metaphor

Cognitive Linguistics, as developed in the 1970s and 1980s, theorized a view of linguistic structures "not as if they were autonomous, but as reflections of general conceptual organization, categorization principles, processing mechanisms, and experiential and environmental influences" (Geeraerts and Cuyckens 2007: 3). A fundamental claim is that words do not have stable meanings. Rather, they are cues to potential meaning, or instructions to create meanings as words are used in context (Warren 1992, and especially 1999). These meanings are nondiscrete and have prototypical properties, with core and peripheral readings (Geeraerts 1997). Furthermore, they may have rich polysemic structures (in contrast to monosemous views of semantics such as Relevance Theory, Sperber and Wilson 1995). In Cognitive Linguistics a sharp distinction between semantics and pragmatics is rejected. Although details of the theory vary considerably from author to author, there has been relative convergence among those who do work on historical semantics. The central research questions have concerned metaphor and metonymy, and ways in which semantic change occurs in linguistic contexts.

Sweetser (1990) proposed a theory of metaphor and metaphorical change drawing on theories of embodiment (e.g. Lakoff 1987) and force-dynamics including exertion of force and blockage by barriers (e.g. Talmy 1988). Sweetser argued, for example, that a metaphor such as KNOWING IS SEEING developed in Indo-European languages from embodied perceptual capacities such as seeing, hearing, and grasping, and that mapping from the socio-physical world of embodiment to the abstract epistemic one of reasoning accounted for the directionality of such cross-linguistically attested meaning changes as Proto-Indo-European (PIE) *weid* 'see' > *wit*, and Gk. *oîda* perfective of *eidon* 'to see' > *idea*, or *must* 'be required' (compelled by socio-physical force; deontic) > 'can be inferred' (compelled by reasoning; epistemic). One of Sweetser's hypotheses was that since meaning change is not random, there must be constraints on mapping from one domain to another. These constraints involve "certain abstract and topological aspects of semantic structure, which we have termed *image-schematic structure*, [...] which must be preserved across metaphorical mappings" (Sweetser 1990: 59, italics original). Such image-schematic structures may involve barriers, e.g. *may* represents a potential barrier that is not yet in place whether in the socio-physical domain (permission), or the domain of reasoning (possibility).

Much of the initial work on metaphor was synchronic and lexical. Particularly influential in this respect was Reddy's (1993 [1979]) study of the conduit metaphors used for language, which accounts for extensive use of expressions concerned with language conceptualized as a physical pipe-line, e.g. *put something into words, the letter contains many typos*. In historical work, however, metaphor came to be noted especially in studies of grammaticalization, understood at the time as the use of lexical expressions to serve a grammatical function. Cross-linguistically, temporal expressions derive from spatial ones (Heine et al. 1991; Haspelmath 1997), e.g. *after* 'behind+COMPR'; (cf. *aft* of a ship); prepositions and adverbs from body parts (e.g. *behind, ahead*), etc. In this work, the two dimensions of semasiology and onomasiology were fruitfully combined. Heine and Kuteva's (2002) *World Lexicon of Grammaticalization* provides an appendix with cross-linguistically attested source > target meaning change; this is a semasiological approach tracking changes of meaning (e.g. BODY > reflexive, cf. *self*). A second appendix outlines target < source meaning change, an onomasiological approach tracking where expressions of a particular meaning derive from (e.g. FRONT < FACE, HEAD, MOUTH).

Metaphor operates on the dimension of choice from among related meanings, and therefore of analogy, iconicity, and paradigmaticity. On the other hand, metonymy, being associative, operates on the dimension of indexicality, linear production, and perception (Anttila 1989: 142). Metonymy and metaphor often intersect at the conceptual level, and indeed the metaphors of embodiment ultimately derive from metonymic associations. Barcelona hypothesizes that "the target and/or source must be understood or perspectivized metonymically for the metaphor to be possible" (Barcelona 2000: 31). On this view, metonymy activates mental access to another domain, e.g. the metaphor SADNESS IS DOWN derives from experiential association with the downward bodily posture that people tend to adopt when they are sad (see also Kövecses and Radden 1998; Panther and Thornburg 2003).

3 Invited inferencing and conceptual metonymy

Sweetser's work engendered tremendous interest in semantic change as metaphorical change. However, challenges and alternative proposals abounded as well. For example, Bybee (2007: 978) points out that image-schema preservation cannot apply to some changes, such as the change from perfect/anterior > present in inchoative (change of state) or state verbs, since there is no plausible image-schema associated with the perfective. In a language like Island Carib, some perfective verbs are used to express present state. Bybee suggests that an expression meaning 'It has turned ripe' is relevant only if it is still ripe at the time of utterance. It is the meaning of "present relevance" that underlies the change. Metaphor cannot be involved here. Rather, what is in operation is the associative, metonymic process called "invited inferencing". We may note that most of the "core" modals in English were once "preterit-presents", i.e. state verbs with past morphology; Gk. *oîda* cited above is the perfective form; and *must* is a past tense form of *mot-* 'be able' (an originally preterit-present verb). In fact, when semantic changes are considered in context, not in the decontextualized format of the examples I have cited above, they may be construed rather differently. What are schematically presented as *see* > 'understand', *must* 'obligation' > 'epistemic conclusion', *be going to* 'motion with a purpose' > 'future' are abstractions over many centuries of micro-changes in very specific contexts. What appears to be a metaphor may be the outcome of a number of changes in which pragmatic inferencing is activated in the flow of speech, as attested by textual data in historical corpora.

The Invited Inferencing Theory of Semantic Change (IITSC) is a usage-based approach founded in the investigation of textual evidence (Traugott and König 1991; Traugott and Dasher 2002). Although sharing many of the assumptions of Cognitive Linguistics, it diverges in several respects, most notably in distinguishing between pragmatics and semantics. The term "invited inferencing" was borrowed from Geis and Zwicky (1971), but used in an extended way to evoke negotiation of meaning between speakers producing or even intending meanings beyond what is said, and hearers inferring such meaning. Likewise it draws on neo-Gricean pragmatics (Grice 1989; Horn 1984; Levinson 2000), and the distinction between particularized and generalized conversational implicatures, but appeals to partially different maxims. The Gricean Maxim that is considered key to change is his Quantity 2 ("Do not make your contribution more informative than is required"), combined with Relevance and rephrased as "Say no more than you must, and mean more thereby" (Horn 1984). Use of this maxim leads to rich interpretations. The hypothesis is that invited inferences that arise on the fly may become conventionalized (commonly activated) as generalized invited inferences. They may be "salient" in the community in that they can be drawn on consciously, cf. the causal implicature of *after*, but for the most part they are used unconsciously (Keller 1994). These generalized invited inferences may continue to be available over centuries, even millennia (cf. *after*). A regularly occurring context which "supports an inference-driven contextual enrichment" of one meaning to another has been called a "bridging context" (Evans and Wilkins 2000: 55). Conventionalization as a bridging context is a pragmatic development. Sometimes such inferences may be absorbed into the meaning of an expression with which they were formerly only pragmatically associated. In this case semantic reanalysis has occurred (Eckardt 2006) and a new coded meaning has become available, as evidenced by the use of an old form with the new meaning in a context which was not available before; e.g., *siþþan* 'since' was originally restricted to temporal 'after' and later came to be used with a causal meaning as well. In other words, semanticization of a formerly pragmatic meaning has occurred.

Although originally discussed mainly with reference to grammaticalization, invited inferencing is conceived as a major motivation for semantic change in general (Traugott and Dasher 2002). It encompasses the changes associated with metonymy and metaphor, but also pejoration and amelioration. In the latter cases, the invited inferences are not only conceptually but also socially motivated. For example, those considered blessed and innocent may be evaluated as ignorant or foolish, cf. OE *selig* 'blessed' > 'silly', or Lt. *nescius* 'unknowing, innocent' (< *ne* + *scius* 'not knowing') > Middle Fr. *nice* 'foolish'.

Semanticization of a speaker's beliefs and/or attitudes to what is being said is called "subjectification" (Traugott 1989, 2010; see also Davidse et al. [eds.] 2010). A partially overlapping, but more restricted, view of subjectification associates it with changes in the cognitive construal of vantage-point (e.g. Langacker 1990, 2006; see also Athanasiadou et al. [eds.] 2006). Subjectification in the first sense encompasses shifts not only from the perspective of the *sujet d'énoncé* 'syntactic subject' to the *sujet d'énonciation* 'speaking subject' (Benveniste 1971), but also a range of meaning developments based in the speaker's perspective: spatial, temporal, metalinguistic, etc. Subjectification is extensively evidenced by the use of phrases like *after all*, *anyway* as discourse markers, and of adjectives like *very* (< 'true', see Fr. *vrai*) as scalar degree modifiers. It is also evidenced by the development of epistemic meanings, and of performative uses of speech act verbs. Many of the latter derive ultimately from past participles of Latin verbs, such as *promise* (< Lt. *pro* + *miss*- 'forward sent'), *suggest* (< Lt. *sub* + *gest*- 'under carried') (note the conduit metaphors in the Latin, and the past participle form which shows these were originally stative and non-agentive).

4 Collocation and collostructional analysis

Cognitive Linguistics and the Invited Inferencing Theory of Semantic Change are both conceptualized as "usage-based" theories. For the most part, the first is exemplified by constructed data, the latter by empirically attested data found in historical texts. Bybee has said of cognitive, usage-based linguistics in general that it is a "framework that allows change to be gradual and specific on various dimensions, such as the lexical, phonetic, and morphosyntactic, while at the same time providing general principles of linguistic organization that explain why change moves in certain directions and not others" (Bybee 2007: 981). Bybee draws attention especially to frequency effects on these dimensions.

Particularly valuable in work on semantic change is the notion of collocation, or relationships among words or groups of words that go together. In a contextualized approach to the change in the meaning of *conceit*, for example, we find that from the beginning it was often associated with negative meanings. For example, of the five examples of *conceit* in Chaucer's work, two are modified by *wrong*, and another is embedded in a context that suggests the opinion held is wanting:

(1) *O sely preest! O sely innocent!*
 With coveitise anon thou shalt be blent!
 O graceless, ful blynd is thy **conceite** *(Canon's Yeoman's Tale 1076–1078)*
 'Oh foolish priest! Oh foolish innocent!
 With covetousness you shall be blinded!
 Oh lacking God's grace, fully blind is your opinion/mind'

Over time, although *conceit* could also be used in the sense of 'good judgment', the negative meaning became semanticized into *conceit*, presumably due to frequency of use in negative contexts.

One of the interesting research questions is how some words become associated with either negative or positive contexts and whether or not these contexts become semanticized into the word. The phenomenon has been called "semantic prosody" (Stubbs 2001) and takes several shapes. One is illustrated by *conceit*, where a word is used so frequently in a negative context that the negative evaluation becomes part of the meaning. Others are preferred collocations, e.g. *a shred of* in the abstract quantifier sense 'some' has come to be used almost exclusively with *not* (hence it is understood as 'not any', and is often analyzed as a negative polarity item).

Speakers often have preconceptions about such collocations, which may or may not be accurate. Invaluable for testing such preconceptions are computer-assisted approaches to corpora that provide "collostructional analysis". Originally developed for synchronic work (Stefanowitsch and Gries 2003), this kind of analysis has been adapted for historical work on grammaticalization (Hilpert 2008), but could be extended to work on semantic change in general. It involves the exhaustive extraction of all tokens of a construction from a corpus while keeping one element constant, e.g. in the construction *be going to*+V, *be going to* with its verbal complements is kept constant. The objective is to determine not only which verbal complements it came to collocate with (this is "host-class expansion", which Himmelmann 2004 considers criterial for grammaticalization), but also the strength of the association between them. It reveals changing selectional restrictions, hence fine-grained meaning change. It can be used to compare similar changes across languages, and to test schematic hypotheses about paths of change. For example, Hilpert (2008) tests Bybee et al.'s (1994: 270) hypotheses about the paths by which futures develop, one of them being (2):

(2) motion → intention → future

Collostructional evidence shows that Swedish *komma at* 'come to', although a motion verb that becomes a future marker, does not do so via intention. It also shows that in English *be going to* was initially used most often with speech act verbs like *answer* and *begin*, and became increasingly attracted to verbs with punctual meaning, especially those that are transitive with agentive meaning (e.g. *get, marry*), but also intransitive (e.g. *die, leave*). On the other hand, Dutch *gaan* 'go', which also became a future marker, was initially used primarily with motion verbs like *laupen* 'walk', and became increasingly attracted to intransitive, durative meanings (e.g. *denken* 'think', and *voelen* 'feel'). Although both *be going to* and *gaan* exemplify (2), they have distinctly different semantic micro-histories, and hence different meanings.

5 Productivity of semantic changes at specific periods

Not many studies have been conducted on semantic changes that affect a large class of items at a specific period of time. However, a few may be mentioned here. In one of the earliest attempts to demonstrate that semantic change can be patterned, Stern (1964 [1931]) showed that around 1300 adverbs meaning RAPIDLY developed the polysemy IMMEDIATELY in the context of perfective, i.e. punctual, verbs "denoting the action as a unit" (185–191), e.g. ME *georne* 'rapidly' > 'immediately'. This change ceased, he said, around 1400, e.g. *fleetly* (1598) and *rapidly* (1727) itself did not undergo this change. Stern's study is a non-quantified precursor of collostructional analysis, showing how change of meaning occurs metonymically in context. The change itself (which he calls a kind of "permutation") is conceptualized as a case of what we would now call invited inferencing and unidirectionality of change: "it is evident that if a person rides rapidly up to another, the action is soon completed; but we cannot reverse the argument and say that if a person soon rides up to another, then the action is also rapidly performed" (Stern 1964: 186). A collostructional analysis would be needed to verify that this change was indeed as particular to the time as Stern claims. It is certainly cross-linguistically attested; Buck (1949: 964) commented that "the majority of words for 'soon' are, or were once, simply 'quickly'" (for examples in Japanese see Traugott and Dasher 2002: 69). But that does not mean that there was a cluster of changes that was highly productive at a particular point in time involving this particular semantic shift in any other language.

Another example of a semantic change among adverbs that has been noted as having occurred particularly frequently at a given time is the development in Early Modern English of "boosters" or degree adverbs out of qualitative and highly evaluative adverbs (e.g. *terribly, horribly, villainous* – as now, some adverbs occurred without *-ly*). Peters (1994: 271) argues that most earlier boosters had developed from "local, dimensional or quantitative adverbs", such as *highly* (dimensional) and *vastly* (quantitative). He hypothesizes that the development of boosters out of qualitative adverbs was associated with the development of more colloquial styles at the period.

A third adverbial domain which is said to have become highly productive at a particular period is that of epistemic adverbs like *probably, alledgedly, reportedly* from the 18th century on. In recent work exploring the relationship between "cultural scripts" and semantics, Wierzbicka (2006) proposed that an increase in the number of epistemic adverbs is correlated with the advent of empiricism, especially under the influence of the philosopher John Locke's *An Essay Concerning Human Understanding* (1690). Likewise, words like *fairness* and *reasonableness* underwent a significant shift. Using collocations as her evidence, Wierzbicka hypothesizes that our modern understanding of reasonableness includes common sense, a standard by which anyone's behavior can be judged (108), and compatibility with reason (134), cf. *reasonable doubt, reasonable care*. However, prior to the enlightenment it meant 'required by reason' (134), or 'having reason', as in (3):

(3) *Man is a* **resonable** *two foted beest* (c.1380–87 Chaucer, *Boece* V. pr. iv. 128; Wierzbicka 2006: 109)

Testing Wierzbicka's hypothesis that prior to the British enlightenment there was a cultural script of faith and certainty, Bromhead (2009) investigates a number of expressions like *I think, in truth, verily*, some of which, like *verily*, are no longer used, or recessive (*in truth*). She supports Wierzbicka's conclusions in general, by providing evidence that the meanings of these expressions prior to the 18th century predominantly expressed certitude and confidence, rather than the doubt associated with the modern empiricist ethos. However, she also shows that the meaning changes Wierzbicka identifies were developing prior to the 18th century and the appearance of Locke's book. This suggests that he was a synthesizer of current views, as well as a catalyst for their spread.

6 Differences between lexical and grammatical changes

While there are similarities with respect to metaphor and metonymy between changes affecting lexical and grammatical (or grammaticalizing) expressions, there are also differences. Most notably, lexical semantic change concerns contentful change, whereas the development of grammatical expressions (see Section 2) is associated with "bleaching" or loss of contentful, lexical meaning: "[a]s grammatical morphemes develop, they lose specific features of meaning and thus are applicable in a wider range of environments" (Bybee 2007: 975). As Peters's (1994) examples of boosters deriving from qualititative adverbs illustrates, grammaticalization may result in such collocations as *terribly happy*, or more recently *pretty ugly*. Bleaching is not found exclusively in grammaticalization. Occasionally lexical items may also lose in substantive content, e.g. OE *þing* 'law court, assembly' by metonymy > 'thing, matter of concern'. But grammaticalization does not only involve loss of lexical meaning. There is enrichment of grammatical meaning as the original abstract implicature is semanticized, thus *terribly* lost the lexical meaning of 'terror', but gained abstract scalar meaning placing its complement high on the scale; *pretty* lost the lexical meaning 'good-looking', but gained scalar meaning, serving to place its complement above the median on a scale of intensity.

Other respects in which semantic change associated with grammaticalization differs from that associated with lexical items is that it is more frequently replicated, and usually cross-linguistically attested. Subjectification occurs in lexical change (see Section 3 above) but it is particularly closely associated with grammaticalization because grammatical markers serve to indicate the speaker's perspective on who does what to whom (case), how the situation is related to speech time (deictic tense) or to the temporality of a reference point other than speech time (relative tense), whether the situation is perspectivized as continuing and open-ended or not (aspect), whether the situation is relativized to the speaker's beliefs (modality, mood), and how utterances are connected to each other (connectives, discourse markers), among other things (Traugott 2010).

7 Changes in the lexicon

As indicated at the end of Section 1, the lexicon is the inventory of form-meaning pairs in a language. These pairs may be conceptualized as on a continuum from substantive, contentful, or "lexical", like *car, shoot*, to "grammatical", procedural, and indexical, like *but, although*. In the lexicon, meaning is often accounted for in terms of lexical relations, such as synonymy, antonymy, hyponymy/hyperonymy (taxonomic relations of member/superordinate set, e.g. *carrots/vegetables*), and meronymy/holonymy (part of/whole of, e.g. *finger/hand*).

Since the inventory of lexical and grammatical items that constitutes the lexicon consists of abstract structures without any inflections, the term "word" is not usually used in discussion of the lexicon. Instead, "lemma" is used for abstract lexemes, and sometimes "gram" for abstract grammatical items. It is usually assumed that the lexicon contains only items that are conventionalized in the sense that they are used by more than one speaker. However, it is particularly difficult in historical work on the earlier periods to know when this criterion is met, since if an item occurs only once, we cannot know whether this is because it was a nonce-item used by just one speaker, or whether it happens to appear in only one surviving manuscript. The debate has been particularly lively with respect to kennings in Old English. Some, especially those related to the sea, recur and may be considered candidates for the lexicon of Old English, e.g. *swānrād* 'swan road'; many others may be nonce-forms. Kennings are usually thought of as metaphors constructed as compounds, but Broz (2008) analyzes them as complex metonymy-metaphor combinations. He illustrates with a productive process of forming kennings that denote the concept of 'body'. In these, *bān* 'bone' is the first element, as in *bāncofa* 'bone-chamber', *bānfæt* 'bone-container' or *bānhūs* 'bone-house'. Broz suggests that several cognitive operations are at work here: a containment image schema which gives rise to conceptual metaphors such as BODY IS CONTAINER (Lakoff 1987), which combines with the PART FOR WHOLE metonymy, bone being the essential part of the body.

Changes affecting items in the lexicon clearly include semantic change, but research into the lexicon also concerns changes to the form of lexemes (e.g. *hlāf weard* 'loaf guardian' > *lord*), and such factors as changes in the size of the lexicon and the consequences of borrowing. The latter two topics provide insight into what meanings were salient at particular periods, and in particular text-types, and will be the focus of this section.

The size of the English lexicon at any period is hard to measure. The only criterion is the number of lemmas and grams listed in dictionaries, a factor highly dependent on tradition, the purposes of a dictionary, social and political changes (see Dossena 2012). Practices differ with respect to whether and when polysemies are counted as separate entries. When there is an academy that regulates language practice, as in France, a dictionary is less likely to include new words and meanings than when there is no such academy. That said, English speakers have been more willing than speakers of many other languages to borrow large amounts of vocabulary. The influence of Scandinavian, French, Latin, and Greek is widely known, but Arabic, Spanish, and more recently Japanese are among the many others that have also contributed to the inventory. No one speaker and no one register makes use of more than a tiny subset of all the possible lexical lemmas recorded in a dictionary. Dictionaries represent the aggregate of items used or usable by the totality of those regarded as speakers of a language.

Since English speakers have been borrowing and inventing words for over a millennium and a half, and surprisingly few words are dropped from collective, as opposed to individual, inventories, the size of the vocabulary has been increasing since the beginning. As might be expected, such increases are not independent of periods of contact or new discourses and lifestyle changes (see borrowing in the 19th century of *jihad* for political and religious discourse, and of *sushi* for life-style discourse). Perhaps the most interesting increase, as shown by the *Chronological English Dictionary*, occurred in the period 1570–1630 (see discussion in Nevalainen 1999). In this case it resulted not from contact, but from a conscious effort to shape English as a national language, no longer second to French or Latin, and from the explosion of new literary works, including the plays of Shakespeare. Many of the words he used never became conventionally used in English e.g. *offendress* 'woman who offends'. Words were borrowed, especially if they were technical (*cerebellum*, *specimen*); derivational affixes were added to native or borrowed words (*uncertitude;* see in contemporary English *überlame*); converted from one part of speech to another, e.g. from noun to verb (*calendar* 'enter on one's calendar'), or coined (*giggle*).

When borrowing occurs, various kinds of consequences can be noted. Narrowing of one of the terms may occur if a native term already exists: compare the generic term *cow* (OE *cu*) with *beef* 'kind of meat' (Fr. *boeuf*). Another is that the vocabulary may become multidimensionally stratified. Dimensions of variation that have received particular attention are region, social group, field of discourse (transaction, homily, letter), medium (spoken or written), and attitude (Kastovsky 2006). An example of social and age stratification is some contemporary teenagers' use of intensifiers like *dead*, often in collocations that differ from those of standard varieties of English such as *dead healthy, pure funny, enough funny* (e.g. Stenström 2000; Macaulay 2005).

Yet another consequence of borrowing is the coexistence of typologically different layers of vocabulary. Because many words have been borrowed into English from French, the lexicon abounds in words that have phonological alternations in the base (e.g. *history, histόric, historίcity*), whereas native words do not (Kastovsky 2006: 212). The lexicon also includes verbs that have been said to be typologically very different from a semantic point of view. Different languages package semantic material into words in different ways (Lehrer 1992: 249). Talmy (e.g. 2000) proposed that there are two basic ways of expressing semantic path and manner/cause of motion in the verb. He distinguishes Chinese and all branches of Indo-European except Romance as languages that encode Motion and Manner/Cause together and treat Path as satellite. In *Jill floated into the cave*, *float* conflates Motion and Manner, in *The napkin blew off the table*, *blow* conflates Motion and Cause (wind). By contrast Romance, Semitic, Polynesian, and Navajo encode Motion and Path together and treat Manner as satellite, as in Spanish *La botella entró a la cueva flotando* 'The bottle entered into the cave floating'. Because French words have been borrowed, we can use both *enter* (French), which treats Manner as satellite, and *swim*, which treats Path as satellite. Very interestingly, Latin, like English, encoded Motion and Manner/Cause. Stolova (2008) attributes the change from Latin to Romance largely to the loss in Late Latin of verb prefixes that encoded Path, cf. *abire* 'out-go', and replacement of them in the Romance languages by verbs derived from nouns that had connotations of direction in them, e.g. Fr. *monter* 'go up, climb' < *mons* 'mountain'. Verbs like *entrare* (< *intra* 'into') that had already become univerbated in Late Latin were not understood as encoding path morphologically, and so were treated like *monter*, as inherently including direction within them. This means that borrowings into English from Latin such as *exit* 'out-go', *ascend* (*ad-scandere* 'at climb') are typologically like English *go up*, while *mount, enter* from French are typologically different – we do not usually *mount up a hill*, though debts may *mount up* (a cumulative, not directional Path use of *up*), nor do we usually *enter into a cave*, although we may *enter into an agreement*, a conduit metaphor).

8 Future prospects

Theoretical work on semantics, pragmatics, and the lexicon is increasing exponentially from many perspectives, among them computational, quantificational, typological, socio-cultural, and rhetorical. We can therefore expect substantial advances in research on semantic and lexical change in English in the near future. As these developments occur, the question of methodology in the use not only of electronic corpora, but also of dictionaries such as the OED will come to be of ever-increasing importance (see Allan and Robynson 2011).

9 References

Allan, Kathryn L. 2008. *Metaphor and Metonymy: A Diachronic Approach*. Malden, MA: Wiley-Blackwell.

Allan, Kathryn and Justyna A. Robinson (eds.). 2011. *Current Methods in Historical Semantics*. Berlin/New York: De Gruyter Mouton.

Anttila, Raimo. 1989 [1972]. *Historical and Comparative Linguistics*. Amsterdam/Philadelphia: John Benjamins.

Athanasiadou, Angeliki, Costas Canakis, and Bert Cornillie (eds.). 2006. *Subjectification: Various Paths to Subjectivity*. Berlin/New York: Mouton de Gruyter.

Barcelona, Antonio. 2000. On the plausibility of claiming a metonymic motivation for conceptual metaphor. In: Antonio Barcelona (ed.), *Metaphor and Metonymy at the Crossroads: A Cognitive Perspective*, 31–58. Berlin/New York: Mouton de Gruyter.

Benveniste, Emile. 1971 [1958]. Subjectivity in language. In: *Problems in General Linguistics*, 223–230. Trans. by Mary Elizabeth Meek. Coral Gables, FL: University of Miami Press. (Originally published as 'De la subjectivité dans le langage'. *Journal de psychologie* 55 [1958]: 267–276.)

Bréal, Michel. 1964. *Semantics: Studies in the Science of Meaning*. Trans. by Mrs. Henry Cust. New York: Dover (Originally published in 1897 in French as *Essai de Sémantique* and in English in 1900.).

Breban, Tine. 2008. Grammaticalization, subjectification and leftward movement of English adjectives of difference in the noun phrase. *Folia Linguistica* 42: 259–306.

Bromhead, Helen. 2008. *The Reign of Truth and Faith: Epistemic Expressions in 16th and 17th Century English*. Berlin/New York: Mouton de Gruyter.

Broz, Vlatko. 2008. Kennings: Riddles of metonymy or metaphor? Paper presented at the 15th International Conference on English Historical Linguistics (ICEHL), Munich, 24–30 August, 2008. https://koha.ffzg.hr/cgi-bin/koha/opac-detail.pl?biblionumber=316072; last accessed 15 January 2017.

Buck, Carl Darling. 1949. *A Dictionary of Selected Synonyms in the Principal Indo-European Languages*. Chicago: University of Chicago Press.

Bybee, Joan. 2007. Diachronic linguistics. In: Geeraerts and Cuyckens (eds.), 945–987.

Bybee, Joan, Revere Perkins, and William Pagliuca. 1994. *The Evolution of Grammar: Tense, Aspect, and Modality in the Languages of the World*. Chicago: University of Chicago Press.

Campbell, Lyle. 2013 [2004]. *Historical Linguistics*. 3rd edn. Cambridge, MA: MIT Press.
Davidse, Kristin, Lieven Vandelanotte, and Hubert Cuyckens (eds.). 2010. *Subjectification, Intersubjectification and Grammaticalization*. Berlin/New York: De Gruyter Mouton.
Dossena, Marina. 2012. Late Modern English: Semantics and lexicon. In Alexander Bergs and Laurel J. Brinton (eds.), *English Historical Linguistics: An International Handbook*. Vol. 1, 887–900. Berlin/Boston: De Gruyter Mouton.
Díaz Vera, Javier E. (ed.). 2002. *A Changing World of Words: Studies in English Historical Lexicography, Lexicology and Semantics*. Amsterdam/New York: Rodopi.
Eckardt, Regine. 2006. *Meaning Change in Grammaticalization: An Enquiry into Semantic Reanalysis*. Oxford: Oxford University Press.
Evans, Nicholas and David Wilkins. 2000. In the mind's ear: The semantic extensions of perception verbs in Australian languages. *Language* 76: 546–592.
Fortson, Benjamin W., IV. 2003. An approach to semantic change. In: Brian D. Joseph and Richard D. Janda (eds.), *The Handbook of Historical Linguistics*, 648–666. Oxford: Blackwell.
Geeraerts, Dirk. 1997. *Diachronic Prototype Semantics: A Contribution to Historical Lexicology*. Oxford: Clarendon Press.
Geeraerts, Dirk and Hubert Cuyckens. 2007. Introducing Cognitive Linguistics. In: Geeraerts and Cuyckens (eds.), 3–21.
Geeraerts, Dirk and Hubert Cuyckens (eds.). 2007. *The Oxford Handbook of Cognitive Linguistics*. Oxford: Oxford University Press.
Geis, Michael L. and Arnold M. Zwicky. 1971. On invited inferences. *Linguistic Inquiry* 2: 561–566.
Grice, H. Paul. 1989. Logic and conversation. *Studies in the Way of Words*, 22–40. Cambridge, MA/London: Harvard University Press. (first published in Peter Cole and Jerry L. Morgan [eds.], *Syntax and Semantics III: Speech Acts*, 41–58. New York: Academic Press, 1975).
Grondelaers, Stefan, Dirk Speelman, and Dirk Geeraerts. 2007. Lexical variation and change. In: Geeraerts and Cuyckens (eds.), 988–1011.
Haspelmath, Martin. 1997. *Temporal Adverbials in the World's Languages*. Munich: LINCOM EUROPA.
Heine, Bernd, Ulrike Claudi, and Friederike Hünnemeyer. 1991. *Grammaticalization: A Conceptual Framework*. Chicago: University of Chicago Press.
Heine, Bernd and Tania Kuteva. 2002. *World Lexicon of Grammaticalization*. Cambridge: Cambridge University Press.
Hilpert, Martin. 2008. *Germanic Future Constructions: A Usage-based Approach to Language Change*. Amsterdam/ Philadelphia: John Benjamins.
Himmelmann, Nikolaus P. 2004. Lexicalization and grammaticalization: Opposite or orthogonal? In: Walter Bisang, Nikolaus P. Himmelmann, and Björn Wiemer (eds.), *What Makes Grammaticalization – A Look from its Fringes and its Components*, 19–40. Berlin/New York: Mouton de Gruyter.
Hock, Hans Henrich and Brian D. Joseph. 2009 [1996]. *Language History, Language Change, and Language Relationship: An Introduction to Historical and Comparative Linguistics*. 2nd edn. Berlin/New York: Mouton de Gruyter.
Horn, Laurence R. 1984. Toward a new taxonomy for pragmatic inference: Q-based and R-based implicature. In: Deborah Schiffrin (ed.), *Meaning, Form, and Use in Context: Linguistic Applications*, 11–42. (Georgetown University Round Table '84.) Washington, DC: Georgetown University Press.
Kastovsky, Dieter. 2006. Vocabulary. In: Richard Hogg and David Denison (eds.), *A History of the English Language*, 199–270. Cambridge: Cambridge University Press.

Kay, Christian, Jane Roberts, Michael Samuels, and Irené Wotherspoon (eds.). 2009. *Historical Thesaurus of the Oxford English Dictionary*. Oxford: Oxford University Press.

Keller, Rudi. 1994. *On Language Change: The Invisible Hand in Language*. Trans. by Brigitte Nerlich. London: Routledge. (Originally published as *Sprachwandel: Von der unsichtbaren Hand in der Sprache*. Tübingen: Francke, 1990.)

Kövecses, Zoltán and Günter Radden. 1998. Metonymy: Developing a cognitive linguistic view. *Cognitive Linguistics* 9: 37–77.

Krug, Manfred G. 2000. *Emerging English Modals: A Corpus-based Approach to Grammaticalization*. Berlin/New York: Mouton de Gruyter.

Lakoff, George. 1987. *Women, Fire, and Dangerous Things: What Categories Reveal about the Mind*. Chicago: University of Chicago Press.

Langacker, Ronald W. 1990. Subjectification. *Cognitive Linguistics* 1: 5–38.

Langacker, Ronald W. 2006. Subjectification, grammaticalization, and conceptual archetypes. In: Athanasiadou, Canakis, and Cornillie (eds.), 17–40.

Lehrer, Adrienne. 1992. A theory of vocabulary structure: Retrospectives and prospectives. In: Mario Pütz (ed.), *Thirty Years of Linguistic Evolution: Studies in Honour of René Dirven on the Occasion of his Sixtieth Birthday*, 243–256. Berlin/New York: Mouton de Gruyter.

Levinson, Stephen C. 2000. *Presumptive Meanings: The Theory of Generalized Conversational Implicature*. Cambridge, MA: MIT Press.

Macaulay, Ronald K. S. 2005. *Talk that Counts: Age, Gender, and Social Class Differences in Discourse*. Oxford: Oxford University Press.

Nevalainen, Terttu. 1999. Lexis and semantics. In: Roger Lass (ed.), *The Cambridge History of the English Language*. Vol. III. *1476–1776*, 332–458. Cambridge: Cambridge University Press.

Panther, Klaus-Uwe and Linda L. Thornburg. 2003. Metonymies as natural inference and activation schemas: The case of dependent clauses as independent speech acts. In: Klaus-Uwe Panther and Linda L. Thornburg (eds.), *Metonymy and Pragmatic Inferencing*, 127–147. Amsterdam/Philadelphia: John Benjamins.

Peters, Hans. 1994. Degree adverbs in Early Modern English. In: Dieter Kastovsky (ed.), *Studies in Early Modern English*, 269–288. Berlin/New York: Mouton de Gruyter.

Pustejovsky, J. 1995. *The Generative Lexicon*. Cambridge, MA: MIT Press.

Reddy, Michael J. 1993 [1979]. The conduit metaphor: A case of frame conflict in our language about language. In: Andrew Ortony (ed.), *Metaphor and Thought*, 164–201. Cambridge: Cambridge University Press.

Sperber, Dan and Dierdre Wilson. 1995. *Relevance: Communication and Cognition*. 2nd edn. Oxford: Blackwell.

Stefanowitsch, Anatol and Stefan Th. Gries. 2003. Collostructions: Investigating the interaction between words and constructions. *International Journal of Corpus Linguistics* 8: 209–243.

Stenström, Anna-Britta. 2000. It's enough funny, man: Intensifiers in teenage talk. In: John M. Kirk (ed.), *Corpora Galore: Analyses and Techniques in Describing English*, 177–190. Amsterdam/Atlanta, GA: Rodopi.

Stern, Gustaf. 1964. *Meaning and Change of Meaning: With Special Reference to the English Language*. Bloomington/London: Indiana University Press. (Reprint of Elanders Boktryckeri Aktiebolag, Göteborg, 1931)

Stolova, Natalya I. 2008. From satellite-framed Latin to verb-framed Romance: Late Latin as an intermediate stage. In: Roger Wright (ed.), *Latin vulgaire, latin tardif: Actes du VIIIème Colloque International sur le Latin Vulgaire et Tardif, Oxford, 6–7 Septembre 2006*, 253–262. Hildesheim: Georg Olms Verlag.

Stubbs, Michael. 2001. *Words and Phrases: Corpus Studies of Lexical Semantics*. Oxford: Blackwell.
Sweetser, Eve E. 1990. *From Etymology to Pragmatics: Metaphorical and Cultural Aspects of Semantic Structure*. Cambridge: Cambridge University Press.
Talmy, Leonard. 1988. Force dynamics in language and cognition. *Cognitive Science* 2: 49–100.
Talmy, Leonard. 2000. *Toward a Cognitive Semantics*. 2 vols. Cambridge: Cambridge University Press.
Traugott, Elizabeth Closs. 1989. On the rise of epistemic meanings in English: An example of subjectification in semantic change. *Language* 65: 31–55.
Traugott, Elizabeth Closs. 2010. (Inter)subjectivity and (inter)subjectification: A reassessment. In: Davidse, Vandelanotte, and Cuyckens (eds.), 29–70.
Traugott, Elizabeth Closs. 2017. Semantic change. In: Mark Aronoff (ed.), *Oxford Bibliographies in Linguistics*. New York: Oxford University Press. http://www.oxfordbibliographies.com/view/document/obo-9780199772810/obo-9780199772810-0155.xml; last accesses 28 June 2017.
Traugott, Elizabeth Closs and Richard B. Dasher. 2002. *Regularity in Semantic Change*. Cambridge: Cambridge University Press.
Traugott, Elizabeth Closs and Ekkehard König. 1991. The semantics-pragmatics of grammaticalization revisited. In: Elizabeth Closs Traugott and Bernd Heine (eds.), *Approaches to Grammaticalization*, Vol. 1, 189–218. Amsterdam/Philadelphia: John Benjamins.
Ullmann, Stephen. 1964. *Semantics; An Introduction to the Science of Meaning*. Oxford: Blackwell.
Warren, Beatrice. 1992. *Sense-Developments: A Contrastive Study of the Development of Slang Sense and Novel Standard Sense in English*. Stockholm: Almqvist & Wiksell.
Warren, Beatrice. 1999. Laws of thought, knowledge and lexical change. In: Andreas Blank and Peter Koch (eds.), *Historical Semantics and Cognition*, 215–243. Berlin/New York: Mouton de Gruyter.
Wierzbicka, Anna. 2006. *English: Meaning and Culture*. Oxford: Oxford University Press.

Gabriele Knappe
Chapter 8:
Idioms and Fixed Expressions

1 Introduction —— 140
2 The concept and scope of phraseology and phraseological research —— 141
3 Approaching historical English phraseology —— 148
4 Metalinguistic sources and their value for the identification of phraseological units in historical texts —— 149
5 Origin, change, and earlier uses of English phraseological units —— 153
6 The impact of phraseology and collocation / string frequency on language change —— 158
7 Summary —— 160
8 References —— 160

Abstract: In order to establish a framework of reference for an approach to historical English phraseology, a brief discussion of the concept and scope of phraseology and phraseological scholarship is provided in Section 2. On this basis, Section 3 approaches historical phraseology in two consecutive steps – always paying special regard to English: an overview of the state of historical phraseology leads to major approaches, which establish the main procedure in Sections 4 to 6. In Section 4, the role of metalinguistic sources for historical phraseology is pointed out, especially with relation to the identification of phraseological units in historical texts. Theories of the origin, rise, and kinds of change of phraseological units as well as the employment of English phraseological units in literary texts are the subjects of Section 5. While Section 5 is thus concerned with change in the phraseological system over time, Section 6, in contrast, finishes off the chapter with an outlook on the influence of frequent word combinations and phraseology on language change in a broader perspective.

1 Introduction

Since about the middle of the 20th century, a branch of linguistics that is concerned with the study of "idioms and fixed expressions" has developed in Europe under

Gabriele Knappe: Bamberg (Germany)

the name of "phraseology". Being the oldest and most comprehensive systematic branch of linguistics dealing with "idioms and fixed expressions", or "formulaic language" – which, however, still lacks a fully developed historical approach – it will provide the point of departure for this chapter. Owing to the developments in American and British linguistics in the past century, the branch of phraseology has only recently started to gain a footing there and to complement existing studies on specific aspects of formulaic language, such as idioms and conversational routines. In fact, the year 2007 stands out with a number of pertinent publications. However, only very few historical studies of English phraseology have been published as yet, while some publications which were not explicitly conceived as belonging to this branch can certainly be viewed from this perspective.

2 The concept and scope of phraseology and phraseological research

The concept and scope of phraseology will be discussed by first approaching phraseology through formulating a description of phraseological units as its objects of study, giving some examples, and pointing out defining criteria and major properties of these units, in particular highlighting the factor of variation. In the main, this subchapter proceeds along lines which now seem to be accepted among phraseologists (cf., e.g., Cowie 1998) after a long period of heated discussion (cf., e.g., Welte 1992). Having thus outlined its content, one major classification of English phraseology that has been suggested will briefly be referred to in order to be able to locate findings of individual (historical) studies within a descriptive system of phraseology. Finally, a rough outline of established approaches of phraseological research will be briefly indicated in order to be able to determine a place for historical (English) phraseology.

2.1 Defining criteria and major properties of phraseological units

"Phraseological unit" seems to be one of the most widely accepted English terms for the linguistic units studied by scholars of phraseology. A description may be given as follows:

Phraseological units are semantically and/or pragmatically fixed units in a language which consist of two or more smaller units that are either lexemes of that language outside these expressions or recognized as unique lexemes within them, and that together do not exceed sentence length.

Therefore, high frequency structural units such as the phraseological unit *as well* in example (1), and pragmatic markers as for instance in (2), belong to phraseology just like infrequent idioms as in (3), or proverbs as in (4).

(1) *as well*
'too; also' (All meaning equivalents quoted in this chapter to explain phraseological units are taken from Cowie et al. (1983) and Cowie and Mackin (1993), if not stated otherwise.)

(2) *you know*
'I am informing, or reminding, you' (but cf. also Brinton [1996: 42], who points out the following functions of *you know*: 'indicating knowledge shared between speaker and hearer', 'indicating general knowledge', and 'presenting new information as if it were old information in order to improve its reception')

(3) *jobs for the boys*
'the provision of paid employment for favored groups within a hierarchy, profession, administration etc. (the implication being that the work of these groups is not really necessary)'

(4) *Let sleeping dogs lie*
'do not provoke, disturb or interfere with somebody/something that is giving no trouble though he/it might, or could, do so'

In linguistic analysis, phraseological units may be marked with regard to their semantics as in the much-quoted opaque expression (5), their lexis (6), syntax (7), or pragmatics (8).

(5) *to kick the bucket*
'(informal) die' (not equivalent to 'to move one's foot violently against a pail')

(6) *to put the kibosh on something/somebody*
'dispose of finally, finish off, do for' (cf. *Oxford English Dictionary* [Proffitt (ed.) 2000–], s.v. *kibosh* n.; the word *kibosh* (of obscure origin) is not used in general English)

(7) *to trip/dance/tread the light fantastic*
'(facetious) dance' (< *Come, and trip it as ye go / On the light fantastic toe*, from John Milton's *L'Allegro*; the phraseological unit lacks the noun)

(8) *an eye for an eye (and a tooth for a tooth)*
'(a warning that) an act of aggression will be met with retaliation of the same kind (especially in personal or national conflicts)' (*Exodus* xxi. 22–24; the meaning is situationally determined)

Phraseological units may carry connotations and may have intensifying and emphatic functions in a text, as Gläser (1986, 1998) points out from the point of view of stylistic analysis, and they can be fruitfully studied from a cultural perspective, too (cf. the contributions in Skandera 2007; for a recent study of the special features of phraseological units, cf. Dobrovol'skij and Piirainen 2009).

For their linguistic study it is important to consider that phraseological units, once they are implemented in a speech community, are reproduced in language use rather than appearing as newly produced structures each time they are employed. What makes them difficult to describe and may render them very hard to identify by means of computer processing in, especially historical, texts are at least four major factors:

Phraseological units are idiomatic to varying degrees; idiomaticity is here understood semantically, referring to the relation of the meanings of the parts to the meaning of the whole expression (semantic [non-]compositionality). Cowie (1983: xiii) distinguishes between three broad categories of phraseological units primarily on the basis of semantic compositionality. Firstly, there are fully idiomatic phraseological units (pure idioms) such as example (5); they have a fixed form and no literal meaning. Secondly, figurative idioms such as the first example in (10) possess a literal and a figurative meaning. Thirdly, restricted collocations such as example (9) are characterized by a combination of one word which appears in a literal sense and another whose meaning is determined by the context. While some members of the third category allow lexical variation, it is rare in the second.

(9) *to jog one's/somebody's memory*
'remind somebody of / about something; help or stimulate somebody to recall something' (*to jog* is used in a transferred sense, *memory* is used literally)

The frequency of use differs for various types of phraseological units (cf. especially Moon 1998b: 88–89).

Phraseological units may show unpredictable transformational behavior, for instance with regard to passivization (10). However, the syntactic behavior of individual expressions follows (strong) tendencies rather than strict rules (cf., e.g., Moon 1998b: 88–90). Thus, while the expression (10a) can be transformed ("⇒") into (10b), for example, there is a strong tendency that the phraseological unit (10c) cannot be transformed into the passive (10d).

(10) a. *to spill the beans*
'(informal) give away information, deliberately or unintentionally' ⇒
b. *the beans are spilled*
c. *to drive a hard bargain*
'(have the means, power, or cunning to) force a bargain; contrive an exchange of goods and services that is either unfair or to one's own advantage' ⇒
d. **a hard bargain is driven*
(the passive transformation is not possible according to Cowie et al. 1983; however, an unmonitored Google search in December 2011 for the expression in the affirmative, including different grammatical forms of the verb phrase, yielded over 3 million hits for the active construction, but also some 560 hits for the passive one, among them the following quotation from *The Telegraph* of 8 November 2006, "'A hard bargain was driven over appearances,' said Jennings of the transfer which paid an initial £5 million". http://www.telegraph.co.uk/sport/columnists/henrywinter/2349920/Walcott-well-up-to-speed-on-his-learning-curve.html; last accessed 19 June 2017)

Above all, phraseological units possess different degrees of formal fixedness (see especially Moon 1998a: 120–177 and Moon 1998b: 90–96; see also the paragraph on idiomaticity, above): in addition to the realization of, e.g., *one's/somebody's* in (9), which depends on the context, and lexical variation and choice in (7) and (11), for instance, phraseological units may also be open to modification and show a striking breadth of creative employment for particular purposes. This may happen to such an extent that even an almost wholly deviant set of words may still be related to one particular phraseological unit (12) (cf. Fiedler 2007: 95–96; Gläser 1998: 142–143). Along similar lines, finally, phraseological patterns such as the combination of subject and predicative constituent in the "Incredulity Response Construction" as exemplified in (13) are constructions with highly idiosyncratic meaning but not much lexical fixation (cf. Fleischer 1997: 130; Sailer 2007: 1069; Huddleston and Pullum 2002: 890, who term these "bare predication polar echo constructions"). This lack of fixedness may make phraseological units difficult to handle by both the speaker and the linguist. In addition, scholars of phraseology have to deal with individual, diastratic, and diatopic variation in a language's store of phraseological units ("phrasicon").

(11) *cap/hat in hand*
'uncovering the head as a sign of reverence, respect, courtesy' (cf. OED, s.v. *cap* n.¹, def. 4h and *hat* n., def. 5a; *cap in hand* in use since the 16th century, *hat in hand* attested in the 19th century)

(12) *Others' Trash Is Now An Architect's Treasure*
(*The New York Times* / *Süddeutsche Zeitung* 13 June 2005; example taken from Fiedler 2007: 96. The sentence's semantics, formal structure, and rhythm unambiguously relate it to the proverb *One man's meat is another man's poison* 'what seems good or pleasing to one person may be bad or unsuitable for another'.)

(13) *Me worry?! Kim resign?! Her a genius?!*
(response construction expressing incredulity)

2.2 Classifying phraseological units

In the light of such a wide and complex range of criteria pertaining to the characterization of phraseological units, it follows that in order to ascertain the scope of phraseology, a comprehensive, "neutral" descriptive framework of reference is called for. Rosemarie Gläser's attempt of 1986 will be introduced at this point (for brief versions in English, cf. Gläser 1998; Knappe 2004: 15–22). Following the earlier Russian tradition and the discussion based on it, Gläser adapts the system to English and distinguishes (beyond the polar notion of idiomaticity and non-idiomaticity as the primary division) between "word-like" units, called "nominations", which form the centre of English phraseology, and "sentence-like" units, called "propositions", which are found on the periphery. The nominations are classified according to word class and include, for instance, nominal phraseological units such as (3) and verbal phraseological units as found in (5), (6), (7), (9), and (10). An example of a proposition is, for instance, the proverb (4), but slogans, commandments, maxims, routine formulae, and quotations belong in this category, too. Between the nominations and the propositions, Gläser establishes a class of "reduced propositions" which are nominations in form but on a deeper level are propositions, such as the fragment of a proverb (14) and the stereotyped comparison (15). These can overlap with the nominations, as in the case of irreversible binomials with *and*, which in (16) should be viewed as one nominal phraseological unit, and sometimes a fragment of a proverb may be hard to identify for native speakers. Although this system is rather comprehensive, further categories can be suggested (cf., e.g., Burger 2015: 30–53).

(14) *a new broom* (< *a new broom sweeps clean*)
 'somebody recently appointed to office or a responsible post' (starts with an energetic programme of reform and change, sometimes not welcomed by those already there)

(15) *as blind as a bat [is]*
 'unable to see, or read, very easily' (but usually not completely blind); (figuratively) unable to see, or perceive, something that is obvious to other people (two underlying propositions in, e.g., *He is as blind as a bat: He is blind* and *A bat is blind*)

(16) *bread and butter*
 'livelihood' (Gläser 1986: 46)

(Sub-)classifications of phraseology may of course fruitfully be tailored to the scholars' research objectives. In order to give just one example, which is also interesting for historical lexicography, Rosamund Moon's (1998a, 1998b) approach will be briefly referred to at this point. She works from a lexicographer's perspective and uses corpus linguistic methods to study "fixed expressions and idioms". Her typology answers the question of which phraseological entries should be included in a monolingual dictionary and to this end addresses three different kinds of non-compositionality in phraseological units: problems of lexico-grammar are inherent in anomalous collocations, such as the "cranberry collocation" in (6), dependence on the discoursal or situational interpretation marks the class of formulae, which is exemplified, for instance, by the "saying" (8), and finally three degrees of semantic transparency are distinguished, (5) being an example of an "opaque metaphor". General difficulties of classifying phraseological units beyond their structure or syntactic function are apparent in Moon's finding that one fourth of the c.6,700 phraseological units which she considers fall into more than one of these categories.

2.3 The study of phraseology, with particular regard to English

Within the framework of phraseological scholarship, phraseological units have been investigated from a wide array of perspectives, which cannot be aptly summarized in this chapter. A handy overview of established approaches may be found in the 20 chapters of the two-volume *Phraseologie/Phraseology*, published in the series Handbooks of Linguistics and Communication Science (Burger et al. 2007).

One important observation is that the number of English contributions in handbooks and collections of papers has increased considerably in recent years. This will certainly further research in English phraseology, as all scholars of English are addressed by the use of this metalanguage (from this perspective, compare Burger et al. 2007 to Burger et al. 1982; cf. also the collections of English articles by Cowie 1998 and Skandera 2007). Norrick (2007) has summarized the state of phraseological research within the main linguistic theories and approaches of modern Anglo-American linguistics (cf. also Sick 1993: 17–54): He found that systematic treatment of phraseological units is rare (Norrick only mentions Makkai 1972; but systematic classifications can also be found in some other studies); American research discusses the issue of idioms within a generative framework; in the British tradition, collocation studies and corpus linguistics have contributed to phraseological research. On the other hand, the studies of English phraseology by Cowie (1983), Gläser (1986, 1998) and Moon (1998a), as well as several contributions in Cowie (1998) such as those by Altenberg, Mel'čuk, and Howarth, and also the monograph *Idiom Structure in English* by Makkai (1972), are to varying degrees indebted to the (Eastern) tradition of phraseology.

Further important publications include, for example, studies from the perspectives of (first and second) language acquisition (e.g. Wray 2002 from a theoretical standpoint, and Nattinger and DeCarrico 1992 from the point of view of language teaching), proverbs (paremiology), pragmatics, metaphor, and psycholinguistics as well as cognitive linguistics, the matter of irreversible binomials and factors influencing the fixedness of word groups (cf. Hudson 1998), to mention but a short selection. Some of these studies show that different theoretical approaches such as stratificational grammar and idiom studies (Makkai), theories of the mental lexicon and formulaic language (Wray), or practical tools such as corpus linguistics and the investigation of phraseology (Moon, Altenberg, Mel'čuk) can be combined in trying to explore the nature and use of idioms and fixed expressions in English.

3 Approaching historical English phraseology

While the phraseological units of present-day English have been given increasing attention, the exploration of historical phraseology has not increased in like degree. In fact, it is still correct to speak of a Cinderella status of historical (English) phraseology: As far as the English collections are concerned, they do not include a single historical article apart from one contribution on the development of English proverb collections (Doyle 2007b; this is the sole focus of Doyle 2007a, too). In book-length studies of English phraseology, concern with the origin and diachronic change of phraseological units is expressed only briefly if at all: thus Welte (1992: 578) judges the historical aspect to be "fascinating" but does not elaborate on it, and Gläser (1986: 51–53) devotes three pages to "diachronic aspects" of phraseology which owe their inclusion in her study of *Phraseologie der englischen Sprache* exclusively to their relevance for present-day usage, with emphasis on relic forms, idiomatization, and word-formation. In Fiedler's (2007) coursebook, historical phraseology has no place at all. Where historical phraseology is treated in its own right in comprehensive surveys and collections – as in Burger et al. (1982: 315–382), Fleischer (1997: 244–246), Häcki Buhofer and Burger (2006: 413–465) and also in the new collection by Burger et al. (2007: 1078–1145, with contributions on English, German, French, Italian and the Slavic languages) – it is striking that it tends to be the final chapter (not, however, in Burger 2015: 131–157 and Thun 1978: 75–84).

The systematic inclusion of historical phraseology in overviews may, however, be interpreted as a sign that scholars are getting ready to explore the place of phraseology in the history of a language in its own right. Historical phraseology with its two branches of synchronic investigation of past systems and diachronic investigation into the development of the language data both re-opens the panorama of phraseological research and at the same time demands methods particularly tailored to historical study.

As far as studies specifically devoted to historical English phraseology are concerned, published studies include papers such as Howarth's (2000) contribution, which highlights pertinent aspects of phraseological variation and change around a model of conventionality, concentrating on the period 1800–1900, and Cowie (2003), which tests the possibilities of the OED for the study of English (historical) phraseology. Dictionaries of idioms and proverbs have also contributed to the study of English historical phraseology (cf. Section 4.2, below). Monographs and collected volumes on aspects of historical English phraseology are rare: examples are Hiltunen (1983), Brinton and Akimoto (1999), Claridge (2000), Moralejo Gárate (2003), Trousdale (2008) within the framework of construction grammar – all on aspects of "multi-word verbs", in particular on the rise of "complex" and phrasal verbs; Prins (1952) on French influence on English phrases; Sontheim (1972) and Aurich (2012) on proverbs and proverbial expressions; Weinstock (1966) on the use of formulaic language in Shakespeare; Knappe (2004) on phraseology in English language study to 1800.

A large-scale survey of historical English phraseology has not been published yet. In fact, a great number of research questions are waiting to be explored. These are too numerous to be listed explicitly and comprehensively in this chapter. Rather, it is hoped that the following systematic (but necessarily not comprehensive) account of possibilities of English historical phraseology, which are presented together with selected references to existing studies, will help to lay a basis for its future exploration within an accepted system of "idioms and fixed expressions" (phraseology).

Three major approaches to historical phraseology have been singled out in the past (cf. in particular Sialm et al. 1982; Burger and Linke 1998; also Howarth 2000), which will be looked at in the following sections:
a. the study of metalinguistic sources such as proverb collections, dictionaries, and grammars and their contribution to the identification of phraseological units in historical texts (Section 4);
b. the investigation of the origin and change of phraseological units (Section 5.1); and
c. their usage and function in earlier texts (Section 5.2).

Another promising area for future research is the study of the impact of phraseological units and frequent collocations on larger issues of language change (Section 6).

4 Metalinguistic sources and their value for the identification of phraseological units in historical texts

Historical metalinguistic sources are relevant for historical English phraseology in a twofold way: first, as representing the scholarship of past ages they are the objects of the historiography of English phraseology both in its own right and with regard to the judgment of the reliability of the works as data sources. Second, both historical and modern collections of historical phraseological language data are, if they are judged to reflect actual language use, major aids in the identification of phraseological units in historical texts.

4.1 The historiography of English phraseology

A book-length survey of the place of phraseology in pre-19th-century English language study is Knappe (2004). Included are:
English proverbs in
- special collections (cf. now also Doyle 2007a, who goes beyond 1800); and
- textbooks; as well as

English phraseological units in
- stylistic treatises;
- handbooks for foreign-language teaching and contrastive language study;
- bilingual and multilingual lexicography with English as the first language entered;
- translation theory;
- philosophical and universal language schemes (including shorthand writing);
- monolingual English lexicography;
- monolingual English grammars; and
- early classifications of phraseological units.

The analysis of the English material showed that particular types of phraseological units stand out as being especially interesting to the early textbook authors. These are proverbs, routine formulae, stereotyped comparisons, binomials, restricted collocations, phrasal verbs, figurative idioms, and idiomatic phraseological units in general. As early as from the time of the Restoration, and partly owing to the endeavors of the Royal Society (especially members of the Society such as John Ray and John Wilkins), scholars writing in the British Isles started approaching the topic in a more analytical way, developing classifications of the phraseological material (cf. also Knappe 2006c) which culminated in George Campbell's *Philosophy of Rhetoric* (1776). Joseph Priestley in the 18th century can be credited with the emancipation of the notion of an "idiom" from its roots in language comparison. For the identification of phraseological units in historical texts it is important to know that the material discussed or entered in these textbooks and dictionaries reflects actual language use (cf. also Section 4.2, below).

It is hoped that future studies will extend and complement the findings in Knappe (2004) and join them up with the beginning of the scholarly study of phraseology in the 20th century. In the long run, the history of English phraseology will have to be viewed in a European perspective (for German, cf. also Burger et al. 1982: 360–382 and Weickert 1997).

4.2 The identification of phraseological units in historical texts

Several criteria have been singled out that may lead to a proper judgment of whether a given historical word combination – found by targeted reading, corpus search, or a combination of the two – may claim phraseological status (cf., e.g., Friedrich 2007: 1093; Burger in Sialm et al. 1982: 346-360). These criteria may be deduced both from linguistic considerations and from metalinguistic sources. Thus, a linguistic criterion may be the fact that a modern parallel of the expression exists, as in (11), the communicative function may betray a routine formula (17), formal criteria such as alliteration are typical of some expressions (18), word-formations are sometimes based on earlier phraseological units, such as the de-phraseological formation in (19), the degree of idiomaticity (semantic non-compositionality) of the whole expression is a strong indicator of phraseological status, as in (20), and there are cases where the original composition of the phraseological unit has become opaque (21). The exact meaning of the components at particular times can be difficult to determine, and thus it may be hard to distinguish idioms from restricted collocations in past stages of the language (22). Finally, in the case of translated texts, word combinations which are (recurrently) different from the original may be further investigated for their phraseological status, and the high frequency of occurrence of structural units or pragmatic markers is an indication of phraseological status, too, as it is in present-day language.

(17) *How do you?*
'How are you?' "God be thanked for you, How do you?", quotation 1570 (cf. OED, s.v. *do* v., def. 19) > *How do you do?* (cf. OED, s.v. *how* adv., def. 2a and *how-do-you-do, how-d'ye-do* phr. and n.; first quotation: 1697)

(18) *kith and kin*
'country and kinsfolk' > 'acquaintance and kinsfolk' > 'relatives' (cf. OED, s.v. *kith* n., def. 5)

(19) *fence-sitter < to sit on the fence*
(cf. Gläser 1986: 52; cf. OED, s.v. *fence* n., def. C2 and *sit* v., def. B3c, in quotation 1887: "Those who sit 'on the fence' – men with impartial minds, who wait to see ... 'how the cat will jump'"; first occurrences: *fence-sitter* 1905, slightly earlier: *fence-sitting* 1904)

(20) *to bear in/on hand*
'bring forth something wrong against someone' (14th–16th century; cf. OED, MED, early dictionaries)

(21) *good-bye* < *God be with you/ye*
 (cf. OED, s.v. *good-bye*)

(22) *at non hond*
 'in no way, not at all', figurative use of Middle English *hond* as 'a position or direction to one side or the other'? (cf. MED, s.v. *hōnd(e* n., def. 7; last quotation of *at no hand* in OED, s.v. *hand* n¹., def. 25g: 1690)

Metalinguistic indications, such as the comments "literally" or "proverbial" in a text (e.g. 1835: "We came in literally *neck and neck*"; 1880: "The Burials Bill is thought to resemble the proverbial *chip in porridge*, which does neither good nor harm"; Howarth 2000: 226), or the inverted commas in the quotation in (19), are helpful for the identification of phraseological units to a certain extent, but reliable larger collections, which we possess from the 17th century onwards (and for proverbs also earlier than this), are certainly profitable resources for historical English phraseology: it was not only the analytic spirit which developed in Restoration England, but this period may also be seen as the time when collectors started to restrict themselves to the inclusion of authentic English language material. Thus, from the 17th century onwards contrastive handbooks for foreign language teaching and dictionaries stand out as rich and to a large extent unexploited storehouses of language data, which in the future will be highly useful in the investigation of the historical development of English phraseological units.

Late 19th, 20th, and early 21st-century historical lexicography, in particular the OED and the *Middle English Dictionary* (Kurath et al. 1952–2001), which both are now searchable online, as well as efforts of phraseography (dictionaries of idioms and fixed expressions) and especially paremiography (dictionaries of proverbs) (cf. Apperson 1929; Tilley 1950; Whiting 1968; Mieder et al. 1992; Speake 2003) provide information on language data which is of paramount importance for the study of the historical development of phraseological units. As far as the great OED is concerned, Cowie (2003) found that much phraseological material can be retrieved from its text but that this material is often neither prominently displayed nor consistently handled. Earlier alphabetic and topical dictionaries can usefully complement these modern lexicographical endeavors, as has for instance been shown in a pilot study on Roget's *Thesaurus* (cf. esp. Knappe 2006a, but also 2006b) – although here the exact meaning and potential formal variations of a given phraseological unit may not be found in the collections, but will have to be deduced from actual texts.

Reliable and comprehensive collections of phraseological units from all periods of English are most important for the study of historical phraseology. Such an historical database of phraseological units can then fruitfully be employed as the point of departure for corpus-based investigation along the lines of the approach adopted in Moon's research (1998a, 1998b), who gathered her material on the basis of the phraseological entries in the first edition of the *Collins Cobuild English Language Dictionary* of 1987 (cf. also Moon 2007). Even if researchers choose not to adopt this "consultation paradigm" which starts from a prefabricated list of phraseological units but prefer an "analysis paradigm" (on these terms, cf. Sailer 2007: 1064) by retrieving hypothetical phraseological units from text corpora by various means, a database of accepted forms will finally be necessary for the evaluation of the potentially phraseological findings. As far as the "analysis paradigm" is concerned, a large amount of work on the available electronic corpora and their annotations will still be necessary before phraseological units which do not match the criterion of frequent lexical co-occurrence can be retrieved from them (cf., e.g., also Degand and Bestgen 2003 on the automatic retrieval of idioms; cf. also Gray and Biber 2015). The problems and challenges of corpus-based phraseological study outlined by Sailer (2007: 1067–1069) for the analysis of Present-day German, for instance with regard to the variation in phraseological units, will have to be reviewed from the point of view of historical (English) corpora. Problems relating to the rare occurrence of many phraseological units and the comparatively small size of the databases are of course even more severe for historical than for present-day databases.

5 Origin, change, and earlier uses of English phraseological units

Next to the identification of phraseological units in older texts, historical phraseological research has addressed questions of the origins and change of phraseological units through time. Many of these points are connected to key issues of historical linguistics. In addition, the uses of phraseological units in literary texts have been addressed, mainly with the aim to assess the literary language of individual authors or the style of particular text types in the past. These studies, however, also contribute to our knowledge of the forms, meanings and functions of phraseological units at particular points in time.

5.1 Origin and change of phraseological units as linguistic signs

It seems safe to say that all phraseological units, once they are accepted parts of the language, share the feature of "conventionality". It seems also safe to say that at the basis of all phraseological units lies the pragmatic feature of "usefulness". These "useful units", then, may develop from several origins (cf. Howarth 2000). Some idiomatic phraseological units may have started out from a free or restricted collocation, such as suggested by the semantic change of the complex predicate in (23). In these cases, classification criteria in typologies which have been suggested for the description of the rise of a phraseological unit are the structure from which the unit developed and the kind of semantic change of the basis compared to the result (cf. Munske 1993). Other phraseological units such as proverbs (4), oaths or the metaphorical phraseological unit in (24) are probably coined expressions with no original literal use. Some phraseological units which are in common use today originate from literary texts, that is, they can be traced back to one creative mind, as in (7). Borrowing, too, is another source of phraseological units – a source not to be underestimated for English as a mixed language – such as the foreign phrase in (25) or, more commonly, adapted or translated ones (26). However, one has to be aware that it can be difficult to distinguish borrowed units from common-source and polygenetic ones (cf. the detailed study by Piirainen and Balázsi 2012–2016).

(23) *to take steps*
'walk' > 'perform a move or moves in a course of action' (17th century) > 'take action or measures towards attaining an end' (from 18th century) (cf. also OED, s.v. *step* n.[1], def. 6d)

(24) *to be in (another person's) shoes*
'be in his position or place' (from 18th century according to OED, s.v. *shoe* n., def. 2k)

(25) *vice versa*
'contrariwise, conversely' (first attestation: 1601; cf. OED, s.v. *vice versa* adv.)

(26) *to keep company*
'give a person one's company' (first attestation: 1509; < *tenir compaignie*, according to Prins 1952)

In cases when phraseological units develop from free collocations, the question of how such a phraseological "fixation" arises must be addressed. For the explanation of the rise of English adverbial phraseological units, for example, Jean Hudson (1998) has suggested a cyclical model of fixation which draws on discussions in cognitive linguistics, pragmatics, discourse analysis, grammaticalization theory, and other research in language change. Her model is unidirectional and circular. Put in a nutshell, Hudson proposes that at the level of *discourse*, an ad hoc expression, that is, an expression formed on the principle of open choice, turns into a unit with a different (new?) meaning through pragmatic inferencing. This unit is not yet fixed. Due to this pragmatic inferencing, however, salience reduction of the constituent parts occurs on the second level, which is *conceptualization*. Hudson replaces the notion of "semantic decompositionality" by "cognitive analyzability", which depends on salience. Reduced salience, in its turn, fixes the expression to some degree on the level of *realization*. Symptoms of fixedness are unexpected syntactic constraints on the constituent parts, such as *the other day* but **the other days*, and unexpected collocational restrictions within the expression, e.g. *first of all* but **second of all*. On a less theoretical level, signs of a fixation process have, among other things, been named by Burger and Linke (1998: 747–750) as the reduction of lexical variants, of possibilities of modification, and of variety in morphosyntactic structure (cf. also Forgács 2004 on aspects of lexicalization; cf. also Levin and Lindquist 2015).

With regard to the choice and establishment of a phraseological unit's canonical form in the history of English, Voitl (1969) has tentatively suggested influence of prescriptive linguistics. However, the tension between convention and variation, as well as creative exploitation, can readily be seen as typical of living phraseological units. It is obviously a major challenge for historical phraseology to distinguish synchronic variation from diachronic change.

The investigation of the formal and semantic change of English phraseological units, too, addresses key issues of historical linguistics. In Burger and Linke (1998) and Friedrich (2007), several distinctive changes are discussed. These changes affect, for example, the order of the elements within the unit (27), the reduction or increase in the number of elements (28), the exchange of lexemes (29), the change in syntactic structure (17), the change in meaning and use (23), and finally the death of a phraseological unit (20). While examples for changes of these kinds can partly be suggested by the entries in the OED and MED, these entries are, after all, highly selective and not intended to give precise phraseological details. In-depth studies focussing on English phraseological developments, based on a wide coverage of lexicographical sources and the use of a large corpus of historical texts, are wanting.

(27) *heels over head* (from 14th century)
 'upside down' > *head over heels* (from 18th century, with development of figurative sense; cf. OED, s.v. *heel* n.^{1}, def. 15a, *head* n.^{1}, def. 46b)

(28) *a bird in hand* [*is better than / worth two in the wood / bush*] (15th–18th century) > *a bird in the hand* [...] (from 15th century)
 (cf. OED, MED, other dictionary sources)

(29) *to know (best) where one's shoe wrings (one)*
'know where (a person's) difficulty or trouble is' (from 14th century; last quotation 1887) > *to know (best) where one's shoe pinches (one)* (from 16th century; cf. OED, s.v. *pinch* v., def. 5b, *shoe* n., def. 2f, *wring* v., def. 4b)

Restrictions of space forbid a detailed review of further studies pertaining to the origin of phraseological units and their change over time. Therefore, a selection of the published ones will only be briefly mentioned, and one unpublished study will be referred to in some more detail.

Thus, for example, foreign influence on the rise of English phraseological units is the subject of Prins (1952), who devoted a book-length study and several articles to the *French Influence in English Phrasing*. The traces left by Latin phrases in Old English were investigated by Gneuss (1955), and Gustaf Stern (1931: 224) in his model of semantic change included fixed expressions which are influenced by foreign languages.

Several formal subtypes of phraseological units (see Section 2.2, above) that are of specific interest to English linguistics have become the object of study, too. Thus, the structural and semantic rise and historical development of phrasal verbs (e.g. *to give up*) and complex predicates (e.g. *to take a bath*) have been given a rather large amount of attention (cf. the monographs cited in Section 3, above). The problem of differentiating noun + noun compounds from syntactic groups with phraseological status has been tackled by Marchand (1969: 20–30), also in a historical perspective. Among studies investigating subtypes are Ross's (1975) article on "alliterative phrases" and Sontheim's (1972) and Aurich's (2012) monographs addressed to the historical development of English proverbs and proverbial phrases.

Apart from individual formal subtypes, the potential of smaller phraseological units, such as the adverbial phraseological units *in hand* and *on hand*, for example, as elements in the formation of larger phraseological units (Fleischer's 1997 *phraseologische Reihe* 'phraseological chain'), such as in *to take in hand* or *a bird in hand* [*is better than / worth two in the wood / bush*] (28), for example, can fruitfully be explored in the history of English, too. An as yet unpublished study by the present author based on lexicographical sources has uncovered 62 phraseological units in which *in hand* and *on hand* appear in the history of English. Two of the results will be briefly mentioned here: First, a "phraseological semantic force" (my own term) of *in hand* and *on hand* can be found, for instance in the development of *take in hand*. All main semantic features of *in hand* seem to have gained control over the unit *take in hand* almost simultaneously until the feature [PROCESS] prevailed from the 16th century on. Thus, from the literal meaning 'in the hand' the feature [PROXIMITY] took hold (e.g.

'to take with one'), also [POWER, CONTROL] 'to bring under control', and finally [PROCESS] 'to carry out', 'to undertake'. The second conclusion relates to the "phraseological binding force" (my own term) of adverbial phraseological units such as *in hand*, which may vary over time. According to my data, most of the new units with *in hand* and *on hand* were formed in the 16th century, a period marked by unprecedented interest in the creative potential and rhetorical force of the mother tongue, aided above all by a desire for rhetorical *copia*, that is, full and variable English expression (on the latter aspect, cf. Knappe 2004: 49–111).

The historical development of phraseological units can also be explored from an onomasiological point of view. Thus Anders (1995) has studied lexical and phraseological realizations of the concept of "dying", also in a historical perspective.

And finally, connecting this section up to Section 5.2, the historical change in form and function of English routine formulae can be studied. Thus, Wyld (1936) included as the tenth chapter of his history of modern colloquial English a discussion of the historical development of routine formulae and finds, for instance, that greetings and farewells in the 16th century were less "stereotypical" than in his own day. A useful synchronic collection and classification from which systematic studies of routine formulae from a diachronic perspective could start is the monograph on *Conversational Routines in English* by Karin Aijmer (1996).

5.2 The use of phraseological units in historical texts: aspects of pragmatics

Phraseological units have always been employed by writers in a variety of functions, and canonical poetry, vice versa, can itself act as the source of phraseological units, as in (7) (cf. also MacKenzie 2003). In addition to finding out what the employment of formulaic language means for the literary text, it can also give evidence on the (creative) use of phraseology at a given time in the history of a language. The stylistically motivated employment of phraseological units in literary texts has been emphasized in the Russian and (Eastern) European study of historical phraseology. English writers of the past have selectively been studied, too.

To start at the beginning, it is well-known that the oral style in medieval poetry is characterized by formulaic expressions (cf. the classical article by Magoun 1953). These have received much attention in scholarship, and are examples for the construction and transmission of artistic texts by help of pre-set formulas, sometimes employed creatively.

In later texts, the use of proverbs in particular has been investigated (cf. especially the bibliography on international proverb scholarship by Mieder 1982). To mention just a few examples, Weinstock (1966) looked at Shakespeare's use of proverbs and found that in his later works, the great writer employed proverbs to mark dramatic turns, and they also served to characterize persons. Reuter (1986) studied Deloney from this perspective, and both Brewer (1986: 229–232) and Windeatt (1992: 332–335, 345–354) comment on Chaucer's use of set phrases (e.g. *bold as blind Bayard*), oaths (e.g. *God so my soule save*) and proverbs (e.g. *The blind man cannot judge in colors*) in the discussion of his poetic style. Thus, for instance, one of Chaucer's favorite lines (adapted from the Italian) is *For pitee renneth soone in gentil herte* 'because pity flows swiftly in a noble heart', which he uses in the *Canterbury Tales* and in the *Legend of Good Women* to reinforce "our sense of humane values", according to Brewer (1986: 230). Brewer adds that in using a large number of familiar phrases Chaucer created a traditionalist diction and aimed at familiar effects, ready communication, and sympathetic attention. The sententiousness in Chaucer's *Troilus and Criseyde*, particularly the use of proverbs, however, which cluster at important points of persuasion and self-persuasion, creates distinct ambiguity which questions the limitations and value of prudential wisdom (cf. Windeatt 1992: 345–354).

These are only a few examples of employment of phraseological language in literary texts. Again, more work needs to be done along these lines.

6 The impact of phraseology and collocation / string frequency on language change

By way of an outlook one further interesting line of research in historical English phraseology will be mentioned: this is the effect that multi-word combinations can have on language change. To this end, frequently repeated word combinations (frequent collocations) and phraseological units will be discussed together. First, the common ground of both concepts will be addressed.

A description of a phraseological unit was given above (Section 2.1). The use of "collocation" as addressed here needs further explanation. As defined by Sinclair (1991: 170), collocation is "the occurrence of two or more words within a short space of each other in a text". Typically, these co-occurrences are frequently repeated or statistically relevant in a corpus (cf. also Bartsch 2004: 65; Moon 2007: 1046–1047). Research into conceptual structures may help us understand the common ground of both collocations as described above and phraseological units in language processing and use, which is important for the question of their influence on language change. Both frequent word combinations and phraseological units are characterized by their degree of entrenchment (cf. Harris 1998): it is either based on the form only or on the semantic/pragmatic unity of a string with certain formal characteristics.

The effect of frequently recurring word form combinations (string frequency) on language change has received attention in scholarship, such as seen in coalescence phenomena and the phonological effect of word-boundary liaison as the trigger for the "Great Vowel Shift" (cf. Krug 1998, 2003, 2012). So if the frequent co-occurrence of lexical items affects language change, as research in string frequency claims, it may be suggested that phraseological units, too, may have an impact on it.

Thus, Knappe and Schümann (2006) have investigated the influence of both collocations (as described above) and phraseological units on the sudden switches of pronouns of address between the singular and the plural in the address of a single person in dialogues in Chaucer's *Canterbury Tales*. About 90 such switchings occur in the text. The use of the plural pronoun for formal address was introduced on the model of French but was by the time of Chaucer not yet vigorously applied. For about one third of the cases of sudden pronoun switch we claim that a "collocational-phraseological" force was the trigger. This force is so strong that it may even override the pragmatically preferred choice of the pronouns of address in the particular situation (cf. Jucker, Chapter 9). For instance, terms for body parts (e.g. *thy eyen*) tend to co-occur with the singular pronoun of address and may provoke a pronoun switch. The verb *prayen* 'I pray you/thee' occurs more often with the plural (62 instances) than with the singular pronoun (14 instances). To give an example, the more common combination of *pray* + *you* may account for the shift from the singular to the plural in Absolon's speech to Alisoun in the *Miller's Tale* (3361–3362), as seen in (30):

(30) *"Now, deere lady, if **thy** wille be,*
 *I praye **yow** that **ye** wole rewe on me ..."*
 ' "Now, dear lady, if it be your will,
 I beseech you to have mercy on me ..." '

In (31) the formula used for the opening of sermons *Heere may ye se* 'By this may you see, i.e. understand' is a phraseological unit. In the *Friar's Tale* (1567) it can account for the insertion of the plural form in the yeoman's (i.e. the devil's) address to the summoner (1566–1568):

(31) *"Lo, brother," quod the feend, "what tolde I **thee**?*
*Heere may **ye** se, myn owene deere brother,*
The carl spak oo thing, but he thoghte another."
' "Lo, brother", said the devil, "what did I tell you?
By this may you see, my own dear brother,
the fellow spoke one thing, but he thought another" '

(The quotations in [30] and [31] are taken from Benson [ed.] 1987.) Starting from here, the role of entrenched structures in the introduction of a distinctive system of pronouns of address in Middle English could be studied.

7 Summary

To sum up, a great amount of work in the retrieval and analysis of phraseological material from the history of English still needs to be done. Some first studies and research from other languages and in different traditions of scholarship can provide a basis from which to start with the systematic investigation of the phraseological past of the English language. In the long run, the aim of scholarship in historical English phraseology should be the description of all facets of the origin and historical development of the phraseological system, or systems, of English. Moreover, at a time when the impact of "formulaic language" on language acquisition, use, and change is increasingly being studied in linguistic theory, historical English phraseology in its interaction with other related approaches of scholarship and methods such as collocation studies, corpus linguistics, cognitive linguistics, grammaticalization and lexicalization theories, and also construction grammar, will open up large, promising fields of research possibilities.

8 References

Aijmer, Karin. 1996. *Conversational Routines in English: Convention and Creativity*. London: Longman.
Anders, Heidi. 1995. *"Never say die"– Englische Idiome um den Tod und das Sterben*. Frankfurt: Peter Lang.
Apperson, George Latimer. 1929. *English Proverbs and Proverbial Phrases: A Historical Dictionary*. 2 vols. London/Toronto: J. M. Dent and Sons; New York: Dutton & Co.
Aurich, Claudia. 2012. *Proverb Structure in the History of English: Stability and Change. A Corpus-Based Study*. Baltmannsweiler: Schneider-Verlag Hohengehren.
Bartsch, Sabine. 2004. *Structural and Functional Properties of Collocations in English: A Corpus Study of Lexical and Pragmatic Constraints on Lexical Co-occurrence*. Tübingen: Narr.

Benson, Larry D. (ed.). 1987. *The Riverside Chaucer*. 3rd edn. Oxford: Oxford University Press.
Brewer, Derek. 1986. Chaucer's poetic style. In: Piero Boitani and Jill Mann (eds.), *The Cambridge Chaucer Companion*, 227–242. Cambridge: Cambridge University Press.
Brinton, Laurel J. 1996. *Pragmatic Markers in English: Grammaticalization and Discourse Functions*. Berlin/New York: Mouton de Gruyter.
Brinton, Laurel J. and Minoji Akimoto (eds.). 1999. *Collocational and Idiomatic Aspects of Composite Predicates in the History of English*. Amsterdam/Philadelphia: John Benjamins.
Burger, Harald. 2015. *Phraseologie: Eine Einführung am Beispiel des Deutschen*. 5th edn. Berlin: Erich Schmidt.
Burger, Harald, Annelies Buhofer, and Ambros Sialm. 1982. *Handbuch der Phraseologie*. Berlin/New York: Mouton de Gruyter.
Burger, Harald, Dmitrij Dobrovol'skij, Peter Kühn, and Neal R. Norrick (eds.). 2007. *Phraseologie/Phraseology: Ein internationales Handbuch der zeitgenössischen Forschung / An International Handbook of Contemporary Research*. 2 vols. Berlin/New York: Mouton de Gruyter.
Burger, Harald and Angelika Linke. 1998. Historische Phraseologie. In: Werner Besch, Anne Betten, Oskar Reichmann, and Stefan Sonderegger (eds.), *Sprachgeschichte: Ein Handbuch zur Geschichte der deutschen Sprache und ihrer Erforschung*. 2nd edn. Vol. I, 743–755. Berlin/New York: Walter de Gruyter.
Claridge, Claudia. 2000. *Multi-word Verbs in Early Modern English: A Corpus Based Approach*. Amsterdam/Atlanta, GA: Rodopi.
Cowie, A. P. 1983. General introduction. In: Cowie, Mackin, and McCaig, Vol. II, x–xvii.
Cowie, A. P. (ed.). 1998. *Phraseology: Theory, Analysis, and Applications*. Oxford: Clarendon Press.
Cowie, A. P. 2003. Some aspects of the treatment of phraseology in the *OED*. In: Cornelia Tschichold (ed.), *English Core Linguistics: Essays in Honour of D. J. Allerton*, 205–224. Bern/Berlin: Peter Lang.
Cowie, A. P., R. Mackin, and I. R. McCaig. 1983. *Oxford Dictionary of Current Idiomatic English*. Vol. II. *Phrase, Clause & Sentence Idioms*. Oxford: Oxford University Press. [Repr. 1993 under the title: *Oxford Dictionary of English Idioms*]
Cowie, A. P. and R. Mackin. 1993. *Oxford Dictionary of Phrasal Verbs*. Oxford: Oxford University Press. [= 2nd edn. of *Oxford Dictionary of Current Idiomatic English*. Vol. I. *Verbs with Prepositions & Particles*]
Degand, Liesbeth and Yves Bestgen. 2003. Towards automatic retrieval of idioms in French newspaper corpora. *Literary and Linguistic Computing* 18: 249–259.
Dobrovol'skij, Dmitrij O. and Elisabeth Piirainen. 2009. *Zur Theorie der Phraseologie: Kognitive and kulturelle Aspekte*. Tübingen: Stauffenburg.
Doyle, Charles Clay. 2007a. Historical phraseology of English. In: Burger, Dobrovol'skij, Kühn, and Norrick (eds.), 1078–1092.
Doyle, Charles Clay. 2007b. Collections of proverbs and proverb dictionaries: Some historical observations on what's in them and what's not (with a note on current "gendered" proverbs). In: Skandera (ed.), 181–204.
Fiedler, Sabine. 2007. *English Phraseology: A Coursebook*. Tübingen: Narr.
Fleischer, Wolfgang. 1997. *Phraseologie der deutschen Gegenwartssprache*. 2nd edn. Tübingen: Niemeyer.
Forgács, Tamás. 2004. Grammatikalisierung und Lexikalisierung in phraseologischen Einheiten. In: Christine Palm-Meister (ed.), *Europhras 2000: Internationale Tagung zur Phraseologie vom 15.–18. Juni 2000 in Aske / Schweden*, 137–149. Tübingen: Stauffenburg.

Friedrich, Jesko. 2007. Historische Phraseologie des Deutschen. In: Burger, Dobrovol'skij, Kühn, and Norrick (eds.), 1092–1106.

Gläser, Rosemarie. 1986. *Phraseologie der englischen Sprache*. Leipzig: VEB Verlag Enzyklopädie. Tübingen: Niemeyer.

Gläser, Rosemarie. 1998. The stylistic potential of phraseological units in the light of genre analysis. In: Cowie (ed.), 125–143.

Gneuss, Helmut. 1955. *Lehnbildungen und Lehnbedeutungen im Altenglischen*. Berlin: Erich Schmidt.

Gray, Bethany and Douglas Biber. 2015. Phraseology. In: Douglas Biber and Randi Reppen (eds.), *The Cambridge Handbook of English Corpus Linguistics*, 125–145. Cambridge: Cambridge University Press.

Häcki Buhofer, Annelies and Harald Burger (eds.). 2006. *Phraseology in Motion I: Methoden und Kritik. Akten der Internationalen Tagung zur Phraseologie (Basel, 2004)*. Baltmannsweiler: Schneider-Verlag Hohengehren.

Harris, Catherine L. 1998. Psycholinguistic studies of entrenchment. In: Jean-Pierre Koenig (ed.), *Discourse and Cognition: Bridging the Gap*, 55–70. Stanford, CA: CSLI.

Hiltunen, Risto. 1983. *The Decline of the Prefixes and the Beginnings of the English Phrasal Verb: The Evidence from Some Old and Early Middle English Texts*. Turku: Turun Yliopisto.

Howarth, Peter. 2000. Describing diachronic change in English phraseology. In: Gloria Corpas Pastor (ed.), *Las lenguas de Europa: Estudios de fraseología, fraseografía y traducción*, 213–230. Granada: Editorial Comares.

Huddleston, Rodney and Geoffrey K. Pullum. 2002. *The Cambridge Grammar of the English Language*. Cambridge: Cambridge University Press.

Hudson, Jean. 1998. *Perspectives on Fixedness: Applied and Theoretical*. Lund: Lund University Press.

Knappe, Gabriele. 2004. *Idioms and Fixed Expressions in English Language Study before 1800: A Contribution to English Historical Phraseology*. Frankfurt: Peter Lang.

Knappe, Gabriele. 2006a. The treasury of phrases in Peter Mark Roget's *Thesaurus of English Words and Phrases* (1852). In: Christoph Houswitschka, Gabriele Knappe, and Anja Müller (eds.), *Anglistentag 2005 Bamberg: Proceedings*, 475–487. Trier: Wissenschaftlicher Verlag.

Knappe, Gabriele. 2006b. Peter Mark Roget's *Thesaurus of English Words and Phrases*: A mid-nineteenth century example of the place of phraseology in the history of linguistic theory and practice. In: Christian Mair and Reinhard Heuberger (eds.), in collaboration with Josef Wallmannsberger, *Corpora and the History of English: Papers Dedicated to Manfred Markus on the Occasion of His Sixty-Fifth Birthday*, 205–220. Heidelberg: Winter.

Knappe, Gabriele. 2006c. Phraseology in English language study before 1800 and Lewis Chambaud's *Idioms of the French and English Languages* (1751). In: Häcki Buhofer and Burger (eds.), 413–423.

Knappe, Gabriele and Michael Schümann. 2006. *Thou* and *ye*: A collocational-phraseological approach to pronoun change in Chaucer's *Canterbury Tales*. *Studia Anglica Posnaniensia* 42: 213–238. http://ifa.amu.edu.pl/sap/files/42/17Knappe.pdf

Krug, Manfred. 1998. String frequency: A cognitive motivating factor in coalescence, language processing and linguistic change. *Journal of English Linguistics* 26: 286–320.

Krug, Manfred. 2003. (Great) vowel shifts present and past: Meeting ground for structural and natural phonologists. *University of Pennsylvania Working Papers in Linguistics: Papers from NWAV 31* 9(2): 107–122. http://repository.upenn.edu/cgi/viewcontent.cgi?article=1456&context=pwpl

Krug, Manfred. 2012. The Great Vowel Shift. In Alexander Bergs and Laurel J. Brinton (eds.), *English Historical Linguistics: An International Handbook*, 756–776. Berlin/New York: De Gruyter Mouton.

Kurath, Hans, Sherman M. Kuhn, John Reidy, and Robert E. Lewis. 1952–2001. *Middle English Dictionary*. Ann Arbor: University of Michigan Press. http://quod.lib.umich.edu/m/med/

Levin, Magnus and Hans Lindquist. 2015. *Like I said again and again and over and over*: On the ADV1 *and* ADV1 construction with adverbs of direction in English. In: Sebastian Hoffmann, Bettina Fischer-Starcke, and Andrea Sand (eds.), *Current Issues in Phraseology*, 7–34. Amsterdam: John Benjamins. [Originally published in *International Journal of Corpus Linguistics* 18(1) (2013).]

MacKenzie, Ian. 2003. Poetry and formulaic language. In: Christine Michaux and Marc Dominicy (eds.), *Linguistic Approaches to Poetry*, 75–86. Amsterdam/Philadelphia: John Benjamins.

Magoun, Francis P. 1953. The oral-formulaic character of Anglo-Saxon narrative poetry. *Speculum* 28: 446–467.

Makkai, Adam. 1972. *Idiom Structure in English*. The Hague/Paris: Mouton.

Marchand, Hans. 1969. *The Categories and Types of Present-Day English Word-Formation: A Synchronic-Diachronic Approach*. 2nd edn. Munich: Beck.

Mieder, Wolfgang. 1982. *International Proverb Scholarship: An Annotated Bibliography*. New York: Garland.

Mieder, Wolfgang, Stewart A. Kingsbury, and Kelsie B. Harder (eds.). 1992. *A Dictionary of American Proverbs*. New York: Oxford University Press.

Moon, Rosamund. 1998a. *Fixed Expressions and Idioms in English: A Corpus-Based Approach*. Oxford: Clarendon Press.

Moon, Rosamund. 1998b. Frequencies and forms of phrasal lexemes in English. In: Cowie (ed.), 79–100.

Moon, Rosamund. 2007. Corpus linguistic approaches with English corpora. In: Burger, Dobrovol'skij, Kühn, and Norrick (eds.), 1045–1059.

Moralejo Gárate, Teresa. 2003. *Composite Predicates in Middle English*. Munich: LINCOM.

Munske, Horst Haider. 1993. Wie entstehen Phraseologismen? In: Klaus J. Mattheier, Klaus-Peter Wegera, Walter Hoffmann, Jürgen Macha, and Hans-Joachim Solms (eds.), *Vielfalt des Deutschen*, 481–515. Frankfurt am Main: Peter Lang.

Nattinger, James R. and Jeanette S. DeCarrico. 1992. *Lexical Phrases and Language Teaching*. Oxford: Oxford University Press.

Norrick, Neal R. 2007. English phraseology. In: Burger, Dobrovol'skij, Kühn, and Norrick (eds.), 615–619.

Piirainen, Elisabeth and József Attila Balázsi. 2012–2016. *Widespread Idioms in Europe and Beyond*. Vol. I (by Elisabeth Piirainen): *Toward a Lexicon of Common Figurative Units*. Vol. II (by Elisabeth Piirainen and József Attila Balázsi): *Lexicon of Common Figurative Units*. New York: Peter Lang.

Prins, A. A. 1952. *French Influence in English Phrasing*. Leiden: Universitaire Pers.

Proffitt, Michael (ed.). 2000–. *The Oxford English Dictionary*. 3rd edn. online. Oxford University Press. www.oed.com

Reuter, O. R. 1986. *Proverbs, Proverbial Sentences and Phrases in Thomas Deloney's Works*. Helsinki: Societas Scientiarum Fennica.

Ross, Alan S. C. 1975. "Run and Reve" and similar alliterative phrases. *Neuphilologische Mitteilungen* 76: 571–582.

Sailer, Manfred. 2007. Corpus linguistic approaches with German corpora. In: Burger, Dobrovol'skij, Kühn, and Norrick (eds.), 1060–1071.
Sialm, Ambros, Harald Burger, and Angelika Linke. 1982. Historische Phraseologie. In: Burger, Buhofer, and Sialm, 315–382.
Sick, Christine. 1993. *Adverbiale Phraseologismen des Englischen*. Tübingen: Narr.
Sinclair, John. 1991. *Corpus, Concordance, Collocation*. Oxford: Oxford University Press.
Skandera, Paul (ed.). 2007. *Phraseology and Culture in English*. Berlin/New York: Mouton de Gruyter.
Sontheim, Kurt. 1972. *Sprichwort, sprichwörtliche und metaphorische Redewendungen: Synchronische und diachronische Studien zu semantisch-idiomatischen Konstruktionen im Englischen*. Ph.D. dissertation, University of Erlangen-Nürnberg.
Speake, Jennifer (ed.). 2003. *The Oxford Dictionary of Proverbs*. 4th edn. Oxford: Oxford University Press.
Stern, Gustaf. 1931. *Meaning and Change of Meaning: With Special Reference to the English Language*. Westport, CT: Greenwood Press.
Tilley, Morris Palmer. 1950. *A Dictionary of the Proverbs in England in the Sixteenth and Seventeenth Centuries: A Collection of the Proverbs Found in English Literature and the Dictionaries of the Period*. Ann Arbor: University of Michigan Press.
Thun, Harald. 1978. *Probleme der Phraseologie: Untersuchungen zur wiederholten Rede mit Beispielen aus dem Französischen, Italienischen, Spanischen und Romanischen*. Tübingen: Niemeyer.
Trousdale, Graeme. 2008. Constructions in grammaticalization and lexicalization: Evidence from the history of a composite predicate construction in English. In: Graeme Trousdale and Nikolas Gisborne (eds.), *Constructional Approaches to English Grammar*, 33–67. Berlin/New York: Mouton de Gruyter.
Voitl, Herbert. 1969. Probleme der englischen Idiomatik. *Germanisch-romanische Monatsschrift*, N.F. 19: 194–212.
Weickert, Rainer. 1997. *Die Behandlung von Phraseologismen in ausgewählten Sprachlehren von Ickelsamer bis ins 19. Jahrhundert: Ein Beitrag zur historischen Phraseologie*. Hamburg: Kovac.
Weinstock, Horst. 1966. *Die Funktion elisabethanischer Sprichwörter und Pseudosprichwörter bei Shakespeare*. Heidelberg: Winter.
Welte, Werner. 1992. On the properties of English phraseology: A critical survey. In: Claudia Blank (ed.), *Language and Civilization: A Concerted Profusion of Essays and Studies in Honour of Otto Hietsch*. Vol. II, 564–591. Frankfurt: Peter Lang.
Whiting, Bartlett Jere, with the collaboration of Helen Wescott Whiting. 1968. *Proverbs, Sentences, and Proverbial Phrases: From English Writings Mainly Before 1500*. Cambridge, MA: Belknap Press of Harvard University Press.
Windeatt, Barry. 1992. *Troilus and Criseyde*. Oxford: Oxford University Press.
Wray, Alison. 2002. *Formulaic Language and the Lexicon*. Cambridge: Cambridge University Press.
Wyld, Henry Cecil. 1936. *A History of Modern Colloquial English*. 3rd edn., with additions. Oxford: Basil Blackwell.

Andreas H. Jucker
Chapter 9:
Pragmatics and Discourse

1 Introduction —— 165
2 Pragmatic explanations in language change —— 168
3 Pragmatics as the study of performance phenomena —— 170
4 Discourse as dialogue —— 174
5 Discourse as a domain of communication —— 176
6 Summary and outlook —— 179
7 References —— 180

Abstract: Pragmatics studies the processes of language use, while discourse analysis is devoted to its product, i.e. discourse. Pragmatics can be understood in a narrow sense focussing on cognitive-inferential aspects of information processing, and it can be understood in a wider sense in which it also includes social aspects of interaction. In historical pragmatics, the former conceptualization lies behind work on pragmatic explanations in language change, while the latter conceptualization studies earlier language use from a social and interactional perspective, including such aspects as inserts (e.g. interjections and discourse markers), speech acts, and terms of address. Discourse, as the product of language use, can be seen as a stretch of conversation (dialogue) or as a domain of communication. In the former conceptualization, research focuses on the structural properties of the dialogue, and in the latter, it deals with the linguistic practices pertaining to particular fields of knowledge or interaction, e.g. courtroom discourse, the discourse of science, and news discourse.

1 Introduction

In a very general sense pragmatics can be defined as the study of language use, while discourse analysis, in an equally general sense, can be defined as the analysis of the result of human communication, viz. discourse.

Andreas H. Jucker: Zürich (Switzerland)

> It has been suggested that discourse analysis is more text-centered, more static, more interested in product (in the well-formedness of texts), while pragmatics is more user-centred, more dynamic, more interested in the process of text production. Discourse analysis is frequently equated with conversational analysis, and pragmatics with speech act theory. It would seem difficult to distinguish the two with any conviction, however (Brinton 2001: 139).

There is certainly a great deal of overlap between the two fields. A large range of topics can be dealt with under either heading. Speech acts, such as greetings and farewells, or discourse markers, such as *well*, *so*, or *you know* have both interactional (pragmatic) functions and text-structuring or discourse functions.

As a field of study, pragmatics has grown very considerably over the last thirty years or so. Traditionally, linguists were mainly concerned with an analysis of language structure at the levels of phonology, morphology, and syntax, but with the pragmatic turn in the late 1970s and early 1980s some of the interest shifted from the structure of language to the language user. At the beginning of this development, pragmatics was often seen as the ragbag of linguistic description (see Mey 1998: 716). As such it covered performance phenomena that could not be handled at the traditional levels of linguistic description, such as speech acts, conversational implicature, deixis, and politeness, but also the structure of conversations.

On the other hand, even in the early days of pragmatics, the discipline was also seen as a perspective. As such it was not a level of linguistic description but a different way of analyzing language. Language was not seen as a system of signs but as a means of communication. "Pragmatics is a *perspective* on any aspect of language, at any level of structure" (Verschueren 1987: 5, italics in original; see also Verschueren 1999: 2). Under the former view, pragmatics was a separate level of linguistic description, parallel to other levels, such as syntax or semantics. Under the latter view, pragmatics was a particular way of doing linguistics that could be applied to all other levels of linguistic description from phonology and morphology to syntax, semantics and, indeed, discourse.

These positions have developed into a more restricted cognitive-inferential conceptualization of pragmatics (adhered to, generally speaking, by Anglo-American researchers) and a broader socio-interactional conceptualization (common among European researchers). Cruse (2000), for instance, gives the following narrow definition of pragmatics:

> For present purposes, pragmatics can be taken to be concerned with aspects of information (in the widest sense) conveyed through language which (a) are not encoded by generally accepted convention in the linguistic forms used, but which (b) none the less arise naturally out of and depend on the meanings conventionally encoded in the linguistic forms used, taken in conjunction with the context in which the forms are used (Cruse 2000: 16).

In this conceptualization, people routinely understand more than what is explicitly communicated. They read between the lines, as it were, and this is the field of the pragmaticist. In her handbook article on historical pragmatics, Traugott (2004: 539) also takes pragmatics "to be non-literal meaning that arises in language use", and Sperber and Noveck (2004: 1) define pragmatics as "the study of how linguistic properties and contextual factors interact in the interpretation of utterances". In their view, pragmatics is not restricted to a study of implicit meanings. In fact, they are at pains to demonstrate that there are many aspects of explicit meaning that require access to contextual information for their interpretation, but they exclude the wider social issues of language use from the scope of pragmatics.

The European tradition adopts a broader, more sociologically based view of pragmatics that includes social and cultural conditions of language use. Trosborg (1994: 37), a representative of this broader European tradition, for instance, states that "sociopragmatics is concerned with the analysis of significant patterns of interaction in particular social situations and/or in particular social systems. For example, speech acts may be realized differently in different social contexts and situations as well as in different social groups within a speech community", while Blakemore, a representative of the Anglo-American tradition, finds it "misleading to include phenomena like politeness, face-saving and turn taking [...] under the general heading of pragmatics" (Blakemore 1992: 47).

The two conceptualizations of pragmatics, obviously, have consequences for the interaction of pragmatics and historical linguistics. The former conceptualization suggests a range of specific performance-related topics, while the latter suggests a specific way of investigating earlier stages of a language and its development.

The term "discourse" is perhaps even more open to different definitions. On the one hand, it can be seen as the spoken equivalent of a text. A (written) text is made up of sentences while a (spoken) discourse is made up of utterances. In this sense, the term "discourse" is more or less synonymous with the term "dialogue" (see below, Section 4). Brinton (2001: 139–140) distinguishes between three discourse analytical approaches to historical data. First, the discourse analyst may use forms, functions, and structures of discourse at historical stages of a language. She calls this approach "historical discourse analysis proper". Second, the discourse analyst may study the discourse-pragmatic factors and motivations behind language change. This approach is called "discourse-oriented historical linguistics". And third, the discourse analyst may focus on the diachronic development of discourse functions and discourse structures over time. She calls this third approach "diachronic(ally oriented) discourse analysis".

However, the term "discourse" can also be used in a much wider sense, not just for a linguistic unit larger than utterances, but as a domain of language. In such a view, a discourse is a collection of linguistic practices characterized by a distinct group of people and a distinct group of genres and text types, e.g. the discourse of science, or more specifically the discourse of medical science or the discourse of modern linguistics.

In the following I shall evaluate how these conceptualizations of the terms "pragmatics" and "discourse" can be applied to the analysis of historical data and in particular to English historical data.

2 Pragmatic explanations in language change

In the Anglo-American conceptualization of pragmatics, pragmatics is mainly a tool to describe and explain patterns of language change. Language is a means of communication and, therefore, the communicative forces that are at work when people use language must be taken into consideration when we analyze, for instance, the syntax of a language and indeed when we analyze diachronic changes in the syntax of a language. Thus, pragmatics becomes a principle of explanation in language change. In Brinton's (2001) terminology this would be "discourse-oriented historical linguistics".

If pragmatics is seen as one level of linguistic description on a par with other levels such as phonology, morphology, syntax and semantics, it is largely restricted to non-truth-conditional aspects of language, and to aspects of language that depend on the context of utterance. Deictic elements, for instance, depend on the situation of use for their interpretation. Speech acts in their early conceptualization of doing things with words were also restricted to non-truth-conditional aspects. Speech act theory took its starting point from Austin's (1962) observation that speech acts are regularly used for purposes other than stating facts that are assessable in terms of true or false.

Meanings are not abstract entities that pertain to linguistic expressions but the result of negotiations between speaker/writer and addressee/reader, which – through repetition of use – have become conventionalized. A theory of meaning change, therefore, must take into account the communicative situation of speaker/writer and addressee/reader. Traugott and Dasher (2005), for instance, argue that it is ad-hoc negotiations of meanings that may lead to meaning change if they are invoked repeatedly until they become conventionalized in the entire speech community. They call such ad-hoc meanings "invited inferences", a term borrowed from Geis and Zwicky (1971). However, Traugott and Dasher use it in a broader sense and do not restrict it to generalized implicatures. It signals the speaker/writer's role in inviting the addressee to infer the intended ad-hoc meaning. As an example they cite the case of *as/so long as* (Traugott and Dasher 2005: 36–37). In Old and Middle

English the spatial meaning ('of the same length as') co-existed with the temporal meaning ('for the same length of time as'). In some contexts, the meaning invited the conditional meaning 'provided that', as for instance in (1).

(1) *wring þurh linenne clað on þæt eage **swa lange swa** him ðearf sy.*
 wring through linen cloth on that eye as long as him need be-SUBJ
 'squeeze (the medication) through a linen cloth onto the eye as long as he needs.' (850–950 Lacnunga, p. 100; example, gloss, and translation from Traugott and Dasher 2005: 36, ex. 19)

The medicine is to be applied for the duration that it is needed, which invites the inference that it is to be applied only if it is needed. According to Traugott and Dasher all examples of *as/so long as* in Old and Middle English are either spatial or temporal, and while some allow a conditional reading, the conditional reading is never predominant. This changes in Early Modern English, when examples occur in which the invited inference of conditionality has been generalized to contexts of reasoning and cognition in which a temporal reading does not make sense or is at least not salient as in (2).

(2) *They whose words doe most shew forth their wise vnderstanding, and whose lips doe vtter the purest knowledge, so **as long as** they vnderstand and speake as men, are they not faine sundry waies to excuse themselues?* (1614 Hooker, p. 5; Traugott and Dasher 2005: 37, ex. 20)

Here the conditional reading is salient, while the temporal meaning is still available. Traugott and Dasher paraphrase the temporal meaning as "for the time that they understand and speak as men", i.e. "as long as they live". From the mid-19th century there are examples in which the conditional is the only possible meaning as in (3).

(3) *"Would you tell me, please, which way I ought to go from here?"*
 "That depends a good deal on where you want to get to," said the Cat.
 "I don't much care where–" said Alice.
 "Then it doesn't matter which way you go," said the Cat.
 *"– **so long as** I get **somewhere**," Alice added as an explanation.* (1865 Carroll, Chapter 6, p. 51; Traugott and Dasher 2005: 37, ex. 21a)

Thus meaning change is the result of the interaction between speakers/writers and addressees/hearers in communicative situations. Speakers/writers use established coded meanings (e.g. the temporal reading of *so/as long as*) in creative ways to invite inferences. Through repeated use, such invited inferences become conventionalized and ultimately they become new coded meanings (Traugott and Dasher 2005: 38).

Thus language change is seen as the result of what Keller (1994) has called an "invisible hand process". Language change comes about as a causal effect of the accumulation of individual speakers' action, who – individually – did not intend this effect.

3 Pragmatics as the study of performance phenomena

Performance phenomena pertain mostly to the spoken language, i.e. to language that is produced under the constraints of online production. Such phenomena were shunned as irrelevant for a long time. For historical linguists they were doubly irrelevant. They were irrelevant because they were not part of the language system itself, and they were irrelevant because historical linguists did not have access to the spoken language of the past. The communicative turn in the '70s and '80s of the 20th century turned performance phenomena into legitimate objects of investigation for synchronic linguistics. Pragmaticists focused their attention on transcriptions of spoken interaction. They studied the minutiae of the turn-taking system, the form and function of individual utterances (speech acts), and so on. But these studies were restricted to present-day data. Pragmaticists saw written language as secondary and therefore as uninteresting for pragmatic analyses.

Today performance phenomena have made their way into standard descriptions of the English language (e.g. Biber et al. 1999, who spend a considerable amount of space on such phenomena within the confines of a structural description of the English language), and within the last decade or so, significant progress has been made on the description of performance phenomena from a diachronic perspective. I shall briefly mention three examples which have received a considerable amount of attention from historical pragmaticists, inserts, speech acts and terms of address. To the extent that the analyses of these elements rely on references to social conditions of their use, they clearly go beyond the narrow Anglo-American conceptualization of pragmatics.

3.1 Inserts

Biber et al. (1999: 1082) use the term "inserts" to refer to "stand-alone words which are characterized in general by their inability to enter into syntactic relations with other structures. [...] They comprise a class of words that is peripheral, both in the grammar and in the lexicon of the language". They distinguish nine different types of inserts: interjections (*oh, ah*), greetings and farewells (*hi, hello, goodbye*), discourse markers (*well, right*), attention signals (*hey, yo*), response elicitors (*right?, eh?*), response forms (*yeah, yep*), hesitators (*um, er*), various polite speech-act formulae (*thanks, sorry*), and expletives (*shit, good grief!*). Not all of these are equally amenable to a historical analysis. Biber et al. (1999: 1096–1098) provide some statistics about their distribution in American English and British English conversations, but they do not say anything about their occurrence in written genres. It seems reasonable to assume that some of them are relatively infrequent in the texts that have survived from earlier centuries. While some inserts, such as interjections or discourse markers, have been analyzed in their own right, others, like *thanks* and *sorry*, have been investigated in larger contexts of speech act studies of thanking and apologizing (e.g. Jacobsson 2002; Jucker and Taavitsainen 2008b), and expletives have been investigated in the context of the language of insults (e.g. Craun 1997).

Taavitsainen (1995) investigates the form, function, and distribution of exclamations, such as *alas, ey, ah, harrow*, and *O* in Late Middle and Early Modern English (see also Hiltunen 2006; Person 2009). Their distribution is clearly genre specific. In the *Helsinki Corpus*, which was used for the investigation, exclamations were particularly frequent in the genres comedy and fiction. They also occurred in trials and in Bible texts. In other genres they were rare. Exclamations were used more widely and with a broader variety of functions than in Present-day English. They were regularly used as vocatives and as appeals to the addressee. The interjection *O*, for instance, is often prefixed to an exclamatory sentence and it often combines with a vocative as in example (4), which is taken from a sermon.

(4) ***O my God, my God*** why haste thou forsaken me? (1614 Hooker, *Two Sermons Upon Part of S. Judes Epistle*, 1614, p. 7; *Helsinki Corpus*, Taavitsainen 1995: 453)

Discourse markers have received considerable attention in historical pragmatics. Brinton (1996), for instance, analyzed a broad range of discourse markers, or "pragmatic markers", as she calls them, including Old English *hwæt*, Middle

English *gan*, and Middle and Early Modern English *anon*. She is interested not only in the developing discourse functions of these elements but also in the grammaticalization processes that they instantiate. In more recent publications she has added analyses of *only* (Brinton 1998), *I say* (Brinton 2005) and *I mean* (Brinton 2007) (see also Jucker 1997, 2002; Fischer 1998; Brinton 2006).

3.2 Speech acts

Speech acts are not easily amenable to historical investigations because the traditional research methods developed for present-day languages cannot be applied to historical data. Originally the concept was developed by philosophers who investigated the nature of speech acts on the basis of careful considerations of what it means to name a ship, to make a promise, to issue a command, to ask a question, or to greet somebody (Austin 1962; Searle 1969). Later, empirical methods, such as discourse completion tests and role-plays, were developed to investigate speech acts and their realizations by different groups of speakers (e.g. Blum-Kulka et al. 1989; Trosborg 1994). For obvious reasons, none of these methods can be applied to historical data.

More recently, corpus-based research methods have been improved and developed to such an extent that various avenues of investigations of historical speech act material have become available. It is, of course, possible to search for verbs denoting specific speech acts. Such speech act verbs are sometimes used performatively to carry out the speech act they denote. Kohnen (2008a), for instance, argues that in Old English explicit performatives were typically used to issue requests and commands as in (5):

(5) *Ic bidde eow þæt ȝe ȝymon eowra sylfra, swa eowere bec eow wissiað.* (Ælfric, *Letter to Wulfsige*, 26; *Helsinki Corpus*, Kohnen 2008a: 30)
 'I ask you to take care of yourselves, as your books teach you.'

The Old English verb *biddan* 'ask, bid' is here used performatively. By saying *Ic bidde eow* 'I ask you' the speaker carries out the speech act of asking or requesting (see in particular Kohnen 2000).

However, many verbs that describe a speech act are not normally used performatively. They are used to talk about the speech act they name. They may occur in narratives with an account that a particular speech act had been performed, or in negotiations when the precise speech act value of an utterance is being discussed.

(6) *If eny man wolde* **challenge** *a frere of Seint Frauncessis ordre and seue ... Frere, thou louest money as myche as othere men [...]* (c.1449 Pecock Repr.; Taavitsainen and Jucker 2007: 113)

'If any man were to challenge a friar of the order of St. Francis and to say ... "Friar, you love money as much as other men [...]"'

In (6) the speech act verb "challenge" is used together with an example of an utterance with this speech act value.

Many speech acts, perhaps most, are carried out without the relevant speech act verb. In order to locate relevant speech acts, the researcher has to rely on the philological method of actually reading the source texts. Jucker and Taavitsainen (2000) have used this method to describe insults in the history of English. But the method obviously precludes any statistical results. The findings can only be very selective based on the available research time.

Some speech acts show recurrent surface patterns. Deutschmann (2003), for instance, has shown that apologies in English are mostly formulaic. They can be traced with corpus-linguistic tools by searching for a small number of expressions that typically occur in apologies, such as *sorry*, *pardon*, and *excuse* together with related and expanded forms. The same method has recently been used to trace apologies (Jucker and Taavitsainen 2008b), promises (Valkonen 2008) and compliments (Jucker et al. 2008).

3.3 Terms of address

In the 13th century under the influence from French, English started to use the second person plural pronoun *ye* not only for two or more addressees but – under certain circumstances – also for one single addressee. Many Indo-European languages still have this distinction between two pronominal forms of address for a single addressee. On the basis of Latin *tu* and *vos*, the pronoun choices are usually abbreviated as T and V (Brown and Gilman 1960: 254). The conditions under which one pronoun or the other is chosen have been the object of extensive research in recent years (see, for instance, the volume by Taavitsainen and Jucker 2003). Brown and Gilman (1960) in their seminal article on the topic tried to find a common denominator for all languages with such a system. They argue that this common denominator is the semantics of power and solidarity. In medieval Europe, according to this theory, the power semantics accounted for a non-reciprocal use of T from the more powerful to the less powerful. The more powerful received V in return from the less powerful. Equals of the upper classes exchanged mutual V, while equals of the lower social classes exchanged mutual

T. The power semantics of medieval Europe has been replaced by the solidarity semantics in which mutual V signals distance and mutual T solidarity.

A significant body of research has shown that social conditions for the choice of T or V in specific situations are considerably more complex. Mazzon (2000), Honegger (2003), and Jucker (2006), for instance, have shown that Chaucer's system of pronoun choices is much more situationally governed than the usual present-day systems in languages such as German, French, or Italian. In the present-day forms of these languages, choices are more or less fixed for any given dyad of speakers, and a switch from mutual V to mutual T is a noticeable event, often accompanied by some kind of ritual (a switch from mutual T to mutual V, i.e. from informal to formal, would be very unusual). In Chaucer's English, the characters of his fictional work used a more complex system that was based not only on social status between the characters but also on the basis of situational dominance or subjugation. Such approaches have replaced the earlier accounts of Chaucer's use of personal pronouns by such scholars as Nathan (1959), Wilcockson (1980), and Burnley (1983), who tried to explain the choices largely on the basis of fixed social relationships.

By the time of Shakespeare, it does no longer seem possible to provide an account that explains individual pronoun choices. Researchers, therefore, generally focus on frequencies and on co-occurrence patterns of nominal and pronominal terms of address. U. Busse (2002, 2003), for instance, shows that titles of courtesy, such as *Your Grace, Your Ladyship, (my) liege*, or *sir*, are more likely to occur together with a V pronoun than any of the other categories of nominal terms of address, while terms of endearment, such as *bully, chuck, heart, joy*, or *love* are most likely to occur together with a T pronoun (see also Stein 2003; B. Busse 2006).

4 Discourse as dialogue

Discourse can be seen as a stretch of conversation or as a domain of language. In this section, I will use the term "dialogue" to refer to the former and the term "domain of discourse" for the latter. The terms "discourse" and "dialogue" imply an interaction between a speaker or writer and a recipient. Written texts, although there is no regular exchange of roles between speaker/writer and hearer, do have an addressee, even if the addressee is only a recipient and cannot actively contribute to the interaction. They are what Kilian (2005: 102) identifies as a "functional" dialogue.

Fritz (1995: 469) distinguishes three stages of what he calls "historical dialogue analysis". The first stage is characterized by analysis of the pragmatic structure and function of a historical dialogue in its social and historical context. The second stage is characterized by a contrastive comparison of earlier dialogue forms with later dialogue forms. The third and most advanced stage is characterized by an investigation of the evolution and dissemination of specific forms of dialogue.

In the first stage, the researcher can use the same conversation analytical or dialogue analytical tools that are employed in modern data in order to investigate older forms of dialogue. The analysis can either adopt a macro perspective or a micro perspective. Under the macro perspective, the researcher focuses on the structure of the dialogue under analysis. Levinson (1983) reserved the term "discourse analysis" for such macro analyses of dialogue structures. Under the micro perspective, the researcher focuses on individual pragmatic elements, such as greetings, address terms, discourse markers and so on; or on local structures, e.g. adjacency pairs, such as question-answer sequences. Levinson (1983) used the term "conversation analysis" for this type of investigation.

An analysis of individual pragmatic elements in individual dialogues of earlier periods coincides with the pragmatic research interests sketched out above. And indeed, a considerable amount of research has been published, e.g. on address terms in Chaucer's narratives or in Shakespeare's plays (see Section 3.3). But researchers have also adopted the larger perspective of looking at the inventory of pragmatic elements making up a specific type of historical dialogue. Watts (1999), for instance, investigates in detail two dialogues that were printed in 16th-century English language coursebooks for the benefit of learners of English as a foreign language.

However, in practice it is not always easy to distinguish between the different stages envisaged by Fritz. Jucker and Taavitsainen (2000), for instance, investigate the use of insults in the history of English. The aim is to show a development or an evolution from the earlier forms to the later forms, but at present all that seems to be possible is a contrastive analysis of selected examples at different periods in the history of English. It is not yet possible to trace a continuous evolution of specific speech acts, such as insults. Archer in various publications (e.g. Archer 2005, 2006, 2007) gives a detailed picture of Early Modern English courtroom dialogue and thus carries out research at the first stage of historical dialogue analysis, but she also compares these findings to the present-day courtroom, representing the second stage. And finally she also draws attention to developments within the period under investigation, and thus contributes to stage three of historical dialogue analysis. She focuses mainly on the question-answer sequences in the courtroom dialogues and uses these to pinpoint the (changing) discursive roles of the active participants in the English courtroom, i.e. the judges, lawyers, witnesses, and defendants.

Taavitsainen (1999) also investigates the evolution of a particular form of dialogue. She assesses medical dialogues in Late Middle and Early Modern English and traces the evolution of these dialogues between 1375 and 1750. She describes two traditions that are evident in Early English medical dialogues: the scholastic formula, based on the format of debates by Greek philosophers, and the mimetic dialogues, in which material is presented in fictional conversations between the author and the reader or between fictional characters. Taavitsainen shows how these traditions develop over the centuries and how, in the 18th century, medical dialogues merge with the new pamphlet tradition, in which social matters, such as health-care for the poor or polite conversations, are treated.

5 Discourse as a domain of communication

As pointed out in Section 1, the term "discourse" can also be used in a more general sense as the totality of linguistic practices that pertain to a particular field of knowledge or to a particular occupation. Such discourses consist not of utterances but of typical text types, characterized by specific lexical items, idiosyncratic syntax, and particular routinized patterns of interaction. In such a context, researchers also ask more general questions about the dissemination of information within groups of speakers. Three such domains of communication in particular have received a fair amount of scholarly attention for the Early Modern English period: courtroom discourse, the discourse of science and news discourse.

5.1 Courtroom discourse

A considerable amount of research has appeared on courtroom discourse in the Early Modern English period. The Early Modern English courtroom differed considerably from its modern equivalent. While modern courts presume a defendant to be innocent until proven guilty, the Early Modern courtroom expected the defendants to prove their innocence. Archer (2005: 85) demonstrates how this leads to a more active involvement on the part of the defendant. It was only in the later part of the Early Modern period that courtrooms introduced defence counsels who started to speak on behalf of the defendant.

Koch (1999: 410–411), in his analysis of excerpts of three early Romance court records, draws attention to the communicative complexity of such records. The records written by a court scribe and addressed to a future reader are legal documents with appropriate formality of expression especially in the ritualistic elements pertaining to the formalities of the proceedings. These parts of the court records are characterized by the "language of distance" as Koch calls it. Embedded in this formal document there is a transcription of the verbal interaction taking place in the courtroom between the judge, the witnesses, the defendants and the lawyers. These utterances, even if they are written down, are closer to spoken language, or the "language of immediacy". There may even be further embeddings, especially if the court cases dealt with libel, in which courtroom interactants report utterances that were spoken outside the courtroom. Such reported utterances are even closer to the language of immediacy.

In her work on the Early Modern English courtroom Archer (2005, 2006, 2007) draws a detailed picture of the strategies adopted by the judge, the lawyers, the defendants, and the witnesses. She concludes that the frequency of questions, their function and their interactional success depended on a number of sociopragmatic factors, such as the speech event, the position of the question, and the discursive roles of the speaker and the addressee as well as the date of the trial (2005: 281). Culpeper and Semino (2000) extend the scope of courtroom discourse. They use two types of data, learned treatises on the topic of witchcraft and courtroom witness depositions. In their analysis, they deal with speech act verbs, such as *to curse* and they show how such verbs could be used to reinterpret trivial arguments within a village community into a witchcraft event.

The witch trials that took place in 1692 in the Puritan village of Salem in the colony of Massachusetts have attracted a considerable amount of research into the discourse strategies adopted by the participants and the functional and structural properties of the trials as such. Kahlas-Tarkka and Rissanen (2007), for instance, investigated the discourse strategies of "successful" and "unsuccessful" defendants in the Salem witch trials, while Hiltunen and Peikola (2007) focus on the material evidence of these trials, i.e. the handwritten records and the printed editions. Their contribution demonstrates vividly how important it is not to forget the communicative role of the scribe who commits the spoken words in the courtroom to writing and thus makes it available for future generations (see also Doty and Hiltunen 2002; Hiltunen 2004; Doty 2007).

5.2 The discourse of science

In the late medieval world, the discourse of science was multilingual. The main language for written texts was Latin, but texts started to be translated into the vernacular and the Greco-Roman tradition provided a model for scientific writing in the vernacular.

In modern linguistics, "medical discourse" refers collectively to the communicative practices of the medical profession, both written and spoken. In the late medieval period, the medical profession consisted of heterogeneous groups of practitioners, including physicians, surgeons, barbers, midwives, itinerant specialists (e.g., bonesetters and oculists), herbalists, apothecaries, wisewomen, and others. They can be roughly divided into clerical and elite practitioners and tradespeople or ordinary practitioners; literacy was restricted mostly to the elite group (Taavitsainen 2006: 688).

Taavitsainen (2006) gives an overview of genres that were important for this discourse community. Compilations and commentaries of earlier studies were important for the dissemination of scholastic knowledge. Texts in question-and-answer format and pedagogical dialogues were also popular genres of scientific and medical writing that were adopted from Latin models into the vernacular. The volume edited by Taavitsainen and Pahta (2004) contains a range of detailed studies of medical and scientific writing in Late Medieval English. Mäkinen (2004), for instance, describes Middle English herbal recipes and recipes in manuals for medicinal plants and shows the textual traditions that link them together.

Valle (1999: vii) takes the view that "science has at least since the seventeenth century taken place within a knowledge-producing discourse community, and that this community will in some way be 'represented' in scientific texts, in forms which can be linguistically identified and studied". The totality of texts produced by this discourse community is, therefore, the discourse of science. In her study, Valle describes the discourse community of the Royal Society on the basis of a corpus of texts drawn from the *Philosophical Transaction*, spanning the three centuries from the beginning of publication in 1665 to 1965 (see also Valle 1997, 2006). Gotti (2006), too, deals with the discourse community of the Royal Society in London and illustrates some of the methods that were used by this community to spread the news about new discoveries and other scientific findings. Letters exchanged between scholars played an important role. They were not only exchanged between individuals, but they were frequently copied and passed on to new recipients. Some influential scholars at the centre of scientific networks regularly received, sent, and resent a large number of letters and thus had the role of clearing houses.

5.3 Early English news discourse

With the invention of the printing press it became possible to publish accounts of recent events and to disseminate them to a large audience. In the 16th and 17th centuries pamphlets and newsbooks were used for this purpose (Raymond 2003). The first newspapers in the modern sense appeared in the early 17th century, first on the continent but soon also in England (Brownlees 1999; Studer 2008). The first newspapers or corantos, as they were originally called, consisted mainly of dispatches from correspondents from important places throughout Europe. These letters were inserted into the newspaper in the order in which they arrived at the editorial office in London. There was no other structural principle. It took another century for the first daily newspapers to be published in the early 18th century. As Sommerville (1996) has pointed out, the revolutionary aspect of this kind of news discourse consisted in the fact that newspapers appeared in regular intervals, weekly at first, twice or three times a week later, and then daily. Thus, news was no longer reported in response to important events, but a certain amount of space had to be filled with news on a regular basis.

The early news discourse has attracted a fair amount of research recently not only in collections of articles, such as Ungerer (2000), Herring (2003), Raymond (2006) or Brownlees (2006) but also in monographs. Studer (2008), for instance, develops a larger picture of the development of news discourse on the basis of the Zurich English Newspaper Corpus (ZEN). He argues that news discourse is shaped by such external factors as the historical context and technological innovations. News discourse both adopted and adapted generic conventions; that is to say, it used existing genres, e.g. in the form of the letters from correspondents in the early newspapers, and it transformed and shaped them for its own needs.

6 Summary and outlook

It is not possible to draw a principled distinction between historical topics that are treated with pragmatic tools of investigation and those that are treated with discourse analytical tools. Traditionally, those approaches that focus on the interactional and dynamic aspects of language belong to pragmatics while those that focus on the structural aspects of dialogues, conversations or discourses belong to discourse analysis. The application of pragmatic and discourse analytical tools to historical data has uncovered a rich area of investigation and thrown new light on much familiar data.

But a lot still needs to be done. At present, three areas of research appear to be particularly promising. First, the research on the history of speech acts has only just started to attract more than just occasional research efforts. In the volume edited by Jucker and Taavitsainen (2008a) a number of researchers have joined forces to investigate a range of different speech acts in the history of English and to develop the necessary methodologies. Recent advances in corpus technology have made it increasingly possible to locate some speech acts automatically.

Second, the research of the evolution of forms of dialogue is still in its infancy. Kilian (2005) has presented an introduction into historical dialogue research, in which he develops a detailed typology of historical types of dialogues and some methodologies to investigate a broad range of such dialogues, i.e. dialogues in which speakers and addressees take turns in their roles. Culpeper and Kytö (2010: 2) ask: "what was the spoken face-to-face interaction of past periods like?" in a systematic way and approach this question from various angles. In particular they look at the structure of conversations, at what they call "pragmatic noise", i.e. pragmatic interjections or discourse markers, and social roles and gender in interaction.

And third, the evolution of domains of discourse appears to be a very promising field of research. The existing work on courtroom discourse, the discourse of science and news discourse needs to be continued, and other domains should be tackled. The discourse of religion, for instance, would be an obvious candidate because there is wealth of historical material available consisting of many different text types, such as sermons, prayers, treatises and saints' lives. The compilation at the University of Cologne of a *Corpus of English Religious Prose* is very likely to be a first significant step in this direction (see Kohnen 2007).

Thus it seems that the new corpora and advances in corpus linguistics have had and are having a considerable impact on historical pragmatics and historical discourse analysis. The cooperation between corpus linguists and historical pragmaticists/discourse analysts has only just started, but it promises considerable advances in our understanding of human interaction and communication from a historical perspective.

Acknowledgments: I thank Thomas Kohnen, Daniela Landert, and Elizabeth C. Traugott for valuable comments on a draft version of this paper. The usual disclaimers apply.

7 References

Archer, Dawn. 2005. *Questions and Answers in the English Courtroom (1640–1760)*. Amsterdam/Philadelphia: John Benjamins.
Archer, Dawn. 2006. (Re)Initiating strategies: Judges and defendants in Early Modern English courtrooms. *Journal of Historical Pragmatics* (Special Issue on Historical Courtroom Discourse, ed. by Barbara Kryk-Kastovsky) 7(2):181–211.
Archer, Dawn. 2007. Developing a more detailed picture of the English courtroom (1640–1760): Data and methodological issues facing historical pragmatics. In: Fitzmaurice and Taavitsainen (eds.), 185–217.
Austin, J. L. 1962. *How to Do Things With Words*. Oxford: Oxford University Press.

Biber, Douglas, Stig Johansson, Geoffrey Leech, Susan Conrad, and Edward Finegan. 1999. *Longman Grammar of Spoken and Written English*. London: Longman.
Blakemore, Diane. 1992. *Understanding Utterances. An Introduction to Pragmatics*. Oxford: Blackwell.
Blum-Kulka, Shoshana, Juliane House, and Gabriele Kasper (eds.). 1989. *Cross-Cultural Pragmatics: Requests and Apologies*. Norwood, NJ: Ablex.
Borgmeier, Raimund, Herbert Grabes, and Andreas H. Jucker (eds.). 1998. *Anglistentag 1997 Giessen. Proceedings*. Trier: Wissenschaftlicher Verlag.
Brinton, Laurel J. 1996. *Pragmatic Markers in English. Grammaticalization and Discourse Functions*. Berlin/New York: Mouton de Gruyter.
Brinton, Laurel J. 1998. "The flowers are lovely; only, they have no scent": The evolution of a pragmatic marker in English. In: Borgmeier, Grabes, and Jucker (eds.), 9–33.
Brinton, Laurel J. 2001. Historical discourse analysis. In: Deborah Schiffrin, Deborah Tannen, and Heidi E. Hamilton (eds.), *The Handbook of Discourse Analysis*, 138–160. Oxford: Blackwell.
Brinton, Laurel J. 2005. Processes underlying the development of pragmatic markers: The case of *(I) say*. In: Janne Skaffari, Matti Peikola, Ruth Carroll, Risto Hiltunen, and Brita Wårvik (eds.), *Opening Windows on Texts and Discourses of the Past*, 279–299. Amsterdam/Philadelphia: John Benjamins.
Brinton, Laurel J. 2006. Pathways in the development of pragmatic markers in English. In: Ans van Kemenade and Bettelou Los (eds.), *The Handbook of the History of English*, 307–334. Oxford: Blackwell.
Brinton, Laurel J. 2007. The development of *I mean*: Implications for the study of historical pragmatics. In: Fitzmaurice and Taavitsainen (eds.), 37–79.
Brown, Roger and Albert Gilman. 1960. The pronouns of power and solidarity. In: Thomas A. Sebeok (ed.), *Style in Language*, 253–276. Cambridge, MA: MIT Press.
Brownlees, Nicholas. 1999. *Corantos and Newsbooks: Language and Discourse in the First English Newspapers (1620–1641)*. Pisa: Edizioni ETS.
Brownlees, Nicholas (ed.). 2006. *News Discourse in Early Modern Britain. Selected Papers of CHINED 2004*. Bern: Peter Lang.
Burnley, David. 1983. *A Guide to Chaucer's Language*. London: Macmillan.
Busse, Beatrix. 2006. *Vocative Constructions in the Language of Shakespeare*. Amsterdam/Philadelphia: John Benjamins.
Busse, Ulrich. 2002. *Linguistic Variation in the Shakespeare Corpus. Morpho-Syntactic Variability of Second Person Pronouns*. Amsterdam/Philadelphia: John Benjamins.
Busse, Ulrich. 2003. The co-occurrence of nominal and pronominal address forms in the Shakespeare corpus: Who says *thou* or *you* to whom? In: Taavitsainen and Jucker (eds.), 193–221.
Craun, Edwin D. 1997. *Lies, Slander, and Obscenity in Medieval English Literature. Pastoral Rhetoric and the Deviant Speaker*. Cambridge: Cambridge University Press.
Cruse, Alan. 2000. *Meaning in Language. An Introduction to Semantics and Pragmatics*. Oxford: Oxford University Press.
Culpeper, Jonathan and Merja Kytö. 2010. *Early Modern English Dialogues: Spoken Interaction as Writing*. Cambridge: Cambridge University Press.
Culpeper, Jonathan and Elena Semino. 2000. Constructing witches and spells: Speech acts and activity types in Early Modern England. *Journal of Historical Pragmatics* 1(1): 97–116.
Deutschmann, Mats. 2003. *Apologising in British English*. Umeå: Institutionen för moderna språk, Umeå University.

Doty, Kathleen L. 2007. Telling tales: The role of scribes in constructing the discourse of the Salem witchcraft trials. *Journal of Historical Pragmatics* 8(1): 25–41.

Doty, Kathleen and Risto Hiltunen. 2002. "I will tell, I will tell": Confessional patterns in the Salem witch trials, 1692. *Journal of Historical Pragmatics* 3(2): 299–336.

Fischer, Andreas. 1998. *Marry*. From religious invocation to discourse marker. In: Borgmeier, Grabes, and Jucker (eds.), 35–46.

Fitzmaurice, Susan M. and Irma Taavitsainen (eds.). 2007. *Methodological Issues in Historical Pragmatics*. Berlin/New York: Mouton de Gruyter.

Fritz, Gerd. 1995. Topics in the history of dialogue forms. In: Jucker (ed.), 469–498.

Geis, Michael and Arnold M. Zwicky. 1971. On invited inferences. *Linguistic Inquiry* 2: 561–566.

Gotti, Maurizio. 2006. Disseminating Early Modern science: Specialized news discourse in the Philosophical Transactions. In: Brownlees (ed.), 41–70.

Herring, Susan C. 2003. Media and language change: Introduction. *Journal of Historical Pragmatics* (Special Issue on Media and Language Change, ed. by Susan C. Herring) 4(1): 1–17.

Hiltunen, Risto. 2004. Salem, 1692: A case of courtroom discourse in a historical perspective. In: Risto Hiltunen and Shinichiro Watanabe (eds.), *Approaches to Style and Discourse in English*, 3–26. Osaka: Osaka University Press.

Hiltunen, Risto. 2006. "Eala, geferan and gode wyrhtan": On interjections in Old English. In: John Walmsley (ed.), *Inside Old English: Essays in Honour of Bruce Mitchell*, 91–116. Oxford: Balckwell.

Hiltunen, Risto and Matti Peikola. 2007. Trial discourse and manuscript context: Scribal profiles in the Salem witchcraft records. *Journal of Historical Pragmatics* 8(1): 43–68.

Honegger, Thomas. 2003. "And if ye wol nat so, my lady sweete, thanne preye I thee, [...]": Forms of address in Chaucer's Knight's Tale. In: Taavitsainen and Jucker (eds.), 61–84.

Jacobsson, Mattias. 2002. *Thank you* and *thanks* in Early Modern English. *ICAME Journal* 26: 63–80.

Jucker, Andreas H. (ed.). 1995. *Historical Pragmatics. Pragmatic Developments in the History of English*. Amsterdam/Philadelphia: John Benjamins.

Jucker, Andreas H. 1997. The discourse marker *well* in the history of English. *English Language and Linguistics* 1(1): 91–110.

Jucker, Andreas H. 2002. Discourse markers in Early Modern English. In: Richard Watts and Peter Trudgill (eds.), *Alternative Histories of English*, 210–230. London/New York: Routledge.

Jucker, Andreas H. 2006. "Thou art so loothly and so oold also": The use of *ye* and *thou* in Chaucer's *Canterbury Tales*. *Anglistik* 17(2): 57–72.

Jucker, Andreas H., Gerd Fritz, and Franz Lebsanft (eds.). 1999. *Historical Dialogue Analysis*. Amsterdam/Philadelphia: John Benjamins.

Jucker, Andreas H., Gerold Schneider, Irma Taavitsainen, and Barb Breustedt. 2008. Fishing for compliments: Precision and recall in corpus-linguistic compliment research. In: Jucker and Taavitsainen (eds.), 273–294.

Jucker, Andreas H. and Irma Taavitsainen. 2000. Diachronic speech act analysis: Insults from flyting to flaming. *Journal of Historical Pragmatics* 1(1): 67–95.

Jucker, Andreas H. and Irma Taavitsainen (eds.). 2008a. *Speech Acts in the History of English*. Amsterdam/Philadelphia: John Benjamins.

Jucker, Andreas H. and Irma Taavitsainen. 2008b. Apologies in the history of English: Routinized and lexicalized expressions of responsibility and regret. In: Jucker and Taavitsainen (eds.), 229–244.

Kahlas-Tarkka, Leena and Matti Rissanen. 2007. The sullen and the talkative: Discourse strategies in the Salem examinations. *Journal of Historical Pragmatics* 8(1): 1–24.
Keller, Rudi. 1994. *On Language Change. The Invisible Hand in Language*. London: Routledge.
Kilian, Jörg. 2005. *Historische Dialoganalyse*. Tübingen: Niemeyer.
Koch, Peter. 1999. Court records and cartoons: Reflections of spontaneous dialogue in Early Romance texts. In: Jucker, Fritz, and Lebsanft (eds.), 399–429.
Kohnen, Thomas. 2000. Explicit performatives in Old English: A corpus-based study of directives. *Journal of Historical Pragmatics* 1(2): 301–321.
Kohnen, Thomas. 2007. From Helsinki through the centuries: The design and development of English diachronic corpora. In: Päivi Pahta, Irma Taavitsainen, Terttu Nevalainen, and Jukka Tyrkkö (eds.), *Studies in Variation, Contacts and Change in English,* Vol. 2. http://www.helsinki.fi/varieng/series/volumes/02/kohnen/; last accessed 27 June 2017.
Kohnen, Thomas. 2008a. Directives in Old English: Beyond politeness? In: Jucker and Taavitsainen (eds.), 27–44.
Kohnen, Thomas. 2008b. Tracing directives through text and time: Towards a methodology of a corpus-based diachronic speech-act analysis. In: Jucker and Taavitsainen (eds.), 295–310.
Levinson, Stephen C. 1983. *Pragmatics*. Cambridge: Cambridge University Press.
Mäkinen, Martti. 2004. Herbal recipes and recipes in herbals: Intertextuality in early English medical writing. In: Taavitsainen and Pahta (eds.), 144–173.
Mazzon, Gabriella. 2000. Social relations and forms of address in the *Canterbury Tales*. In: Dieter Kastovsky and Arthur Mettinger (eds.), *The History of English in a Social Context. A Contribution to Historical Sociolinguistics*, 135–168. Berlin/New York: Mouton de Gruyter.
Mey, Jacob L. 1998. Pragmatics. In: Jacob L. Mey (ed.), *Concise Encyclopedia of Pragmatics*, 716–737. Amsterdam: Elsevier.
Nathan, N. 1959. Pronouns of address in the *Canterbury Tales. Mediaeval Studies* xxi: 193–201.
Person, Raymond R., Jr. 2009. Oh in Shakespeare: A conversation analytic approach. *Journal of Historical Pragmatics* 10(1): 84–107.
Raymond, Joad (ed.). 2006. *News Networks in Seventeenth Century Britain and Europe*. London: Routledge.
Raymond, Joad. 2003. *Pamphlets and Pamphleteering in Early Modern Britain*. Cambridge: Cambridge University Press.
Sommerville, John. 1996. *The News Revolution in England. Cultural Dynamics of Daily Information*. New York/Oxford: Oxford University Press.
Sperber, Dan, and Ira A. Noveck. 2004. Introduction. In: Ira A. Noveck and Dan Sperber (eds.), *Experimental Pragmatics*, 1–22. Houndmills: Palgrave Macmillan.
Stein, Dieter. 2003. Pronominal usage in Shakespeare: Between sociolinguistics and conversational analysis. In: Taavitsainen and Jucker (eds.), 251–307.
Studer, Patrick. 2008. *Historical Corpus Stylistics. Media, Technology and Change*. London: Continuum.
Taavitsainen, Irma. 1995. Interjections in Early Modern English: From imitation of spoken to conventions of written language. In: Jucker (ed.) 439–465.
Taavitsainen, Irma. 1999. Dialogues in Late Medieval and Early Modern English medical writing. In: Jucker, Fritz, and Lebsanft (eds.), 243–268.
Taavitsainen, Irma. 2006. Medical discourse: Early genres, 14th and 15th centuries. In: Keith Brown (ed.), *Encyclopedia of Language and Linguistics*, 2nd edn., 688–694. Oxford: Elsevier.

Taavitsainen, Irma and Andreas H. Jucker (eds.). 2003. *Diachronic Perspectives on Address Term Systems*. Amsterdam/Philadelphia: John Benjamins.

Taavitsainen, Irma and Andreas H. Jucker. 2007. Speech act verbs and speech acts in the history of English. In: Susan M. Fitzmaurice and Irma Taavitsainen (eds.), *Methods in Historical Pragmatics*, 107–138. Berlin: Mouton de Gruyter.

Taavitsainen, Irma and Päivi Pahta (eds.). 2004. *Medical and Scientific Writing in Late Medieval English*. Cambridge: Cambridge University Press.

Traugott, Elizabeth Closs. 2004. Historical pragmatics. In: Laurence R. Horn and Gregory Ward (eds.), *The Handbook of Pragmatics*, 538–561. Oxford: Blackwell.

Traugott, Elizabeth Closs and Richard B. Dasher. 2005. *Regularity in Semantic Change*. Cambridge: Cambridge University Press.

Trosborg, Anna. 1994. *Interlanguage Pragmatics. Requests, Complaints and Apologies*. Berlin/New York: Mouton de Gruyter.

Ungerer, Friedrich (ed.). 2000. *English Media Texts Past and Present*. Amsterdam/Philadelphia: John Benjamins.

Valkonen, Petteri. 2008. Showing a little promise: Identifying and retrieving explicit illocutionary acts from a corpus of written prose. In: Jucker and Taavitsainen (eds.), 247–272.

Valle, Ellen. 1997. A scientific community and its texts: A historical discourse study. In: Britt-Louise Gunnarsson, Per Linell, and Bengt Nordberg (eds.). *The Construction of Professional Discourse*, 76–98. London/New York: Longman.

Valle, Ellen. 1999. *A Collective Intelligence. The Life Sciences in the Royal Society as a Scientific Discourse Community, 1665–1965*. Turku: University of Turku.

Valle, Ellen. 2006. Reporting the doings of the curious: Authors and editors in the *Philosophical Transactions* of the Royal Society of London. In: Brownlees (ed.), 71–90.

Verschueren, Jef. 1987. The pragmatic perspective. In: Marcella Bertuccelli-Papi and Jef Verschueren (eds.), *The Pragmatic Perspective: Selected Papers from the 1985 International Pragmatics Conference*, 3–8. Amsterdam/Philadelphia: John Benjamins.

Verschueren, Jef. 1999. *Understanding Pragmatics*. London: Arnold.

Watts, Richard J. 1999. *Refugiate in a strange countrey*: Learning English through dialogues in the 16th century. In: Jucker, Fritz, and Lebsanft (eds.), 215–241.

Wilcockson, Colin. 1980. *Thou* and *ye* in Chaucer's *Clerk's Tale*. *The Use of English* 31(3): 37–43.

Carole Hough
Chapter 10: Onomastics

1 Introduction —— 185
2 Toponyms —— 186
3 Anthroponyms —— 191
4 Transmission of names —— 195
5 Summary —— 197
6 References —— 197

Abstract: Names provide evidence for language history in two main respects: firstly, as regards lexical and semantic content when first coined; and secondly, as regards phonological and morphological development over the course of time. In neither respect is there widespread agreement as to the extent to which evidence from names can be extrapolated to other areas of language. On the one hand, both place-names and personal names testify to areas of vocabulary and registers of language sparsely represented in other sources; on the other, it is sometimes unclear whether these reflect ordinary language or a specialized onomastic usage. Factors pertaining to the formation and transmission of names are in some respects unique, and will be outlined in this chapter alongside a discussion of the main types of linguistic evidence preserved in the onomasticon.

1 Introduction

Onomastics is the study of names, its two main branches being toponymy (the study of place-names) and anthroponymy (the study of people's names). Traditionally regarded as a sub-class of nouns having reference but no sense, names occupy a special position within language in that they can be used without understanding of semantic content. Partly for this reason, they tend to have a high survival rate, outlasting changes and developments in the lexicon, and easily being taken over by new groups of speakers in situations of language contact. Since most names originate as descriptive phrases, they preserve evidence for early lexis, often within areas of vocabulary sparsely represented in other sources. Many place-names,

Carole Hough: Glasgow (UK)

and some surnames, are still associated with their place of origin, so the data also contribute to the identification of dialectal isoglosses. Moreover, since names are generally coined in speech rather than in writing, they testify to a colloquial register of language as opposed to the more formal registers characteristic of documentary records and literary texts. Much research has been directed towards establishing the etymologies of names whose origins are no longer transparent, using a standard methodology whereby a comprehensive collection of early spellings is assembled for each name in order to trace its historical development. These spellings themselves can then be used to reveal morphological and phonological changes over the course of time, often illustrating trends in non-onomastic as well as onomastic language. The relationship between the two is not always straightforward, however, since the factors pertaining to the formation and transmission of names are in some respects unique. This chapter will discuss the main types of linguistic evidence preserved in names of various kinds, and will also consider the relevance of this evidence to other areas of language.

2 Toponyms

2.1 The origins of place-names

The names of most villages, towns and cities in England were coined during the Anglo-Saxon period from Old English or (in areas of Scandinavian settlement) Old Norse. Others derive from the Celtic languages more strongly represented in Scotland, Wales and Ireland, while survivals from pre-Celtic linguistic strata are mainly found in the names of large topographical features. The names of major rivers are among the most ancient toponyms, and parallels between British and European river-names appear to reflect a system of hydronymy in use on the continent and brought to Britain by pre-Celtic immigrants. These river-names preserve evidence for the earliest form of language spoken in the British Isles, although it remains controversial whether this language was Indo-European – the majority view – or non-Indo-European.

The names of smaller features tend to be later, dating from the medieval or early modern periods, and the same applies to the field-names given to units of cultivated land. Names for new urban developments continue to be created up to the present day, with street-names still being coined in large numbers. Nevertheless, even street-names can be more than a thousand years old in the medieval parts of cities such as Derby, London, Nottingham and York.

Research into the origins of English place-names has been carried out systematically on a county-by-county basis since the 1920s by the English Place-Name

Society (1924–), and is published in a series of annual volumes known collectively as the English Place-Name Survey (EPNS). Whereas the Survey initially focused on names of historical significance such as medieval settlement-names, a growing recognition of the linguistic interest of the material led to coverage being expanded to include other types of names and those dating from later periods. This means that early volumes are not only less up-to-date than those currently being produced, but more limited in scope. Supplementary publications, including a field-name series, aim to redress the balance; and regional studies and dictionaries are also underway to provide coverage of the major names of all parts of England in advance of completion of the full Survey. Volumes 25–26 of the EPNS series comprise a dictionary of place-name terminology, a successor to which is currently in progress (Parsons, Styles, and Hough 1997–), and EPNS collections also form the basis for Field's (1972) dictionary of field-names.

2.2 The structure of place-names

Most English settlement-names are made up of one or (more usually) two elements, identical or closely related to vocabulary words. Most represent a description of a landscape feature or man-made structure, as with the single element or "simplex" names Dean or Deane (OE *denu* 'main valley'), Ford (OE *ford* 'ford, river-crossing'), Ham (OE *hamm* 'hemmed-in land'), Hope (OE *hop* 'small enclosed valley'), Lea or Leigh (OE *lēah* 'wood, clearing'), Stoke (OE *stoc* 'outlying farmstead'), Wick (OE *wīc* 'specialized farm') and Worth (OE *worth* 'enclosure'). The corpus is highly repetitive, and each of the above examples occurs several times in different parts of England. Compound names provide a more precise description by including information on such aspects as appearance, ownership, usage, flora, or fauna. Examples include Abbotsley 'Ealdbeald's clearing', Bagley 'badger clearing', Bradford 'broad ford', Bulwick 'bull farm' and Cotterstock 'dairy farm'. Here, as in most non-Celtic place-names, the descriptive element or "specific" precedes the defining element or "generic". Whereas the generic usually identifies a topographical feature or habitation, specifics have a much wider range, including personal names, older place-names, descriptive adjectives, animal, bird, and plant names, and occupational terms. Some names also contain an additional element generally known as an "affix" (although the term "distinguisher" might be more accurate), as with Stoke Mandeville, from the Mandeville family, and Stoke on Trent, from its position on the River Trent.

In field-names and street-names, the generic is often a term for a field or street, with specifics again being more varied. In London, Chancery Lane refers to the chancellor's office (ME *chauncerie*), Mincing Lane to nuns (OE *myncen*), and

Sherborne Lane to a privy (ME *shite-burgh*), while Mansfield Hill and Markfield Road preserve earlier field-names meaning 'common field' (OE *(ge)mæne*) and 'boundary field' (OE *mearc*) respectively (Mills 2010). However, non-literal formations are also common. Bare Arse, Labour in Vain, and Small Gains are recurrent field-names referring to unproductive land; irony may be suspected in some of the many fields called Paradise; the ubiquitous Hundred Acres almost invariably designates a very small field; and at least one Mount Pleasant refers to a refuse tip. A tendency for landscape features to receive metaphorical names is illustrated by the recurrent Cow and Calf Rocks (large and small), and by various hill-names from the Scandinavian-derived *carline* 'old woman', including Carling Howe, Carling Knott and Fishcarling Head.

2.3 The language of place-names

Many place-names are coined from terms also on record elsewhere, while others contain elements that are otherwise unknown, and for which the only evidence is the toponymicon. The repetitive nature of the corpus makes it possible to assemble a collection of names containing the same term in order to analyze its range of use. This applies particularly to generics. The most common element in English settlement-names, OE *tūn* 'farmstead, village', occurs in hundreds of names, and some of those mentioned above in more than a hundred. Many topographical generics can still be compared directly with the features described, and this has led to one of the main insights of place-name scholarship in recent years. The examination of places named from the same generic has identified subtle distinctions between the use of terms previously thought to be synonyms, revealing that the Anglo-Saxons had a more extensive and nuanced vocabulary for landscape features than has survived into later stages of English (Gelling and Cole 2000). Definitions given in Section 2.2 are summary only, and do not fully reflect the distinction between, for instance, OE *denu*, the standard term for a main valley, and OE *hop*, a small and often remote enclosed valley. Both differ from OE *cumb* 'short, broad valley with three fairly steep sides', OE *slæd* 'flat-bottomed valley', OE *halh* 'nook' (often referring to a less firmly-shaped valley than *cumb* or *denu*), and so on. Similarly precise usages have been established for other areas of topographical lexis, including terms unattested outside the place-name corpus such as OE **hlenc* 'extensive hill-slope' and OE **ofer* 'flat-topped ridge with a convex shoulder'. Evidence from other Germanic languages may assist interpretation. A meaning of OE *halh* as 'slightly raised ground in marsh' is suggested by some place-name occurrences and supported by a similar use of the North Frisian cognate.

Specifics represent a wider cross-section of open class vocabulary than generics, and contain a higher proportion of unattested words. Again the profile of use throws light on meaning. The specific of Bagley is an unattested OE *bagga. The range of generics with which it combines, including references to natural habitat and snares, as in Bag Hill (OE *hyll* 'hill'), Bagshot (OE *scēat* 'projecting land') and Bawdrip (OE *træppe* 'trap'), suggests a wild animal such as the badger, and this is supported by Germanic cognates. The specific of Grazeley (OE *sol* 'wallowing-place'), Gresty (OE *stīg* 'path') and Greywell (OE *wella* 'spring, stream') is a substantive use of OE *grǣg* 'grey (animal)' thought to refer to the wolf, as does an OE *wearg in place-names such as Warnborough and Wreighburn (both OE *burna* 'stream').

Other words are attested in the place-name corpus earlier than in literary sources. OE *bagga may be the root of PDE *badger*, although this is uncertain. The specific of Bulwick is an OE *bula, the etymon of PDE *bull*, on independent record only from c.1200. Carling Howe is first recorded c.1170, whereas the earliest occurrence of *carline* 'old woman' recorded in the OED dates from c.1375. The compound *fish-carline 'fish-wife', attested in Fishcarling Head, is otherwise unknown.

In some instances, place-names support other types of evidence for word meanings. The *Dictionary of Old English* (Cameron et al. 2016) tentatively suggests a meaning "'churn, or even 'dairy'" for three gloss occurrences of OE *corþer*, and this is confirmed by a toponymic use as the specific of Cotterstock (OE *stoc* 'farm'). A substantive use of OE *brūn* 'brown' recorded as a nonce occurrence within a riddle appears to refer to a brown animal, possibly the pig, and again this is confirmed by its use in place-names such as Broomden (OE *denn* 'woodland pasture, especially for swine') and Brownwich (OE *wīc* 'specialized farm').

Certain types of words, including animal names, bird names, and topographical terms, are particularly well represented in place-names. So too are plant names (Hough 2003). The toponymic corpus considerably extends our knowledge of these areas of lexis, as of the colloquial range of vocabulary. Several of the above examples may represent demotic terms as opposed to the more formal registers of language represented in written sources.

However, it is unclear to what extent the place-name corpus as a whole is representative of ordinary vocabulary. Some elements, particularly generics, are thought to belong to an onomastic register common to the northwest Germanic languages, which may have diverged from ordinary lexis at an early date (Nicolaisen 1995). Parallels between OE *halh* and its North Frisian cognate are mentioned above, and there are similar instances where pairs of generics in the West and North Germanic toponymica have more in common with each other than with the corresponding lexical terms. OE *hām* 'homestead, estate', one of the earliest habitative generics in English place-names, is cognate with ON *heimr*, and this may help to explain why it appears to have been in use as a place-name forming element earlier than as a common noun. Other generics also have a different chronological or geographical profile from their lexical counterparts, while the fact that some elements (e.g. OE *lēah*) occur as generics only, apparently not being available for use as specifics, further supports the theory that they were not selected freely from the lexicon. It may therefore be appropriate to regard such elements as cognate with, rather than identical to, vocabulary items, deriving from a common ancestor but developing along different lines. When they began to develop separately is uncertain, but evidence from river-names suggests that a so-called "onomastic dialect" may already have emerged early in the history of Indo-European (Kitson 1996).

Specifics may be closer to ordinary lexis, but again develop uses in place-names which are not necessarily the same as those in non-onomastic language. Analogy is common in place-name formation, and this limits the value of toponymic evidence for word geography as well as for historical semantics. The place-name distribution of *carline*, for instance, suggests a wider currency in northern dialects of Middle English than is supported by lexical evidence, extending to the north-west of England outside the Danelaw, but it is possible that this is due to the conventional use of the term for landscape features. As Scott (2016: 488) observes, "the comparison of dialect maps with maps of place-name elements frequently reveals a lack of parallelism between the distribution patterns of lexical elements and their onomastic counterparts". Another factor is the high level of repetition within the name stock, which suggests that even some compounds may have been drawn from an existing pool. Ekwall (1960) includes 40 occurrences of Burton from OE *burh-tūn* 'settlement by a fortification', 29 of Charlton from OE *cēorla-tūn* 'settlement of freemen', and 20 of Easton from OE *ēast-tūn* 'east settlement', and it is unlikely that they were coined afresh on each occasion.

Field-names and street-names preserve much vocabulary from the medieval and later periods, and comprise the bulk of the evidence for Middle English terms attested uniquely or earliest in place-names (Hough 2002). Street-names are a particularly rich source of occupational terms. Birchin Lane in London, recorded from the 12th century, derives from an unattested ME **berdcherver* 'beard-cutter, barber'; Felter Lane in York, recorded from the 13th century, contains the term *felter* 'felt-maker' attested in the OED only from 1605; and Fletcher Gate in Nottingham, recorded in 1335 as *Flesshewergate*, is the earliest occurrence cited by the OED of the obsolete term *flesh-hewer* 'butcher'. Again there is much repetition within the corpus. Some names are transferred directly from one place to another (e.g. Piccadilly, now found in Manchester and York as well as London), while some are coined by analogy with others. Street-names in -*gate* are common in areas of urban settlement within the former Danelaw, where they often derive from ON *gata* 'street'; but in other instances they have simply been modelled on the original Viking names (Fellows-Jensen 2007). They cannot therefore be used as evidence for the currency of the term *gata* itself, nor for Scandinavian influence on the language.

Nonetheless, microtoponyms make an important contribution to the study of Old and Middle English dialectology by offering a large quantity of data for analysis. On a national scale, they facilitate the mapping of synonyms, an approach taken in Kitson's (1995) investigation of Old English dialect isoglosses, and in studies of the distribution of complementary terms such as *whin*, *gorse*, and *furze* (e.g. Cameron 2008). On a regional scale, they reflect a mix of languages more accurately than the smaller number of settlement names. This has been exploited in studies using the ratio between field-name elements of Old English and Old Norse origin to measure the extent of Scandinavian impact on local dialect (e.g. Cameron 1996, Watts 2002, Parsons 2006).

3 Anthroponyms

3.1 Personal names

Like place-names, Anglo-Saxon personal names are made up of one or (more usually) two elements drawn from a corpus corresponding closely to a subset of the lexicon. Animal names, abstract nouns, and descriptive adjectives are particularly well represented, as is the semantic field of warfare. Masculine and feminine names are formed along parallel lines, with the grammatical gender of the second element or "deuterotheme" often coinciding with the gender of the person. Examples include Æthelgar 'noble-spear', Guthfrith 'battle-peace', and Wulfstan 'wolf-stone' (all masculine), Æthelflæd 'noble-beauty', Æthelthryth 'noble-strength', and Wulfgifu 'wolf-gift' (all feminine). These and other names do not make literal sense, but may have signalled family relationships. Members of a kin group characteristically have names with alliterating (sometimes identical) first elements or "protothemes", while the deuterotheme of a parent's name may be passed on to children of the same sex.

The naming system goes back to Common Germanic. Links have been identified with the vocabulary of heroic poetry, and here even more than with place-names there is reason to regard name elements as cognate with, rather than identical to, their lexical counterparts. Whereas most place-names were literally descriptive of their referents in Anglo-Saxon England, personal names clearly were not, and this lack of sense suggests that elements were drawn from an anthroponymicon rather than from the lexicon. The impression of an older system reflected but no longer motivated in the Anglo-Saxon naming tradition is strengthened by instances where the correlation between natural and grammatical gender is not consistently maintained. Elements corresponding to feminine nouns such as OE *mund* 'protection' and OE *nōth* 'boldness' form masculine names (e.g. Byrhtnoth 'bright-boldness', Sigemund 'victory-protection'), as do elements corresponding to neuter nouns such as OE *cild* 'young person' (e.g. Leofcild 'dear-child') and to adjectives such as OE *beald* 'bold' and OE *beorht* 'bright' (e.g. Æthelbeald 'noble-bold', Ealdbeorht 'old-bright'). Although some elements function both as protothemes and as deuterothemes, others appear to be restricted to one position only, and this lack of flexibility – together with the fact that not all vocabulary words appear to have been available for use in coining names – again points to some fossilization of the system. This means that where a name element is unattested in literary sources from the Anglo-Saxon period, as with *flæd*, whose meaning is reconstructed from Germanic cognates as "elegance or daintiness as of a courtly lady" (Kitson 2002: 97), it cannot be assumed that it was ever in use as a lexical item in Old English.

Anglo-Saxon personal names were largely replaced by Continental Germanic and Biblical names after the Norman Conquest, and are sparsely represented in the present-day name stock. Although personal names have occasionally been coined from vocabulary words, as with the "virtue" names associated with the Puritan movement in post-Reformation England (e.g. Hope, Joy, Patience), and others referring to precious stones, plants, and the like (e.g. Ruby, Heather, Holly), the vast majority of names in current use are of Biblical or classical origin, and even those that remain semantically transparent are generally used without reference to etymological meaning. Recent research has emphasized the importance of social and cultural factors in present-day and early modern name giving, with linguistic origin being a lesser consideration.

3.2 Bynames

Prior to the evolution of surnames, bynames were used to differentiate between people with the same personal name. Already in use in Anglo-Saxon England, they became much more common during the early Middle English period, partly because of the dwindling number of baptismal names in general use. By the late 13th century, most personal names were routinely qualified by a byname.

The four main categories of bynames are local, familial, occupational, and characteristic. Examples from Clark's (1983) study of King's Lynn bynames are *atte Ling* 'beside the heather' (local), *Lellesmai* 'Lelle's kinsman' (familial), *Le Blekestere* 'the bleacher' (occupational) and *Le Longe* 'the tall' (characteristic). Bynames differ from the other types of names discussed above in being literally descriptive, and drawn freely from the lexicon. Despite having much in common with surnames, they were not hereditary (nor shared with siblings), and hence did not lose their lexical meaning. Because of this, they can be taken to represent contemporary language rather than fossilized forms. Nonetheless, they may be difficult to interpret. Bynames such as *Ioie* 'joy' and *Trouthe* 'truth' may be understood literally or ironically, and Clark discusses ambiguities surrounding others such as *Baril* 'barrel' and *Peper* 'pepper', which may be occupational referring to a barrel-maker and spicer, or characteristic referring to corpulence and hot temper.

Like place-names, bynames preserve a number of words unattested elsewhere or on record only from a later date. Tengvik's seminal study of Old English bynames identifies 58 antedated words (Tengvik 1938: 24–26), and others have since been added. Some are animal- or bird-names used as characteristic bynames. Otherwise unknown terms include OE **gor-pyttel* 'dung-hawk', recorded as the byname of *Gotselin Gorpittel* (c.1100–1130). Occupational bynames are an important source of Middle English occupational terms, and several of the King's Lynn bynames either antedate or are close to antedating the earliest documentation in literary sources. These include *Oylman* (a worker at the town's oil-mills) and *Habertasker* 'haberdasher'. Previously unrecorded occupational terms from the same corpus include **candelwif* and **chesewoman*, referring to women involved in the candle- and cheese-making industries. Topographical terms are preserved in local bynames, again often providing antedatings (e.g. Carlsson 1989: 146–147). The languages represented in bynames also make it possible to trace linguistic influences on local dialect. *Le Blekestere* is based on a Scandinavian loanword, while trading links with France are reflected in the definite article and in French forms such as *Baril*.

3.3 Surnames

Like bynames, surnames evolved to differentiate between people with the same personal name; but unlike bynames, they were passed on from one generation to the next, functioning as markers of relationship rather than as descriptions of individuals. Surnames began to come into use in England during the late 11th century, partly as a result of changes in society following the Norman Conquest, but the system was not fully established until about 1400. The main types of surnames correspond to the main types of bynames: local, familial, occupational, and characteristic. The earliest were local surnames held by landowning families, some imported from Normandy and others taken from the names of estates in England. The use of surnames gradually spread down the social scale, with occupational surnames associated particularly with skilled craftsmen, and characteristic surnames with the lower classes.

Local surnames – those referring to place of origin, or to ownership of land – can themselves be divided into two categories: locative and topographical. Locative surnames derive from place-names, topographical surnames from lexical words. Thus the surname Glasgow is locative, from the Scottish city, while the surname Hough is topographical, from OE *hōh* 'spur of land'. The latter type can reflect regional variation in morphology as well as lexis. Examples such as Bridger and Bridgeman 'dweller by the bridge' and Weller and Wellman 'dweller by the stream' show the morphemes *-er* and *-man* suffixed to a topographical term to indicate place of residence. This type of surname is common in central and southern England, but rare in the north, where the morphemes do not seem to have been productive in this sense.

Familial surnames, or surnames of relationship, most commonly derive from parents' forenames. Those from a father's name are known as "patronymics"; those from a mother's name as "metronymics". The earliest derive from unaffixed personal names, whether from Old English, as with Godwin, or from the continental name stock introduced to England after the Conquest, as with Allen, Maude, and Thomas. Surnames with the suffix *-son* are slightly later and often formed from shortened, or hypochoristic, forms of personal names, as with Dobson and Robson (Robert), Ibbotson and Ibson (Isabel), and Wilson and Wilkinson (William). Again there are regional variations. Most surnames in *-son* originated in the north and north midlands of England, and in southern Scotland. In southern and central England, the suffix *-s* was more common, as in Andrews, Roberts and Williams.

Occupational surnames reflect lexical variation in different areas (McKinley 1990: 143–147). Surnames relating to the same trade within the cloth industry are Fuller (south and south-east), Tucker (south-west), and Walker (north); while Barker (north) and Tanner (south) are synonyms. This group is also a primary source of information on Middle English occupational terms. Thuresson (1950) deals with about 850 words, of which 271 were not recorded in the OED, and Fransson (1935) also provides a number of new words and predatings.

Some surnames from characteristics are based on English or French phrases which appear to have had a wide currency in Middle English despite being rarely if at all recorded elsewhere. Examples such as Fairwether, Goodall 'good ale', Makehate 'make joy', Parlebien 'well spoken', Passavaunt 'go before', Proudfoot, and Spendlove are suggested by McKinley (1990: 166) to "perhaps convey some flavour of the ordinary man's spoken English as it was in the 13th and 14th centuries, when most of these names arose".

Lexicographers are increasingly utilizing data from surnames and other types of names (McClure 2011; Grant 2016), and the recent completion of a major new surname dictionary significantly strengthens this evidence base (Hanks et al. 2016).

4 Transmission of names

The lack of sense that is widely considered a defining characteristic of names allows them to preserve fossilized forms of words that have long since disappeared from the lexicon. Moreover, the fact that most place-names are locatable in space, and many personal names locatable in time, gives them an advantage over texts preserved in manuscripts of uncertain provenance. Forms of moneyers' names on Anglo-Saxon coins can be ordered chronologically by coin-types, providing closely datable material for studies of Old English phonology (e.g. Colman 1984, 1992), while the range of spellings relating to individual place-names and place-name elements can reveal dialectal and morphological variation. In East Anglia, <a> spellings in place-names from OE *strēt/strǣt* 'Roman road' (e.g. Stradsett, Stradbroke, Stradishall) testify to a development from Saxon *ǣ*-forms rather than Anglian *ē*-forms in early Old English (Kristensson 2001); variation between Scandinavian and English lexical terms in spellings of individual topographical names from the 14th to 16th centuries throws light on local dialect during the Middle English period (Sandred 2001: 51); and 13th- and 14th-century forms of the field-names *Hanging Furlong* and *Hanging Wong* with the present participle in <-ande> reflect Scandinavian morphological influence (Sandred 2001: 51–52).

This type of evidence needs to be handled with care, however, as it is also widely recognized that names may behave differently from vocabulary items. Lass (1973) points out that many surnames could not have developed their modern form through standard processes of phonological change, and illustrates this through a detailed analysis of the surname Shuttlebotham and its variants Shipperbottom, Shuflebotam, Shovelbottom, Shoebotham, Shoebottom, and Shubotham. Colman (1988) too urges caution in the use of names as evidence for linguistic reconstruction and historical dialectology. Some name spellings become fossilized, failing to reflect phonological variation, while others reflect the influence of more than one etymon. Here as in the initial formation of names, analogy plays a key role. Following the loss of semantic meaning, element substitution may occur, with familiar elements tending to replace less familiar ones. The common element *wulf* 'wolf', often spelled <ulf> in Old English personal names, replaces the original deuterotheme *col* 'coal' of the moneyers' names Sæcol and Swartcol in the later spellings <Sæcolf> and <Swarcolf>; the topographical place-name generic OE *lēah*, often surviving as <ley>, influences the development of names such as Hawksley and Notley from *hafoces hlewe* 'hawk's tumulus' and *hnut clyf* 'nut slope' (Gelling 1997: 202–205), and of Grazeley from *grægsole*; and the development of Warnborough from *weargeburnan* shows interference from the habitative generic OE *burh* 'fortification'. It is particularly common for place-names to be influenced by neighbouring ones, and Coates (1987: 329) cites 24 pairs of place-names, mostly less than five miles apart, where one has developed along non-standard lines through the influence of the other.

Analogy also operates at the level of the whole name. The ubiquitous Burton, from OE *burh-tūn*, has attracted to itself place-names from different specifics. Burton Bradstock contains the name of the River Bride, Burton in Sussex contains an Old English personal name Budeca, and Burton Salmon contains an adjective OE *brād* 'broad'. Similarly, a Middlesex place-name containing a personal name Ceolred has developed into another Charlton, and a Devon place-name containing a personal name Ælfric or Æthelric into another Easton. In each case, the influence of analogy has overridden standard processes of phonological change.

Spelling patterns may also be affected by the medium in which the names are recorded, an area explored by Anderson and Colman (2004) in relation to wraparound conventions and the transposition of graphs in the representation of personal names on Anglo-Saxon coins. Another factor is the role of government in regulating coinage and documenting names. The recurrence of certain forms on coins may reflect not pronunciation but an attempt to regularize spelling (Smart 1983); while students of place-names discriminate carefully between local spellings and those emanating from a centralized administration.

The compound structure characteristic of both personal and place-name formations may also lead them to develop differently from their lexical cognates. In some instances, phonological changes are reflected earlier than in written texts. The loss of /d/ from word-final /nd/, common in written texts from the 15th century onwards, is attested as early as the late 12th and 13th centuries in the stressed (first) syllable of place-names and surnames, where it is attributed to the influence of the consonant initial in the second part of the compound (Wełna 2005). Consonant loss at the juncture of compound personal names is discussed alongside other issues specific to compounds by Colman (1984: 126–136), who demonstrates the value of Old English name-spellings as evidence for phonological developments in obscured compounds (i.e. compounds that have undergone phonological reduction and semantic obscuration).

In general, motivated change affects names more than ordinary lexis. Personal names and surnames are subject to idiosyncratic choices as regards both pronunciation and spelling, and place-names too may be "improved", as with Sherborne Lane in London mentioned above. Early spellings show that it preserves an unattested ME *shite-burgh* 'privy', but this has been changed for reasons of delicacy. In other instances, an element that has become semantically opaque is reshaped to conform with known lexis, or simply replaced by a word that appears to make more sense. Mincing Lane in London derives from the obsolete word *myncen* 'nun', and Fletcher Gate in Nottingham from *flesh-hewer* 'butcher' – apparently associated with the later occupational term *fletcher* 'arrow-maker', itself now obsolete but plausible as a street-name specific. The same process of folk etymology accounts for the development (from a Lancashire place-name) of the surnames Shovelbottom, Shoebottom, and so on. So too the loss of much of the Anglo-Saxon personal name stock following the Norman Conquest led to the names becoming unfamiliar and being reshaped where they appear in surnames or place-names. The surname Freelove derives from an Old English personal name Frithulaf, while the first element of Abbotsley is an Old English personal name Ealdbald. Because names are so often affected by folk etymology, they do not always follow standard patterns of phonological or morphological development. For the same reason, however, they provide evidence for the operation of folk etymology itself.

5 Summary

In sum, the relationship between names and lexis is not straightforward, but this does not diminish the value of onomastic material in the study of historical linguistics. Although neither the initial formation nor the subsequent transmission of names directly parallels the lexicon, the differences are themselves enlightening and reveal information unavailable from other sources. Handled with appropriate caution, onomastic evidence provides insights which both supplement and extend those offered by other areas of language.

6 References

Anderson, John and Fran Colman. 2004. Non-rectilinear name-forms in Old English and the media of language. In: Gunnar Bergh, Jennifer Herriman, and Mats Mobärg (eds.), *An International Master of Syntax and Semantics: Papers Presented to Aimo Seppänen on the Occasion of his 75th Birthday*, 31–42. Göteborg: Acta Universitatis Gothoburgensis.

Cameron, Angus, Ashley Crandall Amos, Antonette diPaolo Healey et al. 2016. *Dictionary of Old English: A to H Online*. Toronto: Dictionary of Old English Project. https://www.doe.utoronto.ca/pages/index.html

Cameron, Jean. 2008. The distribution of whin, gorse and furze in English place-names. In: O. J. Padel and David N. Parsons (eds.), *A Commodity of Good Names: Essays in Honour of Margaret Gelling*, 253–258. Donington: Shaun Tyas.

Cameron, Kenneth. 1996. The Scandinavian element in minor names and field-names in north-east Lincolnshire. *Nomina* 19: 5–27.

Carlsson, Stig. 1989. *Studies on Middle English Local Bynames in East Anglia*. Lund: Lund University Press.

Clark, Cecily. 1983. The early personal names of King's Lynn: an essay in socio-cultural history. Part II – by-names. *Nomina* 7: 65–89.

Coates, Richard. 1987. Pragmatic sources of analogical reformation. *Journal of Linguistics* 23: 319–340.

Colman, Fran. 1984. Anglo-Saxon pennies and Old English phonology. *Folia Linguistica Historica* 6: 91–143.

Colman, Fran. 1988. What *is* in a name? In: Jacek Fisiak (ed.), *Historical Dialectology: Regional and Social*, 111–137. Berlin/New York: Mouton de Gruyter.

Colman, Fran. 1992. *Money Talks*. Berlin/New York: Mouton de Gruyter.

Ekwall, Eilert. 1960. *The Concise Oxford Dictionary of English Place-Names*. 4th edn. Oxford: Clarendon Press.

English Place-Name Society. 1924–. *The Survey of English Place-Names*. Vols. 1–. Cambridge/Nottingham: Cambridge University Press and English Place-Name Society.

Fellows-Jensen, Gillian. 2007. The Scandinavian element *gata* outside the urbanised settlements of the Danelaw. In: Beverley Ballin Smith, Simon Taylor, and Gareth Williams (eds.), *West Over Sea: Studies in Scandinavian Sea-Borne Expansion and Settlement Before 1300. A Festschrift in Honour of Dr Barbara E. Crawford*, 445–459. Leiden/Boston: Brill.

Field, John. 1972. *English Field-Names. A Dictionary*. Newton Abbot: David & Charles.

Fisiak, Jacek and Peter Trudgill (eds.). 2001. *East Anglian English*. Cambridge: D. S. Brewer.

Fransson, Gustav. 1935. *Middle English Surnames of Occupation 1100–1350*. Lund: Gleerup.

Gelling, Margaret. 1997. *Signposts to the Past: Place-Names and the History of England*. 3rd edn. Chichester: Phillimore.

Gelling, Margaret and Ann Cole. 2000. *The Landscape of Place-Names*. Stamford: Shaun Tyas.

Grant, Alison. 2016. Names and lexicography. In: Hough (ed.), 572–584.

Hanks, Patrick, Richard Coates, and Peter McClure. 2016. *The Oxford Dictionary of Family Names in Britain and Ireland*. 4 vols. Oxford: Oxford University Press.

Hough, Carole. 2002. Onomastic evidence for Middle English vocabulary. In: Peter J. Lucas and Angela M. Lucas (eds.), *Middle English from Tongue to Text. Selected Papers from the Third International Conference on Middle English: Language and Text, held at Dublin, Ireland, 1–4 July 1999*, 155–167. Frankfurt: Peter Lang.

Hough, Carole. 2003. Place-name evidence for Anglo-Saxon plant-names. In: C. P. Biggam (ed.), *From Earth to Art. The Many Aspects of the Plant-World in Anglo-Saxon England*, 41–78. Amsterdam/New York: Rodopi.

Hough, Carole (ed.). 2016. *The Oxford Handbook of Names and Naming*. With the assistance of Daria Izdebska. Oxford: Oxford University Press.

Kitson, Peter R. 1995. The nature of Old English dialect distributions, mainly as exhibited in charter boundaries. In: Jacek Fisiak (ed.), *Medieval Dialectology*, 43–135. Berlin/New York: Mouton de Gruyter.

Kitson, Peter R. 1996. British and European river-names. *Transactions of the Philological Society* 94: 73–118.

Kitson, Peter R. 2002. How Anglo-Saxon personal names work. *Nomina* 25: 91–131.
Kristensson, Gillis. 2001. Language in contact: Old East Saxon and East Anglian. In: Fisiak and Trudgill (eds.), 63–70.
Lass, R. 1973. Review of P. H. Reaney, *The Origin of English Surnames*, Routledge and Kegan Paul, London, 1967. *Foundations of Language* 9: 392–402.
McClure, Peter. 2011. Surnames as sources in the OED. www.oed.com/public/surnames assources; last accessed 5 January 2017.
McKinley, Richard. 1990. *A History of British Surnames*. London/New York: Longman.
Mills, A. D. 2010. *A Dictionary of London Place Names*. 2nd edn. Oxford: Oxford University Press.
Nicolaisen, W. F. H. 1995. Is there a Northwest Germanic toponymy? Some thoughts and a proposal. In: Edith Marold and Christiane Zimmermann (eds.), *Nordwestgermanisch*, 102–114. Berlin/New York: Walter de Gruyter.
Parsons, David N. 2006. Field-name statistics, Norfolk and the Danelaw. In: Peder Gammeltoft and Bent Jørgensen (eds.), *Names Through the Looking-Glass: Festschrift in Honour of Gillian Fellows-Jensen July 5th 2006*, 165–188. Copenhagen: C. A. Reitzels.
Parsons, David N. and (for Vols. 1 and 2) Tania Styles with (for Vol. 1) Carole Hough. 1997–. *The Vocabulary of English Place-Names: 1 (Á–Box); 2 (Brace–Cæster); 3 (Ceafor–Cock-pit)*. Nottingham: Centre for English Name Studies (Vols. 1 and 2) and English Place-Name Society (Vol. 3).
Sandred, Karl Inge. 2001. East Anglian place-names: Sources of lost dialect. In: Fisiak and Trudgill (eds.), 39–61.
Scott, Margaret. 2016. Names and dialectology. In: Hough (ed.), 488–501.
Smart, Veronica. 1983. Variation between Æthel- and Ægel- as a name-element on coins. *Nomina* 7: 91–96.
Tengvik, Gösta. 1938. *Old English Bynames*. Uppsala: Almqvist & Wiksells.
Thuresson, Bertil. 1950. *Middle English Occupational Terms*. Lund: Gleerup.
Watts, Victor. 2002. Medieval field-names in two South Durham townships. *Nomina* 25: 53–64.
Wełna, Jerzy. 2005. "Now you see it, now you don't" once more: The loss and insertion of dental stops in medieval English. *Studia Anglica Posnaniensia* 41: 71–84.

Hanna Rutkowska
Chapter 11: Orthography

1 Theoretical approaches to language, speech, and writing: between referentiality and autonomy —— 201
2 Definitions of orthography and related terms —— 203
3 Classification of writing systems and principles governing English orthography —— 204
4 Units of writing systems: terminological evolution —— 207
5 The inventory and distribution of English graphemes from the synchronic and diachronic perspective —— 209
6 Orthography as the source of phonological evidence —— 211
7 Sociolinguistic aspects of orthography —— 212
8 Summary —— 213
9 References —— 214

Abstract: This chapter offers a critical overview of some of the most influential ideas concerning writing in general, and orthographic systems, with particular attention paid to English orthography and its intricate structure. It also presents and explains the terminology which can be found in literature dealing with this subject. Section 1 gives an account of different attitudes to writing and the two main theoretical approaches, relational and autonomistic, which they have motivated. It is followed by a summary of selected definitions of orthography and related terms in Section 2. Section 3 examines various types of writing systems, places the English orthographic system in that taxonomic context, and discusses its governing principles. Section 4 deals with the evolution of terms used to denote units of writing systems. In Section 5 all the graphemes of English orthography are listed and selected historical aspects of their evolution are mentioned. Section 6 contains a brief evaluation of orthography as the source of evidence for phonological change. Finally, the sociolinguistic aspects of orthography are identified, including its role as a binding norm within a language community, and the significance of orthographic variation.

Hanna Rutkowska: Poznań (Poland)

1 Theoretical approaches to language, speech, and writing: between referentiality and autonomy

In order to provide a definition of orthography and put it in the appropriate theoretical context, one must first consider and define the general terms to which it is related. These are, most importantly, "language", "speech", and "writing". It seems quite clear at present that speech and writing differ in numerous ways, including, for instance, the purely physical properties, as well as the communicative situations and the purposes for which each of them is used. Thus, speech is time-bound, fleeting, spontaneous, used to express opinions and emotions, whereas writing is space-bound, permanent, planned, edited, and used to record and convey information (detailed accounts of these differences can be found, e.g., in Crystal 2003: 291–293 and Cook 2004: 31–53). In fact, both speech and writing can be treated as complementary ways of using language, where the latter is understood as "a complex system residing in our brain which allows us to produce and interpret utterances" (Rogers 2005: 2). However, there is no general agreement among linguists as regards the relation between speech and language on one hand, and writing and language, as well as writing and orthography, on the other.

Since the beginning of the 20th century, these notions have been viewed from two main points of view labelled as "relational" and "autonomistic" by Sgall (1987: 2–3; see also Ruszkiewicz 1976: 37–44). The structuralists, representing the relational perspective, equated speech with language, and considered writing as an extra-linguistic phenomenon:

- "Language and writing are two distinct systems of signs; the second exists for the sole purpose of representing the first" (Saussure 1993: 41a).
- "The written forms are secondary symbols of the spoken ones – symbols of symbols" (Sapir 1921: 20).
- "Writing is not language, but merely a way of recording language by means of visible marks" (Bloomfield 1933: 21).
- "The linguist distinguishes between *language* and *writing*" (Hockett 1958: 4).

These quotations, to some extent, echo the classical theories of writing, which assumed a close dependence of written language on spoken language. For example, "[i]n *De Interpretatione*, Aristotle (1963, 43) states that 'spoken sounds are symbols of affections of the soul, and written marks [are] symbols of spoken sounds'" (Liuzza 1996: 35). Also Quintilian claimed that "spelling should follow pronunciation because the text is a repository for the *vox*" (1920, 1:144; quoted in Liuzza 1996: 35).

Because of the influence exerted by Saussure, Bloomfield, and other early structuralists, the validity of their statements has mostly been taken for granted. According to Venezky (1970: 27), "Bloomfield is responsible probably more than any other contemporary linguist for the view that writing is secondary and subservient to speech", because he consistently expressed this opinion in several publications.

In contrast to Saussure, Bloomfield, and others, scholars adhering to the autonomistic point of view, e.g., Vachek, Bolinger, Stetson, McIntosh, McLaughlin, and Venezky, have claimed that "[m]uch is written that is not pronounced" (Stetson 1981 [1937]: 35), and that "writing does more than represent speech" (Cook 2004: 32). More precisely, according to them "[w]riting is any manifestation of language in visible signs; a written language is a code that may not need preliminary decipherment into speech to be understood" (Vachek 1982: 38). In this view, the written language "has to a great extent become an instrument for the direct expression of meaning, co-ordinate with audible language. The result of this has been that the written language has in part been developed on lines of its own, independent of the development of oral speech" (Bradley 1919 [1913]: 14–15; quoted by Liuzza 1996: 27).

Although the preoccupation with spelling as the reflection of speech was the dominant feature of discussions on orthography in the 20th century, the adherents of the autonomistic approach to writing also had some forerunners to draw upon. Already in the 16th and 17th centuries, some scholars (e.g. William Bullokar, Alexander Gil, Alexander Hume, and John Wallis) realized that orthography carried some non-phonemic information. Venezky (1970: 18, 23–25) mentions also the writings of Goold Brown (especially his comprehensive grammar published in 1850), which clearly expressed the idea that "words are not mere sounds, and in their orthography more is implied than in phonetics or phonography. Ideographic forms have, in general, the advantage of preserving the identity, history, and lineage of words" (quoted in Venezky 1970: 18, 24). Brown did not deny the close relationship between letters and sounds, but he also emphasized the relative autonomy of the writing system: "The deaf [...], to whom none of the letters express or represent sounds, may be taught to read and write understandingly. [...] Hence it would appear that the powers of the letters are not, of necessity, identified with their sounds" (both quotations found in Venezky 1970: 23–24). The second citation is reminiscent of a much earlier paper written by Wallis (on teaching the deaf to speak), where the author claims that "there is nothing, in the nature of the Thing it self, why Letters and Characters might not as properly be applyed to represent Immediately, as by Intervention of Sounds, what our Conceptions are" (Wallis: 1670: 1091).

The linguists' varying attitudes to written language clearly correspond to different expectations of its aims and functions. The early structuralists' disparaging view of writing has influenced the definitions of orthography, with which writing has commonly been confused (Vachek 1976 [1945–49]: 128). It motivated the treatment of orthography as an imperfect device for obtaining information about speech, and popularized and somewhat fossilized the perception of orthography as a non-linguistic subject. As a result, the English orthographic system has rarely been devoted separate sections, let alone chapters, in historical grammars of English and handbooks of linguistics. Obviously, as it has been impossible to ignore orthography completely, elements of it have been mentioned in discussions of English phonology (see Kniezsa 1991 for an overview of histories of English spelling).

Summing up, the main differences between linguists expressing their views about the written language and its connection to speech concern the level of autonomy and the linguistic status of writing systems. Because the purely relational perspective seems biased and limited, in what follows, I have taken the more balanced, autonomistic view towards writing, and consequently towards orthography, but I will also refer to the existing competing views wherever necessary (see, especially, Section 4 on the units of writing systems).

2 Definitions of orthography and related terms

According to the OED (Proffitt [ed.] 2000–), the word *orthography* came into English from Old French *ortografie*, but it originates in Greek. Since its appearance in English in the mid-15th century, it has retained the prescriptive sense of a spelling norm, where *spelling* is 'the manner of expressing words with letters'. In the 16th century, it also acquired the descriptive meaning of 'that part of grammar which treats of the nature and values of letters and of their combination to express sounds and words'.

The term *orthography* has also been defined in various other ways, and its meaning at least partly overlaps with that of other expressions. For example, although in everyday usage *orthography* is often understood as synonymous only with *spelling*, in a more technical sense, the orthography of a specific language comprises spelling as well as the capitalization, punctuation, and word division permitted in that language. Spelling is most closely connected with the levels of phonology, morphology, and lexicon, whereas capitalization, punctuation, and word division show some correspondences also with syntax, semantics, and stylistics. Thus, in accordance with this broader sense, one can assume the following definition: "[t]he standardized writing system of a language is known as its *orthography*" (Crystal 2003: 257).

Another term associated with *orthography* is *graphology*, introduced by McIntosh (1961: 107) to denote the study of orthographic systems. The advantage of that term is the parallelism to other linguistic levels, such as phonology and morphology. That term was defined further by Halliday et al. (1964: 50) as "orthography, punctuation, and anything else that is concerned with showing how a language uses its graphic resources to carry its grammatical and lexical patterns". In this sense, *graphology* and *orthography* can also be considered synonymous to the *writing system*. *Graphemics*, first recorded in 1951, by analogy to *phonemics* (Pulgram 1951: 19, see also Stockwell and Barritt 1951 on the relational view of graphemics) is another synonym of *orthography*. It is defined in the OED as 'the study of systems of written symbols (letters etc.) in their relation to spoken languages'. However, some linguists have suggested that "the term graphemics should be confined to the study of systems of writing only" (Bazell 1981 [1956]: 68), as well as postulated the introduction of the term *graphophonemics* for "[t]he discipline concerned with the study of the relationship between graphemics and phonemics" (Ruszkiewicz 1976: 49). The term *graphotactics*, in turn, usually refers to the syntax of graphemes (understood as units of an orthographic system) (see Haas 1970: 59, Carney 1994: 66–69), defined also as "the laws governing [the] combination of graphemes" (Vachek 1973: 9).

All the expressions mentioned above are still found today in descriptions of writing systems, and the choice of particular terminology usually depends on the specific focus and theoretical approach of the writer.

3 Classification of writing systems and principles governing English orthography

It is currently assumed that writing systems (or "scripts") can be classified according to what linguistic level is represented by the written symbols (or graphemes). Thus, the writing systems of natural languages can be divided into "morphographic" and "phonographic" (Rogers 2005: 272). In morphographic systems, the symbols are related primarily to morphemes. Some morphemes may constitute words, and therefore such systems have been often referred to as "logographic" (from Greek *logos* 'word', OED; see Sampson 1985; Venezky 1999). Chinese and Sumerian are typical examples of writing systems showing this type of relationship. In phonographic systems, the symbols relate to phonological units. Depending on the type of unit represented, they are divided into "syllabic", "moraic", and "phonemic" (or "alphabetic") (Rogers 2005: 272). In moraic writing, graphemes correspond to morae, where a "mora" is "either a syllable-initial CV sequence or a codal (final) consonant" (Rogers 2005: 250). Moraic systems, such as the Japanese *katakana*, and Cherokee, have traditionally (though rather imprecisely) been called "syllabic" systems (Sampson 1985; Venezky 1999). In phonemic systems, graphemes represent mainly phonemes, or segments, including consonants and vowels. This type of representation has also been referred to as "alphabetic" (Venezky 1999: 4). The phonemic (or alphabetic) principle implies "biuniqueness", which "requires not only that a given phoneme is represented by a constant symbol but also that the symbol involved does not represent other phonemes" (Carney 1994: 15; see also Lass and Laing 2007: Section 2.2.1). However, total observance of such one-to-one correspondence between sound and symbol is not recorded among the writing systems of natural languages. Scripts classified as the closest to this principle are classical Greek and Finnish (Rogers 2005: 274).

The problem with the classification of writing systems is that they are never purely morphographic or phonographic. In fact, the longer a given script is used by a speech community or a nation as an everyday means of communication, the more it evolves, and the more mixed characteristics it acquires (Sampson 1985: 42; Rogers 2005: 272). Examples of taxonomical mixtures "regularly using both morphographic and phonographic symbols" are Egyptian, Maya, and the mixed use of morphographic *kanji* and two types of phonographic *kana* in Japanese (Rogers 2005: 272). Even such systems as Sumerian and Chinese, where the morphographic principle is clearly the dominant one, show a limited level of phonography (Sampson 1985: 54; Rogers 2005: 274–275).

Writing systems differ not only by their amount of morphography, but also by their "orthographic depth". The more different morphemes are distinguished in spelling, the higher the level of morphography of a given system (Rogers 2005: 275). For example, English is classified as a phonemic system, but it shows the distinctions among different homophonous morphemes, e.g., *you – yew – U – ewe, right – rite – wright – write* (Bradley 1904: 214; Rogers 2005: 273; see also Craigie 1928: 1, Bolinger 1946: 335; Vachek 1973: 43–44 for discussions on the distinction between homophones). That property of English spelling has also been referred to as the "lexical principle" (Chomsky and Halle 1968: 49). On the other hand, "[o]rthographic depth is greater if different allomorphs of the same morpheme are written the same" (Rogers 2005: 275). Accordingly, a final <-ed> in English can be related directly to {past tense}, because it does not show systematic differentiation between its allomorphs /ɪd/ (*pointed*), /d/ (*played*) and /t/ (*washed*). Constant spelling for a morpheme, irrespective of its spoken variants, can also be found in heterophonous, but etymologically and semantically related words, such as *child-children, south-southern,* and *sign-signature* (Francis 1958: 562; Venezky 1970: 42–43, 108; Vachek 1973: 25). Such a preservation of morpheme constancy may be considered consistent with the "morphophonemic principle" (Hall 1981 [1960]: 74). Morphemic and morphophonemic spellings breach the "alphabetic principle", because they lead to a multiplication of sound-symbol (or grapho-phonemic) correspondences, and by the same measure contribute to the opacity, or orthographic depth, of a phonographic system. On the basis of the pairs of etymologically related words provided above, <i> may correspond to /aɪ/ and /ɪ/, <ou> to /aʊ/ and /ʌ/, and <g> to /g/ or zero, and these sets are by no means exhaustive lists of all the permissible correspondences. Thus, English orthography can be called "deep", in contrast to, e.g., the Spanish orthographic system, which shows less divergence from the alphabetic principle, and consequently can be referred to as "shallow". In fact, "the deep/ shallow contrast is a gradient rather than all-or-none distinction" (Sampson 1985: 45), and morphemic and morphophonemic spelling is not an exceptionless rule in English. Rather, English orthography "represents a level intermediate in depth between the phonemic and the morphophonemic level" (Sampson 1985: 44; see also Hockett 1958: 542). For example, the vowel in the plural suffix (as in *pitches*) is represented by <e>, but the difference in voicing between /s/ and /z/ (as in *cats* vs. *dogs*) is not represented at all. A maximally deep orthography would then have *pitchs instead of *pitches*. However, the sequence <tchs> is not permitted in English, and would violate the "graphotactic principle", determining the permissible letter sequences (Carney 1994: 67).

The English writing system also contains a few marginal, non-phonemic, and non-morphemic, but rather iconic (or pictographic) elements, including, e.g., the symbols <&>, <@> and <%>, which represent the words *and*, *at*, and the phrase *per cent*, respectively (Sampson 1985: 34; Lass and Laing 2007: Section 2.2.1).

It is noteworthy that the identification of different principles governing the English writing system, and orthographic systems in general, is not a recent discovery. Already in the late 19th and early 20th centuries Jan Baudouin de Courtenay elaborated a set of rules governing orthographic systems. They included three principles: phonetic, etymological, and historical. Thus, he related orthography to what he believed were its three determining factors, pronunciation, origin (referring to morphology), and tradition (Ruszkiewicz 1981: 24–25; Sgall 1987: 2–3). The idea of multi-level principles and correspondences according to which orthography operates has been further elaborated upon and modified by numerous linguists. For example, Firth (1935: 61) wrote about the notion of "polysystem", or system of systems, referring to the co-existence of and interaction between phonological, grammatical, and lexical systems of orthographic representation. Overviews of the investigations on the interaction of principles in English orthography and in other orthographic systems can be found, e.g., in Ruszkiewicz (1976), Sgall (1987), and Liuzza (1996). They are summarized by Sgall (1987: 12) thus: "In the literature one often speaks about an orthography being based on several principles, the main among which is the phonemic one, while the others underlie the deviations from this basic principle and can be classed more or less exactly in accordance with the levels of the language system".

4 Units of writing systems: terminological evolution

In the course of time and investigation into the nature of relationships between written characters and other levels of language, not all linguists have been satisfied with the simple, traditional terms *letter* and *sound*, and consequently, there has gradually developed a whole set of terms and definitions in order to make descriptions of the writing system more precise. The terminology used by particular linguists has been developed in close connection with their specific approaches to orthography and their perception of its structure and functions. The following sections discuss some of the most important terms and the ideas behind them.

4.1 The doctrine of *littera*

The most characteristic feature of the early attempts at defining the unit of the writing system is the apparent lack of a clear distinction between letters and sounds. The term *letter* was used to refer both to written alphabetic marks and to sounds. One can consider, for example, the statement "The *Elements* of Language are Letters, viz. Simple discriminations of Breath or Voice" (Holder 1669; quoted by Abercrombie 1981 [1949]: 10). What at first sight may seem to be the result of utter confusion, can, in fact, show the impact of the classical notion of *littera*, introduced by the Stoic grammarians, and described by Aelius Donatus in his Latin grammar in the 4th century CE. *Littera* referred to the smallest element of language, combining three attributes, *nomen* (name used for identification), *figura* (shape or visual configuration), and *potestas* (power to signify sound). (Abercrombie 1981 [1949]: 14; Henderson 1985: 142). Thus, the visual mark and the sound could be viewed as different aspects of the same entity.

In spite of its significant and long-lasting influence on numerous generations of grammarians, the concept of *littera*, in the course of time, proved insufficient for the description of both spoken and written systems of language, at least partly due to its potential for misinterpretation. Quotations such as: "Letters are Signes of Sounds, not the Sounds themselves" (Brightland 1711; quoted by Abercrombie 1981 [1949]: 11) demonstrate that the complexity of the concept of *littera* was not transparent and could lead to ambiguity. However, after years of abandonment in the 20th century, the notion has recently been revived by linguists and it has inspired the development of such concepts as "litteral substitution sets" (LSS), which have proved useful in the description of early Middle English writing systems (see, e.g., Benskin 1991: 226; Laing 1999; Laing and Lass 2003, 2009; Lass and Laing 2007: Sections 3.3.1 and 2.3.2).

The word *letter* is still in use both in everyday language with reference to a character of an alphabet, or in more technical descriptions, usually as part of a definition of the distinctive unit of the orthographic system.

4.2 Grapheme

Since the introduction of the term *grapheme* by Baudouin de Courtenay in 1901 (Ruszkiewicz 1976: 24–37, 1981 [1978]: 20–34), it has been defined in various ways:
- "the class of graphs which denote the same phoneme" (Hammarström 1981 [1964]: 97);
- "the class of letters and other visual symbols that represent a phoneme or cluster of phonemes" (OED);
- "any minimal letter string used in correspondences" (Carney 1994: xxvii);
- "[t]he unit of writing" (Stetson 1981 [1937]: 35);
- "the minimal functional distinctive unit of any writing system" (Henderson 1984: 15); and
- "a purely distinctive visual unit, part of an autonomous semiotic system" (Liuzza 1996: 28).

As can be seen from these quotations, the available definitions can be divided into two groups, corresponding to two main senses, and reflecting "conflicting linguistic views of the status of writing" (Henderson 1985: 142):
a. a letter or cluster of letters referring to or corresponding with a single phoneme;
b. the minimal distinctive unit of a writing system.

The former sense, evident in the first three quotations above, assumes that orthography is mainly, if not exclusively, a means of notation for representing speech, and is usually adopted by the proponents of the relational approach to orthography. The latter sense, in turn, is more typical of the adherents to the autonomistic approach to writing (see Section 1 above). It emphasizes the contrastiveness of the grapheme within the orthographic system as one of its necessary features. Moreover, definitions associated with this sense also occasionally point to the analogy which can be drawn between the status of graphemes and that of phonemes within their respective systems: "the graphemes of a given language – like its phonemes – remain differentiated from one another, i.e. [...] they do not get mixed up" (Vachek 1976 [1945–49]: 128–129). Pulgram (1951: 15) even proposed a comprehensive list of correspondences between the graphemes and phonemes of a language. He was also one of the first linguists to use the term *allograph*, by analogy to *allophone*. According to him, "all graphs identifiable as members of one grapheme are its allographs". This definition was later developed by McLaughlin: "an allograph or allographic set which contrasts significantly with all other allographs or allographic sets or with zero will be called a GRAPHEME", where an allograph is "a group of similar characters, modifications, or features [i.e. *graphs*] classed together [...] in graphemic analysis" (McLaughlin 1963: 29). Within the graphemic system, a *graph* can be defined as "each hic et nunc realization of a grapheme" (Pulgram 1951: 15).

It is cogently argued by Henderson (1985) that the autonomistic definition of the grapheme, in comparison to the relational one, "lends itself to the most coherent and principled use. It also allows the term to be applied across the range of writing systems, including irregular alphabetic systems, syllabaries and logographic systems" (Henderson 1985: 146).

5 The inventory and distribution of English graphemes from the synchronic and diachronic perspective

The inventory of graphemes used in modern English comprises "alphabetic" and "non-alphabetic" graphs. The former refer to the twenty-six letters of the alphabet <a, b, c, d, e, f, g, h, i, j, k, l, m, n, o, p, q, r, s, t, u, v, w, x, y, z>. Each letter has also a capitalized counterpart, e.g., <A, B, C, ... Z>, so altogether we can distinguish 52 alphabetic characters. Opinions about the graphemic significance of capital letters are divided. According to Haas (1970: 22–23), since the lower-case and upper-case alphabetic graphs occur in complementary distribution, they can be described as allographs of a particular grapheme, e.g., <a, A> or <k, K>. Taking this point of view, we could distinguish 26 (not 52) graphemes in English. However, Henderson points to the fact that in sentences such as "The archer was called Archer" *archer* and *Archer* are different lexical identities and "so the contrast expressed by capitalization has graphemic status" (Henderson 1985: 144).

The non-alphabetic graphic symbols appear in combination with the alphabetic ones, and are subdivided into four types (McLaughlin 1963: 30):

- "punctuation marks", usually helping to indicate grammatical structure, including, e.g., < , . : ; ' ? ! - – … ' ' " " ( ) < > [ ] { } >;
- "graphic components" referring to diacritics, conjoined to other graphs and used to distinguish different values of the same letter, including accent marks, dots, cedillas, subscript hooks, macrons, e.g. <é, ö, å, ç, ū> (these appear in English only occasionally, in borrowings);
- "tachygraphs" (found mainly in medieval manuscripts), used only with alphabetic symbols, and standing for one or more of them, e.g., a bar through the descender of the letter <p>, functioning as an abbreviation for <-er-> or <-ar-> in, e.g., *person*; and
- "word signs", e.g. <&> (an ampersand), standing for the word *and*, or the symbol <@>, which stands for *at*.

Moreover, Francis (1958: 436) suggests including a space in the writing system, as a sort of zero grapheme (see also Venezky 1970: 47 and Carney 1994: 5, cf. Sgall 1987: 7 who uses the expression "blank").

Viewed from a diachronic perspective, the inventory of English graphemes should also include several additional symbols, particularly *thorn* <þ>, *eth* <ð>, *wynn* <p>, *ash* <æ>, and *yogh* <ʒ>. Thorn and wynn were "borrowed" from the runic alphabet (*futhorc*) in medieval times. Ash was a ligature derived from the Roman alphabet, eth was an Irish modification of <d> to represent, along with thorn, the dental fricatives, and yogh originated as the insular *open g* (ʒ), borrowed from the Irish. All these characters had been replaced by other symbols by modern times. On the other hand, the differentiation between <i> and <j>, as well as between <u> and <v> as separate letters of the alphabet is a comparatively new invention in the English inventory of graphemes. (OED; Scragg 1974: 2, 8, 10 passim).

Over the centuries, changes affected not only the composition of the inventory of symbols used for writing in English. Graphotactics and grapho-phonemic correspondences have also evolved over time, making English orthography more and more inconsistent with the alphabetical principle governing phonemic writing systems. For example, the Old English <c> corresponded to /tʃ/, and /k/, but never to /ʃ/, and <sc> corresponded to /ʃ/, but hardly ever to /sk/. Likewise, punctuation, capitalization, and word division patterns have been modified over the centuries.

The reasons for the changes have been multiple and diverse, but a few important events and influences are particularly noteworthy in the development of English graphemics. For example, the arrival of Christianity at the end of the 6th century CE brought the adoption of the Latin alphabet (with some modifications), and the Norman Conquest resulted in the appearance of numerous French-derived spelling conventions, which partly replaced the previous practices. For example, the Norman scribes introduced the doubling of letters to indicate long vowels in words such as *goose* and *meet*, and also replaced <c>, <cp>, <hp>, and <sc> with <ch>, <qu>, <wh>, and <sh>, respectively. The introduction of printing contributed to the fixing and standardization of English spelling, or at least to the dissemination of standardized practices; and extensive borrowing from various languages explains the diversity of spelling patterns.

Readers interested in more detail on the structure and the rules governing English orthography, can consult a number of books outlining the synchronic and diachronic aspects of English orthography. The most recent synchronic summaries include Rollings (2004), Carney (1994), Venezky (1970, 1999), and Wełna (1982). However, the only relatively reliable comprehensive studies devoted to the history of English spelling published so far is Scragg (1974) and Upward and Davidson (2011), but the latter seems intended for a general non-academic audience.

6 Orthography as the source of phonological evidence

In view of the depth of English orthography, due to the variety and complexity of principles governing it (discussed in the previous sections), a linguist studying the phonology of an older text cannot take orthographic evidence at face value as the source of information about pronunciation, while one studying the morphology or syntax will find relevant evidence much easier to obtain from a written text.

Penzl (1957: 197–200) provides a classification of the types of evidence available for students of previous pronunciation, dividing it into orthographic, orthoepic (referring to the comments of phoneticians, grammarians, and spelling reformers), metrical, comparative, and contact evidence. The evaluation of various sources of information about the phonemic change can be found, apart from Penzl (1957), also in Kökeritz (1953), Dobson (1957–68), Wrenn (1967), Wolfe (1972), Liuzza (1996), Stenroos (2002, 2004, 2006), and in earlier works, e.g., Zachrisson (1913) and Wyld (1936). Orthography is thus one of several sources of evidence for historical phonologists, and should at best be analyzed in conjunction with the information gathered from the examination of other types of evidence.

Orthographic evidence comprises occasional spellings (sometimes referred to as naive spellings), e.g. *douter* for *daughter*, or *ruff* for *rough*, and back spellings (also called reverse spellings or hypercorrections), e.g. *quight* for *quite* (by analogy to *light, night*). Unfortunately, the interpretation of such orthographic evidence is fraught with problems:

- not every change in spelling means a change in pronunciation; e.g. the etymologizing insertion of <b> in *doubt* did not result in assigning any sound value to that letter;
- not all changes in pronunciation are reflected in spelling; e.g. the diphthongization of Middle English [iː] and [uː], as in *mice* and *house*, is not;
- occasional spellings may be due to (typo)graphical errors, especially if one deals with a single instance of a given form; and
- the value of the same spellings may vary according to the period and regional dialect.

Nevertheless, a linguist can minimize the risks connected with such types of evidence by gathering a large number of examples before drawing conclusions, by comparing orthographic evidence with other types of evidence, and, most importantly, by examining thoroughly the orthographic rules of the relevant writing system with due attention paid to the period and regional variety, before starting the analysis (see, e.g., Penzl 1957: 197–203; Wolfe 1972: 110–130; Stenroos 2002: 445–468; Smith 2006: 136). Liuzza (1996: 33) emphasizes particularly the last measure mentioned above: "Only by reconstructing the orthographic rules practiced by a writer can one determine anything about the spoken language behind the text; the evidence, otherwise, is mute".

7 Sociolinguistic aspects of orthography

As has been indicated in the previous sections, orthography can be treated as one of the subjects of linguistic research. Nevertheless, in the estimation of an average language user, orthography functions nowadays mainly as a spelling norm. Such a norm is binding within a language community and non-compliance with it can have social consequences. It applies particularly to public domains, such as education and official written media. Someone using non-standard forms and making spelling mistakes in these contexts is likely to be socially punished by being judged uneducated or even unintelligent.

The notion of spelling error is a relatively recent development. In the Middle Ages, there was no orthographic standard in English in the modern sense. Instead, dialectal variation was abundant. In the 15th century the situation started to evolve towards standardization. This process took more than two centuries to complete, including the stages of selection, acceptance, functional elaboration, and codification (Haugen 1972: 110). The process of codifying those orthographic forms which were viewed as proper was advocated by the spelling reformers, grammarians, and lexicographers. It is often assumed that their proposals were essential for the regularization of spelling in English (Brengelman 1980; Salmon 1999: 18), but recent research has also pointed to the role of early printers in this process (Rutkowska 2013). Spelling books, grammars, and dictionaries, which were printed and disseminated by a growing number of publishing houses, contributed to the elimination of most orthographic variants and to the considerable increase in orthographic consistency. This increase was so substantial that it is usually recognized that by the end of the 17th century English orthography had become standardized (Scragg 1974: 80, Görlach 2001: 78). However, it has recently been emphasized that the completion of standardization can be applied mainly to printed documents, whereas "[d]eviant spelling continued in letters and diaries, even among the educated" (Görlach 2001: 78; see also Salmon 1999: 44; Tieken-Boon van Ostade 2009: 46–50). Furthermore, also in the 19th-century English, "while public printed texts manifest greater stability, even these are not devoid of change" (Mugglestone 2012: 346).

In present times, with well-established orthographic standards, orthographic variation still exists. In English, there is the codified and politically sanctioned diatopic division into two spelling systems, British and American, including the respective use of such spelling variants as those in *honour/honor*, *centre/center*, *monologue/monolog*, and *aeroplane/airplane*. The spelling can differ also depending on the particular reference of the word in a given context. For example, in British English, the form *program* is reserved for computing-related contexts, and *programme* is used in the other meanings, whereas American English uses *program* in all senses of that lexical item (OED, Simpson [ed.] 2000–).

In today's languages, the use of non-standard orthographic variants can also be deliberate (Beaugrande 2006: 43), or even constitute "a powerful expressive resource" capturing some of the "immediacy, the 'authenticity' and 'flavor' of the spoken word in all its diversity" (Jaffe 2000: 498). One can experience the effectiveness of non-standard orthography in daily contexts, for example in tradenames, television commercials and in computer-mediated communication (Crystal 2006). It can also be found in printed texts, for instance in poetry (e.g. Tom Leonard), or popular fiction (e.g. Irvine Welsh), where it is used for stylistic as well as ideological reasons.

8 Summary

Orthography differs in many ways from the other levels of linguistic description. It does not enjoy a stable and generally accepted terminology, partly because in numerous natural languages, such as in English, it is governed by a set of heterogeneous principles, and partly due to the fact that linguists differ significantly as regards the aims and functions which they ascribe to orthographic systems. The existence of diverse definitions of the term *orthography* itself reflects the complexity typical of writing systems. This term is employed to denote, on one hand, a system of graphemes as contrastive units, and, on the other, a set of rules governing the correspondences between the graphemes, phonemes, and morphemes. It also functions as a social code which needs to be observed under the pain of stigmatization.

In the outline offered above, I have attempted to present some of the important aspects of the controversy concerning the relationship between speech and writing, discuss the different levels of linguistic representation in orthography, and describe the main principles according to which the English writing system operates. The characteristics of this system are adequately expressed by Venezky (1999: 4): "English orthography is not a failed phonetic transcription system, invented out of madness or perversity. Instead, it is a more complex system that preserves bits of history (i.e. etymology), facilitates understanding, and also translates into sound".

9 References

Abercrombie, David. 1981 [1949.] What is in a "letter"? In: Ruszkiewicz (ed.), 9–19 [Reprinted from *Lingua* 2: 54–63].
Bazell, Charles E. 1981 [1956]. The grapheme. In: Ruszkiewicz (ed.), 66–70 [Reprinted from *Litera* 3: 43–46].
de Beaugrande, Robert. 2006. Speech versus writing in the discourse of linguistics. *Miscelánea: A Journal of English and American Studies* 33: 31–45.
Benskin, Michael. 1991. In reply to Dr Burton. *Leeds Studies in English: New Series* 22: 209–262.
Bloomfield, Leonard. 1933. *Language*. New York: Holt, Rinehart, and Winston.
Bolinger, Dwight. 1946. Visual morphemes. *Language* 22: 333–340.
Bradley, Henry. 1904. *The Making of English*. London: Macmillan.
Bradley, Henry. 1919 [1913]. *On the Relations between Spoken and Written Language, with Special Reference to English*. Oxford: Clarendon Press. [Reprinted]
Brengelman, Fred H. 1980. Orthoepists, printers, and the rationalization of English spelling. *Journal of English and Germanic Philology* 79: 332–354.
Carney, Edward. 1994. *A Survey of English Spelling*. London/New York: Routledge.
Chomsky, Noam and Morris Halle. 1968. *The Sound Pattern of English*. New York: Harper and Row.
Cook, Vivian. 2004. *The English Writing System*. London: Hodder Arnold.
Craigie, William A. 1928. *English Spelling: Its Rules and Reasons*. London: George G. Harrap.
Crystal, David. 2003. *The Cambridge Encyclopedia of the English Language*. 2nd edn. Cambridge: Cambridge University Press.
Crystal, David. 2006. *Language and the Internet*. 2nd edn. Cambridge: Cambridge University Press.

Dobson, E. J. 1957–68. *English Pronunciation: 1500–1700*. Vols. I and II. Oxford: Clarendon Press.
Firth, John R. 1935. The technique of semantics.*Transactions of the Philological Society*, 36–72.
Francis, W. Nelson. 1958. *The Structure of American English*. New York: The Ronald Press Company.
Görlach, Manfred. 2001. *Eighteenth-century English*. Heidelberg: C. Winter.
Haas, William. 1970. *Phono-graphic Translation*. Manchester: Manchester University Press.
Hall, Robert A. 1981 [1960]. A theory of graphemics. In: Ruszkiewicz (ed.), 71–80 [Reprinted from *Acta Linguistica* 8: 13–20].
Halliday, Michael A. K., Angus McIntosh, and Peter Strevens. 1964. *The Linguistic Sciences and Language Teaching*. Bloomington: Indiana University Press.
Hammarström, Göran. 1981 [1964]. Type and typeme, graph and grapheme. In: Ruszkiewicz (ed.), 89–99 [Reprinted from *Studia Neophilologica* 36: 332–340].
Haugen, Einar. 1972 [1966]. Dialect, language and nation. In: John Pride and Janet Holmes (eds.), *Sociolinguistics*, 11–24. Harmondsworth: Penguin .
Henderson, Leslie. 1984. Writing systems and reading processes. In: Leslie Henderson [Reprinted from *Anthropologist* 68(4): 922–935]. (ed.), *Orthographies and Reading: Perspectives from Cognitive Psychology, Neuropsychology, and Linguistics*, 11–24. London: Lawrence Erlbaum.
Henderson, Leslie. 1985. On the use of the term "grapheme". *Language and Cognitive Processes* 1(2): 135–148.
Hockett, Charles F. 1958. *A Course in Modern Linguistics*. New York: The Macmillan Company.
Jaffe, Alexandra. 2000. Introduction: Non-standard orthography and non-standard speech. *Journal of Sociolinguistics* 4(4): 497–513.
Kniezsa, Veronika. 1991. "The due order and reason": On the histories of English spelling. *Folia Linguistica Historica* 12(1–2): 209–218.
Kökeritz, Helge. 1953. *Shakespeare's Pronunciation*. New Haven: Yale University Press.
Laing, Margaret. 1999. Confusion „wrs" confounded: Litteral substitution sets in early Middle English writing systems. *Neuphilologische Mitteilungen* 100: 251–270.
Laing, Margaret and Roger Lass. 2003. Tales of the 1001 nists: The phonological implications of litteral substitution sets in some thirteenth-century South-West Midland texts. *English Language and Linguistics* 7: 257–278.
Laing, Margaret and Roger Lass. 2009. Shape-shifting, sound-change and the genesis of prodigal writing systems. *English Language and Linguistics* 13(1): 1–31.
Lass, Roger and Margaret Laing. 2007. Introduction. Part I: Background. Chapter 2: Interpreting Middle English. In: Margaret Laing. 2013–. *A Linguistic Atlas of Early Middle English, 1150–1325* (LAEME). Version 3.2. Edinburgh: © The University of Edinburgh. http://www.lel.ed.ac.uk/ihd/laeme2/laeme_intro_ch1.html; last accessed 6 January 2017.
Liuzza, Roy M. 1996. Orthography and historical linguistics. *Journal of English Linguistics* 24(1): 25–44.
McIntosh, Angus. 1961. "Graphology" and meaning. *Archivum Linguisticum* 13: 107–120.
McLaughlin, John C. 1963. *A Graphemic-phonemic Study of a Middle English Manuscript*. The Hague: Mouton.
Mugglestone, Lynda. 2012. English in the nineteenth century. In: Mugglestone (ed.), 340–378.
Mugglestone, Lynda (ed.). 2012. *The Oxford History of English*. Updated edn. Oxford: Oxford University Press.
Penzl, Herbert. 1957. The evidence for phonemic changes. In: Ernst Pulgram (ed.), *Studies Presented to Joshua Whatmough on his Sixtieth Birthday*, 193–208. The Hague: Mouton.

Proffitt, Michael (ed.). 2000–. *The Oxford English Dictionary*. 3rd edn. online. Oxford University Press. www.oed.com

Pulgram, Ernst. 1951. Phoneme and grapheme: A parallel. *Word* 7: 15–20.

Rogers, Henry. 2005. *Writing Systems: A Linguistic Approach*. Malden: Blackwell.

Rollings, Andrew G. 2004. *The Spelling Patterns of English*. München: Lincom.

Ruszkiewicz, Piotr. 1976. *Modern Approaches to Graphophonemic Investigations in English*. Katowice: Uniwersytet Śląski.

Ruszkiewicz, Piotr. 1981 [1978]. Jan Baudouin de Courtenay's theory of the grapheme. In: Ruszkiewicz (ed.), 20–34 [Reprinted from *Acta Philologica* 7: 117–135].

Ruszkiewicz, Piotr (ed.). 1981. *Graphophonemics: A Book of Readings*. Katowice: Uniwersytet Śląski.

Rutkowska, Hanna. 2013. *Orthographic Systems in Thirteen Editions of the* Kalender of Shepherdes *(1506–1656)*. Frankfurt am Main: Peter Lang.

Salmon, Vivian. 1999. Orthography and punctuation. In: Roger Lass (ed.), *The Cambridge History of the English Language*. Vol. III. *1476–1776*, 13–55. Cambridge: Cambridge University Press.

Sampson, Geoffrey. 1985. *Writing Systems: A Linguistic Introduction*. Stanford: Stanford University Press.

Sapir, Edward. 1921. *Language: An Introduction to the Study of Speech*. New York: Harcourt, Brace & World.

de Saussure, Ferdinand. 1993. *Troisième Cours de Linguistique Générale (1910–1911): d'après les cahiers d'Emile Constantin./Third Course of Lectures on General Linguistics (1910–1911): From the Notebooks of Emile Constantin*. Eisuke Komatsu (ed.) and Roy Harris (trans.). Oxford: Pergamon Press.

Scragg, Donald G. 1974. *A History of English Spelling*. New York: Manchester University Press and Barnes & Noble.

Sgall, Petr. 1987. Towards a theory of phonemic orthography. In: Philip A. Luelsdorff (ed.), *Orthography and Phonology*, 1–30. Amsterdam/Philadelphia: John Benjamins.

Smith, Jeremy J. 2012. From Middle to Early Modern English. In: Mugglestone (ed.), 147–179.

Stenroos, Merja. 2002. Free variation and other myths: Interpreting historical English spelling. *Studia Anglica Posnaniensia* 38: 445–468.

Stenroos, Merja. 2004. Regional dialects and spelling conventions in Late Middle English: Searches for (th) in the LALME data. In: Marina Dossena and Roger Lass (eds.), *Methods and Data in English Historical Dialectology*, 257–285. Bern: Peter Lang.

Stenroos, Merja. 2006. A Middle English mess of fricative spellings: Reflections on thorn, yogh and their rivals. In: Marcin Krygier and Liliana Sikorska (eds.), *To Make his Englissh Sweete upon his Tonge*, 9–35. Frankfurt am Main: Peter Lang.

Stetson, Raymond H. 1981 [1937]. The phoneme and the grapheme. In: Ruszkiewicz (ed.), 35–44 [Reprinted from *Mélanges de linguistique et de philologie offerts à Jacq. van Ginneken*, 353–356].

Stockwell, Robert P. and C. Westbrook Barritt. 1951. *Some Old English Graphemic-Phonemic Correspondences – ae, ea and a*. (Studies in Linguistics, Occasional Papers, 4.) Norman, OK: Battenburg Press.

Tieken-Boon van Ostade, Ingrid. 2009. *An Introduction to Late Modern English*. Edinburgh: Edinburgh University Press.

Upward, Christopher and George Davidson. 2011. *The History of English Spelling*. Chichester: Wiley-Blackwell.

Vachek, Josef. 1973. *Written Language: General Problems and Problems of English*. The Hague: Mouton.
Vachek, Josef. 1976 [1945–49]. Some remarks on writing and phonetic transcription. In: Vachek (ed.), 127–133 [Reprinted from *Acta Linguistica* 5: 86–93].
Vachek, Josef (ed.). 1976. *Selected Writings in English and General Linguistics*. The Hague: Mouton.
Vachek, Josef. 1982. English orthography: A functional approach. In: William Haas (ed.), *Standard Languages: Spoken and Written*, 37–56. Manchester: Manchester University Press.
Venezky, Richard L. 1970. *The Structure of English Orthography*. The Hague: Mouton.
Venezky, Richard L. 1999. *The American Way of Spelling*. New York: The Guildford Press.
Wallis, John. 1670. A Letter of Doctor John Wallis to Robert Boyle Esq. concerning the said Doctors Essay of Teaching a person Dumb and Deaf to speak, and to understand Language, together with the success thereof, made apparent to his Majesty, the Royal Society, and the University of Oxford. *Philosophical Transactions* 61: 1087–1099.
Wełna, Jerzy. 1982. *English Spelling and Pronunciation*. Warszawa: Państwowe Wydawnictwo Naukowe.
Wolfe, Patricia. 1972. *Linguistic Change and the Great Vowel Shift in English*. Berkeley: University of California Press.
Wrenn, Charles L. 1967. The value of spelling as evidence. In: Charles L. Wrenn (ed.), *Word and Symbol: Studies in English Language*, 129–149. London: Longmans.
Wyld, Henry. 1936. *A History of Modern Colloquial English*. Oxford: Basil Blackwell.
Zachrisson, Robert. 1913. *Pronunciation of English Vowels 1400–1700*. Göteborg: W. Zachrissons boktryckeri.

Claudia Claridge
Chapter 12:
Styles, Registers, Genres, Text Types

1   Introduction —— 218
2   A selective history of registers —— 220
3   Stylistic developments in English —— 224
4   Approaches to historical texts —— 228
5   Summary —— 233
6   References —— 234

Abstract: The chapter surveys research on registers, styles, text types and genres in the history of English. The presence of registers is connected with socio-cultural conditions, such as the structure of society, multilingualism, the practice of translation, academic traditions, and technological progress. The legal and the scientific registers are described in more detail. The stylistic development of English is treated here as linked to standardization (elaboration in syntax and lexicon) and the orality-literacy continuum (increasing development of more literate characteristics). The curial style of the 14th/15th century and the plain style of the 17th century are highlighted. Three approaches to genre and to text types are presented. Inventories of genre labels highlight the presence, nature and development of genres throughout English history. Changes in texts, and genres across periods can also be studied through looking at their conventional structure (e.g. letters) or their linguistic features (e.g. discourse deixis). Lastly, text types/genres can also play a role in language change.

1 Introduction

Looking through books on the history of English, one will as a rule not find separate sections on texts and registers (with the exception of Görlach 1999a, 2001a; Claridge 2017). Looking at language in use, in contrast, it is obvious that it "exists in texts" (Diller 2001: 3). Individual linguistic features are realized *in* texts and *for the sake of* creating coherent and effective texts, so that language history can not only be investigated by studying texts but is actually only constituted by

---

Claudia Claridge: Augsburg (Germany)

texts and changing textual needs. Any linguistic history that is textless, therefore, ignores a very important perspective on the development of English. The interrelationship between the development of linguistic features and their textual uses has only relatively recently received more attention on a firmer theoretical and methodological basis than before. The collection edited by Diller and Görlach (2001) and the special issue of the *European Journal of English Studies* (ed. Moessner 2001) dealing with genre and text types in a historical perspective bear witness to this.

Unfortunately, the definitions of the terms in the title are quite varied in the literature (cf. Diller 2001 for a discussion). This chapter is based on the following understanding of the terminology. While registers and styles are inventories of linguistic devices, genres and text types are classes of texts. Genre is primarily based on text-external considerations (cf. Biber 1989: 5–6) and refers to aspects such as the functions, conventional shape, and structure of texts. Genres are linked to expectations on the part of text users about the (proto-)typical functions and (surface) features of texts belonging to the genre; thus competent speakers have fairly clear ideas about what a fairy tale, a letter, a prayer, or a weather forecast is like. As folk categories, genres are not necessarily defined by a strict and homogeneous set of criteria. Text types, on the other hand, are defined by text-internal linguistic criteria, which to a certain extent go along but do not completely overlap with genre distinctions (cf. Taavitsainen 2002: 220). Text-typological approaches (e.g. Longacre 1996; Werlich 1983) have presented broad categories such as narrative, descriptive, expository, instructive or procedural/behavioral, and argumentative, which are characterized by a typical (co-)occurrence of linguistic features, e.g. narrative: past tense verbs, time adverbials; procedural: imperatives. Such internal text-type features can be present in a given text to varying extents, thus making it more or less expository/narrative/etc. in nature, and features from different types can combine, producing, for example, an expository-argumentative hybrid.

Register is a more general term, comprising both oral and written productions based in particular on situational, social, and professional contexts and the field or domain of discourse. Thus the domains of religion, law, science, journalism, etc., constitute the religious, legal etc. registers, all of which exhibit a certain cohesion in terms of possible interaction types, aims, and contents, producing lexico-grammatical similarities on a more general level than text types. Registers usually comprise various genres. Style is the vaguest of all these terms and potentially cuts across all the other distinctions. Diller (1998: 155–156) defines style as used by textual stylistics as the idiosyncratic "characteristic linguistic features of a text", and that of linguistic stylistics as "different ways of saying the same thing". From the point of view of the language user, style implies aspects like choice between linguistic items, perceptions of appropriateness going *beyond* register conventions, ideas of norm vs. deviance, and (potentially prescriptive) aesthetic notions. A given style can go with an individual, a group of people, or a time period.

A note on the application of some of these concepts in a commonly used source in historical linguistics, namely *The Helsinki Corpus* (HC) (Rissanen et al. 1991), may be in order here. The corpus encodes what it calls "text type" (<T>) and "prototypical text category" (<Z>). The latter refers to (broad) text types as explained above, containing such labels as "expository", "instruction religious", and "narration imaginative", to which it adds register information (religious) or the more general Volume 3 distinction of (non-)fictionality in some cases. *The Helsinki Corpus* text types, in contrast, in some cases are rather genres (e.g. handbook, sermon, preface, comedy) and in others are reminiscent of registers (e.g. science medicine, history).

2 A selective history of registers

Some registers are attested throughout the history of English, albeit perhaps in varying strength and internal variety. The religious register is one of those with a long history, for example, and also with a certain breadth of representation. Apart from the Bible, the register is represented by – both original and translated – sermons and homilies, texts related to the liturgy like prayers, the Creed, the psalter or hymns, lives of saints, hortative and instructional writing, and academic theological/exegetical writing. Except for the last type, all are attested from Old English onwards. Other registers, in contrast, have only emerged at some later point in history (e.g. newspaper language). Late evolution may have to do with extralinguistic developments, such as the possibilities offered by the printing press or the rise of modern natural science, but also with the different status of English vis-à-vis other languages in different periods. As to the latter aspect, in domains like religion, the law, and scientific/academic writing, Latin, in particular, and French played important roles during the Middle Ages and also beyond, thus competing with, sometimes dominating, English in the respective registers (cf. Görlach 1999b: 462). This will also be visible in the short outline of the registers of law and science which follows.

2.1 Legal English

Like the religious register, legal (and administrative) English is a long-standing variety with a remarkable functional stability and a very distinctive form of English. Hiltunen (1990) provides a historical survey of legal English, but without covering all periods equally (Early Modern English is particularly neglected, for this cf. Lehto 2015). The oldest extant legal texts are the laws of King Ethelbert of Kent (635 CE), which are followed by various other law codes up to the reign of Cnut in the 11th century (cf. Liebermann 1903–16). Old English legal language already shows the complex structures present in the modern variety, even if to a lesser extent, such as conditional, relative and adverbial subordination, and multiple embedding. But it also lacks some modern characteristics, such as the emphasis on unambiguous reference and precision, and thus also its repetitiveness.

With the Norman Conquest, however, English ceased to exist as a language of the law for about four centuries, until the 1362 Statute of Pleading re-established English as the oral legal language, and the first Act of Parliament to be written in English was passed in 1483. During the Middle English period, legal writing had used first "Law Latin", later French, while pleading had taken place in French, thus adopting not only foreign legal procedures, but also the linguistic patterns of legal Latin and French. Similar linguistic mixtures are also found in administrative or business records, whose macaronic writing style (mixing Latin, French, and English) has been termed a "deliberate, formal register" by Wright (1992: 769). The full establishment of English in all spheres of law was gradually carried through during the Early Modern English period, involving again translation of important texts into English. From about the 16th century there is no shortage of legal texts in English. Through trial transcripts and proceedings (cf. Huber et al. 2016) we also have an insight into the oral forms of historical legal discourse; studies on Early Modern English courtroom language have been carried out by Archer (2005) on British data and by, e.g., Grund (2007) on the Salem Witchcraft Trials.

As a consequence of its history, Hiltunen (1990: 52) has characterized modern legal language as "essentially a kind of 'creole', where the formative elements go back to an amalgamation of native resources and extensive borrowing". One of the noteworthy characteristics of legal English is its lexicon reflecting the influence of the various legal traditions throughout its history, from Anglo-Saxon terminology (which has mostly disappeared, often together with the concepts, e.g. *wergeld*), via Norse terms, to French and Latin words (Mellinkoff 1963). Modern law language is further characterized by archaic lexical usages, such as *aforesaid*, *theretofore* and similar elements, which are fossils from the Early

Modern English period. Throughout its English history, the register seems to have followed a trend towards ever more specificity and explicitness, thus increasing its linguistic complexity. Partly, this complexity has been made more accessible by structure-building visual arrangements, which had not been used in the past; this last point shows that the visual aspect of texts should also play a role in textual studies.

2.2 Scientific language

The "vernacularisation boom of the fourteenth century" (Taavitsainen 2001: 189) was certainly important for law, and so it was for another register, i.e. scientific writing. In contrast to law, science is a younger discipline and thus also a newer register. Anglo-Saxon science and an Old English scientific register in a proper sense do not exist; what is extant is rather texts of a practical nature, such as astrological texts, herbals, and medical recipes (e.g. *Bald's Leechbook*). In general the scientific or academic community of the Middle Ages, which was an international one, used Latin, not only as a written but also as a spoken language, e.g. within the universities. This custom was slow to die, extending into the 17th and 18th centuries in England, when Latin works were still being written, although to an ever-decreasing extent. From an extralinguistic point of view, science – in the modern understanding of an empirical (also experimental) and rationalist undertaking in search of new knowledge, which is prototypically represented by the natural sciences – is a product of the 17th and 18th centuries (Hunter 1981). What we find before that is the more traditional and conservative scholastic tradition as well as various precursors of modern science from the late Middle Ages onwards, both with regard to thinking, method, and language use. This development is being charted by the "Scientific Thought-styles" project centering on the exemplary investigation of medical writing, which revealed a shift from argumentation founded on established authorities to more evidence-based argumentation. The split of the domain into a learned-popular continuum, emerging from late ME (Taavitsainen 2005), can be seen in this connection; while the learned end is characterized by expository and argumentative texts, the popular side tends to be practically oriented and instructive in style.

Taavitsainen (2001) presents a survey of the early development of the scientific register. Vernacular writing in medicine, followed by other scientific fields (e.g. astronomy), emerged in the 14th century. Some forms of writing in this field had a continuous vernacular history, e.g. recipes, rules of health, charms, prognostications, and remedy books (Taavitsainen 2005). Generally, however, the developing English register took as its model the Latin academic and scientific register (termed "modelling from above" by Taavitsainen 2001: 188), which was aided by the fact that many texts were either translations (e.g. by Trevisa in the 14th century) or adaptations of foreign sources. Newly introduced genres, such as specialized treatises or surgical texts, often made their way into English through translations. In particular the conventions for the learned genres were apparently taken over from the Greco-Roman tradition, but research in this area is complicated by the fact that the relevant genres in Latin and Greek have not been sufficiently investigated (Taavitsainen 2005). Taavitsainen mentions that the classical format of questions and answers, which was simplified in English, developed from fairly irregular early attempts to fixed and regular structures in the 16th century, and remained in use in handbooks for centuries. The scientific vocabulary is thus also based on extensive borrowing from Romance sources (increasing from the 14th century onwards), with the respective greater use of native vs. foreign lexical resources corresponding to more practical/popular writings vs. more theoretical/academical writing in the medical field, for example. While the Helsinki research group around Taavitsainen and Pahta concentrated on medical writing, Halliday (1988) charted the development of physics writing as a representative of the scientific register. He shows how the major propositional points are over time increasingly presented in nominalized forms, easily allowing both objectivization, categorization, and fore-/backgrounding, while verbs are progressively more restricted to expressing relational or existential aspects of the nominal arguments. In parallel, though starting somewhat later than the just mentioned aspects, the depersonalization of scientific discourse is in progress.

Let me end this section with two general points. First, translations have played a role in various registers. This means that register and textual studies will have to pay attention to how foreign models influenced English developments, and thus, more cross-linguistic studies and also more text-oriented studies on languages such as Medieval Latin are necessary. Second, a link can be made between register development and standardization in English (cf. also Section 3), as different registers had a differing impact on the standard and also were receptive to the standard to various extents. The administrative register in the form of Chancery writings was one input into the emerging English standard (Fisher 1996), Lollard texts within the religious register have been connected with another important strand of standardizing varieties (Samuels 1963), with which ME scientific writing also had certain affinities, although this register seems to have resisted the standard somewhat more (Taavitsainen 2001). In EModE times, the *Book of Common Prayer* and the *Authorized Version* also had a standardizing impact.

3 Stylistic developments in English

Styles are at least partly linked to the orality-literacy continuum, with oral and literate features mixing in particular ways in texts. In this connection, standardization, especially the process of elaboration (Haugen 1972 [1966]), is important for stylistic developments, as standardization will emphasize the literate end of the continuum. Another important aspect is the varying impact of foreign models, French and in particular Latin, which goes together with the long-standing but ultimately waning influence of (classical) rhetoric. Furthermore, specific stylistic changes are sometimes embedded in certain registers and genres, literary as well as non-literary, which also accounts for the substantial contributions to historical stylistics from literary studies. A last aspect of note is the fact that most studies of style deal with the (early) modern period, at the most extending into late Middle English. Gordon (1966), still the only large-scale historical study of prose style extant, shows this bias as well, the Middle Ages being dealt with in a mere 35 pages.

3.1 Standardization processes and their stylistic effects

The syntactic elaboration of English proceeding especially during the 16th to 18th centuries ultimately produced more complex, ordered, and explicit structures, all of them principally useful for complex writing and thus essentially literate (e.g. Rissanen 1999 for an overview of syntactic developments). Such stylistically relevant structures include greater and more sophisticated use of hypotactic and embedded structures (adverbial and relative clauses, non-finite constructions, innovations in the conjunction class) and emerging and/or expanding use of topicalizing constructions (e.g. passive, clefting), as well as more discriminate use of prepositions and prepositional phrases, enabling a tighter information structure. In Chafe's (1982) terms, these characteristics make for the more integrated and detached characteristics of modern writing. Despite the fact that it is difficult to clearly attribute individual changes to foreign, especially Latin, models, the general attitude towards Latin as a model of grammatical precision and stylistic elegance fostered the stylistic "improvement" of English in order to make it "equal" to Latin (cf. the varying assessment of English reported e.g. by Rusch 1972). What also played a role in this context is the humanistic rediscovery of the original classical texts and the influence of classical rhetoric in English education (cf. the works of Erasmus and, in English, Wilson; cf. Plett 2004).

The lexical elaboration of English, going on since the early Middle Ages but consciously intensified particularly in the 16th and 17th centuries (cf. Nevalainen

1999; Barber 1997), produced stylistic levels within the lexicon, with the Romance elements tending towards more impersonal, abstract, and formal expression versus the native elements' potentially more down-to-earth, emotive, and colloquial impact. While the lexical division is partly linked to register (e.g. *cardio-/cardiac* in the medical register vs. *heart* elsewhere), it can also be exploited for stylistic effects. Hughes (2000) illustrates how (quasi-) synonymous doublets and triplets differ stylistically depending on etymology and time of borrowing. In general one can say that the style of a given piece of writing or passage from at least about the 15th century onwards is in no small part determined by the percentage of Romance and classical vocabulary used (Gordon 1966). The so-called "aureate" style of Lydgate and others in the 15th century is created by a conscious use of elevated Romance lexis, and partly also by complex noun phrases and Latinate syntax. How Shakespeare exploited these lexical distinctions for characterizing persons and situations as well as changing relationships and generally for stylistic effect was shown by Schäfer (1973). Besides expanding the means of the language in general, lexical growth had a stylistic aim from the start in being crucially linked to the rhetorical concept of copiousness, i.e. lexical variety through amplification, synonymy, repetition, and paraphrasing.

3.2 Oral vs. literate styles

The connection between standardization, writing, texts and the orality-literacy cline was investigated in particular by Biber (1995; cf. also Biber and Finegan 1989, 1992). He examined the development of eight English genres, called "registers" by him (personal essays, medical research articles, science research articles, legal opinions, fiction, personal letters, and dialogue from drama and from fiction) from the 17th to the 20th century based on the three dimensions:
- Involved vs. Informational Production,
- Situation-dependent vs. Elaborated Reference, and
- Non-abstract vs. Abstract Style.

These dimensions are characterized by the significant presence or absence of the following features:
a. private verbs, 1p and 2p pronouns, present tense verbs, demonstrative pronouns, *be* as main verb etc.,
b. *wh*-relative clauses, pied piping, nominalizations, phrasal coordination,
c. conjuncts, passives, past participles, adverbial subordinators (cf. Biber 1988 for a comprehensive feature listing).

The features of (a) represent the oral/spoken end of the continuum and those of (b) and (c) the written/literate end. Biber's results show that all prose registers are clearly non-oral in character already at the beginning of his time frame and that most of them become increasingly more literate during the next 100 or 200 years, especially more informational and elaborated. The 18th century in particular is characterized by very pronounced literate textual realizations. According to Biber (1995: 298), such a development is typical of the early stages of the introduction of writing in a language. As this does not really apply to English in the 17th century, it is rather the combined result of ongoing standardization, in particular the culmination point of its normative phase in the 18th century, and perhaps the requirements of the more "public" genres. McIntosh's (1998) "gentrification" thesis confirms and complements Biber's results, by tracing a development towards a more literate and elegant prose in the course of the 18th century, a process that is driven by class-consciousness and a feeling of propriety. The resulting "gentrified" style is marked by complex but very orderly sentences, passives, nominalizations, as well as polysyllabic and abstract vocabulary. While Biber's genres develop largely in parallel until the 18th century, they start to diverge from the 19th century onwards. Medical, scientific, and legal prose consistently proceeded to develop towards even more literate styles up to the 20th century, while the popular, non-expository genres (essays, fiction, drama, letters) gradually and increasingly reversed towards more oral, i.e. involved, non-abstract, and situation-dependent, realizations. In the modern period there is thus a clear stylistic split between the two groups.

While the research just summarized deals with a long-range perspective and uses the stylistic dimensions originally produced on the basis of 20th-century material, Biber (2001) reapplied factorial analysis to 18th-century data, thus producing the stylistic dimensions typical for that time. The results point to the fact that there was a more pronounced distinction between spoken and written registers in the past than there is today, with drama but none of the other types being marked as extremely oral. It is also possible that this result is an artefact of the missing spoken dimension, thus making drama stand out in peculiar ways.

3.3 Historical styles: two examples

Any literary history will abound with styles, be it the aureate diction of the 15th century, Euphuism in the 16th century or Milton's Latinate style. Some of these may be of literary interest only, while others are relevant to both literary and linguistic scholars, among which are the clergial or curial style, the so-called "plain style" and the stylistic shift taking place in the 18th century mentioned above. The clergial style, found in the 14th and 15th centuries, derives ultimately from medieval chancellary Latin, the dictaminal arts in general, and more directly from French vernacular models, which were imitated and developed by English writers. It eventually turned into a courtly prose style. It can be found in Chaucer's prose (Bornstein 1978, with a long list of examples), in writings of the English royal administration and in Caxton's works (Burnley 1986; Blake 1992). Features of this style include Latinate words and constructions, extensive clausal qualifiers, and long complex sentences, synonymous doublets, anaphoric cohesive devices, epithets, and a preference for the use of the passive.

The plain style emerging in the 17th century needs to be looked at in a larger context, as it is partly a reaction against other stylistic models. According to Sprat's well-known formulation about the discourse of the Royal Society the motivation for the plain style was

> to reject all the amplifications, digressions, and swellings of style: to return back to the primitive purity, and shortness, when men deliver'd so many things, almost in an equal number of words. [...] a close, naked, natural way of speaking; positive expressions; clear senses; a native easiness: bringing all things as near the Mathematical plainness, as they can: and preferring the language of Artizans, Countrymen, and Merchants before that, of Wits, or Scholars (Sprat 1667: 113).

In spite of Sprat's testimony neither the genesis, the characteristics, nor the type of users of the plain style are entirely clear; partly this may also be due to the fact that the 17th century itself used the term to refer to opposing styles (Adolph 1968: 130). Taavitsainen (2001: 196) characterizes the "house style" of the *Philosophical Transactions*, the organ of the Royal Society, as marked by first-person narration, subjective point of view, and expressions of low modality. Hüllen's (1989) analysis of some of the descriptive adjectives Sprat uses (e.g. *plain, naked, easy*) shows that apart from conveying the senses 'generally understandable' and 'unadorned' they have a number of meanings linking linguistic style to thought, and more generally life styles (e.g. 'not intellectual, objective, frank, theoretical, contentedness'). For Gordon (1966: 127), this style embodied a rejection of Latinate syntax (Ciceronian and Senecan), of rhetorical figures, and of metaphor and simile, as well as a return to Anglo-Saxon sentence structures – i.e. it is *one* form of the speech-based prose using ordinary vocabulary and the "grammar of spoken English" (Gordon (1966: 122) that he identified in the 17th century. It is, however, the genteel and polite form produced by educated gentleman, which is what Sprat's early scientists were; it is not necessarily the speech of merchants or artisans (Gordon 1966: 128; Atkinson 1996: 362–364; Hüllen 1989: 84). While Sprat linked the new style to the Royal Society and thus to natural science, it is better seen as a larger and manifold process. A plain style is also found with authors such as John Wilkins, John Webster, and Joseph Glanvill, and in fields such as law, religion, and travel literature, which do not belong to the new science (Hüllen 1989: 70), and needs to be seen in the context of a larger development from a rhetoric of persuasion to one of exposition (thus linking up with text types) from the end of the 16th century onwards (Howell 1956: 388).

Various authorities, while agreeing on the overall stylistic shift, have emphasized different aspects and times as being decisive for the new style. Fish (1952) stressed the importance of puritan preaching style, shifting the emergence back to as early as 1570, and Warner (1961: 97) saw the likelihood of an influence of the *Authorized Version* of the Bible; science figures prominently in other explanations. Adolph (1968), placing the shift around 1600, saw the scientific and puritan notions of utilitarianism as decisive for its development. Picking the same time frame, Croll (1921) opted for Francis Bacon's personal anti-Ciceronian style as the foundation of the new plain style. Jones (1953) came closest to Sprat by identifying the Restoration period and the emerging sciences and rationalism as the crucial aspects for the new style. Despite the disagreements, some things seem clear: new communicative needs, based on diverse religious practices and on an emerging natural science, but also on newly arising economic and social conditions (e.g. rise of the "middle classes"), led to a new style. This style was less overtly influenced by Latin rhetorical models, broke with "scholastic" (thought) styles (cf. also Taavitsainen 2001), and was potentially more focused on the author. Gordon's characterization of this style as speech-based, however, conflicts with Biber's (1995) and Biber and Finegan's (1989, 1992) findings of the already largely literate character of this period's prose (cf. above).

4 Approaches to historical texts

Kohnen (2012) distinguishes three approaches to the investigation of historical texts:
- historical text linguistics proper,
- diachronically oriented text linguistics, and
- text-oriented historical linguistics.

The first of these approaches is the study of texts, genres and discourse domains in historical periods of a language, which crucially includes genre inventories. The second approach studies changes in texts, genres and discourse domains across periods, e.g. conventional text structure, or the link between macro-categories and specific text types. The third approach deals with the functions of texts, genres and discourse domains in language change.

4.1 Historical text linguistics: genre histories

Görlach (1992, 2001b, 2002, 2004) takes an external approach to the question of genres, although he uses the term "text type". His suggestion is to collect genre names existing at a given time or throughout the history and to conduct a componential analysis on the lexical field found. Görlach (2001b, 2004) gives the following 24 parameters (thought of as equivalent to semantic markers) for distinguishing text types, to which I add in brackets his characterization of the genre "contract": field (law), intention (binding), act/action connected to text (none), accompaniment by music or visual material (no), conglomerate (no), composite (yes), boundness (free), cohesion/coherence (yes), original (yes), nativeness (yes), general/regional (standard), time (present-day), medium (written), style (formal), form (prose), formulaicness (yes), orientation (content-oriented), specialization (technical), truth (non-fictional), spontaneity (no: revised), publicness (yes), length (n.a.), and official (yes). Görlach (2004) provides two alphabetical lists of English genre terms based on entries in the *Shorter Oxford English Dictionary* (with dates) and on the *Thesaurus of Old English*. Examples of genre terms from Görlach's list are eulogy, handbook, invoice, joke, lecture, parable, report, and small talk. He also illustrates his approach with an exemplary componential analysis of genre terms beginning with <c>, from which the contract example above was taken. The presence or absence of a genre term at a given time, extractable from Görlach's list, and its understanding by contemporaries themselves highlight the cultural determinacy of the concept genre. Genres and text types may remain fairly stable over a long time (e.g. the sonnet), but equally they may be falling into disuse (e.g. those marked by a dagger in Görlach's list, or the telegram at present) or be newly emerging (e.g. the essay in the 16th century) (cf. Görlach 2002). Some types evolve only within (newly established) media, registers, or publication types, such as dedications within books (15th century), and a whole variety within newspapers (e.g. editorial 1830, obituary 1828, weather forecast 1883; Görlach 2004), though sometimes taking existing genres as models (e.g. early dedications and news reports being connected to letters).

4.2 Diachronically oriented text linguistics

Conventional and changing textual structures have been investigated for the genre of letters, for example. Richardson (1984) describes Chancery and other letters, based on Latin style, to be structured as follows:
– address,
– salutation,

- notification,
- exposition,
- disposition / disjunction,
- final clause,
- valediction,
- attestation and
- date.

Davis (1965), in contrast, argues for a French model to be followed in correspondence, consisting of
- address,
- commendation formula,
- health formula at the beginning of the letter, and
- closing formula.

Nevalainen (2001) explores the use of these formulae in the letters of the Johnson merchant family written 1542–1552. She finds that the Johnson letters follow six of the nine medieval letter-writing conventions, namely date (and place), salutation, address, "health" formula, notification, and (a form of) valediction, but they do this to varying degrees, with great individual variation and with additions and modifications. Okulska (2006) deals with structural letter elements, but also with topic development and information structure in the sub-genre of the diplomatic narrative report letter, from the 15th to the 18th century. With regard to the latter aspect, the letters represent discursive hybrids combining narrative (past orientation, topic-based) and reporting (present tense, person-centered) elements, the latter also frequently triggering evaluative-argumentative comments in the early, but not the later, part of the period. As to the presentation of information in these letters, there is a shift from inductive topic-delayed to deductive topic-first thesis presentation from the 16th century onwards, which puts the focus more clearly on the information itself than on the persons interacting.

Another approach with regard to text types is to follow the diachronic development of the prototypical text types, such as narrative or exposition, or, as there are hardly pure types, of genres which are typically dominated by one of these, e.g. works on language as representing the instructive type. This has not been done for any of the types on a broad scale so far, but smaller-scale treatments exist (e.g., Peikola et al. 2009). Taavitsainen (2004), for example, deals with genres of secular instruction from Old English to Early Modern English, in particular with how they are made more pleasant and entertaining for the readers. This means the inclusion of other than purely instructive features, such as the use of verse form, narrative passages, dialogues, typical involvement features, and a conventional fictionalized frame. Taavitsainen found both considerable variation within the text category and interesting diachronic continuities, as well as a "circular movement" of features moving from learned texts to more popular texts, thus again leaving space for innovation at the learned end of the continuum. With regard to narrative discourse, for example, Wårvik (1990a and 1990b) describes the history of grounding markers in English narratives. She finds that English has undergone a change from a foreground-signalling language in Old English (by use of the more or less obligatory marker þa 'then') to a background-signalling language in modern English (by means of, e.g., subordination, non-finite forms). Whereas marking in Old English is fairly specific and, in a certain sense, monodimensional, the modern system is more fuzzy, being characterized by a variety of non-obligatory, partly stylistic options.

A further avenue of research investigates the aspect that certain text categories or genres seem to prefer certain text-level features rather than others. One good example for this is discourse deixis, which has been investigated by Fries (1993, 1994), Claridge (2001), and Kilpiö (1997). Fries (1993, 1994) found deictic elements marking text location very or most commonly in the text categories instruction (religious and secular), non-imaginative narration, and exposition in Old English and Early Modern English. The markers *afore* and *the said* very clearly dominate in statutory texts. Statutory and similar texts also figure prominently in Kilpiö's (1997) diachronic investigation, which concentrates on participial adjectives of the type *(a)forementioned* in the entire *Helsinki Corpus* (HC) (thus using *The Helsinki Corpus* text-labelling terminology). While these discourse-deictic elements are rare in Old English and early Middle English, they become more frequent from 1350 onwards with genres like official letters, documents, and law heading the frequency lists (joined by history and science in Early Modern English). In contrast, Old English law does not use such features. Of interest are also the kinds of genres which make do without these discourse-deictic elements, namely Middle English and early Modern English rule, Bible, homily, drama, comedy, and those that use them very rarely, namely sermons, fiction, and education. Sermons and religious treatises also show the lowest instance of discourse-deictic terms in Claridge's (2001) study, while the legal register, represented by many different genres in the corpus, has the highest number. Early Modern English scientific genres show a high number of items indicating present location and forward-indicating items, pointing to the importance of commenting on the ongoing discourse procedure of the author.

The study of connective devices is another case in point for text-level feature preferences insofar as it illuminates the kinds of explicit cohesive relationships typical for certain genres. Kohnen (2007) investigated what he termed "connective profiles", i.e. the overall use of the whole range of coordinating and subordinating conjunctions/complementizers. Comparing 17th-century sermons and statutes he found quite distinct profiles: a fairly high and heterogeneous number of connectives in sermons and a much lower, less varied use in statutes. Partly this seems to be due to a stylistic preference for conjunctionless non-finite subordination in statutory language. But it is also based on the communicative functions common of statutes. Rare *but* and non-existent *for* are expendable because contrastive viewpoints and the provision of justifications are hardly found in these texts, whereas moderately common *and* is useful for enumerations. All subordinators are less common in statutes than in sermons, except for manner/comparison markers, which is due to the legal formulaic use of introductory *whereas/as* clauses. A notable frequency is furthermore only exhibited by nominal clause connectives (especially *that*) and by conditional clauses. Kohnen also looked at the diachronic development of sermons over the 15th, 16th, 17th, and late 20th century, and sums up the general pattern as a decrease in oral features and simultaneous increase in literate features in Early Modern English, followed by the reverse development in the 20th century.

4.3 The role of texts in language change

Kohnen (2001) sees genres ("text types" in his terminology) as catalysts in language change, i.e. they facilitate change and are responsible for the spreading of a construction, his example being the adverbial first participle construction. He showed how this construction spread across text types over a period of two centuries, its textual frequency first increasing in religious treatises around 1340, then about 1390 in both homilies/sermons and petitions/statutes, by roughly 1470 in chronicles, and finally by around 1520 in narrative prose and private letters. In each instance the construction fulfils an important functional requirement of the text type, e.g. introducing explanatory passages in Biblical exegesis (treatises), providing vivid descriptions in sermons, petitions, and narrative prose, or encoding formulaic speech acts in the introductory sections of letters. According to Kohnen, the particular chronological adoption of the feature by the genres is due to the following three aspects. Early or well-established vernacular types, such as religious treatises and sermons, make use of the participle construction earlier than types which are found only later as vernacular forms, e.g. letters. So do genres close to Latin and/or French traditions (both of which had the construction in question) and those that are more formal in character, such as religious prose and petitions/statutes. Lastly, the linguistic features adopted by genres with considerable social relevance and a prestigious status, i.e. religious treatises, statutes, and documents, are more likely to spread to other text types later than features adopted first by less prestigious texts.

5 Summary

The above presentation has somewhat artificially separated things that intimately belong together. A style is found in a text which belongs both to a register and to a genre. Ideally, these aspects should be treated together then, but this would increase the complexity to such an extent that larger-scale and diachronic investigations would be difficult. Thus, particular research efforts tend to concentrate on only one of these aspects, even if this necessarily means simplifying. Another complicating factor, also visible in the extant research, is the variable usage of the basic terminology – what is one researcher's style may be another's register, which makes comparisons across works difficult. Furthermore, despite Kohnen (2012) quoted above, there is as yet no historical or diachronic text linguistics as an established field. Researchers in this field may at the moment tend to place themselves vaguely in the paradigm of historical pragmatics.

In contrast to the theoretical difficulties, actually researching historical texts may be getting increasingly easier. Many of the researchers quoted above approach the field with the help of corpus linguistics. A range of historical corpora is available by now, all of which use some kind of register, text type or genre coding system. *A Representative Corpus of Historical English Registers* (ARCHER) (Biber and Finegan 1993/2002/2007/2010/2013/2016) has been compiled and is being extended by Biber and various affiliates. *The Helsinki Corpus of English Texts* (HC) (Rissanen et al. 1991) contains texts from all the registers mentioned. As more general corpora often do not contain individual registers in sufficient numbers, single-register corpora are a particular asset. The *Zurich English Newspaper Corpus* (ZEN) (Fries et al. 2015), *The Lampeter Corpus of Early Modern English Tracts* (pamphlets) (Claridge et al. 1999) and *The Lancaster Newsbook Corpus* (McEnery and Hardie 2001–07) can be used together to investigate the origins of the press register. Similarly, the *Corpus of Early English Medical Writing* (CEEM) (Taavitsainen et al. 2005, 2010), compiled at Helsinki University, charts the development of a scientific writing based on the medical prototype. The *Corpus of Early English Correspondence Sampler* (CEECS) (Nevalainen et al. 1998) could be called a single-genre corpus. Not all of the above-mentioned corpora contain complete texts, however, which would be of especial importance for the genre or text-type approach.

6 References

Adolph, Robert. 1968. *The Rise of Modern Prose Style*. Cambridge, MA: MIT Press.
Archer, Dawn. 2005. *Questions and Answers in the English Courtroom (1640–1760)*. Amsterdam/Philadelphia: John Benjamins.
Atkinson, Dwight. 1996. The Philosophical Transactions of the Royal Society of London, 1675–1975. *Language in Society* 25: 333–371.
Barber, Charles. 1997. *Early Modern English*. Edinburgh: Edinburgh University Press.
Biber, Douglas. 1988. *Variation Across Speech and Writing*. Cambridge: Cambridge University Press.
Biber, Douglas. 1989. A typology of English texts. *Linguistics* 27(1): 3–43.
Biber, Douglas. 1995. *Dimensions of Register Variation*. Cambridge: Cambridge University Press.
Biber, Douglas. 2001. Dimensions of variation among 18th-century registers. In: Diller and Görlach (eds.), 89–109.
Biber, Douglas, and Edward Finegan. 1989. Drift and the evolution of English style: A history of three genres. *Language* 65: 487–517.
Biber, Douglas, and Edward Finegan. 1992. The linguistic evolution of five written and speech-based English genres from the 17th to the 20th centuries. In: Rissanen et al. (eds.), 688–704.
Biber, Douglas and Edward Finegan. 1993/2002/2007/2010/2013/2016. *A Representative Corpus of Historical English Registers* version (ARCHER). Version 3.3. Consortium of fourteen universities. http://www.projects.alc.manchester.ac.uk/archer/; last accessed 6 January 2017.
Blake, Norman. 1992. The literary language. In: Norman Blake (ed.), *Cambridge History of the English Language,* Vol. II. *1066–1476,* 500–541. Cambridge: Cambridge University Press.
Bornstein, Diane. 1978. Chaucer's *Tale of Melibee* as an example of "style clergial". *The Chaucer Review* 12: 236–254.
Burnley, J. David. 1986. Curial prose in England. *Speculum* 61(3): 593–614.
Chafe, Wallace. 1982. Integration and involvement in speaking, writing, and oral literature. In: Deborah Tannen (ed.), *Spoken and Written Language: Exploring Orality and Literacy*, 35–53. Norwood, NJ: Ablex.
Claridge, Claudia. 2001. Structuring text: Discourse deixis in Early Modern English Texts. *Journal of English Linguistics* 29(1): 55–71.
Claridge, Claudia. 2017. Discourse-based approaches. In: Laurel J. Brinton (ed.), *English Historical Linguistics: Approaches and Perspectives*, 185–217. Cambridge: Cambridge University Press.
Claridge, Claudia, Josef Schmied, and Rainer Siemund. 1999. *The Lampeter Corpus of Early Modern English Tracts*. http://www.helsinki.fi/varieng/CoRD/corpora/LC/; last accessed 29 June 2017.
Croll, Morris W. 1921. "Attic Prose" in the seventeenth century. *Studies in Philology* 18: 79–128.
Davis, Norman. 1965. The Litera Troili and English letters. *Review of English Studies, New Series* 16: 233–244.
Diller, Hans-Jürgen. 1998. Stylistics: Linguistic and textual. *European Journal of English Studies* 2(2): 155–174.
Diller, Hans-Jürgen. 2001. Genre in linguistic and related discourses. In: Diller and Görlach (eds.), 3–43.

Diller, Hans-Jürgen and Manfred Görlach (eds.). 2001. *Towards a History of English as a History of Genres*. Heidelberg: Winter.
Fish, Harold. 1952. The Puritans and the reform of prose-style. *A Journal of English Literary History* 19: 229–248.
Fisher, John. 1996. *The Emergence of Standard English*. Lexington: University Press of Kentucky.
Fries, Udo. 1993. Towards a description of text deixis in Old English. In: Klaus R. Grinda and Claus-Dieter Wetzel (eds.), *Anglo-Saxonica: Beiträge zur Vor- und Frühgeschichte der englischen Sprache und zur altenglischen Literatur*, 527–540. Munich: Fink.
Fries, Udo. 1994. Text deixis in Early Modern English. In: Dieter Kastovsky (ed.), *Studies in Early Modern English*, 111–128. Berlin/New York: Mouton de Gruyter.
Fries, Udo, Hans Martin Lehmann et al. 2015. *Zurich English Newspaper Corpus* (ZEN). Version 1.0. Zurich: University of Zurich. http://www.es.uzh.ch/en/Subsites/Projects/zencorpus.html; last assessed 6 January 2017.
Gordon, Ian A. 1966. *The Movement of English Prose*. London: Longman.
Görlach, Manfred. 1992. Text-types and language history: The cookery recipe. In: Rissanen et al. (eds.), 736–761.
Görlach, Manfred. 1999a. *English in Nineteenth-century England*. Cambridge: Cambridge University Press.
Görlach, Manfred. 1999b. Regional and social variation. In: Lass (ed.), 459–538.
Görlach, Manfred. 2001a. *Eighteenth-century English*. Heidelberg: Winter.
Görlach, Manfred. 2001b. A history of text types: A componential analysis. In: Diller and Görlach, 47–88.
Görlach, Manfred. 2002. What's in a name? Terms designating text types and the history of English. In: Andreas Fischer, Gunnel Tottie, and Hans-Martin Lehmann (eds.), *Text Types and Corpora. Studies in Honour of Udo Fries*, 17–28. Tübingen: Narr.
Görlach, Manfred. 2004. *Text Types and the History of English*. Berlin/New York: Mouton de Gruyter.
Grund, Peter. 2007. From tongue to text: The transmission of the Salem Witchcraft Examination Records. *American Speech* 82: 119–150.
Halliday, M. A. K. 1988. On the language of physical science. In: Mohsen Ghadessy (ed.), *Registers of Written English*, 162–178. London: Pinter.
Haugen, Einar. 1972. Dialect, language, nation. In: J. B. Pride and Janet Holmes (eds.), *Sociolinguistics*, 97–111. Harmondsworth: Penguin.
Hiltunen, Risto. 1990. *Chapters on Legal English. Aspects Past and Present of the Language of the Law*. Helsinki: Suomalainen Tiedeakatemia.
Howell, W. S. 1956. *Logic and Rhetoric in England, 1500–1700*. New York: Russell & Russell.
Huber, Magnus, Magnus Nissel, and Karin Puga (comp.). 2016. *The Old Bailey Corpus 1720–1913*, Version 2.0. http://corpora.clarin-d.uni-saarland.de/cqpweb/.
Hughes, Geoffrey. 2000. *A History of English Words*. Oxford: Blackwell.
Hüllen, Werner. 1989. *"Their Manner of Discourse": Nachdenken über Sprache im Umkreis der Royal Society*. Tübingen: Narr.
Hunter, Michael. 1981. *Science and Society in Restoration England*. Cambridge: Cambridge University Press.
Jones, Richard Foster. 1953. *The Triumph of the English Language*. Stanford: Stanford University Press.
Kilpiö, Matti. 1997. Participial adjectives with anaphoric reference of the type *the said, the (a) forementioned* from Old to Early Modern English: The evidence of the Helsinki Corpus. In:

Terttu Nevalainen and Leena Kahlas-Tarkka (eds.), *To Explain the Present: Studies in the Changing English Language in Honour of Matti Rissanen*, 77–100. Helsinki: Société Néophilologique.

Kohnen, Thomas. 2001. Text types as catalysts for language change: The example of the adverbial first participle construction. In: Diller and Görlach (eds.), 111–124.

Kohnen, Thomas. 2007. "Connective profiles" in the history of English texts. In: Ursula Lenker and Anneli Meurman-Solin (eds.), *Connectives in the History of English*, 289–308. Amsterdam/Philadelphia: John Benjamins.

Kohnen, Thomas. 2012. Historical text linguistics: Investigating language change in texts and genres. In: Hans Sauer and Gaby Waxenberger (eds.), *English Historical Lingustics 2008: Selected Papers from the Fifteenth International Conference on English Historical Linguistics (ICEHL), Munich, 24–30 August 2008*. Vol. II. *Words, Texts and Genres*, 165–188. Amsterdam/Philadelphia: John Benjamins.

Lass, Roger (ed.). 1999. *The Cambridge History of the English Language,* Vol. III. *1476–1776*. Cambridge: Cambridge University Press.

Lehto, Anu. 2015. *The Genre of Early Modern English Statutes: Complexity in Historical Legal Language*. Helsinki: Société Neophilologique.

Liebermann, Felix. 1903–16. *Die Gesetze der Angelsachsen*. 3 vols. Halle an der Saale: Max Niemeyer.

Longacre, Robert E. 1996. *The Grammar of Discourse*. 2nd edn. New York: Plenum Press.

McEnery, Tony and Andrew Hardie. 2001–07. *The Lancaster Newsbooks Corpus*. UCREL and Linguistics and English Language, University of Lancaster. http://www.lancaster.ac.uk/fass/projects/newsbooks/. Available through the *Oxford Text Archive*: http://ota.ox.ac.uk/desc/2531; last accessed 6 January 2017.

McIntosh, Carey. 1998. *The Evolution of English Prose, 1700–1800: Style, Politeness, and Print Culture*. Cambridge: Cambridge University Press.

Mellinkoff, David. 1963. *The Language of the Law*. Boston: Little, Brown.

Moessner, Lilo (ed.). 2001. *Special Issue of European Journal of English Studies* 5(2).

Nevalainen, Terttu. 1999. Early Modern English lexis and semantics. In: Lass (ed.), 332–458.

Nevalainen, Terttu. 2001. Continental conventions in early English correspondence. In: Diller and Görlach (eds.), 203–224.

Nevalainen, Terttu, Helena Raumolin-Brunberg, Jukka Keränen, Minna Nevala, Arja Nurmi, and Minna Palander-Collin. 1998. *Corpus of Early English Correspondence Sampler* (CEECS). University of Helsinki. https://www.helsinki.fi/en/researchgroups/varieng/corpus-of-early-english-correspondence. Also http://www.helsinki.fi/varieng/CoRD/corpora/CEEC/ceecs.html; last accessed 6 January 2017.

Okulska, Urszula. 2006. Textual strategies in the diplomatic correspondence of the Middle and Early Modern English periods: The narrative report letter as a genre. In: Marina Dossena and Susan Fitzmaurice (eds.), *Business and Official Correspondence: Historical Investigations*, 47–76. Bern: Lang.

Peikola, Matti, Janne Skaffari, and Sanna Kaisa Tanskanen (eds.). 2009. *Instructional Writing in English: Studies in Honour of Risto Hiltunen*. Amsterdam/Philadelpia: John Benjamins.

Plett, Heinrich F. 2004. *Rhetoric and Renaissance Culture*. Berlin/New York: Mouton de Gruyter.

Richardson, Malcolm. 1984. The dictamen and its influence on fifteenth-century English prose. *Rhetorica* 2: 207–226.

Rissanen, Matti. 1999. Syntax. In: Lass (ed.), 187–331.

Rissanen, Matti, Merja Kytö, Leena Kahlas-Tarkka, Matti Kilpiö, Saara Nevanlinna, Irma Taavitsainen, Terttu Nevalainen, and Helena Raumolin-Brunberg. 1991. *The Helsinki Corpus of English Texts* (HC). http://www.helsinki.fi/varieng/CoRD/corpora/HelsinkiCorpus/; last accessed 6 January 2017.

Rissanen, Matti, Ossi Ihalainen, Terttu Nevalainen, and Irma Taavitsainen (eds.). 1992. *History of Englishes: New Methods and Interpretations in Historical Linguistics*. Berlin/New York: Mouton de Gruyter.

Rusch, Jürg. 1972. *Die Vorstellung vom Goldenen Zeitalter der englischen Sprache im 16., 17., und 18. Jahrhundert*. Bern: Francke.

Samuels, M. L. 1963. Some applications of Middle English dialectology. *English Studies: A Journal of English Language and Literature* 44: 81–94.

Schäfer, Jürgen. 1973. *Shakespeares Stil: germanisches und romanisches Vokabular*. Frankfurt: Athenäum.

Skaffari, Janne, Matti Peikola, Ruth Carroll, Risto Hiltunen, and Brita Wårvik (eds.). 2005. *Opening Windows on Texts and Discourses of the Past*. Amsterdam/Philadelphia: John Benjamins.

Sprat, Thomas. 1667. *The history of the Royal-Society of London for the improving of natural knowledge by Tho. Sprat*. London: Printed by T. R. for J. Martyn …, and J. Allestry … (accessible via EEBO: http://eebo.chadwyck.com/home).

Taavitsainen, Irma. 2001. Language history and the scientific register. In: Diller and Görlach (eds.), 185–202.

Taavitsainen, Irma. 2002. Historical discourse analysis: Scientific language and changing thought-styles. In: Teresa Fanego, Belén Méndez-Naya, and Elena Seoane (eds.*)*, *Sounds, Words, Texts and Change*, 201–226. Amsterdam/Philadelphia: John Benjamins.

Taavitsainen, Irma. 2004. Genres of secular instruction: A linguistic history of useful entertainment. *Miscelánea: A Journal of English and American Studies* 29: 75–94.

Taavitsainen, Irma. 2005. Genres and the appropriation of science: Loci communes *in English in the late medieval and early modern period*. *In:* Skaffari . (eds.), 179–196.

Taavitsainen, Irma, Päivi Pahta, and Martti Mäkinen (comps.). 2005. *Middle English Medical Texts* (CD-Rom). Amsterdam/Philadelpia: John Benjamins.

Taavitsainen, Irma and Päivi Pahta (eds.). 2010. *Early Modern English Medical Texts: Corpus Description and Studies* (incl. CD-Rom). Amsterdam/Philadelpia: John Benjamins.

Warner, Alan. 1961. *A Short Guide to English Style*. Oxford: Oxford University Press.

Wårvik, Brita. 1990a. On grounding in English narratives: A diachronic perspective. In: Sylvia Adamson, Vivien Law, Nigel Vincent, and Susan Wright (eds.), *Papers from the 5th International Conference on English Historical Linguistics, Cambridge, 6–9 April 1987*, 559–575. Amsterdam/Philadelphia: John Benjamins.

Wårvik, Brita. 1990b. On the history of grounding markers in English narrative: Style or typology? In: Henning Andersen and Konrad Koerner (eds.), *Historical Linguistics 1987*, 531–542. Amsterdam/Philadelphia: John Benjamins.

Werlich, Egon. 1983. *Text Grammar of English*. 2nd edn. Heidelberg: Quelle & Meyer.

Wright, Laura. 1992. Macaronic writing in a London archive, 1380–1480. In: Rissanen et al. (eds.), 762–779.

Claudia Lange
Chapter 13:
Standards in the History of English

1   Introduction —— 238
2   English standards —— 244
3   Summary —— 250
4   References —— 250

Abstract: Standardization may be regarded as a process or as an ideology, but in adopting a historical perspective on standards of English, the two approaches can hardly be kept apart. The aim of this chapter is to provide an overview of how standardization in general has been conceptualized and how the relevant concepts have been applied to the development of English standards in different periods of the history of the language.

1 Introduction

Accounts of the history of English generally agree on the following: the language spoken in England which in retrospect is called Old English already possessed a (West Saxon) written standard, a remarkable achievement in comparison with other European vernaculars. The further development of this standard language was, however, interrupted by the Norman Conquest in 1066, when writing in the vernacular effectively ceased, giving way to Latin and Norman French as the languages of record. When English re-emerges as a written language early in the Middle English period, it is characterized by such a degree of dialectal diversity that the period is frequently labelled "transitional". It is the Early Modern English period that is largely credited as the era in which the development towards standard English gained momentum, and in which overt efforts at codification began to have a notable impact on the speech community and the ongoing development of both spoken and written English. Late Modern English then saw the further dissemination of the standard due to the rapid increase in literacy and the advent of universal schooling. Our Present-day English standard, then, can be traced back to late Middle English, but the most momentous events for a historio-

---

Claudia Lange: Dresden (Germany)

graphy of English standardization are clustered in the Early and Late Modern English periods.

This chapter provides a perspective on standardization throughout the history of English. It does so by tracing and, wherever applicable, intertwining several strands of research pertaining to English standard(ization)s. One way of approaching the topic has already been alluded to above, namely the longstanding concern with searching for the roots of the current (British English) standard, i.e. trying to (re)construct a more or less unbroken tradition for English. This research tradition cuts across the distinction made by, among others, Mugglestone [2003], between "processes" of standardization and "ideologies" of standardization. The most influential taxonomy of standardization processes comes from Haugen (1966), who also insisted that standardization is inseparably bound up with the written language (although this may not universally be the case, cf. Singh (2003) for South Asia). The developments observable in the ME period, discussed in Section 2.2, will make it exceptionally clear that "for the process of linguistic standardization the use of a language in writing is both its prerequisite and its trigger" (Schaefer 2006: 4). Haugen's classification will be the topic of Section 1.1.

Section 1.2 will introduce research focussing on ideologies of standardization. As I will argue, standard ideologies are a post-hoc phenomenon in that they are predicated on an already existing standard; that is, they can only emerge at a relatively late stage in the history of English standard(ization)s. Synchronically, standard ideologies inform speakers' attitudes, which in turn drive the dissemination and maintenance of standard English. Diachronically, the influence of the standard ideology is apparent in the body of knowledge produced by historical linguists: Milroy (2000: 15–16) sees it at work in the "historicisation" of English, i.e. the conferring of legitimacy upon the (standard) language by writing its history.

Section 2 will disentangle the polysemy of the term "standard" as it has been applied throughout the history of English. We will see that in different periods, various levels of linguistic organization were prominent in undergoing standardization, and the term "standard" as established by scholars for a particular variety in a particular period therefore varies widely in its scope. Section 2.1 will deal with what has been labelled "Standard Old English" or "West Saxon (literary) standard". Section 2.2 will focus on the trilingual communicative space in the Middle English period and the re-emergence of English vernacular writing as a precondition for further standardization. Early Modern and Late Modern standardization processes and ideologies will be the topic of Sections 2.3 and 2.4, respectively.

1.1 Processes of standardization

Being in possession of a standard is neither a necessary nor a sufficient condition for a language, if we look upon "language" as the property of a speech community with shared norms (cf. Labov 1972: 27). A standard combines the two requirements of "minimal variation in form" and "maximal variation in function" (Haugen 1966: 931) and thus goes far beyond the notion of shared norms. In order to get a clearer understanding of the polysemous terms "language" and "norm" and their correspondences, it is helpful to recollect Coseriu's model of language (Coseriu 1971), as e.g. put forward by Koch (1988).

Coseriu distinguishes three levels of language: first, there is the universal level of language as the common property of all humans. Human linguistic activities are typically realized in a particular language such as English or French (which he labels $language_{d[escriptive]}$) and, more specifically, in individual discourses. A $language_d$ is marked by "historicity": "external historicity" accounts for the indubitable fact that there are different languages, and "internal historicity" is related to the variation within a $language_d$ (Koch 1988: 330). A $language_d$, then, can be conceptualized as a variational space, where each (regional, social, etc.) variety has its own norms: "In dieser Hinsicht ist eine $Norm_d$ eine historisch-sozial *begrenzt gültige* sprachliche Tradition innerhalb einer $Sprache_d$ (die ihrerseits historisch begrenzt ist)" [In this respect, a $norm_d$ is a historically and socially *limited* tradition within a $language_d$ (which in turn is historically limited)] (Koch 1988: 330).

Over the last centuries, most European languages with a written tradition have been affected by standardization processes. This development coincided with the rise of the nation-state, so that a language without a standard is nowadays hardly conceivable: "Nation and language have become inextricably intertwined. Every self-respecting nation has to have a language. Not just a medium of communication, a 'vernacular', or a 'dialect', but a fully developed language. Anything less marks it as undeveloped" (Haugen 1966: 927).

Haugen also provides the four main reference points for a discussion of standardization processes, namely
a. selection of norm;
b. codification of form;
c. elaboration of function;
d. acceptance by the community (Haugen 1966: 933).

Whereas (a) necessarily represents the first step in any standardization process and (d) its final stage, (b) and (c) may apply to different degrees at different times during the process, depending on the actual level of the language undergoing standardization (for a different view on the sequence of steps, see Deumert and Vandenbussche 2003: 4–7). In Coseriu's terms, step (a) typically extends the range of one of the norms$_d$ that form part of language$_d$, such that, eventually, one norm$_{d(escriptive)}$ becomes coextensive with the norm$_{p(rescriptive)}$ for language$_d$: "the process of standardization works by promoting invariance or uniformity in language structure [...] standardization consists of the imposition of uniformity upon a class of objects" (Milroy 2001: 531). Step (b), codification of form, is typically accomplished by dictionaries, grammars, usage guides, and in some cases academies; again, this stage is inconceivable without a high degree of literacy. Elaboration of function may happen before or parallel to codification; another common term for this process is *Ausbau* (following Kloss 1967, 1978), a notion that has recently been reconceptualized by Fishman (2008). Whereas steps (a) and (b) satisfy the demand of "minimal variation in form", *Ausbau* operates mainly on the level of syntax and the lexicon and is the precondition for an incipient standard language to achieve "maximal variation in function". Acceptance, finally, marks the last stage in the development towards uniformity in language: once the standard language is generally accepted, any further development is arrested or at least slowed down considerably, and linguists typically turn to non-standard varieties to track down signs of language change.

Haugen's four dimensions of standardization provided the frame of reference for individual as well as comparative studies of standardization processes (e.g. Nevalainen 2003; Deumert and Vandenbussche 2003; Schaefer 2006). An alternative taxonomy comes from Milroy and Milroy (1991), who have identified "selection", "acceptance", "diffusion", "maintenance", "elaboration of function", "codification", and "prescription" as constitutive of standardization processes (see Nevalainen and Tieken-Boon van Ostade [2006] for an application of this model to standardization in English). Milroy and Milroy go beyond Haugen in adding "diffusion", "maintenance", and "prescription" to their model, the latter two terms reflecting their focus on the effect of standard ideologies. Before I turn to these, it is necessary to discuss to what extent Haugen's classification has stood the test of time.

Haugen's step (1), the selection of a norm, might be taken to imply that it is one clearly demarcated variety of a language$_d$ that is selected as the input to all further standardization processes. However, research has shown that "[m]ost standard languages are composite varieties which have developed over time, and which include features from several dialects" (Deumert and Vandenbussche 2003: 5), an insight which can be captured with Haugen's refined notions of "the unitary thesis of selection" and "the compositional thesis of selection" (Haugen 1972), or, in Deumert and Vandenbussche's terms, "monocentric selection" and "polycentric selection" (Deumert and Vandenbussche 2003: 4).

Work by Nevalainen (e.g. 2003, 2006) has drawn attention to a process which she calls "supralocalisation" and which tends to precede selection as the first step in Haugen's model:

> Supralocalisation is here used as an umbrella term to refer to the geographical diffusion of linguistic features beyond their region of origin. When supralocalisation takes place, it typically results in dialect levelling, loss of marked and/or rare elements. In this respect it achieves the chief goal of standardisation, to reduce the amount of permissible variation. However, and this should be stressed, many processes of supralocalisation in English, both today and in the past, have been induced naturally by dialect contacts without any conscious effort toward producing an official standard language (Nevalainen and Tieken-Boon van Ostade 2006: 288).

Supralocalization is thus akin to "accommodation" in face-to-face-interaction, but with an additional diachronic dimension. Nevalainen and Tieken-Boon van Ostade stress that supralocalization happens "naturally" in contact situations: to apply Coseriu's terms again, supralocalization falls out naturally from the universal level of language, as all human linguistic activity is marked by "reflexivity", i.e. it is intersubjective and typically directed at some "alter ego" (Koch 1988: 337). Implicit in the definition above is the notion that dialect contact is just as natural (that is, "universal" in Coseriu's sense) as supralocalization; and there has indeed been a growing recognition in recent years that English has to be conceptualized as a contact language throughout its history (cf. Trotter 2000; Mesthrie 2006).

1.2 Ideologies of standardization

Prior to standardization, the variational space of a language is largely unstructured, where "unstructured" is not meant to imply one large homogeneous space; rather, it designates the absence of a hierarchical ordering of varieties. Each variety within language$_d$ has its own norms$_d$ and its range of functions. Once the standard is in place, however, the variational space is restructured: the standard variety serves as the focal point within that space, and other varieties are demoted to the status of dialects:

> The establishment of the idea of a standard variety, the diffusion of knowledge of this variety, its codification in widely used grammar books and dictionaries, and its promotion in a wide range of functions – all lead to the devaluing of other varieties. The standard form becomes the **legitimate** form, and other forms become, in the popular mind, illegitimate. Historical linguists have been prominent in establishing this legitimacy, because, of course, it is important that a standard language, being the language of a nation state and, sometimes, a great empire, should share in the (glorious) history of that nation state (Milroy 2001: 547).

One effect of the standard ideology which has become engrained in the historiography of English historical linguistics is the "historicization" of English: "The historicization of the language requires that it should possess a continuous unbroken history, a respectable and legitimate ancestry and a long pedigree. It is also highly desirable that it should be as pure and unmixed as possible" (Milroy 2001: 549). Historicization is instrumental in bestowing legitimacy on a language: the language is conceptualized as essentially the same entity throughout centuries, even millennia, abstracting away from obvious linguistic change. Thus reference to the people's common language may serve to establish the link to some collective ancestry, and it may further serve to justify political and/or territorial claims based on this apparent collective property.

At first sight, Milroy's use of the term "historicization" seems to clash with Koch's notion of "historicity":

> Der Standard ist einerseits als eine der Normen$_d$ und damit als begrenzt gültig anzusehen. Er muß andererseits aber auch als Norm$_p$ gesehen werden, was seine Historizität ansatzweise relativiert, denn die Norm$_p$ lebt im Raum einer Einzelsprache von der Fiktion ihrer unbegrenzten Gültigkeit, also ihrer Befreiung von der Historizität (Koch 1988: 332).
> 'On the one hand, the standard has to be seen as one of the norms$_d$ and therefore as of limited validity. On the other hand, it has to be seen as norm$_p$, which partly serves to relativize its historicity, since norm$_p$ thrives on the fiction of its unlimited validity within the [variational] space of a language$_d$, thus its liberation from historicity'.

Milroy's "historicization" refers to the assertion that a language$_d$ such as English has essentially been around forever: historicization downplays what Coseriu called the internal and external historicity of language, for example by privileging internal motivations for linguistic change over external motivations (cf. Milroy 2000: 15). Similarly, when a descriptive norm$_d$ turns into norm$_p$, i. e. the standard, it becomes an ideological construct, and it is "conceived of as unmarked, stable, and uniform" (Johnston and Lange 2006: 192).

Milroy and Milroy (1991) stress the negative consequences of the standard ideology: once the standard is in place, it imposes a binary distinction between legitimate and illegitimate forms of the language. This awareness of the standard is not restricted to language specialists, but affects the whole speech community: "An extremely important effect of standardization has been the development of consciousness among speakers of a 'correct', or **canonical**, form of a language" (Milroy 2001: 535). Adherence to the standard typically becomes imbued with ideological underpinnings. The devaluing of non-canonical varieties entails the devaluing of their speakers: language use becomes available as a social symbol that may be enlisted to express and maintain inequalities in society. The standard can be used as a gatekeeper, granting or preventing access to the linguistic marketplace. These manifestations of the standard ideology are particularly evident from the 19th century onwards, as will be shown in Section 2.4.

Another noteworthy perspective on linguistic standardization comes from Geeraerts (2003). He identifies two "cultural models" pertaining to standardization and nationalism: the "rationalist" and the "romantic" model. A romantic model of standardization is based on the view that

> languages are primarily expressive rather than communicative. They express an identity, and they do so because they embody a particular conception of the world, a world view or 'Weltanschauung' in the sense of Herder. [...] if languages or language varieties embody a specific identity, then a preference for one language or language variety rather than another implies that the specific identity of a specific group of people is neglected or denied. [...] A correlative of this position is the positive evaluation of variety (Geeraerts 2003: 37).

In Geeraerts' terminology, the Milroys' approach would be "romantic" in that it conceives of the standard primarily as a medium of social exclusion, to the detriment of linguistic – and ultimately social – diversity. From the rationalist perspective, a language is simply a medium of communication, and the endorsement of the standard as a neutral medium of social participation becomes a democratic ideal (Geeraerts 2003: 40). Geeraerts traces the development of the two cultural models of standardization throughout the history of European nation states into the modern globalized world, where romanticists despise the global spread of English as a threat, whereas rationalists cherish it as an opportunity (Geeraerts 2003: 55).

2 English standards

This section will bring to bear the preceding general considerations on processes and ideologies of standardization on the history of standard(izations) in English. As elsewhere in this volume, the customary periodization of the history of English is adopted (cf. Curzan, Chapter 2).

2.1 Old English

From a European perspective, English is remarkable in being the first vernacular committed to writing. The first Old English texts date from the 8th century. Most of the texts that have come down to us are written in the West Saxon dialect, and if the term "standard" is applied to Old English, it is generally used with reference to this variety. Nevalainen and Tieken-Boon van Ostade (2006: 271) claim that "the earliest standardisation attempts, which go back as far as King Alfred (b. 849–901 [sic]) and even beyond, aimed at making English – or rather West Saxon – the official language". There is, however, consensus in the literature that "[i]f Old English did acquire a standard language, then it is to be found, not in the works of Alfred, but in those of Ælfric, a century later" (Hogg 2006: 399). King Alfred and his scribes may surely be credited with establishing West Saxon alongside Latin in the Anglo-Saxon communicative space as a written language, thereby contributing to its subsequent elaboration, but tracing the standard to their time "and even beyond" seems to be exaggerated – or, in Milroy's terms, evidence for the standard ideology.

"Standard Old English" as conceived of by Gneuss (1972) is the variety of late West Saxon written by bishop Æthelwold, his prolific disciple Ælfric, and others in the scriptorium at Winchester. Gneuss' evidence for a standard is lexical: he identified a lexical set which he called "Winchester words" in the writings of the Winchester scribes and traced the supralocal dissemination of this vocabulary. Further evidence for the claim that "Ælfric aimed at standardizing Old English in its written form" (Gretsch 2006: 171) comes from an examination of the manuscript revisions being carried out by Ælfric, which showed a high degree of consistency in the spelling of e.g. inflectional endings. In meticulously editing his manuscripts and regularizing variants, Ælfric was acting in the spirit of the Benedictine reform: the sacred word had to be kept unchanged (cf. Kornexl 2000: 266).

Both notions of "standard Old English", however, have been open to criticism. Kornexl (2000: 261) points out that the concept of "Winchester words" has been overgeneralized to justify the claim that there is indeed a standard Old English: the confusion surrounding the notion "standard Old English" is largely due to a misunderstanding of Gneuss' original contribution. Whether Ælfric's carefully revised language may be called a standard language is also doubtful. Gretsch (2006: 172) acknowledges that "what Ælfric wrote was not 'Standard Old English' *per se*, but 'Ælfric's Standard Old English', and that this existed side by side with other standards, though perhaps none as systematic as his was". Accordingly, there is no meaningful way of attributing a "standard" to Old English in the sense outlined in Section 1.1 above: "Ælfric's language was neither selected nor codified by others" (Hogg 2006: 401). Hogg therefore suggests discarding the notion "standard" with reference to Ælfric's language and following Smith (1996) in referring to "standard*ised* or to focused written language: such usages remind us that we are dealing with a process of normative focusing rather than with a fixed set of forms" (Smith 1996: 67).

Writing in Old English came to an abrupt end with the Norman Conquest in 1066:

> Most scholars agree that the late West Saxon *Schriftsprache* was an artificial standard which masked both dialectal variation and the development of the changes which distinguish Middle from Old English [...] Such a standard language could be kept in place only by careful scribal training in English; the end of such training was the beginning of 'Middle English'. The appearance of characteristically Middle English spellings in twelfth-century manuscripts may be regarded as the shredding of a tattered veil, not the manifestation of new developments (Liuzza 2000: 144–145).

There is thus no direct continuity between Old English and the emerging standards of later periods; again, English is unusual among the European vernaculars in undergoing *Ausbau* twice.

2.2 Middle English

The Middle English period is generally neglected in accounts of English standardizations, and for good reasons: the Norman Conquest in 1066 caused, among other things, a far-reaching rearrangement of the communicative space. The highly developed tradition of vernacular writing collapsed: English effectively ceased to be used as the language of government record and was once more confined to spoken registers. Written records were kept in Latin and French, and it is only in the 14th century that the vernacular resurfaced in the written mode to any extent. When it did so, writing in the vernacular was "particular and local", and consequently, "the Middle English period is, notoriously, the time when linguistic variation is fully reflected in the written mode" (Smith 1996: 68). We therefore have to deal mainly with the preconditions for standardization that characterized the Middle English period, namely textualization of the vernacular and processes of supralocalization. Nevertheless, a precursor of the present-day standard has been identified in the Middle English communicative space: the so-called "Chancery standard", which will briefly be discussed below.

As Schaefer (2006) has shown, the "boost of literacy" in English in the 14th century marked "the decisive step toward a future standard as the function of English was extended" (Schaefer 2006: 9). English simultaneously underwent "extensive" and "intensive" elaboration: the vernacular was used in more and more domains which were hitherto reserved for Latin and French, extending its functional range within the trilingual communicative space of medieval England. Accordingly, the language, in transition from orality to literacy, had to acquire the structural means that were appropriate for the written medium. The notion of "textualization" captures the fact that the transfer from the spoken to the written medium involves much more than just "scripting", i.e. creating a verbatim written version of the spoken word (cf. also chapter 2 of the introduction to *A Linguistic Atlas of Early Middle English, 1150–1325* [LAEME]; Lass and Laing 2007). From the 14th century onwards, "English gained ground by being elaborated with the help of those languages that had already achieved a more or less long institutional standing as carriers of literate discursive practices" (Schaefer 2006: 12).

These processes of structural elaboration, ultimately serving the goal of "maximum variation in function" were sustained by the literate minority; in a sense, they constitute "language change from above", even if they did not necessarily entail a conscious decision on the part of the writers to impose their usage on others. Those processes of supralocalization that are apparent in the Middle English period, on the other hand, are clearly instances of "change from below": first steps towards reduction of variation and thus towards "minimum variation in form" were taken when a levelled "colourless language" emerged, following the large-scale migration throughout the period with London as the centre of gravity. The *Linguistic Atlas of Late Mediaeval English* (LALME) (McIntosh et al. 1986) maps testify to the gradual diffusion of such supraregional dialectal features in the late Middle English period. Nevalainen (2006) has examined this process for several morphosyntactic features, likewise noting a tendency towards reduction in variation. However, in the period under discussion "supralocalisation did not equate to standardisation" (Nevalainen 2006: 130).

This conclusion may also be drawn when considering the accumulated evidence which calls for a reassessment of the notion "Chancery English", a term that goes back to Samuels (1963) and was subsequently endorsed by Fisher (1984, 1996). "Chancery English" and its position within the communicative space of medieval England have been extensively discussed; suffice it to say here that the term designates "a form of fifteenth-century London English identified as the direct ancestor of the modern written standard" (Benskin 2004: 1). Smith (1996: 68–73) has already drawn attention to the fact that Chancery English admitted of much more spelling variation than one would expect from a "standard", and Benskin (2004) effectively delivers the *coup de grâce* to the notion of "Chancery standard", listing a host of inaccuracies and misrepresentations in Fisher's account and concluding:

> Chancery's ordinary administrative practice did nothing to promote English of any sort, but rather, for the purposes of government, retarded it. [...] Chancery Standard was Latin, and save for nine years during the Commonwealth, it remained so until 1731 (Benskin 2004: 37–38).

Following Benskin's carefully assembled evidence, we can safely shift the notion of a "Chancery Standard" from the realm of "processes of standardization" towards the realm of "ideologies of standardization". Benskin suggests taking a fresh perspective on the beginnings of standard English that discards the fixation on Chancery English – and, we may add, the fixation on spelling with respect to standardization processes.

2.3 Early Modern English

Even though the writers of earlier periods did not abstain fully from commenting upon language and evaluating language varieties, it is in the Early Modern period that metalinguistic comments start to proliferate, providing evidence for the social indexing of linguistic variation. Such comments frequently appear in dictionaries and grammars, the prototypical instruments of codification whose publication is also on the rise throughout the period, culminating towards the end of the 18th century (cf. Nevalainen 2003: 143). Contributing cultural factors were the advent of printing and the rapid rise of a literate middle class.

The first level of linguistic organization to achieve a fairly high degree of uniformity was spelling: the "efflorescence of different English writing systems" (Smith 2008: 215) which characterized the Middle English period gave way to a consistent orthography by 1650 (cf. Nevalainen 2003: 138). Smith suggests seeing this as a more or less natural consequence of the extensive elaboration of English: variation became "inconvenient, and a communicatively driven process of dialectal muting began to reduce the range of written variation" (Smith 2008: 215).

Similar processes of supralocalization converged to reduce variation in morphosyntax, as Nevalainen and Tieken-Boon van Ostade (2006: 291–299) have shown. Features that originally were restricted to a regional variety of English lost their regional marking over time and gained currency in a composite supralocal variety. Again, there is no uniform source for the morphosyntactic features that eventually emerged as the standard features. One tentative conclusion is that "most grammatical features that made their way to the supralocal *Gemeinsprache* during the sixteenth and seventeenth centuries diffused from the capital region to the rest of the country" (Nevalainen and Tieken-Boon van Ostade 2006: 295).

In terms of standardization processes, the EModE period is probably best known for the conscious attempts at elaboration and codification of the lexicon. When it comes to the lexicon, the notion of standardization as promoting uniformity and invariance becomes slightly paradoxical: by definition, the lexicon is open-ended and cannot be subject to reduction of variation in the same way as, say, orthography. Likewise, "codification" with respect to the lexicon in the Early Modern English period does not mean "fixing once and for all"; it rather pertains to intensive elaboration with the help of (mainly) Latin, which made the many "hard-word-dictionaries" of the period necessary. In the cultural context of the Renaissance, the importance of Latin as the prestige language in the contemporary communicative space was renewed.

Finally, it should be noted that while the development towards "minimal variation in form" accelerated considerably in the early Modern English period, this period also marked the beginning of a trend in the opposite direction: with the dawn of colonial expansion, English became "transplanted" to new territories, where the language rapidly – and naturally – developed separate norms, and, in some cases, eventually separate standards. Just as domestic variation converged, so the incipient globalization of English provided for the modern pluricentricity of the language.

2.4 Late Modern English

The 18th and 19th centuries are generally regarded as the age of prescriptivism *par excellence*. Unlike countries such as France, England never established an academy for "correcting, improving and ascertaining the English tongue", as Swift famously demanded in 1712. The enterprise of codifying English in grammars and usage books was thus not entrusted upon a single recognizable institution, but carried out by individuals, for a variety of reasons. In a sense, the first institution which actively promoted the standard – as well as the standard ideology – is the school: it is schooling for all that firmly establishes the "standard language culture" (Milroy 2001: 530) in the speech community as a whole.

Whatever their motives, the "codifiers" of English clearly met a growing demand in a society in which language became a resource for social distinction. This is reflected in a shift of emphasis: whereas Early Modern grammars did not endorse specific usages, grammars of the late-18th and 19th centuries took pains to identify the "proper" forms and condemn "improper" usages (cf. Nevalainen 2003: 142–146). It is at this stage that the goal of "minimal variation in form" in the structure of the language is most actively pursued, and where the standard ideology comes to the fore in the grammar writers' justifications for proscribing their choices. Their pronouncements on usage changed markedly in this period: in the 19th century, the Victorian obsession with morality was transferred to language use, and "incorrect" language becomes "*morally* reprehensible. Those who speak in this way are committing offences against the integrity of the language" (Milroy 2000: 16).

Pronunciation was the last level of linguistic organization to be subjected to standardization. The late 19th and early 20th century witnessed the selection and codification of Received Pronunciation (RP), as set out in detail in Mugglestone (2003). Nevalainen (2003: 148) suggests that pronunciation could only be successfully codified when the International Phonetic Alphabet (IPA) became available. However, Milroy's functional explanation seems to be more in line with the internal dynamics of standardization processes: "[...] *standardization is implemented and promoted primarily through written forms of language*. It is in this channel that uniformity of structure is most obviously functional. In spoken language, uniformity is in certain respects dysfunctional, mainly in the sense that it inhibits the functional use of stylistic variation" (Milroy 2000: 14).

3 Summary

The preceding discussion has shown that "there is no single ancestor for Standard English, be it a single dialect, a single text type, a single place, or a single point in time. Standard English has gradually emerged over the centuries, and the rise of the ideology of the standard arose only when many of its linguistic features were already in place" (Wright 2000: 5–6). If we look at the current state of the art in English historical linguistics, then the standard ideology is clearly losing its grip. For one thing, editorial practices have changed considerably: it is now hardly acceptable to artificially create uniformity by normalizing variants when editing a manuscript. Similarly, one of the monuments of late 19th century scholarship, the *Oxford English Dictionary*, is now committed to broadening its database: the third edition aims to overcome the original edition's "Britocentricity" (http://www.oed.com/public/update0903/march-2009-update; last accessed 3 July 2017) and will be based on a much more diversified body of texts, not only for Present-day English, but also for earlier periods of English (cf. "Documentation" http://public.oed.com/the-oed-today/preface-to-the-third-edition-of-the-oed/; last accessed 3 July 2017). Further, research in historical linguistics is increasingly turning to varieties of English that have hitherto been neglected or altogether excluded from consideration, and new sources are being tapped for a more integrated approach to the history of English. Meanwhile, the English language continues to change, and it will be highly instructive to see how and when such changes eventually become part of the standard.

4 References

Benskin, Michael. 2004. Chancery Standard. In: Christian Kay, Carole Hough, and Irené Wotherspoon (eds.), *New Perspectives on English Historical Linguistics. Selected Papers from 12 ICEHL, Glasgow, 21–26 August 2002*. Vol. II: *Lexis and Transmission*, 1–40. Amsterdam/Philadelphia: John Benjamins.

Coseriu, Eugenio. 1971. System, Norm und "Rede". In: Uwe Petersen (ed.),*Sprache: Strukturen und Funktionen. XII Aufsätze zur allgemeinen und Romanischen Sprachwissenschaft*, 53–72. Tübingen: Gunter Narr.

Deumert, Ana and Wim Vandenbussche. 2003. Standard languages: Taxonomies and histories. In: Deumert and Vandenbussche (eds.), 1–14.

Deumert, Ana and Wim Vandenbussche (eds.). 2003. *Germanic Standardizations: Past to Present*. Amsterdam/Philadelphia: John Benjamins.

Fisher, John H. 1996. *The Emergence of Standard English*. Lexington: University Press of Kentucky.

Fisher, John H., Malcolm Richardson, and Janet L. Fisher (eds.). 1984. *An Anthology of Chancery English*. Knoxville: University of Tennessee Press.

Fishman, Joshua A. 2008. Rethinking the Ausbau-Abstand dichotomy into a continuous and multivariate system. *International Journal of the Sociology of Language* 191: 17–26.

Geeraerts, Dirk. 2003. Cultural models of linguistic standardization. In: René Dirven, Roslyn Frank, and Martin Pütz (eds.), *Cognitive Models in Language and Thought. Ideology, Metaphors and Meanings*, 25–68. Berlin/New York: Mouton de Gruyter.

Gneuss, Helmut. 1972. The origin of standard Old English and Æthelwold's school at Winchester. *Anglo-Saxon England* 1: 63–83.

Gretsch, Mechthild. 2006. A key to Ælfric's standard Old English. *Leeds Studies in English* 37: 161–177.

Haugen, Einar. 1966. Dialect, language, nation. *American Anthropologist* 68: 922–935.

Haugen, Einar. 1972. The Scandinavian languages as cultural artifacts. In: Anwar S. Dil (ed.), *The Ecology of Language. Essays by Einar Haugen*, 265–286. Stanford: Stanford University Press.

Hogg, Richard. 2006. Old English dialectology. In: Ans van Kemenade and Bettelou Los (eds.), *The Handbook of the History of English*, 395–416. Malden, MA/Oxford: Blackwell.

Johnston, Andrew James and Claudia Lange. 2006. The beginnings of standardization – an epilogue. In: Schaefer (ed.), 183–200.

Kloss, Heinz. 1967. Abstand-languages and Ausbau-languages. *Anthropological Linguistics* 9: 29–41.

Kloss, Heinz. 1978. *Die Entwicklung neuer Germanischer Kultursprachen seit 1800*. 2nd rev. edn. Düsseldorf: Schwann.

Koch, Peter. 1988. Norm und Sprache. In: Harald Thun (ed.), *Energeia und Ergon: Sprachliche Variation – Sprachgeschichte – Sprachtypologie. Band II: Das sprachtheoretische Denken Eugenio Coserius in der Diskussion*, 327–354. Tübingen: Narr.

Kornexl, Lucia. 2000. "Concordes equali consuetudinis usu" – monastische Normierungsbetrebungen und sprachliche Standardisierung in spätaltenglischer Zeit. In: Doris Ruhe und Karl-Heinz Spieß (eds.), *Prozesse der Normbildung und Normveränderung im mittelalterlichen Europa*, 237–273. Stuttgart: Franz Steiner.

Labov, William. 1972. *Sociolinguistic Patterns*. Philadelphia: University of Pennsylvania Press.

Lass, Roger and Margaret Laing. 2007. Introduction. Part I: Background. Chapter 2: Interpreting Middle English. In Margaret Laing. 2013–. *LAEME: A Linguistic Atlas of Early Middle English*,

1150–1325. Version 3.2. Edinburgh: © The University of Edinburgh. http://www.lel.ed.ac.uk/ihd/laeme2/laeme_intro_ch2.html; last accessed 5 January 2017.

Liuzza, Roy. 2000. Scribal habit: The evidence of the Old English gospels. In: Mary Swan and Elaine M. Treharne (eds.), *Rewriting Old English in the Twelfth Century*, 143–165. Cambridge: Cambridge University Press.

McIntosh, Angus, Michael L. Samuels, and Michael Benskin. 1986. LALME: *A Linguistic Atlas of Late Mediaeval English*. 4 vols. Aberdeen: Aberdeen University Press. See http://www.lel.ed.ac.uk/ihd/elalme/elalme.html; last accessed 5 January 2017.

Mesthrie, Rajend. 2006. World Englishes and the multilingual history of English. *World Englishes* 25(3–4): 381–390.

Milroy, James. 2000. Historical description and the ideology of the standard language. In: Wright (ed.), 11–28.

Milroy, James. 2001. Language ideologies and the consequences of standardization. *Journal of Sociolinguistics* 5(4): 530–555.

Milroy, James and Lesley Milroy. 1991. *Authority in Language: Investigating Language Prescription and Standardisation*. 2nd edn. London/New York: Routledge.

Mugglestone, Lynda. 2003. *"Talking Proper": The Rise of Accent as Social Symbol*. Oxford: Oxford University Press.

Nevalainen, Terttu. 2003. English. In: Deumert and Vandenbussche (eds.), 127–156.

Nevalainen, Terttu. 2006. Fourteenth-century English in a diachronic perspective. In: Schaefer (ed.), 117–132.

Nevalainen, Terttu and Ingrid Tieken-Boon van Ostade. 2006. Standardisation. In: Richard Hogg and David Denison (eds.), *A History of the English Language*, 271–310. Cambridge: Cambridge University Press.

Samuels, M. H. 1963. Some applications of Middle English dialectology. *English Studies* 44: 81–94.

Schaefer, Ursula. 2006. The beginnings of standardization: The communicative space in fourteenth-century England. In: Schaefer (ed.), 3–24.

Schaefer, Ursula (ed.). 2006. *The Beginnings of Standardization: Language and Culture in Fourteenth-Century England*. Frankfurt: Peter Lang.

Singh, Rajendra. 2003. The languages of India: A bird's-eye-view. In: Rajendra Singh (ed.), *The Yearbook of South Asian Languages and Linguistics*, 173–181. Berlin/New York: Mouton de Gruyter.

Smith, Jeremy. 1996. *An Historical Study of English: Function, Form and Change*. London: Routledge.

Smith, Jeremy. 2008. Issues of linguistic categorisation in the evolution of written Middle English. In: Graham D. Caie and Denis Renevey (eds.), *Medieval Texts in Context*, 211–224. London: Routledge.

Swift, Jonathan. 1712. *A proposal for correcting, improving and ascertaining the English tongue; in a letter to the most Honourable Robert Earl of Oxford and Mortimer, Lord High Treasurer of Great Britain. Eighteenth Century Collections Online*. Gale Group. https://quod.lib.umich.edu/e/ecco/; last accessed 5 January 2017.

Trotter, David (ed.). 2000. *Multilingualism in Later Medieval Britain*. Cambridge: D. S. Brewer.

Wright, Laura. 2000. Introduction. In: Wright (ed.), 1–8.

Wright, Laura (ed.). 2000. *The Development of Standard English 1300–1800: Theories, Descriptions, Conflicts*. Cambridge: Cambridge University Press.

Index

address term 159, 160, 173, 174
adverb, development of 81, 118, 131, 132
alliteration 37, 59, 60, 62–67, 151, 156
allophonic variation 46–49
analogy 117, 118
Anglo-Saxon (language), *see also* 14, 16, 18, 20
– Old English
anthroponym 191–195
– by-name 192, 193
– personal name 191, 192
– surname 193–195

borrowing
– lexical 48, 49, 60, 70–73, 94, 134, 135, 154, 156
– syntactic 112

Celtic 42, 103, 112, 186, 187
collocation 129–132, 135, 143, 146, 147, 150, 151, 154, 155, 158, 159
collostructional analysis 118, 130, 131
consonant inventory, changes in 41–43
contact, language 103–105
determiner, development of 116, 117
discourse 154, 155, 167, 168, 174–179
– analysis 154, 166, 175
– courtroom 176, 177 *see also* register, legal
– news 178, 179
– science 177, 178 *see also* register, scientific
do, auxiliary 103
Dutch 19, 38, 41, 44, 45, 48, 52, 130

Early Modern English 12, 16–18, 20, 29, 30, 33, 44, 46, 63, 72, 73, 84, 94, 98, 117, 131, 169, 171, 172, 174–177, 221, 223, 230–232, 238, 248, 249

French 45, 48, 49, 70, 128, 134, 135, 148, 149, 156, 159, 173, 174, 193, 194, 211, 220, 221, 224, 227, 230, 233, 240, 246

genre 171, 178, 179, 219, 229, 230–232
– letters 229, 230
– and language change 232, 233
German (Modern) 41, 44, 45, 48, 86, 98, 174
Germanic 14, 21, 22, 24, 31, 40–44, 46–48, 52, 60, 66, 73, 78, 80, 81, 84, 85, 89, 91, 93, 95, 96, 98, 188, 189, 191, 192
Germanic Stress Rule (GSR) 60, 69, 71, 73
Gothic 92
grammars, competing 107, 114, 115
grammaticalization 87, 91, 110, 113, 114, 116–119, 124, 126, 128, 130, 132, 133, 154, 172
grapheme 208, 209
– English inventory 209–211
graphology *see* orthography
Greek 19, 45, 70, 72, 86, 88, 126, 127, 134, 203–205, 223

Half-(Semi-) Saxon 14, 16, 18, 20
have causative 115, 116

idiom/idiomaticity/idiomaticization 141–145, 147, 148, 150–154
Indo-European 41, 42, 77, 78, 81, 83, 86, 90, 91, 95, 124–126, 135, 173, 186, 190
inference, invited 127, 128, 155, 168–170
insert 171, 172

Late Modern English 20, 238, 239, 249
Latin (Lt.) 17, 19, 22, 29, 40, 41, 45, 46, 70–73, 78, 86, 88, 98, 112, 128, 129, 135, 156, 173, 177, 178, 207, 210, 220, 221–225, 227, 229, 232, 245, 246, 249
Latin Stress Rule 70, 72, 73
lexicon, change in 133–135
littera (letter) 207, 208

metaphor 123, 125–127, 128, 129, 132–135, 146, 147, 154, 188, 227
metonymy 123, 126, 128, 132–134
Middle English 13–21, 23, 25–29, 43, 44, 47, 48, 50, 59, 67–72, 83, 84, 92, 94, 95,

98, 99, 105, 108, 112, 113, 116, 131, 152, 169, 171, 174, 176, 178, 188, 190, 192, 194, 208, 212, 221, 224, 231, 246–248
– boundary dates 25–27, 31–33
modal 84, 107–109, 113, 114, 116, 125, 127
– double 108, 109
morphology
– inflectional 81–84
– inflectional, changes in 91–97
– root-based 78, 80, 81
– stem-based 78, 80–82, 85, 90, 91, 97
– typology 79–81
– word-based 78, 80–82, 95–97

names, evidence provided by 185, 186, 188–191, 195–197
Norman Conquest 11, 17, 19, 25, 27, 28, 30, 32, 67, 192, 193, 197, 210, 221, 238, 245, 246

Old English 13, 14, 16–21, 25, 27, 28, 30–32, 43–49, 59–66, 78–80, 83–86, 88, 92–98, 105, 106, 108, 116, 124, 128, 132, 133, 135, 156, 171, 172, 186–197, 210, 220, 221, 222, 230, 231, 244–246
Old Norse 19, 25, 44–46, 105, 112, 186, 191, 221
orthography 203, 204
– as source of phonological evidence 211, 212

periodization
– canonical periods of English 13–21
– criteria for, internal 21–23, 25–28, 31
– criteria for, external 21, 22, 24, 26
– critique of 11–13
– rationale for 10, 11
phoneme 37–39
phonotactics 43–46, 49, 50, 55
phraseological unit
– definition of 141–145, 151, 152
– impact on language change 158, 159
– origin and change of 153–157
– treatment in metalinguistic sources 149–153
– types of 145, 146, 156

pragmatics 142, 143, 157, 158, 165–168, 170, 175, 176
Present-day English 38, 47, 50, 59, 60, 63, 65, 69, 70, 74, 108, 110, 148, 171, 189, 238
prosody 57, 58
– Middle English 67–72
– Old English 60–66
– Present-day English 72–75
proverb 142, 145–150, 152, 154, 156, 158

reanalysis 112–117
– formal approach 113–115
– functional approach 115, 116
register 116, 125, 134, 186, 189, 219, 220
– legal 221, 222, 226 *see also* discourse, courtroom
– scientific 222, 223, 226 *see also* discourse, science
rhyme 37, 60, 67, 68, 70, 72

semantic change, lexical 123, 124, 154, 155
semantic prosody 129, 130, 132, 133
Spanish 45, 134, 135, 206
speech act 128, 130, 166, 171–173, 175, 177, 232
spelling, norms of 212, 213
standard, English 12, 15, 18, 28, 29, 53, 106, 107, 135, 212, 213, 223
– Early Modern English 248, 249
– Late Modern English 249
– Middle English 30, 246–248
– Old English 30, 244–246
standardization 22, 26, 50, 211–213, 223–226, 239–244
stress 39, 40, 47–49, 58–60, 62–68, 69–75, 78, 89–91, 96, 97, 108, 196
style 219, 220, 224, 225
– oral vs. literate 157, 225–227
– plain vs. clergial 227, 228
subject, category of 109–111
subjectification 128, 129, 133
syllable structure 58, 59

toponym 186–191
Transition(al) English 15–18, 20
Tudor English 16–18, 20, 30

word formation
– changes in 98, 99
– processes of 85–89
word order, changes in 106, 107, 113

writing system
– classification of 205–207
– English 205, 206

www.ingramcontent.com/pod-product-compliance
Lightning Source LLC
Chambersburg PA
CBHW030109010526
44116CB00005B/168